EUGENICS SOCIETY READER 1

Biosocial Man

Studies related to the interaction of biological and cultural factors in human populations

Edited by

DON BROTHWELL

Institute of Archaeology, London, England

1977

Published for the Eugenics Society by the Institute of Biology

The Eugenics Society
69 Eccleston Square
London SW1V 1PJ

Published by the
Institute of Biology
41 Queen's Gate
London SW7 5HU

ISBN: 0 900490 09 8

First published, 1977

© The Eugenics Society, 1977

All rights reserved. No part of this
book may be reproduced, stored in
a retrieval system, or transmitted, in any
form or by any means, electronic, mechanical,
photocopying, or otherwise
without the prior permission of
the copyright holder.

Printed in Great Britain by
Billing & Sons Limited, Guildford, London and Worcester

Contributors

C. O. CARTER, *MRC Clinical Genetics Unit, Institute of Child Health, 30 Guilford Street, London WC1N 1EH.*
ALBERT DAMON (deceased). *Formerly: Department of Anthropology, Harvard University, Cambridge, Massachusetts 02138.*
THEODOSIUS DOBZHANSKY (deceased). *Formerly: Department of Genetics, University of California, Davis, California 95616.*
BRUCE K. ECKLAND, *Department of Sociology, University of North Carolina, Chapel Hill, North Carolina 27514.*
H. J. EYSENCK, *Institute of Psychiatry, Maudsley Hospital, Denmark Hill, London SE5 8AF.*
ROBIN FOX, *The Harry Frank Guggenheim Foundation, Research Office, 17 West Ninth Street, New York, N.Y. 10011.*
C. R. HALLPIKE, *Swallowmead Cottage, Diptford, Nr. Totnes, Devon.*
LEON R. KASS, *The Kennedy Center for Bioethics, Georgetown University, Washington, D.C. 20007.*
WILLIAM S. LAUGHLIN, *Department of Biobehavioral Sciences, The College of Liberal Arts and Sciences, University of Connecticut, Storrs, Connecticut 06268.*
ARNO G. MOTULSKY, *Division of Medical Genetics, University of Washington, Seattle, Washington 98195.*
MONI NAG, *The Population Council, 245 Park Avenue, New York, N.Y. 10017.*
ALAN S. PARKES, *The Galton Foundation, 7 Downing Place, Cambridge CB2 3EL.*
JOHN PEEL, *Department of Social Studies, Teesside Polytechnic, Middlesbrough, Cleveland TS1 3BA.*
MALCOLM POTTS, *Population Services International, Marie Stopes House, 108 Whitfield Street, London W1P 6BE.*
D. F. ROBERTS, *Department of Human Genetics, University of Newcastle upon Tyne, Newcastle upon Tyne NE2 4AA.*
J. M. THODAY, *Department of Genetics, University of Cambridge, Downing Street, Cambridge CB2 3EH.*
LIONEL TIGER, *The Harry Frank Guggenheim Foundation, Research Office, 17 West Ninth Street, New York, N.Y. 10011.*
O. L. ZANGWILL, *The Psychological Laboratory, University of Cambridge, Cambridge CB2 3EB.*

Acknowledgements

Grateful acknowledgement is made to the authors, editors, and publishers of the following works and journals for permission to use their material:

1. Reprinted from *Man*, 2, 415-433 (1967) by kind permission of the author, the Royal Anthropological Institute of Great Britain and Ireland, and the editor of the journal. Copyright 1967 Royal Anthropological Institute.
2. Reprinted from *Impact of Science on Society*, XX, 29-44 (1970) by kind permission of the author, the editor of the journal, and of UNESCO. Copyright UNESCO 1970.
3. Reprinted from *Population Studies*, XXVII, 59-68 (1973) by kind permission of the author, and the editor of the journal.
4. Reprinted from *Journal of Biosocial Science*, 5, 195-204 (1973) by kind permission of the author, and the editor of the journal.
5. Reprinted from *Social Science and Medicine*, 7, 179-190 (1973) by kind permission of the authors, the editor of the journal, and of Pergamon Press Ltd, Oxford.
6. Reprinted from *Eugenics Quarterly*, 15, 71-84 (1968) by kind permission of the author, and the editor of the journal. Copyright 1968 by the American Eugenics Society, Inc.
7. Reprinted from *Eugenics Quarterly*, 13, 326-340 (1966) by kind permission of the author, and the editor of the journal. Copyright 1966 by the American Eugenics Society, Inc.
8. Reprinted from *The American Journal of Human Genetics*, 23, 107-123 (1971) by kind permission of the author, and the University of Chicago Press. Copyright 1971 by the American Society of Human Genetics. All rights reserved.
9. Reprinted from *The Journal of the Royal Anthropological Institute*, 95, 87-103 (1965) by kind permission of the author, the Royal Anthropological Institute of Great Britain and Ireland, and the editor of the journal.
10. Reprinted from *Social Biology*, 16, 69-80 (1969) by kind permission of the Society for the Study of Social Biology, and the editor of the journal. Copyright 1969 by the Society for the Study of Social Biology.
11. Reprinted from *Journal of Biosocial Science*, 1, 71-83 (1969) by kind permission of the author, and the editor of the journal.
12. Reprinted from *The British Journal of Psychology*, 67, 301-314 (1976) by kind permission of the author, the editor of the journal, and the Cambridge University Press. Copyright 1976 by The British Psychological Society.
13. Reprinted from *Journal of Biological Education*, 6, 323-329 (1972) by kind permission of the author, the Institute of Biology, and the editor.
14. Reprinted from *The Advancement of Science*, XX, 1-11 (19636-64) by kind permission of the author, the British Association for the Advancement of Science, and the editor of the journal. Copyright 1973 Royal Anthropological Institute.
15. Reprinted from *Man*, 8, 451-470 (1973) by kind permission of the author, the Royal Anthropological Institute of Great Britain and Ireland, and the editor of the journal. Copyright 1973 Royal Anthropological Institute.
16. Reprinted from *Social Education*, 32, 142-146 (1968) by kind permission of the author, the National Council for Social Studies, and the editor.
17. Reprinted from *Science*, 174, 779-788 (1971) by kind permission of the author, the American Association for the Advancement of Science, and the editor of the journal. Copyright 1968 by the American Association for the Advancement of Science.

Contents

		Page
Contributors		iii
Acknowledgements		iv
Introduction *Don Brothwell*		vi
1	In the beginning: aspects of hominid behavioural evolution *Robin Fox*	1
2	The possible biological origins of sexual discrimination *Lionel Tiger*	23
3	Anthropology and population: problems and perspectives *Moni Nag*	41
4	The social impact of human reproduction *Alan S. Parkes*	57
5	The sociology of population control *John Peel* and *Malcolm Potts*	69
6	Theories of mate selection *Bruce K. Eckland*	85
7	Race: a population concept *William S. Laughlin*	103
8	Human and medical genetics: a scientific discipline and an expanding horizon *Arno G. Motulsky*	121
9	Assumption and fact in anthropological genetics *D. F. Roberts*	141
10	Race, ethnic group, and disease *Albert Damon*	161
11	Spina bifida and anencephaly: a problem in genetic-environmental interaction *C. O. Carter*	177
12	Thought and the brain *O. L. Zangwill*	191
13	Genetics and educability *J. M. Thoday*	209
14	The biological basis of criminal behaviour *H. J. Eysenck*	221
15	Functionalist interpretations of primitive warfare *C. R. Hallpike*	241
16	On genetics and politics *Theodosius Dobzhansky*	265
17	The new biology: what price relieving man's estate? *Leon R. Kass*	273
Index		294

Introduction

The collection of essays which follows is an attempt to indicate the breadth of biosocial science. To my knowledge, there is as yet no article or book which in any way gives a proper indication of the varied ways in which biological man is linked with social man. Of course, the division itself is only one of convenience: man's evolution is the sum of a continuous reciprocal feedback between physical and cultural factors and to view human molecular change without considering differentiation in language or creativity would be to misunderstand evolution.

In using a relatively new term such as 'biosocial science', there will clearly be differences of opinion as to what it comprises. It might even be argued that this is a term and a science which must in the end replace anthropology, sociology, and human biology, which could turn out to be doubtful divisions of the overall 'zoology' of Man. This would in fact be a reversal of the present sad state of affairs where sociological and biological studies of Man have become more and more separated. But, whatever happens at an academic and teaching level, there is no doubt that biosocial studies are here to stay, and probably have a considerable contribution to make in the construction of a proper perspective for our species.

In planning this collection, I have been concerned to represent as many aspects of biosocial investigation as possible in the smallest number of papers. This has value and danger for, in selecting for breadth, there are likely to be many gaps between the studies presented. However at this stage, it is the wide range of studies of a biosocial nature which seem most important to emphasize. Nevertheless some sequence can be seen in the topics, from hominid evolution to aspects of population, the nature of society, physical diversity within and between recent peoples, patterns of disease, human behaviour and ability, and man in relation to the challenges of his material culture and his strategy for the future.

The papers selected are variable in length and, perhaps, in the importance of their content. Such heterogeneity is to be expected in a selection of this nature. However, there is similarity in the fact that each paper makes some point which is a useful extension of what has gone before.

Hominid evolution has probably extended over more than five million years, which gives plenty of chronological 'room' to discuss the complex nature of cerebral, behavioural, and cultural interaction and evolution. Fundamental change has continued through into the more recent phase of increased population density and urban evolution. That our evolution is the sum total of various factors—not always pulling in the same direction—is evidenced by a consideration of the extent of Man's climatic adaptations, and the argument that the elaboration of rituals has had an adaptive advantage, as well as a consideration of the evolution of sexual discrimination.

Remaining at a population level, further matters can be considered. One can review population size in relation to cultural change or stability, and Nag has more to say on the anthropology of population factors. Parkes considers, at a world level, the present social impact of human reproduction, while Peel and Potts elaborate on sociological aspects of population control. One could also argue for possible significant relationships between economic and demographic factors, and the need to assess such links more fully.

If we close in on populations and consider more specific aspects of society and family, further biosocial details emerge. Surnames can be considered in relation to certain family parameters, and one can debate the question of mate selection and the problems of analysis. By reference to variation within a particular population, it is possible to investigate the variable association of social status with other anthropological characteristics. A very different kind of detailed investigation is provided by a consideration of secular changes in dizygotic twinning rates in various communities.

Race is a term which has been abused in the past few decades. At an unemotional level, however, it is concerned with the interesting micro-evolutionary differences which occur within species, and is relevant to studies on, say *Drosophila* as much as Man. In the many papers which have been published on this topic, we see something of the range of comment which has been made in recent years relating to race, from Laughlin's general comments on race at a population level. Relative social isolation of some hybrid groups, aspects of growth, and of the importance of genetic studies in relation to societies are other related factors. Patterns of disease have varied in human groups through time and are linked not only to the human environment, but to population origins and social factors as well. Damon reviews the complexity of these links generally, and of course this can be carried further in many directions, for instance, in the impact of socio-cultural factors on disease in the tropics. Similarly, two categories of disease, adult lactose intolerance and certain malformations of the central nervous system could be considered in relation to factors of population history and variability and to the environment.

For the purposes of this book, studies on human behaviour and ability are linked together with comments on educability. Thoday is concerned with more general aspects, while other contributions are concerned with such specific biosocial phenomena as musical ability, language, visual art in relation to certain defects, criminal behaviour, and the nature of primitive warfare.

Finally, there are some concluding remarks, which, at the same time, pose questions concerned with the future of our species.

DON BROTHWELL

1

IN THE BEGINNING: ASPECTS OF HOMINID BEHAVIOURAL EVOLUTION*

Robin Fox

One of the most exciting developments in anthropology over the last decade has been the revival of interest in human social origins. We are once again very much concerned with what happened 'in the beginning. .', but we are approaching this in a very different way from the nineteenth-century anthropologists who asked the same question. They were concerned to project backwards from primitive society to 'the infancy of mankind'. It would be pointless to parade here all the well-known and correct objections to this procedure. But now a combination of new material from several fields has led some anthropologists to try the reverse procedure; that is, to project 'upwards' from the primates. (This method in turn has dangers not unlike those on which evolutionism foundered). The new material however comes from a more extensive fossil record of primate evolution; an increasing number of excellent field studies of the social behaviour of monkeys and apes; and a realisation of the relevance of the work of the ethologists for an understanding of the evolution of behaviour.

All this I am sure would have delighted Malinowski. One half of his tradition - the detailed scrutiny and contextual examination of particular cultures - has survived and flourished among social anthropologists. But the other half - his concern with 'human nature' and the 'biological basis of culture' has languished. It has been argued, perhaps correctly, that he never really made a convincing connexion between the two, but this is primarily because he had no adequate evolutionary framework into which to put them both. The evolutionism of his predecessors he rightly rejected, and the new biology was in its infancy. But he maintained with characteristic forthrightness that 'We have to base our theory of culture on the fact that all human beings belong to an animal species' (1944:75) and he was always willing to explore what he described as 'The no-specialist's land' between the science of man and that of the animal (1927:x). Although the new knowledge of which I have spoken would have led him to rethink and possibly reject many of his views on the nature of culture, I am sure it would have excited his copious imagination, and that he would have seen its relevance at least. Malinowski's importance for me lies in his

*The Malinowski Memorial Lecture, delivered at the London School of Economics and Political Science on 16 May 1967.

conviction that the 'biological basis of culture' should be at the forefront of our thinking, and not in his tradition of fieldwork nor in his insistence on contextual interpretation of custom.

It is perhaps a sign of the times that my title was suggested neither by the opening words of the Book of Genesis, nor the Gospel according to St John, but by the final sentence of Freud's *Totem and taboo* (1952). This in turn was taken from Goethe's *Faust* (Act I), 'Im Anfang war die Tat' : 'In the beginning was the Deed'. Freud's attempt in this book to account for the origins of 'human nature' was the subject of a long critique by Malinowski (1927) and rarely has any theory been so universally condemned. But the fact that so many eminent, learned and authoritative social scientists have condemned the theory suggests to me that there is an even chance of its being right. I want here to argue that there is more than a germ of truth in it, and to show how the Malinowskian questions about human biological propensities can perhaps best be handled in an evolutionary framework of the kind Freud intuitively saw was necessary.

Let me briefly summarise Freud's theory of the 'Deed' or 'primal event'. In the beginning men lived in family hordes in which a single, dominant, aggressive and jealous male monopolised the females and threw out his sons. The ejected sons (the 'brothers' in Freud's terminology) formed themselves into a homosexual band, until the fatal day arrived. 'One day the brothers who had been driven out came together, killed and devoured their father and so made an end of the patriarchal horde.' He continues, 'Some cultural advance, perhaps command over some new weapon, had given them a sense of superior strength' (1952: 141). However, although they hated the father, the brothers also envied him and admired him and hence at his death they felt guilty as a result of 'delayed obedience'. Consequently, they invented totemic prohibitions on the one hand and incest taboos on the other. The father was identified with a totem animal which could not be slain except in ritual when the brothers reaffirmed their solidarity, and the incest taboos meant the renunciation of the father's women who were the cause of all the trouble. From these beginnings in ritual and renunciation all that is truly human sprang. And, of course, this was the basis of the Oedipus complex, the fundamental feature of human personality.

Freud was asking a fundamentally important question here: how was the breakthrough from non-human primate to fully-human primate achieved? He saw that the roots of our present social behaviour lay in our primate heritage, and yet there was obviously a great difference. His problem was to account for this difference. It was not enough for him to repeat, in the parrot fashion of anthropologists, that man had culture: of course he had - but why? Or as Konrad Lorenz would put it, the great evolutionary question is 'how come?' What had impelled this evolution towards a radically different mode of adaptation?

For Freud the breakthrough was the result of the imposition of taboos on natural tendencies, this imposition being the beginning of culture. Without accepting his specific proposals most anthropologists have accepted this position. For Lévi-Strauss the rules of incest and exogamy are the first 'intrusion' of culture into nature, and totemic thinking is a basic form of articulate taxonomic thought (1949; 1962). For Malinowski also, the opposition of culture and nature was absolute.

For other writers, for example the unjustly neglected Westermarck, this has not necessarily been the case and instead they have attempted to derive features of human social life from features of primate life. That is, they have looked for an explanation in terms of continuity rather than difference. The human family, for instance, was for Westermarck a natural outcome of primate tendencies (1891). This all depends, of course, on the level at which one is working. Thus, Malinowski stressed the rules and customs of marriage and courtship, lacking in animals and present in man. Of this difference there can be no doubt - animals do not have articulate rules. For Freud too the invention of conscious rules and obedience to them was crucial. For Westermarck, however, it was the continuities in the structure of the units that were interesting. The rules of marriage were many and various, but what was interesting was the persistence of the primate familial pattern of mating and socialisation in man.

Thus we are working here at two levels: the structural and the cultural. At the cultural level there are by definition quite pronounced differences, but at the structural level this is not so clear.

This raises another problem. Many of the anthropological arguments concerning the differentiation of man from the non-human primates concentrate almost exclusively on the 'nature-culture' distinction, and the 'substitution' of culture for nature. But man differs from the other primates not only in terms of learned cumulative traditional behaviour (and even this difference is one of degree not kind); he also differs in genetic endowment - he is a different genus. The hominid line has had a history independent of the other hominoidea for anything up to 30 million years and perhaps more (see, for example, Leakey, 1967). Hence many of the differences which we can observe between the most basic behaviours of men on the one hand and monkeys and apes on the other, may not stem from man's superior cultural achievements but rather from his expression of a completely different biological nature. Moreover this difference need not be a recent one in evolutionary terms but may stem from the remote hominid past. We must not therefore too readily assume that any crucial difference is necessarily the result of cultural adaptations. I will return to this point, which is very relevant to the question of whether or not differences between ourselves and the monkeys and apes are a result of the overthrow of our primate natures, or simply a reflection of the fact that we are a different primate which has evolved a different nature. It should also make us wary, as we shall see, of taking as models for 'pre-human' hominid behaviour, the behaviour of particular contemporary non-human primates.

The whole picture is complicated by the fact that culture did not appear, as Malinowski thought, all of a piece. He never thought to justify this position, and indeed he scarcely needed to do so, as it was subscribed to by most anthropologists as a matter of course. Keith's 'cerebral rubicon' (750 c.c.'s) before which was animal and after which was man, was supplemented by Kroeber's 'critical point' theory, which he likened to the freezing point of water (Keith, 1948; Kroeber, 1948). These theories were purely deductive rationalisations, and we now know that tools, hunting and probably shelters appeared with the genus *Australopithecus* up to two million years ago, and that the brain size of this little man-ape was no greater than that of the living great apes. The rapid evolution of the brain occurred, in other words, *after* the inception of culture, and the fact that the evolving man-ape became dependent on culture meant that culture itself acted as a selection pressure. In a very real sense then, culture is man's nature (Geertz, 1965).

This raises for us the even more difficult problem of where to start looking for human origins. 'In the beginning was . . .' but when was the beginning? We must here take Freud's point, conveniently overlooked by his critics, that in his 'origin myth' he compressed the time-scale of evolution. He insisted in a footnote to which he drew particular attention, that his treatment involved an 'abbreviation of the time factor', a 'compression of the whole subject matter', and that 'It would be as foolish to aim at exactitude in such matters as it would be to insist upon certainty' (1952: 142-3). We do not need, then, to look for a point in time, but for processes over time. We must examine the social unit among the primates as a clue to the 'raw material of society' (Linton, 1936). We must then look at the fossil record to see if this can help us to understand how the raw material become worked into the typically human society of today.

We cannot, as I have said, necessarily accept any particular contemporary primate as the model for the pre-human hominid. What we can do is to narrow down the range of possibilities. We are beginning to know the full range of possible primate behaviours, and we can narrow down our focus to a part of this range that will represent the possibilities open to the pre-human hominid. In this we are going back to the kind of enquiry that Westermarck, Carveth Read, Freud and others were pursuing. They were struggling with an inadequate biology, a poor fossil record, a mistaken geological time-scale, and almost purely anecdotal material on the social life of primates. Rather than jeering at their theories we should marvel that they achieved so much in at least seeing the problems and attempting to solve them. In any case, they were not always as mistaken as is generally assumed.

Both Westermarck and Freud looked to the unfortunate gorilla for evidence, although Westermarck also examined the chimpanzee. Both in fact depended on the work of Savage (1847), but Freud got this material second-hand from Darwin via Lang and Atkinson (1903). To Westermarck this hearsay evidence (Savage depended on native accounts of gorilla behaviour) suggested that the 'family' - by which he meant the monogamous independent family - was the basis of primate social life, and that the human family was a natural outcome of this. Thus was the hypothesis of 'primitive promiscuity' in early man attacked from the primate angle. Freud also took the gorilla as his model, but came to different conclusions. A single, aggressive, dominant male with a harem of females was seen as the basic group. The 'primal horde' was in fact this cyclopean family.

Derek Freeman (1965) has recently criticised this assumption on the basis of the work of Schaller (1963) on the mountain gorilla. There are several features of gorilla society which do not tally with this picture:

1. There is usually more than one adult male in a group.
2. While there are relations of dominance between the males, there is little aggressiveness and competition.
3. The dominant male is not jealous and allows females to copulate with other males.
4. There is no evidence of young males being driven out, but they may leave and wander for a time and join other bands.

There is no support from the gorilla for Freud's hypothesis, but there is little for Westermarck's either. What of the chimpanzee (Goodall, 1965; Reynolds and Reynolds, 1965; Reynolds, 1965)?

With the chimpanzee we have a somewhat more fluid system in which groups of females seem to be the focus of group cohesion. Within a forest population there will be several such groups with their young, forming the fixed points in a social world of roving male bands. These male bands roam the forest in search of food and when they find it they drum on the trees to attract the females. The males may visit several female groups in turn, spending some time with them. When large parties of chimpanzees gather they indulge in spectacular jamborees. Sexual relations are promiscuous again, with evidence of individual choice and preference being important. Reynolds (1966a) found that some male chimpanzees were more home-loving than others and these tended to hang around the females and children. He refers to them rather charmingly as 'mothers' brothers'.

There is nothing in this behaviour of man's nearest relative to suggest either the bedrock of human familial organisation looked for by Westermarck, or the violent cyclopean family horde that had to be overthrown before a truly human state could be arrived at, sought by

Freud. There is no evidence of permanent or even semi-permanent male-female relationships, even less than among the gorilla; and mating, while not totally random, is still promiscuous. The social unit here is either the forest population as a whole, or the groups of males on the one hand, and females on the other; but not the independent family.

However the chimpanzee is still championed by some as the model for proto-human society. Reynolds (1966b) has recently argued that in terms of common descent he is the best candidate and we must therefore take him seriously. His social structure is seen as an excellent pre-adaptation to life on the savannahs. When the early hominids, during the pliocene drought, moved from the forests to the savannahs, Reynolds argues, they took with them a social structure basically like that of the chimpanzee. The female/young group continued to be the basic unit but the wandering groups of males now became foragers and hunters, using their tool-making and carnivorous proclivities more and more efficiently to this end. The mothers' brothers stayed with the females to guard them, and eventually the individual choice/promiscuous mating pattern settled down, with an increasing division of labour, to a more human pattern of assigned mates and families. Thus for Reynolds an evolution of human patterns would be a normal and progressive development from chimpanzee-like patterns, given the historical transition to savannah hunting. The closeness of relationship of the chimpanzee to ourselves, and his obvious likeness in terms of intelligence, tool-making, individuation, curiosity, emotional liability and high sexual drive, reinforce this view.

But the problem of taking the great apes as models lies in the fact of their forest ecologies. Most modern students of primate evolution agree that we should pay close attention to ecology in order to understand the selection pressures at work on the evolving primate lines. This has been shown to be crucial in understanding somatic evolution, and as this is ultimately a result of behavioural adaptations, then it is crucial to behavioural evolution as well.

As we have seen, Reynolds has to project his chimpanzees *forward* on to the savannah; but this, in evolutionary terms, is a move they never made. They stayed on the forest floor and became highly adapted to a life of relative security and plenty in the forest setting. Thus it may be a mistake to project the contemporary chimpanzee, with his long history of forest-floor living, back to the miocene as a model for the evolving hominids, who may have been doing something quite different. In fact it may have been the ancestors of the great apes - at the time a more successful group of animals than the hominids - who denied the shelter of the trees to the ancestors of man.

The only real counter to this argument would be the theory of Kortlandt and Kooij (1963) that the chimpanzees did move out and adapt to savannah living, moving back into the forest later. This would explain why their capacities exceed their achievements. But this theory is not generally accepted.

Here perhaps we should pause to give the gibbon his due (Carpenter, 1964). He is a puzzle in that while he is classified with the great apes he has remained in the tree-tops. He is the only permanent brachiator left among the Hominoidea. (The orang certainly brachiates, but we know little about his social habits.) He would have pleased Westermarck in that he is impeccably monogamous and lives in defended territories. The pressures leading to the formation of these territorial families, however, are very different from those which have operated during most of the history of the hominids. Indeed, the gibbon is more like some birds than his primate cousins, and closely resembles many of the prosimians. However, the further back we push hominid ancestry - and it now seems to have crept beyond the early miocene - the more likely it is that rather than hominids being offshoots from a pongid stem (which led to the great apes), they are a relatively independent line (Simons, 1964). Gibbons, apes and hominids may have separated early and developed independently (Schultz, 1936). It always remains therefore an open question as to whether any of our behavioural heritage has gibbon-like overtones - including the tendencies to pair formation and the territoriality seemingly absent in the chimpanzee and gorilla. Be that as it may, we must bracket off the gibbon for a moment and return to the ground - and the dry open grassland and desert at that.

Kroeber, when criticising Freud's concept of the primal horde, said, 'It is a mere guess that the earliest organization of man resembled that of the gorilla rather than the trooping monkeys' (1920: 44-50). It in fact turns out to be a poor guess, and the overwhelming majority of anthropological opinion now sides with the trooping, ground-dwelling monkeys as the best model for the proto-human horde. It stresses the importance of parallellism and ecology over close genetic relatedness.

Freeman does not pursue this line in his critique, being content with the negative case. What he does is to suggest that the elements of the Oedipus complex, 'the sexual drive, dominance, aggression and fear, are phylogenetically given and basic to the nature of the human animal and to human behaviour in all known forms of family and procreative groups (1965: 20).' In other words, these are a part of the primate heritage, and he quotes evidence from pig-tailed monkeys and langurs.

If, then, Freud had looked to the ground-dwelling trooping monkeys, what would he have found? He would have discovered a system in which group size could range from 9 to 200 or more individuals, and in which an organisation of troop defence and even rudimentary predation existed. It is commonly accepted that baboons are the most successful of terrestrial primates after man, and baboons have commonly been taken as the closest guide to the kind of life we might have expected to find in hominid groups, at least in the pre-Australopithecine stage. (By 'baboons' I here mean the ground-dwelling monkeys, including, for example, the macaques). The problem here is that we have two rather distinct types of baboon society. The original attempts to compare baboons and early man (e.g. Washburn and Avis, 1958; Sahlins, 1959; Washburn and DeVore, 1962; DeVore and Washburn, 1964; DeVore, 1965a), were based on the woodland-savannah-dwelling common baboons (chacma, olive, cynocephalus, etc.) and the macaques and rhesus monkeys of Japan and India. I shall call this Baboon 1. This society can be described roughly as a series of concentric circles. In the centre circle are the dominant males, most of the females, and the immature young. In the next circle are the less dominant males, while at the periphery are the sub-adult males and those adults not in the dominance hierarchy. The dominance hierarchy is limited in size; no matter how the group's numbers increase, it never seems to exceed six big males. These males monopolise the females and have choice of females in heat in order of precedence. In a small group the dominant male will do practically all the breeding himself. In larger groups females often form 'consort' relationships with dominant males which last for a few days to a week. As a female comes into oestrus she may be mounted by several sub-dominants, but it is only a dominant who can cover her at peak of ovulation. As dominance is characterised by strength, fighting ability, ability to co-operate and even willingness to baby-sit (which leads to acceptance of leadership by the group of females), such a breeding system has obvious survival value. The group then is structured around this core of dominant males who act as leaders and defenders and even in some cases as predators, although they do not provide for the females and young. (For a general survey of baboons see Hall, 1966. For paricular studies of this type (1), see Altmann, 1965; DeVore, 1965b). On the edges of this group are the young adult males. These have a loose dominance order, some bonding processes, and a good deal of homo-erotic behaviour. They may make forays into the group of females and may even be able to mount one who is not in peak oestrus, but they rarely successfully challenge the dominant males who can, and do, combine against them if necessary.

The Japanese macaques certainly have palace revolutions of a sort, and attempts to overthrow dominant males do take place. But usually a male can only get into the hierarchy by patient waiting and by pulling strings. If he has a high ranking mother (for the females have a hierarchy too) then she can keep him close to the centre and he can ingratiate himself with the females and be tolerated by the dominant males. At some point, then, he will get into the court circle. But many of the males must be content with a bachelor existence. Some wander off and become solitaries - the beatniks of the monkey world. Others eventually join other bands where they have more luck. (It is interesting for the theory of exogamy that here it is the females who remain stationary and the males who move between groups.

The same is of course true of the chimpanzees. Thelma Rowell (personal communication) informs me that among three groups of baboons in Uganda studied over five years, all the males have changed groups at least once. The idea of these as relatively (or even absolutely) 'closed' breeding groups is thus disproved).

The full range of complexities and subtleties of social structure among these remarkable terrestrial primates cannot be detailed here, but the overall structure is clear enough. It is not the cyclopean horde with the single jealous male, and indeed such a unit would perhaps not have survived under the conditions we are contemplating; but it does have those elements that Freeman spoke of as basic to the Oedipus complex: the dominance of the adult males, the fear and exclusion of the juveniles, and a whole society held together, in a paradoxical way, by the aggressiveness of the participants.

The other type of baboon social system (which I will call Baboon 2) is quite different, and is only just coming to the forefront of discussion. This type is common to the hamadryas and gelada baboons, and to some extent to the patas monkey. (Kummer and Kurt, 1963; Crook, 1966; Hall, 1966). The first two inhabit harsh arid environments where seasons differ sharply (mostly in Ethiopia). They are found in large herds, possibly as a defence against predators, but the subdivision of the herds and the internal structure of these divisions differ from those of their woodland-savannah cousins. The basic unit is the 'one-male group'. On average there is one adult male to three or four females in each group. These females with their immature young are kept under strict surveillance by their overlord, and reciprocally they are attracted to and follow him. He attacks those who wander too far and accept the approaches of other males (a special 'neck bite' has been developed for this purpose). These one-male groups make up the core of the herd. Again, at the peripheries, there is the group of excluded males. (This superficially represents the organisation of some ungulates, but is different in that the polygynous association of dominant males and females in, for example, the kob, giraffe or red deer, is purely seasonal. With these baboons it is permanent). The group of excluded males is much more of a unit than in the first type, and in times of food scarcity it wanders off in search of food, much like the roving band of male chimpanzees. At maturity the males are expelled from (or at any event, leave) the family, and after that they can only get back to the breeding system by acquiring a harem of their own. Some older males seem to tolerate 'apprentices' who attach themselves to the harem owner and probably eventually take over some of his surplus females. But we do not yet know enough about 1) what happens in the all-male band and 2) how new harems are formed.

The picture here is much more cyclopean, and several writers have seized on it as the obvious model for proto-human society. There is here the jealous, dominant male, herding his females and defending them, as well as the expelled sons banding together into a fraternal horde. But note that the total unit is still the horde itself. The rejected sons may be excluded from breeding; but they remain a part of the horde structure, and as in the first type of baboon system they act as first line of defence against attack. The big males in both systems act as the ultimate defence against predators. Only in the little patas monkey do we approach the independent family acting as a unit - but here the male interestingly enough acts as a rather gentle watch-dog and not as a dominant jealous husband. Hence some form of co-operative behaviour seems built into baboon social structure, and the excluded juveniles can eventually work their way back to the centre of power and marital bliss if they are tough, patient and intelligent enough. There is no real possibility here of sons ganging up against the 'father', because there is not a single father but rather a formidable body of big males with established dominance status.

The year-round association of the males and females in the one-male group has led some writers, Westermarck-fashion, to seek in it the origins of the human type of male-female association (Campbell, 1966). But there are several difficulties about this to which I must turn later.

To put this account into evolutionary perspective and to lead up to the controversial Australopithecines, let us see how geological and climatic changes have been seen as the rungs of the evolutionary ladder, the essential selection pressures which have moulded the development of structure and function. Napier, primarily interested in bipedal walking and other loco-motor functions has charted the spatio-temporal progress of various primate stocks (Napier, 1964). The gibbon stayed in the *forest canopy*, while the other Hominoidea took to the *forest floor*. The chimpanzees and gorillas stayed there, while one of the hominid lines moved out from the *forest edge* to the *tree savannah* as far back as the mid-miocene (20 million years B.C.). Another hominid line stuck to the forest and only moved out much later than its cousin. The first line - the ancestors of *Australopithecus africanus*, and possibly of *Homo erectus* and eventually modern man - broke out into the *open savannah* in the early pleistocene after a long sojourn in the open parklands. The baboons probably followed a line of development through the ecological grades similar to the first hominid line, but stuck to their quadrupedal gait.

The following diagram is an expansion and adaptation of one of Napier's diagrams (Napier, 1967). It shows the 'distances' that the various genera have travelled through the ecological grades, man having moved out into an enormous variety of biomes. The chimpanzee presents a slight problem in that in fairly recent times it has moved into woodland savannah areas; but it is essentially a forest and forest-fringe animal.

Aspects of Hominid Behavioural Evolution

Tropical forest → Forest fringe → Woodland savannah → Open savannah → Other

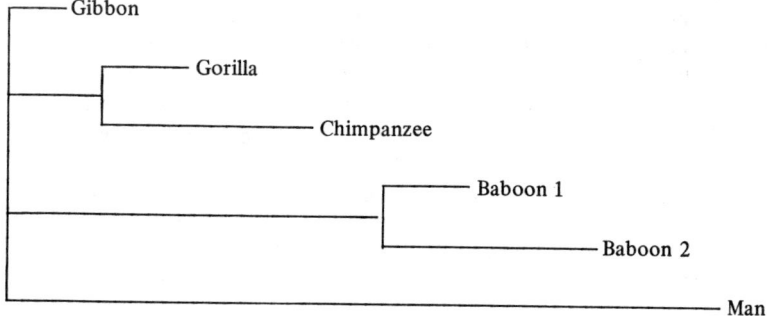

Diagram 1.

Now we have suggested that ecology and social structure are closely interlinked, and indeed Crook and Gartlan (1966) have classified primates in terms, not of morphology, but of habitat, and have shown that social systems are closely linked to environment. They have distinguished five grades of adaptation, as shown in table 1, which is a simplified summary of Crook and Gartlan (1966).

Table 1. Ecological grades of primate evolution

	Grade 1	Grade 2	Grade 3	Grade 4	Grade 5
Habitat	Forest	Forest	Forest/forest fringe	Forest fringe/ tree savannah	Grassland or arid savannah
Species	Galago (Bush-baby) Dwarf lemur	Indri Lemur Gibbon	Howler monkey Guereza Gorilla	Macaque Common baboon Chimpanzee	Hamadryas baboon Gelada Patas monkey
Diet	Insects	Fruit or leaves	Fruit, leaves, stems	Vegetarian-omnivore	Vegetarian-omnivore
Reproductive units	Pairs	'Family parties' (single male)	Multi-male groups	Multi-male groups	One-male groups

Note: Vernacular names of species have been used, and only a few examples from each grade have been taken.

We can see that these grades follow the same kind of sequence as that posited by Napier. The striking fact is that no matter how different the animals within each grade are, their social systems broadly correspond, allowing for overlap, marginal and transitional cases, etc.

There are a number of possible criticisms of this scheme, but to spell these out would take too long here, so let us accept it and look at the interesting transition from Grade 4 to Grade 5. This transition, say Crook and Gartlan, is also characteristic of hominid evolution, a position that parallels Napier's on the move from the woodland savannah to the open savannah. 'Paleontological investigations', they say, 'suggest a radiation of early hominids from dryopithecine stocks in circumstances similar to those controlling the transition from Grade 4 to Grade 5 in the cercopithecids' (1966: 1202). This they relate in the hominids to the adaptation of an omnivorous diet and hence to the development of co-operative hunting and foraging.

Thus it could be argued, as indeed Campbell has done, that we can look for the origins of the human type of reproductive unit in the kind of adaptations that were found necessary for successful breeding in Grade 5. There are, however, certain aspects of baboon 2 behaviour (some of which are shared with baboons generally) that are obviously off on another track from that taken by the hominids, and these animals may therefore not be a good guide to hominid development. For example, females mature at roughly twice the rate of males. Also, the baboon polygynist does not gather as many wives as possible (like the Freudian horde father or some human polygynists) but stops at about four. Both these facts are probably related to ecological adaptation in which a 'one-male group' of this size and composition is the best kind of breeding unit in arid conditions. One large male plus a number of small fast-maturing females is perhaps the most efficient food-utilisation unit in times of maximum aridity. At the limits of their ranges, for example, Japanese macaques are found in small groups of this kind.

Let us look at some factors which have been stressed as particularly 'hominid' characteristics, that is, as end-products of trends in hominid evolution. Such are:

1. year-round breeding and loss of oestrus;
2. growth of co-operation and food-sharing;
3. lack of pronounced sexual dimorphism.

Now if we assume that hominids were moving towards, or alternatively were preserving and developing, these patterns, where does the baboon fit in? The baboon female is still subject to the oestrus cycle, and because of seasonal variations in food supply, breeding in baboon 2 is markedly seasonal. Only 'vigorous seasonal breeding' according to Crook and Gartlan, is compatible with survival in the arid savannahs. As to the second point, Crook and Gartlan argue that under these conditions sexual antagonism *increases* and so does male competition. This also seems to lead to a marked increase in sexual dimorphism.

One feature that does persist even outside the breeding season is the male-female bond. This, as in other primate cases, disproves the theory that only persistent sexual interest of males and females in each other holds the primate group together (Zuckerman, 1932). Nor does this sexual interest seem necessary to hold the primate 'family' together, where such a unit occurs. Oestrus and seasonal breeding notwithstanding, the Baboon type 2 maintains its family structure. But is this maintained on the same basis as it would have been in the early hominids? All factors seem to indicate that the genetic bases for baboon 'familial' behaviour are very dissimilar from those of man, and that these animals moved in a very different direction of behavioural evolution. The hominids must indeed have brought a different biological equipment to bear, or they must have made a fantastic change in a relatively short period.

Crook and Gartlan seem to realise this and make the suggestion that early hominids 'had initially a social organisation not unlike that of the chimpanzee'. What they did was to 'tighten up' the rather free-and-easy social organisation of the chimpanzee-type and toughen it in the face of arid conditions, seasonal fluctuations in food supply, threats from predators and the demands of a predatory existence. The result was to take the latent dominance pattern and weave it into a baboon-like social structure (type 1 and then type 2). This changed social structure, however, retained the pre-adaptations of the chimpanzee-style, including the all male bands which became the foragers and hunters. Weapons, they suggest substituted for gross physical dimorphism, which we know was lacking in the Australopithecines. They are not clear as to exactly how these groups might have been organised, and this, on their theory, might have differed in different habitats. Thus a multi-male dominance hierarchy and its appendages would have characterised the declining number of hominids that remained in the shrinking woodlands, and a one-male-group type of structure those that took to the open grasslands. It is in the latter, where a baboon type 2 structure was grafted onto a chimpanzee-like basis, that we may have the clue to human family origins.

We must pause here to note one or two points. We must remember Kortland's theory that chimpanzees are 'fallen men' and that those chimpanzees able to get to the woodland savannah do indeed tighten up their organisation and display concerted attack on predators, etc. We must also note Rowell's findings that baboons which return to the forests loosen up their social structures and in fact become much more chimpanzee-like with, for example, a much less pronounced dominance hierarchy (Rowell, 1966). All these considerations seem to be leading up to a debate on the relative weights to be attached to genetic and ecological determinants of social structure. It does seem, however, that the harem behaviour of the hamadryas baboon, for example, with such specialisations as the neck bite, is genetically determined and hence phylogenetically old (Jay, 1965: 550).

The theory of Crook and Gartlan inserts a crucial stage into the progession proposed by Reynolds: a stage in which the forest developed a baboon-like social structure (type 2) during the pliocene sojourn on the dry savannahs.

If then what I have outlined is the raw material of the primal horde, what of Freud and Westermarck? We have here some of the features of the cyclopean family, as we have seen, but this is not isolated and the total unit is still the horde and not the individual family. In so far as the hominids veered towards a structure of Baboon 1 type, the family disappeared altogether. There is no question in either case of a 'father versus sons' situation, but there is clearly a 'young expelled males versus older dominant males' situation. In either type of structure the 'fathers' monopolise the 'mothers' and exclude the 'sons'. How far they monopolise the 'daughters' in type 2 is not clear. They probably do, and in type 1 they certainly do. Thus Freud's contention that incest rules were directed primarily towards the maturing male would tally with this situation, and it would tally with the fact that father-daughter incest is by far the commonest type known in man, while mother-son is the least common.

For Westermarck there is a little comfort if type 2 is the model, for here we have a basis for continuity. Even so the basis of hominid polygyny in a one-male group situation must have been different from the baboon basis. This is something we should ponder.

For either hypothesis there are difficulties. Should we try to look for continuities, or should we accept with Freud that something shattering had to happen to jerk the proto-hominid organisation into a human shape? And was that thing the invention of weapons and the killing of the fathers? Did there have to be a period of revolutionary cannibalism acting as a selective process?

Let us look at the kind of creature that our proto-hominid conditions, both ecological and social, were selecting. Here perhaps the work of Michael Chance is the most important (Chance, 1962a; 1962b; Chance and Mead, 1953). He points out that in a troop structure of baboon type 1 (he worked largely with macaques) several processes are at work. There is 'constant mating provocation' in that the females are receptive for a longer period of the year and for a larger fraction of the oestrus cycle than in any other mammal. This constant provocation leads to constant competition among the males and the establishment of a breeding hierarchy. The survival of the individual male and his chances of success in breeding depend on his capacity to 'equilibrate' - roughly speaking, his capacity to control his sexual and aggressive drives. 'Equilibration demands of the animal an intensification of the control over its emctional responses, both facilitatory and inhibitory' (1962b: 125). Because of the number of contrasting stimuli presented and the number of rather close decisions that have to be made, the successful animal has to control its emotional responses rather than simply act them out. Chance then postulates that the enlargement of the neo-cortex was 'an anatomical adaptation to the circumstances requiring an equilibrational response' (125). The proto-hominids had perhaps gone furthest of all the primates in this development and it was therefore an important pre-adaptation giving them a springboard from which to launch themselves, via tools, hunting and language, into the truly human state.

Clearly I am unable to do justice here to the complexity and detail of Chance's argument. If I had time to elaborate it, I could undoubtedly strengthen my case. It is too simple, for example, just to talk in terms of the 'growth of the neo-cortex'. For the present however we must be content with this inadequate summary.

Chance can be criticised on several grounds. His theory, as Etkin (1954) points out, would apply only to the male neo-cortex, and much as we may be mystified at the use made of this organ by the female of the species, she undoubtedly possesses it. It does seem to be the case, however, that in primates male cortical control of sexual behaviour is greater than female. Further, Chance was working on the theory that primates lacked a breeding season; but 'vigorous seasonal breeding' characterises many primates including baboons of both types. Provocation to conflict which requires an equilibrational response, however, can surely occur over other things than sex: food, for example, in times of scarcity. I would also like to make the suggestion that dominance itself has provocative qualities; that the young males desire to get into the hierarchy for its own sake. Indeed, sex cannot be the only provocation, for in some baboons the young males do in fact copulate with females at the commencement of oestrus.

The point here is that if Chance is even partly right, then the selective pressures which produced the 'take-off' stage for the 'transition to humanity' involved a social structure with a dominance hierarchy of males in constant and relatively monopolistic association with females, and with a body of excluded males forming a fraternal band. The whole process of enlarging the neo-cortex to take-off point was based on a competition between the dominant and sub-dominant males in which those which survived were those best able to control and inhibit, and hence time, their responses. Here then are the beginnings of deferred gratification, conscience and guilt, spontaneous inhibition of drives, and many other features of a truly human state. The selection pressures we have outlined were well on the way to producing the creature Freud saw as the outcome of the terrible event.

Now what exactly was the outcome? It was a rule-obeying guilt-feeling creature which could live in groups according to a social code of conduct. The primal horde gave way, in Freud's opinion, to 'the most primitive kind of organisation that we actually came across', and this, 'consists of bands of males' all obeying the same code (1952: 141). If however we cease to take the erroneous gorilla evidence then this particular transition is not necessary, for as Chance (1962a) has also pointed out, the basic social bond of gregarious primates is not the male-female bond, but the bond between the males: males of the hierarchy, males of the roving band, and excluded males of the fraternal band. This bond is ambivalent - threat both repels and attracts the sub-dominants - but it is there. Thus in the normal processes of primate evolution we could have had the basis of human society without the necessity to repeated murder.

Must we therefore dismiss the Freudian theory at least on the murderous issue? We do not know for sure, and we cannot aim at certainty, but Freud himself offers us an alternative. Freeman has contrasted the two solutions as the 'fact and fantasy hypotheses'. Towards the end of his book Freud has second thoughts. Perhaps the transition was not bloody and murderous. He says, 'The mere hostile *impulse* against the father, the mere existence of a wishful *fantasy* of killing and devouring him, would have been enough to produce the moral reaction that created totemism and taboo' (1952: 159-60). He continues, 'The alteration might have been effected in a less violent fashion and none the less have been capable of determining the appearance of the moral reaction'. In consequence, 'No damage would then be done to the causal chain stretching from the beginning to the present day, for psychical reality would be strong enough to bear the weight of these consequences' (1952: 160).

This seems to me to express beautifully in Freud's own language the point I have been labouring here. If Freud had been equipped with the primatological and other information I have quoted, and had not been misled by the erroneous gorilla evidence, his second hypothesis would have been vindicated. There is moreover no clash here with Westermarck. (It has been my experience that whenever Westermarck and Freud seem to disagree the best thing to do is to assume that they are both right. The hypothesis that can accommodate both of their theories is likely to be a good one). For Westermarck then there is indeed a continuity here from the bi-sexual groups of the primate to human social organisation - a continuity that need not have been disrupted by murder and cannibalism. Again it is doubtful that this was a straight continuity in form from a primate type of mating and family system to a human, but the human type was nevertheless a direct evolution from the primate type.

Aspects of Hominid Behavioural Evolution

Here we must pause and take breath and look once more at the chronology of these events. Chance is dealing essentially with the process of events during the pliocene. The picture he paints of hominid groups here tallies with the theories of Crook, for example, who sees various forms of baboon-like adaptations as being necessary for life in the arid savannahs. However, the known fossil hominids of the late pliocene and early pleistocene (that is, one to two million years ago) are the Australopithecines. These small creatures were bipedal and had a very human dentition, but their average brain-size was only equal to that of the great apes. The rapid expansion of the brain occurred in the pleistocene, and largely during the last million years of hominid existence when brain size increased three times - an almost unprecedented rate of evolution. Chance does not say more than that if such a rapid evolution took place, then it argues for 'some special form of breeding system'. By this he means some system based on dominance, in which the more efficient and intelligent creatures did the breeding.

However, we must add to this two other factors. Not only was this a period of growing sophistication in the use of tools, but this hominid - or at least one branch of the stock - was a hunter. Hence both weapons and the chase must enter our consideration at least one million years ago (Washburn, 1959). This has led to a two-pronged attack on the transition problem. Man, it is argued, became a kind of carnivore, and his brain rapidly evolved to cope with the complexities of being a tool-making, symbol-using hunter. Chance does not explore this issue, but even allowing for it his question still stands: whatever the pressures making for a larger brain, by what kind of *breeding system* can such a rapid expansion have occurred? Could a weapon-bearing, flesh-eating hunter have had a social system of a baboon type 1, or 2, or both?

Many authorities doubt this and have argued that the proto-hominids must have lived in territorially independent monogamous nuclear families, thereby taking us back to Westermarck. But these theories were put forward before much of the evidence we have cited was available (Bartholomew and Birdsell, 1953; Etkin, 1954; Eiseley, 1956). Most of their proponents find it necessary to criticise Chance. Etkin goes so far as to say that only as a result of the development of the 'integrated nuclear family' could the brain have evolved at all! Many arguments are used to back up this theory: man's carnivorous tendencies that suggest a wolf-like system; the lack of pronounced sexual dimorphism in man; the helplessness of the human infant; the long period of the child's dependency; the lack of the oestrus cycle in the human female, and year-round breeding; the need for co-operation between males and hence the need to reduce conflict over women; the inability of a male hunter to provide for more than one mate; etc., etc. On careful examination none of these arguments, nor any combination of them, seems adequate to support the conclusion drawn. They are riddled with internal contradictions and their proponents seem uncertain about many features and in particular about the nature of the social unit: was it a single territorially-independent nuclear family, or a large hunting band? Etkin, for example, suggests that the individual hominid families may have 'joined up' for hunting. If this is so, then he must agree that the basic unit was still the hunting band. The internal composition of it is a matter of dispute, but as against those who argue for independent nuclear families, Coon (1963) has argued that the polygynous propensity is uppermost in hominid mating patterns and that a dominance structure in which older males took first preference of females would have characterised archaic mating systems. Here we would have had permanent assignment of mates, and not just a monopoly of sexually receptive ones, but the assignment would have been in terms of dominance status. Only strong, successful, intelligent and sociable young males would also have achieved this status. I cannot here rehearse all Coon's arguments, but if he is right then we would have had a mating structure which would combine developing features of human reproductive physiology (such as the eventual loss of the oestrus phenomenon, the year-round potency of males and the dependence of the human infant) with a type of breeding system compatible with Chance's conditions for rapid cortical development. This breeding system could have evolved from something like either type of baboon structure, which could itself have had its basis in a chimpanzee-like system.

Here I would like to plead for a different approach to this question. It seems to me pointless to try to pin the Australopithecines down to any particular kind of institutional pattern. To wish on to these enterprising creatures a monogamous nuclear-family organisation seems unduly restrictive. The real question should be: what kind of breeding system did there have to be in order for certain crucial developments to take place? Many actual institutional arrangements could have met the criterion of a breeding system that would facilitate and encourage the rapid development of the neo-cortex. The one central fact that we need to grasp is that this system, on Chance's hypothesis, should be based on a dominance hierarchy. As we have seen, there are many variations on this theme, and ecology seems to call the tune.

I can perhaps here suggest one other possibility. The tendency to form pair-bonds for mating purposes seems strong in *Homo sapiens*, yet it is lacking in the great apes and in the baboon 1 types of mating system. (This was pointed out to me by Desmond Morris). Its appearance in baboon 2 is suggestive but is based on gross dimorphism and other features untypical of hominids. Could it be that a tendency to form such mating bonds is part of an ancient heritage stemming from a gibbon-like period of pair-territory existence in the earliest stages of hominid development? Could this have been a piece of equipment carried over from an ancient past, but masked by the exacting conditions of the pliocene? Or is it something that developed as rapidly as the brain itself during the hunting phase? (Wolves, it could be argued, like many carnivores, form pair-bonds).

Even if the latter is the case, how old is hunting? Baboons and chimpanzees do hunt, and there is no reason why the hominids of the pliocene and even the Australopithecines should not have resembled a 'hunting baboon'. After all, a prominent victim of the south African ape-man was a species of ancestral baboon. The dentition of the hominids suggests that adaptation to an omnivorous diet may be quite ancient. Thus a sexual division of labour and some form of pair-bonding, even if these are dependent on carnivorous tendencies and hunting, may have developed earlier than the pleistocene. However, this does not necessarily suggest a monogamous, family-loving animal. Indeed, if the little hominids were hunting powerful pack-living baboons, then it is inconceivable that they could have lived in territorially independent nuclear families. (Etkin sees this point.) And insofar as they were living in hunting hordes themselves, the possibility of the sub-units of these being monogamous nuclear families is remote. The pair-bond only means that there should be a relatively permanent assignment of mates. It does not in fact suggest anything about the domestic unit or the minimal unit of socialisation. It is perfectly compatible with an assignment of mates on a dominance basis, and in fact would probably serve to intensify the struggles and problems of the young males and increase even further the pressures of equilibration. The idea that has been advanced that the assignment of mates effectively 'reduces jealous conflict between males' seems somewhat optimistic.

If the hominid band veered towards the baboon-like structure, then the monogamous tendencies of man, such as they are, may simply be an outcome of changed ecological conditions, and a closer correlation of the male and female growth curves. The argument that monogamy occurred because males must provide for relatively immobile females, and that the males could only cope with one female at a time, is not convincing. There is no reason why the males as a whole should not have protected and provisioned the females as a whole, or why female *gathering* of roots, etc., should not have been important. This has nothing necessarily to do with the assignment of mates, and the case of wolves is a poor analogy. (In fact Chance has argued that the pair-bonding tendency of wolves *prevents* brain development!)

Freud notes that the murderous event might have awaited the advent of weapons. The brothers became cannibal savages, he says. Certainly the advent of weapons (or at least tools) and carnivorous tendencies has been held by many to herald a breakthrough in hominid advance, as we have seen. Cannibalism has been postulated for Pekin man. Certainly it would have been difficult for old males to eject permanently and keep at bay well-armed young males. In any case, as Freud sees, a co-operative body of possibly related males was a basic kind of human group. However, this development of weapons did not necessarily lead to murderous clashes, although the deduction that it did is not unreasonable. What it did lead to was elaborate systems of initiation in which the primate urges to dominance in the young males were tamed and reworked. The capacity to equilibrate was the basis from which rule-obedience developed and this was capitalised on in initiation which, after all, is usually ritually phrased in terms of explusion, exile, and reincorporation (killing, death and rebirth). The impulse to kill the old man is tempered by the impulse to *be* the old man. But as Margaret Mead points out, Freud is wrong to locate this process in the nuclear family alone. That unit is simply one possible focus of it (Mead, 1964). It is a tendency directed by the young males as a body against the old males as a body.

Again Freud is to some extent right about the processes (given the fantasy hypothesis), but misled about the focus of them both by his own ethnocentricism and the fictional family life of the gorilla.

We have skirted the other great problem of totemism and the incest taboos. But as we saw earlier, according to Lévi-Strauss, totemism is not so much an institution as a way of thought; a basic form of articulate thought. Now insofar as a critical advance in the growth of the neo-cortex was an essential pre-requisite for such thought, and insofar as this growth was an outcome of the process foreseen by Freud, to describe totemism as a necessary outcome of the great event may not be so far wide of the mark. Of course this is cheating slightly. As to incest, we must leave that to another time, but sufficient has perhaps been said here to make it clear that many ideas about incest, exogamy and culture will have to be revised and can be revised within the framework of analysis we have used (see, for example, Imanishi, 1965).

My conclusions have been rather diffuse, and I have only been able to give an outline - even a caricature - of the problems involved, For example, it was clearly not *only* equilibration that led to brain growth, but many other pressures as well. We cannot aim at certainty in this field, but we can by patient sifting of evidence and by avoiding too many slick analogies and imaginative leaps, reduce our area of ignorance, reduce the number of possibilities, until we can perhaps reach a fair approximation of what happened 'In the beginning'. This would itself only be a beginning: a beginning, I would hope, of a revival of the Malinowskian questions about biological needs and cultural behaviour. Once again we may see anthropologists asking the *real* anthropological question: not 'what is social structure', but 'what is man?'.

References

Altmann, S.A. (Editor) (1965). *Japanese Monkeys: A Collection of Translations.* Selected by K. Imanishi. Atlanta: Altmann.
Bartholomew, C.A. and Birdsell, J.B. (1953). Ecology and the proto-hominids. *American Anthropologist*, 55, 481-489.
Campbell, B.G. (1966). *Human Evolution: An Introduction to Man's Adaptations.* Chicago: Aldine.
Carpenter, C.R. (1964). *Naturalistic Behaviour of Nonhuman Primates.* Philadelphia: Pennsylvania State University Press.
Chance, M.R.A. (1962a). Nature and special features of the instinctive social band of primates. In *Social Life of Early Man*, edited by S.L. Washburn. London: Methuen.
Chance, M.R.A. (1962b). Social behaviour and primate evolution. In *Culture and the Evolution of Man*, edited by M.F. Ashley Montagu. New York and London: Oxford University Press.
Chance, M.R.A. and Mead, A.P. (1953). Social behaviour and primate evolution. In *Evolution.* Symposium of the Society for Experimental Biology. New York and London: Jonathan Cape.
Coon, C.S. (1963). *The Origin of Races.* London: Jonathan Cape.
Crook, J.H. (1966). Gelada baboon herd structure and movement: a comparative report. *Symposium of the Zoological Society of London*, 18, 237-258.
Crook, J.H. and Gartlan, J.S. (1966). Evolution of primate societies. *Nature*, 210: 5042, 1200-3. London.
DeVore, I. (1965a). The evolution of social life. In *Horizons of Anthropology*, edited by Sol Tax. London: Allen & Unwin.
DeVore, I. (Editor) (1965b). *Primate Behaviour: Field Studies of Monkeys and Apes.* New York: Holt, Rinehart & Winston.
DeVore, I. and Washburn, S.L. (1964). Baboon ecology and human evolution. In *African Ecology and Human Evolution*, edited by F.C. Howell and F. Fourlière. London: Methuen.
Eiseley, L.C. (1962). Fossil man and human evolution. In *Culture and the Evolution of Man*, edited by M.F. Ashley Montagu. New York and London: Oxford University Press.
Etkin, W. (1954). Social behaviour and the evolution of man's mental capacities. *American Naturalist*, 88, 129-142.
Freeman, D. (1965). *Totem and Taboo: A reappraisal.* Mimeo. Canberra: Australian National University.
Freud, S. (1952). *Totem and Taboo.* New York: W.W. Norton.
Geertz, C. (1965). The transition to humanity. In *Horizons of Anthropology*, edited by Sol Tax. London: Allen & Unwin.
Goodall, J. (1965). Chimpanzees of the Gombe stream reserves. In *Primate Behaviour: Field Studies of Monkeys and Apes*, edited by I. DeVore. New York: Holt, Rinehart & Winston.
Hall, K.R.L. (1966). Distribution and adaptations of baboons. *Symposium of the Zoological Society of London*, 17, 49-73.
Imanishi, K. (1965). The origin of the human family: a primatological approach. In *Japanese Monkeys: A Collection of Translations*, edited by S.A. Altmann. Atlanta: Altmann.
Jay, P. (1965). Field studies. In *Behaviour of Nonhuman Primates*, edited by A.M. Schrier, H.F. Harlow and F. Stollnitz. New York and London: Academic Press.
Keith, A. (1948). *A New Theory of Human Evolution.* London: Watts & Co.
Kortlandt, A. and Kooij, M. (1963). Proto-hominid behaviour in primates. *Symposium of the Zoological Society of London*, 10, 61-88.

Kroeber, A.L. (1920). Totem and taboo: an ethnologic psychoanalysis. *American Anthropologist*, 22, 48-55.
Kroeber, A.L. (1948). *Anthropology*. New York: Harcourt, Brace.
Kummer, H. and Kurt, F. (1963). Social units of a free-living population of hamadryas baboons. *Folia primate*, 1, 4-19.
Lang, A. and Atkinson, J.J. (1903). *Social Origins* by A. Lang; *Primal Law* by J.J. Atkinson. London: Longmans Green.
Leakey, L.S.B. (1967). An early miocene member of Hominidae. *Nature*, 213: 5072, 155-163. London.
Lévi-Strauss, C. (1949). Les structures élémentaires de la parenté. Paris: Presses Universitaires de France.
Lévi-Strauss, C. (1962). *Le Totémisme Aujourd'hui*. Paris: Presses Universitaires de France.
Linton, R. (1936). *The Study of Man*. New York: Appleton-Century.
Malinowski, B. (1927). *Sex and Repression in Savage Society*. London: Kegan Paul, Trench & Trubner.
Malinowski, B. (1944). *A Scientific Theory of Culture and Other Essays*. Chapel Hill: University of North Carolina Press.
Mead, M. (1964). Comment on: The human revolution, by C.F. Hockett and T. Ascher. *Current Anthropology*, 5, 160.
Napier, J.R. (1964). The evolution of bipedal walking in the hominids. *Archives de Biologie*, 75 (Suppl.), 673-708.
Napier, J.R. (1967). The antiquity of human walking. *Scientific American*, 216, 56-66.
Reynolds, V. (1965). Chimpanzees of the Budongo forest. In *Primate Behaviour: Field Studies of Monkeys and Apes*, edited by I. DeVore. New York: Holt, Rinehart & Winston.
Reynolds, V. (1966a) *Kinship and the Family in Primates and Early Man*. Mimeo.
Reynolds, V. (1966b). Open groups in hominid evolution. *Man*, 1, 441-452.
Reynolds, V. and Reynolds F. (1965). *Budongo: A Forest and its Chimpanzees*. London: Methuen.
Rowell, T.E. (1966). Forest living baboons in Uganda. *Journal of Zoology, London*, 149, 263-276.
Sahlins, M.D. (1959). The social life of monkeys, apes and primitive man. In *The Evolution of Man's Capacity for Culture*, edited by J.N. Spuhler. Detroit: Wayne State University Press.
Savage, T.S. and Wyman, J. (1847). Notice of the external characters and habits of *Troglodytes gorilla* a new species of orang from the Gaboon river; osteology of the same. *Boston Journal of Natural History*, 5, 417-443.
Schaller, G.B. (1963). *The Mountain Gorilla: Ecology and Behaviour*. Chicago: University Press.
Schultz, A.H. (1936). Characters common to higher primates and characters specific for man. *Quarterly Review of Biology*, 11, 259-283; 425-455.
Simons, E. (1964). The early relatives of man. *Scientific American*, 211, 51-62.
Washburn, S.L. (1959). Speculations on the inter-relations of the history of tools and biological evolution. In *The Evolution of Man's Capacity for Culture*, edited by J.N. Spuhler. Detroit: Wayne State University Press.
Washburn, S.L. and Avis, V. (1958). Evolution and human behaviour. In *Behaviour and Evolution*, edited by A. Roe and G.G. Simpson. New Haven and London: Yale University Press.
Washburn, S.L. and DeVore, I. (1962). Social behaviour of baboons and early man. In *Social Life of Early Man*, edited by S.L. Washburn. London: Methuen.
Westermarck, E. (1891). *The History of Human Marriage*, Vol. 1. London and New York: Macmillan.
Zuckerman, S. (1932). *The Social Life of Monkeys and Apes*. London: Routledge & Kegan Paul.

2
THE POSSIBLE BIOLOGICAL ORIGINS OF SEXUAL DISCRIMINATION

Lionel Tiger

Why is it that in the vast majority of societies men run the show and women are relegated to the smaller domain of the household, that men are almost universally the aggressive and dominant ones and women the passive and dominated? Is it purely because of the persistence of tradition?

From indications found in the group life of non-human primates, our nearest animal relatives, Professor Tiger suggests that the Darwinian law of species survival evolved large, dominant males, forming strong bonds with other males which helped in organizing and managing the community, and evolved females oriented towards the propagation and stabilization of social structures.

The Biological Basis of Behaviour

For too long many social scientists have paid inadequate attention not only to the work and thought of behavioural biologists but also to the biological aspects of human behaviour. Sociologists, political scientists and economists have used a model of man in which biological factors were unimportant, or at least residual; no ready means of assimilating information about other living systems than the human has been available to researchers into human social action.

It thus remains the case (though this will change rapidly in the next decade) that undergraduate and post-graduate students in the social sciences almost never are required to demonstrate any serious proficiency in biology. Though they may be subjected to an immense and sophisticated burden of methodological and mathematical instruction and they will learn very well indeed how to collect and handle data, they are hardly likely to learn what data to gather in the first place - in the sense that students of other animals are guided by biological principles to determine what behaviour patterns and what events in the lives of animals reflect a species' central problems, concerns and adaptations.

One serious social and scientific consequence of this is that - as usual - women have suffered particular deprivation. Because of the blurring of biological distinctions, even the categories 'maleness' and 'femaleness' have been inadequately treated - perhaps much less than the less significant and less provocative categories 'rich' and 'poor'. The overt and surprising reason for this is that it has been tacitly assumed that in all spheres except the explicitly reproductive males and females are much the same. To suggest otherwise implies biases of a quasi-racial kind. Moreover, there was also an implication that female equality in practice might be eroded by the assumption of female difference in theory.

My argument in this essay is that it is necessary to see biological factors as of prime importance in discussing maleness and femaleness. This involves understanding human evolution, human neurophysiology, cross-cultural regularities - in general, the biological infrastructure of human social relationships. Knowing as we do the importance of socio-sexual differences in many mammalian reproductive systems, perhaps it will not surprise if, employing this perspective, we learn that we are a species boasting considerable male-female differences which extend and ramify more widely through our human societies than many of our theories of socialization, organization and action in general would have us recognize and predict.

In this brief essay I want to comment about differences in male-female social organization. The suggestion is that, not unreasonably, these social differences bear relationship to biological realities of the human species which in turn are functions of human evolution and of a particular set of primate adaptations; these adaptations include both those uniquely our own and those we share with some other primates (with whom we find we share behavioural characteristics, just as earlier we were surprised to find that we share significant physical ones). The broad outlines of the argument are more fully presented in my book *Men in Groups* (1969); here, I want to discuss the significance this argument may have for our social theories and action.

In essence, the position derives from the following set of ethnological observations and theories. The behaviour of animals evolves just as physical structure does, and both structure and function (which is a systematic way of saying behaviour) reflect animals' evolutionary adaptation to their material and social environments. This adaptation is always mediated by processes of sexual selection which Darwin first explicitly described. The social behaviour of animals is, hence, not altogether sudden. It is not, in other words, only the expression of particular local and ephemeral circumstances. Even relatively complex social propensities can be programmed genetically - just as the extraordinarily complex life cycle, for example, is programmed by genetic codes and finds its expression in a reciprocity between the particular 'programmed energy' of an organism and the concatenation of habits, practices, situations and likelihoods which is a social culture (Lorenz, 1958).

As far as humans are concerned, the problem of isolating genetically determined, behaviour patterns is magnified because we are fond of creating elaborate and sometimes secretive social systems.

Hunting, The Master Pattern

It could be said that our most elaborate biological adaptation is to create culture. But if culture is our most complex concoction, it remains unchallenged by anthropologists and biologists that hunting is the master pattern of the human species. It is the organizing activity which integrated the morphological, physiological, genetic and intellectual aspects of the individual human organisms and of the population who compose our single species. Hunting is a way of life, not simply a 'subsistence technique', and it involves commitments, correlates and consequences spanning the entire biobehavioural continuum of the individual and of the entire species of which he is a member.

'That man achieved a worldwide distribution while still a hunter reflects the enormous universality of this kind of behavioural adapation . . . he practiced hunting for 99 percent of his history . . .' (Laughlin, 1968). In other words, our practice of hunting was the infrastructural condition of our specialized evolution, and though it is tempting to see in this only a confirmation of theories of human bloodiness and evil, it remains the case that hunting was a co-operative activity and that in the acts of pursuit and slaughter there was selective advantage to those individuals able to work together, attuned to each others' needs, resources and states, and willing to mould their individual behaviour to the collective pattern of the groups (Bigelow, 1969).

The critical subordinate section of this argument (for our purpose here) is that hunting was an all-male enterprise and that just as there was selection *for* co-operative hunting males, there was selection *against* both those females willing to hunt and those males agreeable to female participants in their hunts. The reasons for this proposition depend on a variety of individually disputable bits of evidence. But their over-all implications seem to point forcefully in the direction of an increased differentiation of male-female behaviour through evolution at the same time as there was probably a decreased physical differentiation.

Of course, differences in running methods, throwing skills, temperature adaptability, effects of physiological changes, etc., were clearly both the cause of and the effect of differentiated hunting experience. At the same time, the intriguing hypothesis remains that an important feature of this behavioural differentiation was the development of differing interests in and capacities for social bonding. Just as selection for reproduction operated by establishing and consummating bonds between males and females (and this was broadly programmed - for example, to follow puberty), so selection as a result of hunting depended on the readiness of the organisms concerned to form male-male bonds for these purposes while at the same time rejecting male-female ones during the hunting period. Presumably this applied too during those preliminary and celebratory-recriminatory events which were probably essential to the prosecution of strenuous tasks involving considerable technical and co-operative skills.

The fact that we have been a hunting species for probably one million years and possibly up to 26 million underlines the significance of this hypothesis of male-male linkages for the establishment of species-specific patterns of behaviour. These must remain influential today, if only as parameters in terms of which the force and effect of the patterns may be altered or vitiated by cultural factors and by the existential circumstances of particular individuals.

Biological Determination of Women's Role
But what has all this to do with women today?

At one level the role of biology in constraining the lives of women is obvious. Reproduction involves pregnancy and at least a short period of commitment to highly demanding offspring whose physical needs are not only inconsiderately recurrent but also who make psychological claims on mothers' time and energy. These claims can be avoided only by: (a) inadequate mothering, whose effects on the entire life span of the offspring we are now beginning to appreciate not only from data on humans but in essence from such studies on non-human primates as the Harlows'; (b) by a system of servants which relieves mothers of many of the burdens of rearing children (but not of having and dealing with servants); (c) a communalized system of child-rearing ranging from the kibbutz to a system of crèches and day nurseries - the economic rationale for this, however, is not only to make it easy for women to have children but to make it possible for them to work in the economy more directly than as managers of private households and mothers; and finally (d) a cultural system in which children are raised by kin of either mother or father (social or biological) but in which, in any event, women do raise children at various points in their lives, even if these are not their own offspring.

This much is obvious, and though societies respond in various ways to the problem of aiding and mollifying the stresses of child-rearing, it remains the case that this process constitutes a real (if widely approved) impediment to following the same career pattern as men. A number of communities have provided for this by offering facilities for mothers which allow them time off from work - either on a short-term or long-term basis - opportunities for retaining after an absence, the maintenance of pension and other rights, etc., and the retention of 'equity' in a career line in an organization, industry, or in the community at large. Despite these provisions, however, females typically constitute a more floating segment of the labour market, work at lower rates of pay and in lower-level positions, and are more likely to be dismissed by organizations retrenching their personnel.

In general, it remains the case that females, in virtually every society, are to a large degree excluded from positions of power and substantial reward. They are clearly subdominant and even where they are educated as well as males and possess equal economic resources, they fail to achieve posts, properties or honorific awards in any degree comparable to those of males. Moreover, they find themselves largely outside the major political, economic and military decision-making processes of our time.

Of course, this is not to recommend this situation, but to identify once again the gap between the ideology of sexual equality and the reality of an only tentative and sporadic movement to this equality.

My point is that the reason for this hiatus between wish and reality is not simply the result of male churlishness, chauvinism or fear. Nor is it similar to the differences between the privileges and opportunities of different economic classes or races in stratified societies. Nor is it solely the result of a coercive process of socialization which condemns disadvantaged females to live equably and with misguided self-satisfaction. Simple-minded though it may seem, perhaps the difficulty females have faced arises in good measure because the rhetoric and the dream of equality have allowed communities to avoid coming to terms with real differences between the sexes - differences which go beyond the explicitly reproductive, and which have to do with the conduct of social affairs on even its most abstract and complex levels.

To help understand this suggestion in its proper context, it may be useful to look briefly at the social behaviour of other primate males and females, bearing in mind that we are primates ourselves - though different from all the others - and that it is possible that we share some ancient core patterns of 'genetically programmed behavioural propensity' just as we clearly have in common certain evident physical structures and processes.

Primate Sex Bonds and Group Structure

An obvious feature of primate behaviour to which primatologists pay attention early in their research is male-female differentiation. In some species there is relatively little, except for the bearing and immediate rearing of children. This is particularly so among arboreal creatures for whom the problems of defence are more easily solved by fleeing up a tree than by generating defensive social organization. On the other hand, among terrestrial groups such as the south African baboon, the demands of defence on the savannah have led to the evolutionary selection of males about twice as large as females, with large jaws and sharp canines, and in general physically equipped to defend the females and young of their communities.

A correlate of these defence patterns - which so far as we know involve males only - is that the males, both the dominant ones and the sub-adult ones, form 'bonds' - groups in which the individuals regard themselves as more significant to each other than to non-bond members. These are, in a real sense, 'personal' relationships, as distinct from aggregation-type encounters in which there is no real element of choice.

What is fascinating about these male bonds is that they seem to be associated with political dominance. This is, in turn, directly linked with the dominant males having the greatly preponderant sexual access to oestrus females. Thus, there is the clear implication that selection of males willing and able to form bonds with other males is a constant feature of these primates' reproductive function.

This introduces quite a new element into the whole matter of social bonds and their relationship to reproduction. Not only does a male animal have to want to and be capable of consummating an encounter with a fertile female, but to reproduce himself he must also be able to engage in relatively very long-term and elaborate social relationships with several other males. Though sub-adult males do form weak bonds (rather like human boys' gangs - and, as in the human, there are no female gangs), only dominant adult males seem to be able to form these with political effectiveness. The subdominant males appear to be incapable of forming strong bonds because even four or five of them are unable to combine to overthrow the leadership of the two or three dominants from whose bonds a great deal of super-individual power is generated.

Thus a picture emerges from generalizing about the terrestrial primates; it features the importance of bonds among males for the process of selection. An additional point of equal relevance is that the stability, order and defence of the community depend on the male-bonded individuals: politics and reproduction are closely linked. *Hence the Darwinian processes of natural selection involve a combination of sexual competence with females and social competence with males.* This in turn appears to stabilize communities, provide models for the young males, and seems, indeed, to conduce to the 'health' of females as well as dominant males.

(In one as yet unpublished study, it is noted that in a group of rhesus monkeys in which there was no male, the females were incapable of 'governing' the group and social tension and disorganization were constant. The introduction of but one adult male into the group corrected the situation immediately, and a more normal political and social pattern quickly returned.)

What is relevant in all this to our concern here is that primate females seem biologically unprogrammed to dominate political systems, and the whole weight of the relevant primates' breeding history militates against female participation in what we can call 'primate public life'.

This is not only to say that female primates have no social bonds. Of course they do. First of all, they form intense bonds with their offspring and this bond is as crucial to group survival as the male-male bond seems to be.

Moreover, as we get more and better data about primate life it becomes clearer that there is something similar among some primates to 'kinship systems' among humans (Reynolds, 1968). Particular individuals born of certain females recognize certain inter-generational relationships between each other, and in terms of the group as a whole there is a tendency for the offspring of high-status females to become high-status themselves. Rudimentary but functioning 'class structures' then appear to arise - not in connexion with any particular property or other resource but in terms of social relationships themselves.

That the young of dominant females should be more competent, more confident, and more capable of approaching the dominant males on whom 'advancement' depends, should not surprise us altogether. But that this is also a function of rather elaborate group-kinship structures suggests that even such complex patterns as these may be broadly rooted in a biological foundation and that the contribution of females to these systems is meaningful not only for their offspring but for the entire group and - presumably for the species as a whole.

Further, that this female participation seems to tend toward the formation of stratified rather than egalitarian communities must be an item to consider among those schools of thought which are based on the broad belief that more primitive states of society - such as animals enjoy - are open and pleasant by comparison with human ones, and that the contribution of females to social procedures must be generally wholesome, egalitarian, and contrary - so runs the diagnosis - to the dismal and unhappy hierarchical structures which males create and endlessly refine.

The Genetic Foundation of Masculine Dominance

Let us return to the human case directly. In humans the bonding propensity of males - if it exists - would have been given an additional evolutionary emphasis by the function of hunting. It is important to remember that among non-human primates there is little if any differentiation between the sexes in the food-gathering activity. This is crucial, because if hunting in the human species was for males only, then a pre-existent male bonding pattern which we might have inherited along with the primates may have been strongly and unambiguously accentuated by our special human innovation of co-operative hunting. In other words, while in other primates the sexual division of labour had chiefly to do with defence and politics in the human case this was expanded to include economics too, and herein may lie some of the resistance which human communities appear to show still to even the most sophisticated and ardent efforts to achieve sexual equality.

Every human community displays some sexual division of labour. The allocation of tasks may vary enormously. In one society a particular job will be for men and in another the same job for females. Some jobs will be done by both. But the significant regularity is that there is always some distinction between male and female work for some jobs and on some grounds. Sometimes these are linked to obvious physical factors: they involve speed, danger, muscular strength, etc. None the less, there is often no technological justification for the sexual distinction, and one is driven to the conclusion that the pattern of sexual division of labour may relate not only to real differences in skills, aptitudes and interests, but to a core pattern of the human primate: that in some circumstances, particularly those defined as dangerous, important for the community, or involving matters of high moment, males will exclude females from their groups and engage in male bonding undisturbed.

That this may be both a deliberate and an infra-social, broadly unconscious pattern - in the same sense as the male-female bond, based on sexual attraction and reproduction, is both conscious and infra-social - underlines the difficulty of doing something about this; it aggravates the difficulty of knowing precisely how to go about obtaining female equality in the labour, political, and associated spheres.

In other words, I am suggesting that a species-specific pattern of *Homo sapiens* is the creation of particular bonds between males, that these bonds are intrinsically related to political, economic, military, police and other similarly power - and dominance - centred social subsystems, that equal female colleagues - even one - could interfere with these bonding processes, that one reflection of this principle is the constant division of labour by sex, and that while conscious social management of these processes may of course alter or reverse them, the propensity to behave in this way will continue to manifest itself in each new generation until genetic change 'breeds it out' - a process which even under current circumstances is very improbable in any foreseeable future.

Of course, all this is impossible to prove in the sense that an exact and reproducible cause gives rise to an exact and reproducible effect. However, biologically speaking, a species is an experiment without a control group - except in so far as it bears systematic and acceptable comparison with other species (Tinbergen, 1963) - and in the human case we can use cross-cultural data to point toward items of behaviour which are common to all cultures, thus species-specific, and those which are clearly culture-specific. Hence, I have argued that the ubiquity of the male dominance and female exclusion patterns which can be identified is a serious indication of the possibility that these patterns may originate in our genetic codes, and in the interactions between genetic code and social group and particular circumstances in which individual codes work themselves out.

It should not surprise us that maleness and femaleness as biological categories have elaborate effects on even complex technologically based behaviour. Both are clearly biological features of the core of individual beings, and while there are many similarities between males and females, it is scientifically parsimonious to attend to the possibility that behavioural differences in other spheres are as significant as those in the reproductive.

At the outset of this essay I suggested that social scientists have paid inadequate attention to biological science and noted that this was particularly marked in the matter of male-female differences. It may be of interest to try to overcome this inadequacy and try to follow out some of the consequences of a revised view of control-by-genetic-process of broad social patterns and particularly of the effect of genes on the situation of women as well as on our attitudes.

How Theoretical Equality Causes Factual Inequality

My basic proposition takes the form of a paradox: that the understandable and universally acceptable notion that males and females are equal and should have all equal rights of law, economy, politics, etc., has contributed to the practical inequality of females.

Theoretical sexual equality has forced rejection of any concern about sexual differences. The practical result of this has been the continued deprivation of females and the slowing-up of a process of opening opportunities to women in present structures, of changing the structures and of adding new ones to accommodate women. At the moment, it is women who must accommodate themselves, and they are being asked to compete with men in male-oriented institutions. The net result of this is their continued deprivation and a recently increased resentment and anxiety.

A number of obvious examples come quickly to mind. A variety of researches have confirmed what many other less sophisticated communities have known all along - that the female menstrual cycle has some appreciable and predictable effects on female social, psychological and even technical behaviour. Crime rates, industrial accident rates and incidence of illness, for example, have been correlated with the regular cycle.

A recent report by K. Dalton of the University College Hospital, London, reveals that young women writing examinations are affected by as much as 14 per cent by the time of their cycle at which they undertake some tests. The implications of this simple finding are of course enormous. For example, persons wishing to enter graduate school in the United States of America must take special examinations on a national standard. Should a woman write these during her low-performance time, she begins with virtually a second-class result and the work of her previous years in the educational system and her own personal qualities and skills may be severely devalued. In good part this is because she participates in a system which does not formally recognize her femininity, admitting that it may be the cause of changes in behaviour or performance of direct pertinence to the educational system which has so expensively provided her the opportunity for seeking graduate training.

The same effect will operate less dramatically but with persistent consequences throughout a young woman's educational career; it must also retain its impact during her functions in some job. This can become serious, not only for the individual woman's well-being and occupational success, but for the clients of her particular service or effort. The effect will be more clearly exposed as women increasingly perform tasks involving the exercise of technological judgement upon which depends the safety of other people. The relationship of the cycle to motor-car accidents has been pointed out; it seems inevitable that should women become airline pilots it will be necessary for their work schedules to conform to their biological rhythms - not because accidents are inevitable, but because they become somewhat more likely and hence a risk subject to control by conscientious managers.

Now, the writing of examinations and the flying of airliners are two rather extreme contrasts. But in both cases there is sufficient suggestion of the effects of the male-female difference on performance for sensitive communities to consider ways of mitigating the consequences of these for individual females and for the community at large. It seems likely that communities willing to take these factors into account will respond more suitably and immediately to situations involving real danger and the use of expensive artifacts such as aircraft and heavy industrial machinery.

The subtler and less tangible matter of scheduling educational, commercial, and other activities to take individual women's cycles into account seems much less likely to be implemented easily. Perhaps the two outstanding reasons for this are: (a) to do so would be to recognize formally and overtly real differences between males and females - something which communities have in a curiously successful and tenacious way managed to avoid doing, in the name of the ethic of equality, and (b) there appears to remain a widespread taboo of more or less severity against the formal statement by both men and women of the fact and occurrence of menstruation, though this depends on the attitude of the community involved, of course, It is not clear to what extent this is a function of females' desire to maintain some privacy in this respect, or of males' resentment and perhaps even fear of a process.

A study using the Human Relations Area Files by Young and Bacdayan (1965) describes an unusually bizarre correlation between political authoritarianism and the strength of taboos against various degrees of contact with menstruating females. This suggests that there is considerable variation in this matter (as in any other) between communities and among individuals. It also portends that communities with relatively liberal political attitudes may be more likely to openly acknowledge the existence of the menstrual cycle and cope with its consequences. Yet, at the same time, in some such liberal communities - United Kingdom, the United States and Canada, for example - there is a particular reluctance to deal with such a female-specific matter as the cycle. Perhaps this is indeed for the first reason given above, namely that such an expression of difference might be construed as an expression of inferiority.

The particular reason for stressing the effect of menstrual cycling on work performance is that it is both relatively clear-cut and an excellent example of the general fact that the work patterns of industrial communities in particular are male-oriented. The 7-to-9-hour 5-to-6-day pattern of work of course represents the densest and apparently most efficient way of organizing the time of individual employees.

My point is very simple: were work adjusted to female propensities, as it is now to those of males, a more humane and effective 'fit' between system and individual could follow.

The same principle applies to the relationship of working mothers and children. It is customary that those employees with full privileges are full-time employees. Again, this is defined in male terms. However, there is no special reason, beyond habit, inertia, the reluctance to face complexity, etc., why mothers cannot be treated as full-time employees with full privileges - in proportion to their contribution - even if they work only a few hours a week, or one or two days, or three half-days, or according to any other arrangement which permits them to spend as much time with their young as they regard to be necessary, while participating in the wider tasks available in paid employment.

At the moment, in technologically elaborate communities it is chiefly the unpaid volunteer lady worker who is permitted a flexible participation in the socio-economic network. If such arrangements can be made for volunteer employees, it is not inconceivable that they can be made, too, for paid employees. This is not to say that no part-time job possibilities are open to females, for of course there are. But such employment is always secondary in importance and individuals are discouraged from seeing their work as part of a continuing career; the very fact of their responsibility to their families permits them only a partial commitment to their employers.

The same comment applies to phasing of female work over years as well as days. The community spends great sums of money educating women to undertake jobs which the rigidity of its own structure makes it difficult for them to assume and maintain should they wish to bear children and spend considerable periods of time with them for several years or until they enter school. Similar problems of pension rights, seniority, retraining, and continuity arise for the mother whose working career is interrupted as for the part-time worker.

It is curious that at the same time as various organizations and governments claim difficulty in attracting and retraining committed and competent skilled employees, systematic and seemingly insurmountable barriers are placed in the way of the largest single pool of available personnel to fill these posts. And not only do the pertinent organizations themselves lose, but so does the community in general because of the resentment, confusion and conflict of loyalties between past training and present situation which more and more females experience simply because more and more women are being elaborately and carefully educated.

Male Bonds and Female Exclusion

Menstrual cycles and child-rearing are very obvious factors in any effort to assess the reality and possibility of female participation in what we can call the 'macro-structures of society' - those involving large-scale organization and the major corporate enterprises. More subtle but perhaps even more significant influence are the essentially primate valences - bonding tendencies - to which I referred earlier. I mean by this that the tendency for males to form bonds in work, fighting, politics, etc., and the more obvious but equally pervasive propensity for males and females to form at least ephemeral bonds centring round the process of sexual titillation and consummation, may be as formidable barriers to egalitarian female employment as the obvious ones directly related to reproduction. And an additional factor which has been often overlooked both by ethnographers and students of contemporary politics and economics is the apparent difficulty females have in forming the bonds necessary in order to manage structures involving power and wealth. Let us explore these factors in turn.

It should by now be clear that the proposition here is that if males bond because it is 'in the nature of the beast' to do so, then this places a considerable burden both on women seeking to join these bonds, and on those men willing to allow females into groups when this may signally affect the groups and the relations between group members.

One intriguing example of this phenomenon is the secret society; only exceptionally are these heterosexual. They are mostly all-male and when women do join them, this appears to mark the end of the society's particular drama and effect on its surroundings. This is, again, not to recommend a particular attitude or policy towards secret societies. But it is to suggest that they express certain effective propensities of the human male and that we can observe in these curious and unpredictable organizations a feature of male behaviour in the voluntary world which may find more formal expression in the more overt and legislated worlds of business, politics, etc. (Tiger, 1969. Chap. 6).

Team sport is another example of this phenomenon; with the exception of tennis and skating, team sports are overwhelmingly unisexual. Except for the most violent of sports, there is no reason why rules governing female participation could not be introduced and appropriate numbers of women join teams. But I suggest that team sports depend on the bonding process and that female participation is anathema to this and would severely curtail the enjoyment of both players and spectators because of the disturbance of the male socio-dramaturgy of sport.

Perhaps both secret societies and sports will be seen by some as a wretched and retrogessive failure of males to embrace a modern and wholesome sexual egalitarianism. It may also be sensible to see them as rather complex projections of species-wide (and their incidence is species-wide) propensities for male bonding. In any event, they do exist (though secret societies are under considerable pressure, particularly in the United States) and represent a clue to what many men are concerned about and to the ways in which they willingly choose to spend their time.

If we apply the principles of these forms of association to other areas we can see that the rejection of female co-workers by males may stem from more than retrogressive pique, prejudice, lack of sympathy for females, or some other impetus regarded as malignant and uninformed. This means that coping with this rejection may involve dealing with subconscious processes which are possibly of ancient primate origin and which have for several million years and until just recently served very well for political and economic survival. What we may call 'the anti-female tradition', has its origins, then, not only in belligerent male chauvinist ideology and, in economic exploitation of females, but in a genetic process which evolved because pre-hominids found they could survive and reproduce better if they excluded females from the processes of political dominance, with survival further aided by the exclusion of females from the hunting party.

The Disruptive Male-Female Bond

One obvious reason for such exclusions has to do with the male-female bond. This linkage, we know, can be extremely passionate and vexatious and it is of endless interest to observers of both fictional and real stories of romance. What Desmond Morris has called 'the pair bond' can be as ardently and obsessively maintained as any known among humans. While it can merge the lives of a male and female, it can also disturb class, religious and other social systems. Such is its strength that even the most persuasive rules of these systems are subject to disruption by a male and female caught in the bonding encounter. Yet while this bond can be intense it can also be ephemeral; this is the 'crush', the 'affair', the sporadic, problematic attraction of a male and female who presumably do not marry (though they may reproduce), some form of marriage being, presumably, the social end-product of this private valence. It is ephemerality which is of interest to us here as we consider the role of females in male-dominated structures.

First of all, one may ask Desmond Morris: what about the *'au pair* bond', that common idyllic dilemma of the bourgeois male who finds his home occupied by a young woman with whom he is forbidden to engage sexually despite her proximity and possible attractiveness? After all, she was imported to solve his wife's problems, not add to them. While this is a frivolous example, it none the less underscores a particular feature of the male-female bond: that it is potentially disruptive, volatile, unreasonable, demanding, and very possibly hostile to the purposes which brought the male and female into contact in the first place. This is particularly so where the individuals concerned are relatively young and where they must spend extended periods of time together.

The implications of this for the conduct of socio-economic and political activities are obvious. One of the intriguing features of business organizations and similar structures in Europe and North America is the lack of formal recognition of the problem posed by the pair-bonding impetus. There is, of course, an undergrowth of awareness. Private taboos or understandings abound: teachers may not 'pair-bond' with their student though students of other instructors may be more acceptable; and students at other institutions - why not?

The same rules of prohibited organizational incest are supposed to apply to relations between doctors and nurses, managers and secretaries, scientists and research assistants, and so on. That these are honoured in the breach as well as the observance suggests to some degree the difficulty of governing a highly charged primate pattern by the relatively fragile informal and even formal rules of organizations. And all this also suggests one further disadvantage which women face in their effort to secure comradeship with men in places of work - given the extant male-dominated structure.

The pair-bonding problem is soluble, with whatever strenuous efforts and accommodations that may be necessary, when the encounter is between unequal individuals. Doctors and nurses, actresses and producers, stars and starlets, can perhaps deal better with this disruption of formal relations than individuals in equal or near-equal positions.

Robin Fox has suggested that polygamy is not really about sex but about dominance, that sexual access is more important than sexual action (1968). His point is that polygamy may reflect human retention of the primate pattern where males dominate females and express this dominance in sexual activity. This point is, of course, contentious. But my argument remains that males and females of appropriate age and demeanour will seek some sexual *rapprochement* and that the conflict between formal colleagueship and differential sexual power may be disruptive in work and politics and other large-scale systems.

All this may seem far-fetched, and one dares broach this particular subject in this particular fashion only because of its obvious conflict with the demands of organizations for members to behave in formally sanctioned ways. Understandably, the introduction of this particular manifestation of sexual energy into organizations becomes more hazardous the higher in the hierarchy are the individuals concerned. Perhaps it is this combination - sex as a feature of male dominance, and sex as disruptive of relations between powerful equals - which augments the traditional cultural prejudice in very many communities against the installation of women in posts of power.

The Female-Female Bond

Before concluding, I must make several remarks about another kind of bond, the female-female bond. The groups which females form appear to occupy themselves less with macro-structures of society than with micro-structures. In general, they seem to be less persistent over time and involve fewer people in associations having less organizational and technical complexity, both in humans and the other primates.

Recently there have been several sets of data published about primate groups in which female-managed 'kinship structures' are significant for the continuity of primate bands across several generations, and even for the general guidance of the process of selection of male leaders (Reynolds, 1968). Perhaps further research may reveal the female bonds that exist in the other primates, and that these serve evolutionary functions, particularly in the critical sphere of rearing the young and, through socialization, establishing the continuity of the future with the present. Be that as it may, the fact is that in the human case there is a highly significant division of food-gathering labour - as distinct from non-human primates, among whom all able individuals find their own food - and this suggests that the factor of male bonding among humans may well have been more important than among the other (vegetarian) primates.

Should we find that primate females specialize in social organization and the maintenance of kinship patterns, this could accord with human data about the centrality of the domestic arena for female action. Necessarily, the facts of reproduction govern this at certain stages of the life cycle. Thus, there is the real possibility that selection has always favoured females who have surrounded themselves and their children with a group of kin and other females who provide information, security and the simple and necessary ease of social contact.

As much as solitary hunters face a difficult task, so do solitary mothers. In so far as biological processes can select for such gregarious characteristics, it is possible that a female bonding propensity does exist, with a focus on the relatively intimate matters of families and children rather than on the macro-structures involving war, hunting, defence, sport, religion and so on, which appear in virtually all cultures to obsess and stimulate human males.

A host of present data about the reluctance of females to work for, vote for, or otherwise be associates of other females would then follow from this fact - if it should be proven to be a fact - that females in groups function best when occupied with tasks in the community consistent with those appropriate to their more limited familial ones.

Again, this is not to recommend this situation, nor to excuse the difficulty females have in penetrating male-dominated organizations or in contriving all-female dominated ones. My purpose is to note briefly that just as in pair-bonding or male-bonding, female-female bonding may involve biologically determined infra-social processes. The factor of sexual competition for the attention and (implicitly) breeding potential of males is an additional restraint on the co-operation of females over extended periods of time and under various forms or degrees of social pressure.

I have tried to outline some of the parameters of biology within which efforts at social change may have to operate. Defining or describing a situation is not to excuse it, but presumably to provide some factual and theoretical basis for changing a system once it is understood. That the existing state of affairs is all involved with passionately felt prejudices, aspirations, fears and uncertainties makes it all the more necessary to ask why the position of women in society after society has remained unsatisfactory to idealistic and enterprising men and women.

The conspiracy theory of why this is so, and the class theory - curiously mixed as it is with an overtone of prejudice similar to that of racism - may be insufficient axes around which a discussion can revolve, for such discussion must also take into account what new biological and other data we have which may be pertinent.

Of course, there are limits to the utility of a biological model, too - it is too easy for some to say that what is true because of biology must always remain social reality; but this is just not so. Our human biology is, however, the fundamental foundation on which social reconstitution must perforce be based. There can be no other foundation. And the task of ideologists and makers of public policy must be to incorporate biological reality into the idealism of their programmes and the scope of their extensions of human possibilities.

References

Bigelow, R. (1969). *The Dawn Warriors: Man's Evolution Toward Peace.* New York: Atlantic-Little, Brown.

Fox, R. (1968). The evolution of human sexual behaviour. *New York Times Magazine,* 24 March.

Laughlin, W.S. (1968). Hunting: an integrating biobehaviour system and its evolutionary importance. In *Man the Hunter,* edited by R.B. Lee and I. DeVore, p.304. Chicago: Aldine.

Lorenz, K. (1958). The evolution of behaviour. *Scientific American,* December.

Reynolds, V. (1968). Kinship and the family in monkeys, apes and man. *Man* 3, 209-223.

Tiger, L. (1969). *Men in Groups.* New York: Random House; London: T.Nelson.

Tinbergen, N. (1963). On aims and methods of ethology. *Zeitschrift für Tierpsychologie,* 20, No.4.

Young, F.W. and Bacdayan, A.A. (1965). Menstrual taboo and social rigidity. *Ethnology,* 4, No. 2.

3

ANTHROPOLOGY AND POPULATION: PROBLEMS AND PERSPECTIVES

Moni Nag

The rate of growth of the human population has *not* been uniform throughout history, nor have those of the societies comprising it. Some societies have become extinct, most have experienced periodic ups and downs in population size. While scholars from many fields may contribute substantially towards reconstructing the history of human population dynamics and understanding its determinants and consequences, anthropologists have their own contribution to make. What follows is a brief review of some important contributions which have already been made or can be made by cultural anthropologists in three critical areas of population study: (1) long-term history of population dynamics; (2) demographic processes in primitive and peasant societies; and (3) population (size, density, and pressure) and culture.

Long-Term History of Population Dynamics

Anthropologists have questioned the validity of the human population growth curve usually presented by demographers, which shows a drastic increase in world population since about 1750 or so, and a very slow but gradual increase up to that time (Durand, 1967). They recognize that a population upsurge started with the industrial revolution but tend to agree with Deevey (1960) that humanity experienced at least two other upsurges in population size at the advent of two previous technological revolutions, namely, the tool-making revolution and the agricultural revolution, and that there was an approach towards equilibrium in the two inter-revolutionary periods of the past. Several anthropologists of past generations (Kroeber, 1948; Childe, 1942) found it logical to assume that the agricultural revolution produced a spurt of population growth. Braidwood and Reed (1957) provided some archaeological and ethnological evidence to estimate the population concentration in different development levels of Old World culture history. According to them, the density of population rose sequentially through the stages of 'natural' food-gathering, 'specialized' food-collecting, primary village farming and primary urban community, the figures given being 3.0, 12.5, 2,500 and 5,000 per 100 square miles respectively. These estimates are, however, based on assumptions which require much further research for satisfactory validation. Even though we may recognize a general association between increases in population density and the evolution of subsistence technologies, much controversy remains concerning the causal relationships underlying this association. This issue, central to theories of cultural evolution, will be discussed in a later section.

The modern theory of 'demographic transition' was developed to explain the population dynamics of western countries in the post-industrial period. From high levels of both mortality and fertility in the pre-industrial period, the population of these countries settled down to low levels of mortality and fertility through a transitional stage of low mortality and high fertility levels (Thompson, 1929). One of the underlying assumptions of this theory is that both the mortality and fertility levels of all pre-industrial societies were generally very high. Anthropologists have questioned this assumption. For example, I have shown elsewhere that there is a great variation in the fertility levels of contemporary non-industrial societies (Nag, 1962, pp. 15-18). There is some palaeo-pathological and ethnological evidence to suggest that the mortality level of hunting-gathering societies was not necessarily high (Polgar, 1972).

Demographic Processes in Primitive and Peasant Societies

Anthropologists have traditionally conceptualized the spread of man over the surface of the earth in terms of migratory movements rather than in the framework of population growth which is a result of the balance between the three demographic processes; fertility, mortality and migration. It is only during recent years that anthropologists have been studying the factors which affect these processes through which, and only through which, population size and density can change. As expected, anthropological studies of population have been done mostly with reference to 'primitive' and peasant societies which are generally beyond the purview of sociologically or economically oriented demographers.

Migration
There is no dearth of examples in human history of spontaneous migration induced by natural phenomena, such as glaciation, flood, earthquakes, etc. The recognition of migration as a specific measure of population policy is, however, not a very common phenomenon. It is interesting to note that in ancient China the schools of Confucius and a few other Chinese philosophers held the government primarily responsible for maintaining an ideal balance between land and population by moving people from over-populated to under-populated areas. They noted that governmental action was reinforced by spontaneous migration (United Nations, 1953).

Barbados, a very densely populated plantation island in the Eastern Caribbean, provides a modern example of large-scale emigration which followed the calculated policy of its government, adopted in 1863 after a prolonged drought in the island (Nag, 1970). For Tikopia, a Polynesian island, Firth (1936, p. 414) records the practice of men, especially the young and unmarried, setting out on overseas voyages.

Kasdan (1970) summarizes the history of the continuing interest of anthropologists and sociologists in explaining migrations in terms of social, material, historical and psychological factors. He points out that the shift from a social-psychological approach (Park, 1950) to the sociological approach in the study of migration was probably initiated by anthropologists in an attempt to understand the policies of colonial administrators and the impact of western economic institutions on relatively isolated peasant and tribal societies. The concept of 'networks' (social and spatial connections between individuals and groups), developed by Barnes (1954) and elaborated by Epstein (1961) and Gutkind (1965) in their studies of migration in Africa, has been utilized fruitfully in a number of migration studies presented in a recent symposium on *Migration and Anthropology* (Spencer, 1970).

Mortality
The principal factors held to be responsible for the periodic or occasional increase of mortality rate in pre-industrial societies are those which have been categorized by Malthus as positive checks to population growth: famine, epidemics and war. Anthropologists have very rarely interested themselves in famines and epidemics. It seems that there were many situations in which the risk of famine was greater among the agriculturists and pastoralists than among hunting-gathering peoples because the population units of the former were larger. Moreover, the simple agriculturalists and pastoralists did not have sufficient safeguards against the failure of crops or decimation of flocks (Polgar, 1964). With regard to epidemics, it is generally accepted that these must have been less significant among hunting-gathering peoples because of the smaller size of their social groups and lesser frequency of contact between groups.

Anthropologists have shown some interest in the demographic determinants of war but so far have shown very little interest in its demographic consequences. There is general agreement (Harris, 1971) that the conditions for bringing whole groups into total mutual hostility were probably non-existent throughout most of the palaeolithic period, and hence mortality caused by warfare is believed to have been relatively insignificant during this period. Whatever evidence we have of armed conflicts among the contemporary hunters and gatherers tends to support this view. There is no doubt that relatively stable nucleated settlement and a few other factors associated with agriculture generated conditions favourable to armed conflicts between groups, which can legitimately be called wars. Illustrations of such wars can be found in various articles written recently by anthropologists in a book entitled *War: The*

Anthropology of Armed Conflicts and Aggression (Fried *et al.* 1968). Harris (1971) argues that the principal cause of warfare among simple agriculturists is population pressure, thus viewing warfare primarily as a population-regulating system. Casualties from warfare in pre-industrial societies were probably quite high in some cases, but as a population-regulating system, epidemics must have been more effective, at least in agricultural societies.

The practice of infanticide, a relatively well-recorded phenomenon, seems very often to have been a manifestation of population policy for the family or larger kin group. Until fairly recent times, among the Australian aborigines, when a mother felt that she would be unable to rear a child because she had another small child of breastfeeding age, the newborn was buried in the sand or simply allowed by the mother to die, with the approval of her husband (Spencer and Gillen, 1927). The purpose behind infanticide is very often spacing, necessitated by prolonged dependence of children on breastfeeding and by the difficulty of carrying more than one baby at a time. Among the Netsilingmuit Eskimo, girls were thought to be less economically productive than boys; female infanticide was practised because the parents could not 'afford to waste several years nursing a girl' (Balikci, 1968).

Infanticide is reported to have been practised not only in hunting and gathering societies but also by many peasant societies. Pakrashi (1968) has made a survey of female infanticide in India during the 18th and 19th centuries, and found that it was practised quite widely among certain castes of the states of Uttar Pradesh and Punjab.

Fertility
Carr-Saunders (1922), a British demographer, was the first to make a comprehensive study of the fertility levels of non-industrial societies and the factors affecting them. His survey was based on the fragmentary, and hence largely unreliable, data provided by nineteenth-century anthropologists, missionaries, travellers, etc. One of his generalizations was that the fertility level of what he called 'primitive races' is generally quite low. This he attributed to involuntary factors, he believed, widespread in the population concerned - pre-pubertal sexual intercourse and the prolongation of lactation. The main voluntary factors for low fertility on this level, according to him, were induced abortion and prolonged abstention from intercourse, particularly after childbirth. In a UNESCO-sponsored study of cultural conditions affecting fertility in non-industrial societies, Lorimer *et al.* (1954) offered the following hypotheses, among others: (1) societies emphasizing unilineal (either patrilineal or matrilineal) descent and having corporate kinship groups tend to generate strong cultural motives for high fertility; (2) cohesive groups, such as extended families, do not necessarily stimulate high fertility but tend to enforce

conformity to societal norms; (3) social disorganization may increase or decrease fertility, depending upon whether the disorganization favours 'apathetic acceptance of circumstances' or is associated with sterility-inducing diseases.

The studies made by Lorimer *et al.* and those preceding them did not provide or use any comprehensive framework for the study of factors affecting human fertility. Davis and Blake (1956) provided a useful analytical framework for the comparative study of culture and human fertility. They identified and classified eleven 'intermediate variables', such as age at marriage, fecundity, contraceptives, etc. through which, and only through which, any cultural factors influencing the level of fertility must operate. In my cross-cultural study of factors affecting human fertility in 61 selected non-industrial societies (Nag, 1962), I used the above analytical framework and found that the post-partum abstinence and sterility induced by venereal diseases were two of the important factors having significantly negative association with fertility level.

There seem to exist social institutions and practices in all known human societies which tend to keep fertility levels below biological potential. Perhaps it is also true that there are social institutions and practices in all human societies specifically intended for controlling family size and birth interval. Although these hypotheses still need further cross-cultural testing, there is some supporting historical and anthropological literature already on hand. In their discussions of optimum population, Plato and Aristotle proposed restriction of births, if necessary (United Nations, 1953). Aristotle mentioned abortion and child exposure as suitable means of preventing an excessive number of children. He also mentioned homosexuality as a means of population control, and homosexuality was indeed practised by the Cretans. The ancient Romans, on the other hand, were more alert to the advantages of population growth for military and related purposes. Their writers disapproved of celibacy and defended monogamous marriage. Roman legislation aimed at raising the marriage and and birth rate.

The anthropological literature shows that induced abortion is a very widespread practice in human societies. But is is very difficult to assess from the available literature the extent of the actual practice of abortion and how far it is or was practised for the primary intent of limiting family size or child-spacing (Devereux, 1955). The extent of the practice of abortion seems to vary widely in both non-industrial and industrial societies (Nag, 1962, pp. 77-82). The degree of approval or disapproval of abortion may depend partly on the concept of the phase when the foetus is supposed to be imbued with life. It may also partly depend on the status and freedom enjoyed by women in a given society.

Prolonged abstinence from sexual intercourse is known to have been found to be negatively associated with fertility level in non-industrial societies. Abstinence and the rhythm method are among the main methods responsible for decline of fertility in western societies. The practice of abstinence and rhythm as methods of birth control may vary according to the general attitude toward sex in various societies. It may, for example, be hypothesized that the Hindus in India are more likely to accept the rhythm method than the Muslims, because the Hindus are traditionally used to ritual abstinence on various occasions throughout the year and also because of their general attitude of moderation in sexual behaviour (Nag, 1972).

Coitus interruptus is reported to be the most widely diffused non-appliance method of contraception in the world and 'is probably nearly as old as the group life of man' (Himes, 1936). In the small Polynesian island of Tikopia, until recently, the heads of families were exhorted by the chief once a year to limit their number of children by practising *coitus interruptus* (Firth, 1936, p. 492). Ryder (1959) suggests that it was practised more widely in societies of pre-industrial Europe than in peasant societies of Asia or in contemporary western societies. He argues that in the pre-industrial European societies with conjugal familism and limited agricultural resources, marriage had to be postponed until there was sufficient guarantee for the economic viability of the union. This led unmarried couples to practise *coitus interruptus* in order to avoid pre-marital pregnancy. They continued the practice after marriage when economic difficulties arose. Their (speculated) preference for *coitus interruptus* over abortion and infanticide, Ryder assumes, is a reflection of their 'greater respect for individual life and marriage and the more extended economic horizon' than is prevalent among peoples of lower levels of science and technology. According to Petersen (1961), since the practice of *coitus interruptus* requires that the male be strongly motivated enough to frustrate his desire at the moment of highest excitation, it is expected to be less frequently practised in societies where the economic and social responsibility for the child is borne by the broader kin group, rather than mainly by the father, It seems true that the practice is less prevalent in Asia than in Europe, but we do not have sufficient data to check whether the hypotheses suggested by Ryder and Petersen offer an adequate explanation for this difference.

The fertility-regulating practices of non-industrial societies are often ignored by demographers in their analysis of population dynamics. Population growth in these societies is considered almost exclusively as a consequence of the diminishing effect of mortality-inducing factors. Very little attention is given to the fact that at least part of the population growth may result from the lesser use of fertility-regulating practices. The contact with industrial societies may mean not only the improvement of public health practices, transportation, etc., but also, at the same time, a reduction in the practices of abortion, infanticide, post-partum abstinence,

non-remarriage of widows, etc.
Anthropologists have so far shown more interest in the socio-cultural determinants of fertility than in the socio-cultural consequences of fertility change. One area of research in the consequences of fertility change, which would be of particular interest to cultural anthropologists, is the effect of reduced family size on consanguineous marriages. The temporary rise in the proportion of consanguineous marriages in two French localities at the end of the 19th century is ascribed to the reduction in family size (Sutter, 1968). We do not know whether or not this relationship can be generalized for other societies. Lévi-Strauss (1963) cites a demographic study which estimates the average size of French population 'isolates' (groups of intermarrying people) as varying 'from less than 1,000 to over 2,800 individuals'. This seems to be too small a range compared to that existing in other industrial societies. A reduction in family size among some particular groups in a society or in the society as a whole is expected to have its impact on many aspects of its culture: kinship, economics, social stratification, political organization, ideology, etc. The studies of social change in the modern world cannot afford to overlook or ignore these impacts.

Population (Size, Density, Pressure) and Culture

Most of the anthropological studies on fertility, mortality and migration, either as distinct or as interacting processes, have been conducted in quite recent years. The interest of cultural anthropologists, along with other social scientists, in the relationship between population size and density on the one hand and various aspects of culture such as means of subsistence and social organization on the other, goes back much earlier. However, until recently this interest manifested itself generally in a superficial or casual recognition of population growth as a factor in social and cultural evolution. During the last few years, a number of anthropological studies of greater depth have come out. Those which have dealt with the sociocultural consequences of population growth refer mainly to four specific aspects of culture: (1) means of subsistence, (2) kinship, (3) social complexity and (4) social stratification and political organization. A serious difficulty common to all these studies arises from the fact that the general consensus about the conceptualization and measurement of population characteristics (except population pressure), is not matched by similar agreement in the case of cultural characteristics. The studies reviewed in the following will show how cultural anthropologists have attempted to conceptualize and measure some characteristics of culture and relate them to population.

Means of subsistence
As stated earlier, there is some ethnological and archaeological evidence to

suggest that population size and density increase with the evolutionary sequence of the means of subsistence. In conformity with the principles of Malthus, this relationship has been interpreted by some anthropologists to imply that population size and density are determined by improvement or innovations in the means of subsistence. According to Harris (1971), 'the correlation between increases in techno-environmental efficiency and increases in the rate of population growth suggests that in the long run, production has determined reproduction'. A few others think that the growth of population has not been determined but permitted by the improvement of learned adaptations to the environment. In these anthropological formulations, although the technological knowledge of dealing with other environmental factors is also implied, the usual emphasis is on the acquisition of foodstuffs, perhaps expressed as the harnessing of energy. From an analysis of population growth in pre-industrial Europe, China and Japan, Dumond (1965) suggests that the size and the growth of a population are dependent on the following four elements: (1) fecundity, as culturally modified; (2) incidence of disease; (3) degree of peace obtaining; and (4) subsistence possibilities. According to him, the frequent tendency is to consider the first three elements as approximately constant with variations in the size of pre-industrial population resulting mainly from the variation in the fourth factor. I would like to make two comments here: (1) the four elements mentioned above are not independent of each other; (2) if population growth is affected by an increase in the techno-environmental efficiency related to the acquisition of food, it is important to investigate the relative influences of the processes of fertility, mortality and migration through which any population change occurs.

Some anthropologists and economists maintain that the growth of population is actually the cause of improvement in the means of subsistence rather than being an effect of the latter. White (1959) ascribes the beginning of agriculture in the Old World, that is, the initiation of the attempts to control the growth and reproduction of food-producing plants, to an increased pressure upon food supply caused by population growth. Some anthropologists have argued that specific societies they have studied have changed from shifting to permanent cultivation when faced by population pressure generated by a lack of sufficient land for adequate rotation (Dumond, 1961; Carneiro, 1961; Geertz, 1963). However, significant changes in the technology of food acquisition as well as in population size and density occur gradually over long periods. So it is extremely difficult or impossible to determine through empirical study of most historical sequences whether the change in population size and density is the cause or the effect of the changes in the technology of food acquisition. Boserup (1965) an economist, approaches the question from a different angle. Comparing the labour costs per unit of output in various

Anthropology and Population

systems of non-mechanized agriculture, she concludes that 'it is more sensible to record the process of agricultural change in primitive communities as an adaptation to gradually increasing population densities, brought about by changes in the ratio of natural population growth or by immigration'. One important corollary of her conclusion is that the primitive and peasant societies with sustained population growth may have a better chance to get into a process of genuine economic development than those with stagnant or declining population, 'provided, of course, that the necessary agricultural investments are undertaken'. In some densely populated societies this condition may not be fulfilled, if their rate of population growth is high.

Kinship
We have already noted that kinship organization is considered an important determinant of fertility. Some anthropologists have recently begun to view it as an effect of population size, density or pressure. Eggan (1950) observed among the western Pueblos that the multi-lineage clans were more stable and better capable of organizing a larger population than the single lineages. It led him to think that multi-lineage clans and phratries were devices adopted by societies as a response to population growth. A search for the cultural ecological explanation of the existence of patrilineal 'bands' among a number of tribes led Steward (1955) to conclude that sparse population density is one of the four factors which produce this type of multi-family group. Fox (1967) thinks that the societies with cognatic descent groups can adapt more easily to population pressure than those with unilineal descent groups because the greater flexibility in a cognatic group allows its members to redistribute themselves if it becomes far too large for its land. He finds support for his hypothesis in the popularity of the cognatic principle in small island communities with limited amounts of land. Harner (1970), however, contradicts Fox and postulates that the principle of cognatic kinship results from conditions of lowest population pressure while that of unilineal descent results in response to growing competition under conditions of higher population pressure. He thinks that the island societies with high population pressure (referred to by Fox) have cognatic descent groups because either they have their own class stratification or they operate under colonial administations. Both of these conditions undermine the competitive advantages of the unilinear principle. Harner finds support for his hypothesis in a statistical test of correlation between the principle of descent and the degree of dependence on hunting and gathering, calculated on the basis of the data provided by Murdock *et al.* (1962-67) in the *Ethnographic Atlas.* In order to relate the principle of descent to population pressure he makes an assumption which is not easily testable. It is that an inverse correlation exists between the degree of dependence on hunting and gathering and

the degree of population pressure in societies having any agriculture; and hence, the total degree of dependence on hunting and gathering in such societies provides a scale for measuring population pressure.

The decline in population size of a small society may seriously affect the traditional functions of its kin-based groupings. I cite below two such illustrations from the anthropological literature. Wagley (1951) shows how the rapid depopulation after Luso-Brazilian contact among the Tapirapé Indians of central Brazil seriously affected the normal functioning of their patrilineal ceremonial moieties (divided into three age-grades of men) and their non-exogamous 'feast groups' (patrilineal for man and matrilineal for women). The depopulation caused a lack of necessary representation of these groups in Tapirapé villages, thus making their social structure more vulnerable to disorganization. My second illustration comes from a study of the demographic and ecological influences on aboriginal Australian marriage sections (Yengoyan, 1968) which shows that the population size of an Australian tribe sets definite limitations on the operation of its section system, and that inter-tribal marital exchanges, theft unions and alternative marriages may occur (sometimes with destructive consequences) when ideal marriage partners are infrequent through decreasing tribal size. The relationship between population size and the proportion of marriages considered as ideal or preferred by a society is also corroborated in a computer simulation study of a human population. Kunstadter *et al.* (1963) found that the proportion of matrilateral cross-cousin marriage, which is the ideal in the model population, is positively related to population growth and to marriage rates, and that variability in the proportion of ideal marriages is inversely related to population size.

Social complexity
Herbert Spencer (1885) was perhaps the first social scientist to formulate a principle regarding the relationship between population size and social complexity. He stated that the increase of mass is the causal force in social as well as organic evolution and that as the population size of a society augments, its divisions and sub-divisions 'become more numerous and more decided'. Durkheim (1893) pointed out that the increase in population size is a necessary but not a sufficient condition for the development of division of labour in a society. Integration of a society on the basis of progressive functional differentiation occurs, according to him, when, in addition to the increase in population size there is also an increase in dynamic or 'moral density', which may be interpreted as the degree of communication among its members. Durkheim suggested the use of population density as a measure of 'moral density' because these are positively related.

The formulations of Spencer and Durkheim may be regarded as nothing more than insightful speculations. In any case, they were not immediately followed by adequate empirical investigations. There seem to be two main reasons for this: (1) the relative lack of interest in the study of sociocultural evolution during the first half of this century; (2) the difficulty of devising quantitative measures of socio-cultural complexity. Naroll (1956) takes a lead in devising such measures and applying them to 30 well-documented ethnic units. He finds a correlation between size of the largest community in a society and the following two measures of social complexity: (1) number of craft specialties; (2) number of 'team types'. Naroll defines team as a group of at least three people with clearly defined membership and formal leadership in regular use. The examples of 'team types' based on kinship, territory and association are extended family, village and village council respectively.

Carneiro and Hilse (1967) use a different measure of social complexity and investigate its relationship with total population size in a sample of 46 single-community societies. Their measure is the number of traits in a society which are primarily organizational, that is, which involve the coordinated activity of two or more persons. The graphic representation of the number of organizational traits of the sample societies plotted against their population shows a close relationship between the two variables.

Social stratification and political organization
The role of population pressure in the evolution of social stratification and political complexity has been a subject of empirical investigation by some anthropologists during recent years. Carneiro and Hilse (1966, 1970) suggest that population pressure in simple farming societies living in circumscribed areas with restricted arable land, acts as a stimulus to war and ultimately leads to the development of social stratification and state. They elaborate the process of this development in the coastal valleys of Peru, and think that such developments in the areas of circumscribed agricultural land elsewhere in the world, such as the Valley of Mexico, Mesopotamia, the Nile Valley and the Indus Valley, also occurred in much the same way. They seem to recognize population pressure not only as a necessary but also as a sufficient condition for the development of social stratification and state in societies under specific ecological and cultural conditions.

In a brief review of the anthropological literature on the relevant topic Fried (1967) considers population pressure as one of the necessary conditions for the development of social stratification and 'pristine' states, but explicitly rejects warfare and slavery as essential intervening steps in process. He cites a number of studies of aboriginal societies which indicate that an increasing population density gives rise to an increasing narrowness in granting access to basic resources which, in turn, leads the society towards social stratification.

Two British anthropologists, Fortes and Evans-Pritchard (1940), claimed in their classic introduction to *African Political Systems*, that no demonstrable relationship exists between population density in a society and the complexity of its political system. They supported this assertion with empirical data from six African societies. In a recent study of the relationship between population and political systems in tropical Africa, however, Stevenson (1968) departs from the strictly synchronic functionalist approach which, he feels, was largely responsible for the conclusions of Fortes and Evans-Pritchard. His re-analysis of each of the same six African societies from a historical and evolutionary perspective shows that population density and political complexity are positively related over time and that states are most often associated with denser population than non-states.

In his investigation of the relationship between population pressure and social evolution, Harner (1970) uses the degree of complexity in class stratification and political organization as indices of social evolution. He demonstrates by scatter diagrams and statistical correlation tests that the complexities in class stratification and political organization increase with the decreasing dependence on hunting and gathering. As stated earlier, his assumption that the degree of dependence on hunting and gathering provides a scale for measuring pressure is not easily testable.

Concluding Remarks

In a classic inventory and appraisal of the study of population, Hauser and Duncan (1959) make a distinction between 'demographic analysis' and 'population studies'. The latter, according to them, are concerned not only with population variables but also with relationships between population changes and other variables - social, economic, political, biological, genetic, geographical, and the like. Their volume includes articles relating demography to the following disciplines: ecology, human ecology, geography, physical anthropology, genetics, economics and sociology. The omission of some other disciplines, particularly cultural anthropology and psychology, probably reflects the fact that at the time the amount of work done with respect to population in these disciplines was not really significant.

The present paper shows the increasing interest of cultural anthropologists in population and identifies some significant research issues in population studies which are relevant to their discipline. It has not been possible to include all the areas of population studies to which anthropologists have contributed (Marshall *et al.*, 1972) . Examples of important areas which have not been dealt with in this paper are: (1) palaeo-demography (Angel, 1947; Howells, 1960; Kobayashi, 1967; Vallois, 1960) and (2) estimation of population size and other characteristics through genealogical, historical, and other non-conventional methods (Dobyns, 1966; Hackenberg, 1967, 1974; Thompson, 1966). The reader will not perhaps fail to notice in the paper my own special interest in fertility. My purpose, however, will be served if this brief overview stimulates more anthropologists to apply their disciplinary perspectives, concepts and techniques in population studies, and, at the same time, if it familiarizes population specialists in other disciplines with the contribution (existing and prospective) of anthropologists in this particular field.

References

Angel, J.L. (1947). The length of life in ancient Greece. *Journal of Gerontology*, 2, 18-24.
Balikci, A. (1968). The Netsilik eskimos: adaptive processes. In *Man the Hunter*, edited by R.B. Lee and I. DeVore, p. 81. Chicago: Aldine.
Barnes, J.A. (1954). Class and committees in a Norwegian island parish. *Human Relations*, 7, 39-58.
Boserup, E. (1965). *The Conditions of Agricultural Growth: The Economics of Agrarian Change under Population Pressure*, pp. 117-118. Chicago: Aldine.
Braidwood, R.J. and Reed, C.A. (1957). The achievement and early consequences of food production: a consideration of the archaeological and natural-historical evidence. *Population Studies: Animal Ecology and Demography. Cold Spring Harbor Symposia on Quantitative Biology*, 22, 19-31.
Carneiro, R.L. (1961). Slash-and-burn cultivation among the Kuikuru and its implications for cultural development in the Amazon Basin. In *The Evolution of Horticultural Systems in Native South America*, edited by J. Wilbert. Caracas.
Carneiro, R.L. and Hilse, D.F. (1966). On determining the probable rate of population growth during the Neolithic. *American Anthropologist*, 68, 171-181.
Carneiro, R. L. and Hilse, D.F. (1967). On the relationship between size of population and complexity of social organization. *Southwestern Journal of Anthropology*, 23, 234-243.
Carneiro, R.L. and Hilse, D.F. (1970). A theory of the origin of the state. *Science*, 169, 733-738.
Carr-Saunders, A.M. (1922). *The Population Problem.* Oxford: Clarendon Press.
Childe, G. (1942). *What Happened in History*, p.73. Harmondsworth and New York: Penguin Books.
Davis, K. and Blake, J. (1956). Social structure and fertility: an analytical framework. *Economic Development and Cultural Change*, 4, 211-235.
Deevey, E.S. (1960). The human population. *Scientific American*, 203, 195-204.
Devereux, G.(1955). *A Study of Abortion in Primitive Societies*, pp. 25-26. New York: Julian Press.
Dobyns, H.F. (1966). Estimating aboriginal American population. *Current Anthropology*, 7, 395-449.
Dumond, D.E. (1961). Swidden agriculture and the rise of Maya civilization. *Southwestern Journal of Anthropology*, 17, 301-316.
Dumond, D.E. (1965). Population growth and culture change. *Southwestern Journal of Anthropology*, 21, 302-324.
Durand, J.D. (1967). A long-range view of world population growth. *The Annals of the American Academy of Political and Social Science*, 369, 1-8.
Durkheim, E. (1893). *The Division of Labour in Society*, pp. 256-263. Paris and New York.

Eggan, F. (1950). *Social Organization of the Western Pueblos*, pp. 288, 300. Chicago: University of Chicago Press.
Epstein, A.L. (1961). Network and urban social organization. *Rhodes-Livingstone Journal*, 29, 21.
Firth, R. (1936). *We the Tikopia*, p. 414. London: Allen & Unwin.
Fortes, M. and Evans-Pritchard, E.E. (Editors) (1940). *African Political Systems*, p. 7. London: Oxford University Press.
Fox, R. (1967). *Kinship and Marriage*, p. 153. Harmondsworth: Penguin Books.
Fried, M.H. (1967). *The Evolution of Political Society: An Essay in Political Anthropology*, pp. 196-204. New York: Random House.
Fried, M.H., Harris, M. and Murphy, R. (Editors) (1968). *War: The Anthropology of Armed Conflicts and Aggression*. New York: Natural History Press.
Geertz, C. (1963). *Agricultural Involution: The Process of Ecological Change in Indonesia*, p. 36. Berkeley: University of California Press.
Gutkind, P. (1965). African urbanisism, mobility and social network. *International Journal of Comparative Sociology*, 6, 48-60.
Hackenberg, R.A. (1967). The parameters of an ethnic group: a method for studying the total tribe. *American Anthropologist*, 69, 478-492.
Hackenberg, R.A. (1974). Genealogical method in social anthropology: the foundations of structural demography. In *Handbook of Social and Cultural Anthropology*, edited by J. Honigman. Chicago: Rand McNally.
Harner, M.J. (1970). Population pressure and the social evolution of agriculturists. *Southwestern Journal of Anthropology*, 26, 67-86.
Harris, M. (1971). *Culture, Man and Nature: An Introduction to General Anthropology*, pp. 223-229. New York: Crowell.
Hauser, P.M. and Duncan, O.D. (Editors) (1959). *The Study of Population*, pp. 2-3. Chicago: University of Chicago Press.
Himes, N.E. (1936). *Medical History of Contraception*, p. 184. New York: Gamut Press.
Howells, W. (1960). Estimating population numbers through archaeological and skeletal remains. In *The Application of Quantitative Methods in Archaeology*, edited by R.F. Heizer and S.F. Cook. Viking Fund Publications in Anthropology, No. 28.
Kasdan, L. (1970). Introduction. In *Migration and Anthropology*, edited by R. Spencer. Proceedings of the 1970 Annual Spring Meeting of the American Ethnological Society. Seattle: University of Washington Press.
Kobayashi, K. (1967). Trend in the length of life based on human skeletons from prehistoric to modern times in Japan. *Journal of the Faculty of Science, University of Tokyo*, 3, 107-162.
Kroeber, A.L. (1948). *Anthropology*, p. 389. New York: Harcourt, Brace.
Kunstadter, P., Buhler, R., Stephen, F. and Westoff, C.F. (1963). Demographic variability and preferential marriage patterns. *American Journal of Physical Anthropology*, 22, 511-519.
Lévi-Strauss, C. (1963). *Structural Anthropology*, p. 293. New York: Basic Books.
Lorimer, F. et al. (1954). *Culture and Human Fertility*. Paris.
Marshall, J.F., Morris, S. and Polgar, S. (1972). Culture and natality: a preliminary classified bibilography. *Current Anthropology*, 13, 2.
Murdock, C.P. et al. (Editors) (1962-67). Ethnographic atlas. *Ethnology*, 1-6.
Nag, M. (1962). Factors affecting human fertility in non-industrial societies: a cross-cultural study. *Yale University Publications in Anthropology*, 66, 15-18.
Nag, M. (1970). The influence of conjugal behaviour, migration and contraception on natality in Barbados. In *Culture and Population: A Collection of Current Studies*, edited by S. Polgar. Monograph No. 9. Chapel Hill.

Nag, M. (1972). Sex, culture and human fertility: India and U.S. *Current Anthropology*, 13, 2.
Naroll, R. (1956). A preliminary index of social development. *American Anthropologist*, 58, 687-713.
Pakrashi, K. (1968). On female infanticide in India. *Bulletin of the Cultural Research Institute*, 7, 33-47.
Park, R.E. (Editor) (1950). Human migration and the marginal man. In *Race and Culture*. edited by R.E. Park. Glencoe: Free Press.
Petersen, W. (1961). *Population*, p. 547. New York: Macmillan.
Polgar, S. (1964). Evolution and the ills of mankind. In *Horizons of Anthropology*, edited by Sol Tax. Chicago: Aldine.
Polgar, S. (1972). Population histories and population policies from an anthropological perspective. *Current Anthropology*, 13, 2.
Ryder, N.B. (1959). Fertility. In *The Study of Population*, edited by P.M. Hauser and O.D. Duncan, p. 430. Chicago: University of Chicago Press.
Spencer, B. and Gillen, F.F. (1927). *The Arunta*, pp.39, 221. London: Macmillan.
Spencer, H. (1885). *The Principles of Sociology*, 1, 449-450. New York: Appleton.
Spencer, R.F. (Editor) (1970). *Migration and Anthropology*. Proceedings of the 1970 Annual Spring Meeting of the American Ethnological Society. Seattle: University of Washington Press.
Stevenson, R.F. (1968). *Population and Political Systems in Tropical Africa*. New York: Columbia University Press.
Steward, J. (1955). *Theory of Culture Change: The Methodology of Multilinear Evolution*, pp. 123-135. Urbana: University of Illinois Press.
Sutter, J. (1968). Fréquence de l'endogamie et ses facteurs au 19e siècle. *Population*, 23, 303-324.
Thompson, H.P. (1966). Estimating aboriginal American population: a technique using anthropological and biological data. *Current Anthropology*, 7, 417-424.
Thompson, W. (1929). Recent trends in world population. *American Journal of Sociology*, 29, 959-975.
Vallois, H.V. (1960). Vital statistics in prehistoric populations as determined from archaeological data. In *The Applications of Quantitative Methods in Archaeology*, edited by R.F. Heizer and S.F. Cook. Viking Fund Publications in Anthropology, No. 28.
United Nations (1953). *Determinants and Consequences of Population Trends*. Population Studies No. 17, p. 21. New York: Population Division of Department of Social Affairs.
Wagley, C. (1951). Cultural influences on population: a comparison of two Tupi tribes. *Revista de Museum Pauline* (Nova Serie), 5, 95-104.
White, L.A. (1959). *The Evolution of Culture*, p. 286. New York: McGraw.
Yengoyan, A.A. (1968). Demographic and ecological influences on aboriginal Australian marriage sections. In *Man the Hunter*, edited by R.B. Lee and I. DeVore. Chicago: Aldine.

4
THE SOCIAL IMPACT OF HUMAN REPRODUCTION*

Alan S. Parkes

Man is essentially a gregarious animal and is subject, therefore, to both biological and social pressures. As a result, almost everything he does has biosocial repercussions. This is especially true of reproduction, which is a biological process with an overriding social impact. If human reproduction came to an end, so would the human race. By contrast the present unprecedented combination of a high reproductive rate and a high survival rate is causing widespread concern. One may take the view that mankind, by reason of its exploding numbers, is rushing to a Gadarene doom, or the opposite view that man has brains as well as gonads and will cope with his proliferation. In either case, one must admit that at the present time there is a population problem.

The reason for the problem is obvious. In nature every species combats a low survival rate with a high reproductive rate. In man, in modern times, medical science has raised the one without, so far and taking the world as a whole, having done much to lower the other. The result, as we all know, is an increase in world population which simple arithmetic shows cannot be sustained indefinitely. This conclusion was authoritatively pin-pointed in a forceful report by a committee of the National Academy of Sciences in Washington published nearly 10 years ago. The verdict of the Committee was that 'either the birth rate must come down or the death rate must go back up'. In this situation, which in essence is quite simple, we have our greatest biosocial problem; it is essentially one of adjusting reproductive potential to a level of reproductive performance appropriate to modern conditions of survival.

Man's Reproductive Capacity

First of all, what is this reprodutive capacity which, in association with a high survival rate, is so alarming? Given a normal sex ratio, the average production of one surviving female child per woman would result in a potentially stable population. By contrast, the average production of two surviving female children would double the population every generation,

---

* A lecture delivered under the title 'Biosocial aspects of human reproduction' at a joint meeting of the Australian and New Zealand Association for the Advancement of Science, the members of an IPPF SEAO Region Medical and Scientific Conference and the Family Planning Association of Australia, 17th August 1972.

say every 25 years. A geometric increase of this kind would obviously be castastrophic in an historically short time. Yet human reproductive capacity is well beyond the comparatively modest output of two female children per woman.

A fertile male, during his lifetime, produces untold billions of spermatozoa, and under conditions of polygyny, because of his minor contribution to the reproductive process, could father, and undoubtedly has fathered, many hundreds of children. Similarly, female reproductivity is not usually limited by the supply of germ cells. The human ovary starts with some hundreds of thousands of oocytes which are not added to in later life. This fact has the highly biosocial implication that a woman of 40 years old who produces a child, does so from an egg which is around 40 years old and may by this time not be at its best. The initial oocyte population is rapidly depleted by atresia, but nevertheless, a woman begins her reproductive life with a supply of eggs vastly in excess of the number that can be used. Even if she sheds one egg every 4 weeks for 30 years she is using only around 400 by this means, and the most that could be consumed by pregnancy is, of course, far less.

What then are the limits of female reproductive performance? The world record is said to be held by a Russian peasant woman who is reputed to have produced, in the middle of the last century, sixty-nine children in twenty-seven confinements; sixteen pairs of twins, seven sets of triplets and four sets of quadruplets. This prolific woman was, moreover, only the first wife of the children's father. We may well regard this story as on a par with that of the Russian sesquicentenarians, but Great Britain is well up with the field. The current record appears to be a mere twenty-two or so but it is recorded that a woman living in Hertfordshire in the 17th century married at the age of 16 and had a world record of thirty-eight confinements in which she produced thirty-two daughters and seven sons. Her last son, who died around 1740, became a distinguished surgeon and wrote a book on embalming (*Guinness Book of Records*). In a recent visit to Peru I saw a newspaper heading which, translated, said 'Mother of 24 children refuses the pill'. The Hutterite communities in the US, dedicated to farming and reproduction, have put up some remarkable records. In 1941-50, their birth rate was 45.9 per 1000; in the early 1950s the average completed family size was ten, and their women commonly produced children when over 40 years of age (PRB, 1968). The Amish are almost equally prolific; an Amish man who died in 1961 left 410 living descendants (PRB, 1961). Man's reproductive capacity, therefore, though small in relation to his supply of gametes, is still very great. Why then, has the human race not exploded earlier in its history? The answer is well known.

In nature every species, however high its reproductive rate, is held in check by limiting factors of which the main ones are food supply, disease and predators, and there can be no doubt that until comparatively recent times, such factors, aided often by restrictive social customs, were extremely effective in checking population growth. It took up to half a million years (depending on its antiquity) for the human race to reach an estimated 300 million in the year AD 1000 and more than another 800 years to reach an estimated 1000 million early in the 19th century. Thanks to the efforts of medical and agricultural scientists we are now rushing up to an estimated 7000 million by the end of the 20th century. Such an historically sudden increase in the numbers of so large an animal as man, whose biomass of perhaps 250 million tons is by far the largest among living animals, is indeed a remarkable biological phenomenon and would have been impossible had man remained a food gatherer and hunter like other animals. Remarkable or not, the increase cannot go on indefinitely. Something will happen to stop it. The question is, what will that something be. Is human fecundity declining spontaneously or will it do so under the unnatural pressures of civilization and overcrowding? Will it be left to the limiting factors of nature to assert themselves more vigorously than at present? Finally, and this is the supreme question, will man learn consciously to adjust his fertility to the potentialities of his environment and so distinguish himself from the lower animals in a far more fundamental way than he does by the possession of, say, works of art and nuclear weapons?

Is Human Fecundity Declining?

So few communities now reproduce to their biological limit that it is difficult to answer this question comprehensively but communities such as the Hutterites offer no suggestion of any decline in human fecundity. For the individual fecundity is certainly not declining to a level appropriate to the present and prospective survival rate. In some ways it may even be increasing. Puberty is arriving earlier than it used to do (though the idea that it is doing so by 1 year every 10 years - a truly frightening thought - is a gross exaggeration) and in our permissive society the fecundity of mere children is being amply demonstrated.

In the UK recently a girl of 12 years old had a therapeutic abortion; the boy responsible was said to be a year older. In 1971, about 4000 girls under the age of 16 years in the UK were known to have become pregnant and no doubt many more were unrecorded. Even 20 years ago, well before the state of the present permissive era, Dublin (1951) noted that a few dozen fathers under the age of 15 years were recorded each year in the US, corresponding to fertile intercourse around the age of 14 years or earlier. In this connection it may be recalled that conception before menarche is possible, and has been recorded (Döring, 1962), because in the normal way ovulation precedes menstruation and may do so even with the first cycle at puberty. The ultimate in fecundity is held by a Chilean girl

5 years of age who was delivered of a live child by Caesarian section and so became the youngest recorded mother in human history (Escomol, 1939). This girl started to menstruate at 8 months old and was almost certainly a case of precocious puberty of hypophysial origin. At the other end of the scale, there is no satisfactory evidence that the age of menopause is increasing, i.e. that the reproductive life span is extending at both ends (McKinlay, Jefferys and Thompson, 1972), but, even so, a woman in the US a few years ago, is said to have produced a daughter at the age of 57.

In a different way the time taken to conceive when conception is desired should be a good index of fecundity, since it involves the reproductive efficiency of both male and female. It is difficult to get hard data, but Guttmacher (1956) concluded that three out of four couples, not using contraception, effected conception within 6 months, the median time being 2½ months. Figures of 30% within 1 month and 90% within 1 year have also been recorded. In a recent pilot survey, four of eleven girls studied in detail when requesting a legal abortion had become pregnant from a single or isolated coition (Pearson, 1971). Other figures have, of course, been very different. Pearl (1939) estimated that more than 259 acts of uncontracepted intercourse were, on the average of all ages, required to induce a pregnancy; even with young couples, supposedly at the most fecund age, the figure was reduced only to 175. He may have been correct, but the figure is likely to raise a smile on the face of any woman who became pregnant on her honeymoon. All in all, therefore, it would be difficult to maintain that the fecundity of the human couple shows signs of declining.

Demographically, of course, there is plenty of evidence of a decline in human fecundity in the sense of reproductive performance. The long and steep decline in the birth rate in France during the 18th and 19th century, associated with a decline in family size from over six to about two, is sometimes cited as evidence of declining human fecundity; it is certainly an example of declining demographic fertility, but what connection does this have with biological capacity? Demographers and statisticians must deal in populations, cohorts, age specific rates, projections and such like high level stuff, but what the biologist wants to know is what happens at bed level to give rise to the data which the demographer uses.

Apart from such factors as late marriage, a decline in human reproductive performance can be due only to a decline in fecundity, including a decline in sex drive, to negative or positive contraception or to induced abortion. Few, I think, would suggest that in the 18th and 19th centuries there was an epidemic of abstinence, a catastrophic decline in sex drive or a failure of other components of biological fertility. Negative contraception, in the form of CI was no doubt prevalent, as it still is. Positive contraception was primitive and must have been highly unreliable -

one recommended recipe was a vaginal sponge soaked in brandy. There was also, of course, a brisk trade in appliances made from animal tissues, the aesthetic impact of which can be judged from the fact that they were commonly referred to as 'machines'. Positive birth control, as opposed to positive contraception, in the form of induced abortion must also have been resorted to frequently, and no doubt infertility arising from do-it-yourself methods added its quota to the decline in family size. All in all, therefore, it is not difficult to ascribe the fall in the birth rate in France to causes other than a decline in biological potential.

Similar considerations apply to the decline in the birth rate in England and Wales during the first 30 years of the present century, when family size decreased from around four to two, an all-time low. A committee of the Royal Commission on Population, set up in 1944, of which I had the interesting experience of being a member, could find no evidence that the decline was biological in origin, so that it was presumably due to voluntary birth control by some means or other. This conclusion was confirmed by the fact that the Committee's deliberations were cut short by the post-war baby boom.

The Pressures of Civilization and Overcrowding

If, therefore, the potential reproductivity of mankind is not decreasing spontaneously, is it likely to do so in future in response to evolutionary, physiological or psychological factors inherent in civilization and overcrowding? We have, for instance, the intensive campaign to damp down the fertility of fertile people and the almost equally intensive campaign to remedy the infertility of infertile people. Will these paradoxical efforts cause high fertility to lose its survival value, and, if so, will the ultimate result be a decrease in biological fertility? The answer will obviously depend on many factors, including the extent and nature of infertility, especially of its genetic components, and the extent of the resources which, under present conditions of population pressure, society is willing to devote to remedying it.

Cost-benefit studies are often used to reinforce the massive case for the limitation of fertility, and similar studies will some day have to be used to rationalize the treatment of infertility. For instance, it is difficult to imagine that, for the community as opposed to the individual, procedures such as egg transfer and *in vitro* fertilization, however interesting biologically, could be justified therapeutically on a cost-benefit basis. Much the same applies to the induction of ovulation by treatment with gonadotrophins, for which elaborate control facilities are necessary to avoid super-ovulation and the traumatic experience for the woman of producing a litter. So far, the record in this direction appears to be held by an Italian woman, who had fifteen fetuses removed at the fourth month following hormone treatment.

One thing, however, is clear. Whatever may be the evolutionary result of present trends, not even the most optimistic observer can think that human fecundity will decline, in response to a loss of survival value, in time to solve the present population problem. The re-direction of human evolution, to a point at which the average woman could produce only two or three children in a life-time, is not likely to happen quickly, if ever. But it is possible that the slow processes of evolution will be speeded up by changes in the physical and social environment. We hear a lot about pollution, especially about the chemical insults to which we are constantly subjected. Will these affect human reproductive capacity and, if so, will they do so in time to supplement conscious efforts towards limiting human fertility. It is impossible to say, but there are suggestive reports, as to impotence among pesticide workers.

Of possible relevance here is the decrease in the dizygotic twinning rates which has occurred in many countries, especially in Europe, since 1957 (James, 1972). It is well known that the DZ rate varies greatly in different parts of the world from around 6/1000 in Japan to 50/1000 in parts of Africa, while the MZ rate is remarkably constant at 4-5/1000. Against this background the fall in the DZ rate in the last 10 years is remarkable, especially for Scotland, where the rate slumped from around 10.4/1000 in 1958 to 6.4/1000 in 1968. In England and Wales the fall started from a lower level but was otherwise similar, and much the same applies to Australia. Couples get married earlier than they used to do, and younger mothers have fewer twins than older ones, but this seems not to account for the decrease everywhere. We have here, therefore, evidence of a decline in the frequency of twin ovulations, or in the frequency of coitus necessary to promote the fertilization of two eggs, or in the capacity to carry a twin pregnancy. In short, there may here be some evidence of a decline in fecundity. We have no clue as to the cause, but in this connection it is difficult to avoid thinking of the increasing use over the decade of insecticides, herbicides, and growth stimulants.

Turning now to the social environment, what about the effects of overcrowding? Is there any chance that the psychosexual disturbances of overcrowded rats (Calhoun, 1962) or the physiological infertility of overcrowded mice (Crowcroft, 1966) will appear in man? We can only speculate. The disturbances in Calhoun's rats, kept at double the density required for normal breeding, appeared to be caused by incessant physical contact, and already there is no lack of that in man. On the other hand, Crowcroft's mice, which stopped breeding in a restricted space but started again when the space was increased, were probably affected by a high concentration of pheromones, substances which, in contrast to hormones, are secreted externally and affect other individuals. In Crowcroft's experiments it is likely that substances of this kind produced by the female mice affected the fertility of other females by depressing hypophysial activity through olfactory channels. The study of pheromones of this type, originated by Whitten (1957) in Canberra and Bruce (1959) in London, is only some 15 years old and it is proving to be a most exciting development in biology. So far, however, pheromone effects have not been demonstrated in man, though it may be suggestive that androstenone, an odorous steriod secreted by the salivary glands of the boar, has a powerful effect on the sow, while a closely related compound, androstenol, which has a pleasant musky smell is found in human urine. Discussion of this kind, however, is dominated by the fact that man can and does breed under the most severe conditions of squalor and overcrowding (Solano, 1967), and that sophistication and a high standard of living are often thought, as by Herbert Spencer long ago, to be more damaging to fertility.

The Conscious Control of Human Fertility

Endogenous adjustment of potential human fertility to meet modern conditions of survival cannot, therefore, be expected for a very long time, if ever. What then of the future? Few people would wish to see the problem solved by the harsh limiting factors of nature or by primitive forms of social control, such as human sacrifice, infanticide, cannibalism, self-immolation and the casting out of the old and sick. The inescapable conclusion is that man must learn, and learn faster than he is doing at present, consciously to control his own fertility.

How is this to be done? Let us consider first the oldest method. Abortion for social reasons is now legalized in many countries and one must applaud this triumph of humanity and commonsense - provided that the method is used appropriately. In my view, abortion should be reserved for cases of unforeseen medical or genetic emergency, as a last resort when contraception has failed or for a crash programme of population limitation when the slow spread of contraception would be inadequate. By contrast, I should be very sorry indeed to see so biologically wasteful a process become a routine method of fertility control or to see the use of contraception become more haphazard because of the availability of abortion as a longstop. In saying this, however, I am thinking of indiscriminate abortion without regard for the sex or condition of the abortus, and possibilities are looming up which may make selective abortion socially valuable and scientifically important. I refer to the possibility of diagnosing both the sex and the chromosomal constitution of the embryo by examination of amniotic cells.

Diagnosis of sex at an early stage would permit the removal of an embryo of the unwanted sex, so that people sufficiently motivated to sacrifice an embryo on the altar of the sex ratio could literally choose the sex of their children. With improving techniques this method might be easier and more certain than the alternative possibility of *in vitro* separation of X - and Y - spermatozoa combined with artificial insemination. I need hardly say that any method of choosing the sex of children would initiate a most interesting social experiment. Anne McLaren (1972) is probably correct in thinking that the first result would be a small reduction in the birth rate, because at least some children are produced in the hope of adjusting the sex ratio of the family. By contrast, however, I think the net result on the sex ratio at birth would be slight, because the present ratio of near 50:50 is probably what most parents in the long run would choose for their families. A fashion for boys, for instance, would almost certainly be followed by a fashion for girls, who would have acquired a scarcity value during the glut of boys, and vice versa. I think there would be little chance of the sex ratio of adults adjusting to the reproductive potentials of the two sexes, say one male to twenty females, and little chance therefore, of the social and demographic upheavals which the appearance of such a ratio would cause. But if the swings of the fashion pendulum were slow, the social results could be fascinating to watch. An experiment of this kind has, in fact, been carried out in front of our eyes during recent years. In the past, the slight excess of males at birth was abolished within a few years by higher mortality, so that there was an excess of females of marriageable age. In recent times the decline in child mortality has preserved the excess of males up to marriageable age and girls have now acquired a slight scarcity value. Twenty years ago, when this tendency was already evident, I prophesied that in these circumstances the young males would have to do something to attract attention to themselves. It is pleasant to be a true prophet.

Turning to more serious matters, we have the other possible use of selective abortion - the elimination of at least some types of defective embryos. Diagnosis by amniocentesis would, of course, have its limitations, but it could nevertheless be extremely valuable in reducing the number of defective children. Today, the number of such children is relatively large, and their catastrophic impact, especially on the mother, is exacerbated by the misguided efforts of the medical profession to preserve anything and everything that is born alive, at whatever cost in distress and frustration to the family and in cash to the community.

I shall add very few words to the millions which are written every year about contraception. It is sometimes said that the development of the perfect contraceptive would solve the population problem. This I do not believe. For one thing, there never will be a contraceptive perfect for use at all times, under all conditions, in all parts of the world and in all cultures. For another, the best of methods will be of no value if it is not used, and here we have to face the problem of motivation.

I have already referred to the alarmingly low birth rate in the UK during the 1930s. By that time, knowledge of contraception was spreading widely, but available methods were relatively crude and aesthetically objectionable to many people. The conclusion to be drawn from our low birth rate, therefore, is that if people want small families they will have them, however primitive the methods of control available; conversely, one may assume that large families will not entirely disappear whatever disincentives are applied to, or contraceptives dangled in front of, the parents. Parental and especially maternal urge is strong; even now there are wives who are not happy unless they have young babies to look after. And there will always be accidents even after the desired family size has been achieved. The capacity for forward planning is not universal; few people have a brain packed in ice during the count-down to coitus and we hear a lot these days about the emotional stimulus of risk-taking, erstwhile known as 'taking a chance'. Moreover, in some ways man is still a primitive creature. Seasonal variation in the birth rate in the US points to a peak conception rate at Christmas and the New Year. In England, the peak occurs during the summer holiday period, in spite of the fact that there is a coincident peak in the sale of contraceptives (Parkes, 1968).

Motivation, therefore, not contraceptive technology is the main bottleneck in fertility control, and the situation is complicated by the fact that motivation now has two distinct aspects - the welfare of the family and the welfare of the human race. Family planning was initiated with the idea of limiting and spacing births in the interests of the mother and the family. It had no concern with national or global demographic problems, and even good family planning can result in a size of family much in excess of that implied by considerations of population growth. Ought couples, therefore, to consider wider issues than their own circumstances in deciding how many children they should have? This is not a new question. A.V. Hill in his Presidential Address to the British Association for the Advancement of Science in 1952 specifically asked whether, under modern conditions, couples had the right to unlimited reproduction. In the 20 years since A.V. Hill's address, the far-sighted question has often been debated, but no clear answer has appeared. The Universal Declaration of Human Rights, issued by the UN in 1968, states that men and women have a right to marry and found a family, but ignores the question of family size. The main omission, in my view, however, is the absence of any indication that rights imply obligations and that if one accepts the rights which follow from being a social animal, one must also accept the obligations. Among these, under present conditions, I would give a high place in an obligation not to produce children in demographically excessive numbers and not to take a substantial risk of begetting a defective child. But in the same way as rights imply obligations, obligations imply further rights. Thus, if couples have an obligation to restrict their fertility, they have a right to be fully informed of the methods available for doing so. Similarly, if they have an obligation to avoid producing defective children, they have a right to the best possible genetic counselling, to prenatal diagnosis and, if necessary, to selective abortion.

The idea of quantity control for the family in the form of indiscriminate contraception, and in many countries indiscriminate abortion, is now widely accepted in principle, and, if I may extend the industrial simile, the idea of quality control should be added to it. In saying this, I am not thinking of genetic engineering in the sense of producing supermen or standard men by chromosome manipulation; I am thinking only of the elimination, so far as possible, of mental or physical defectives. But even negative quality control of this kind is going to take a long time to become generally practicable and acceptable. In the meantime, we have the urgent need to extend quantity control from the family to the human race, from planned parenthood to planned population, and sooner or later some consideration for demographic problems will have to be injected into the traditional ideas of family planning. Nations will have to evolve population policies based on global rather than on national considerations. The mutual dependence on each other of the peoples of the world increases year by year, and no individual country should now stand aside in demographic isolation. We have only one world in which to live and in the long run we shall sink or swim together.

References

Bruce, H.M. (1959). An exteroceptive block of pregnancy in the mouse. *Nature*, 184, 105.
Calhoun, J.B. (1962). Population density and social pathology. *Scientific American*, 206, 139.
Crowcroft, P. (1966). *Mice All Over*. London: Foulis.
Döring, G.K. (1962). Schwangenshaft und Gebart vor de Menarche. *Deutsche Medizinische Wochenschrift*, 87, 2514.
Dublin, L.J. (1951). *The Facts of Life from Birth to Death*. New York: Macmillan.
Escomol, E. (1939). La plus jeune mère du monde. *Presses Médicale*, 47, 875.
Guttmacher, A.F. (1956). Factors affecting normal expectancy of conception. *Journal of the American Medical Association*, 161, 855.
James, W.H. (1972). Secular changes in dizygotic twinning rates. *Journal of Biosocial Science*, 4, 427.
McKinlay, S., Jefferys, M. and Thompson, B. (1972). An investigation of the age at menopause. *Journal of Biosocial Science*, 4, 161.
McLaren, A. (1972). The future of the family. In *The Future of Man*, edited by F.J. Ebling and G.W. Heath. London: Academic Press.
Parkes, A.S. (1968). Seasonal variation in human sexual activity. In *Genetic and Environmental Influences on Behaviour*, edited by J.M. Thoday and A.S. Parkes. Edinburgh: Oliver & Boyd.
Pearl, R. (1939). *The Natural History of Population*. London: Oxford University Press.
Pearson, J.F. (1971). Pilot study of single women requesting a legal abortion. *Journal of Biosocial Science*, 3, 417.
Population Reference Bureau (1961). One man's family. *Population Bulletin*, 17, 155.

Population Reference Bureau (1968). Pockets of high fertility in the United States. *Population Bulletin,* **24**, 25.
Solano, F. (1967). A journey of a thousand miles. *Family Planning,* **16**, 48.
Whitten, W.K. (1957). Modification of the oestrous cycle of the mouse by external stimuli associated with the male. *Journal of Endocrinology,* **17**, 307.

5

THE SOCIOLOGY OF POPULATION CONTROL*

John Peel and Malcolm Potts

Ideology and Population Control

This paper is written from an avowedly Malthusian viewpoint; its authors are convinced that rapid population growth is detrimental to economic and social advancement. This is a point of view which is coming to be generally accepted amongst development specialists and by the governments of under-developed societies, although it is still by no means universally regarded as self-evident. Amongst economists and sociologists the situation is less clear. Ideological considerations and a respect for cultural variation have deterred some social scientists from a forthright commitment to population policies. Marx's rejection of Malthusian theory has been especially influential but, as is commonly the case with neo-Marxist exegesis, there is more than one opinion about what Marx, or more appropriately Engels, had to say on the question of population.

The weakest interpretation of Marxist orthodoxy is that fertility control should be a consequence and not a cause of economic development. An alternative construction is that redistribution of the world's resources will render fertility control unnecessary whilst a third, the most extreme, interpretation is that fertility control will remove the most effective incentive to revolution. The reply to the first of these arguments is that today's under-developed countries, unlike 19th century Europe, cannot afford to allow demographic circumstances to be determined by long-term economic events. Many under-developed countries, in any case, already enjoy modern western expectation of life, while retaining high birth rates and have annual growth rates two or three times higher than anything ever experienced in Europe. The second argument is arithmetically wrong; if the world's material resources were divided equally between its population everyone would fall far below the poverty lines accepted by developed countries, having to live on less than two dollars per day per head. Stycos has recently answered the third argument with specific reference to his Latin American experience: 'Poverty and misery do not produce revolutions but modest economic improvements along with disproportionate increases in aspirations do' (1971). Some Marxist thinkers have written explicitly along the same lines as those western development

---

* Text of a paper presented at the Annual Conference of the British Sociological Association, University of York, Wednesday, 12 April 1972.

economists who are interested in the regulation of populations. For example, Fidel Castro, in his 'revolutionary offensive' speech declared: 'What factors constitute the major obstacles (to industrialization)? One factor is population increase ... Any under-developed country which increases its population by 2.2 per cent will triple its entire population in 50 years and will need to invest no less than 12 per cent of the gross product to compensate for the population increase' (Landstreet, 1971). Similarly, E. Arab-Ogly, of the University of Moscow has written: 'Society must choose whether it prefers doubling the prosperity of a constant population, say every 20 years, or doubling the population while maintaining the same standard of living in approximately the same period. One and the same pudding cannot be eaten twice under two different names' (Landstreet, 1971).

Indeed, in the communist world anti-Malthusianism has always been more important as a propagandist stance than as a determinant of actual conduct. In 1913, Lenin condemned 'social neo-Malthusianism' but went on to say: 'It goes without saying that this does not by any means prevent us from demanding unconditional annulment of all laws against abortion or against the distribution of medical literature on contraceptive measures, etc. Such laws are nothing but the hypocrisy of the ruling classes. These laws do not heal the ulcers of capitalism they merely turn them into malignant ulcers that are especially painful for the oppressed masses' (Lenin, 1913). Today in the USSR contraceptive services and legal abortion are freely available: the former being seen as a means of avoiding the latter. 'Prevention of abortions is one of the important objectives in the work of the maternity health centres', writes the author of a common midwifery textbook for nurses. 'To prevent abortions, the workers of the maternity health centre (physician, midwife and nurse) also teach their patients to use contraceptives. The nurse must have a good knowledge of harmless contraceptives, as well as of their proper use'. Moreover, the one country in the world which today is behaving in a thorough-going Malthusian fashion is the People's Republic of China which, as we shall show, may yet provide a model for the under-developed world.

The Pressure for Population Policies
Apart from ideological considerations there is an understandable reluctance on the part of sociologists to concede that people in one place and culture should dictate the patterns of behaviour of people of quite different backgrounds. On the whole, it is more than reasonable to avoid attempting to engineer major sociological changes in other cultures. Should population policies be an exception? Three things may be said in support of such a contention. The first is that the fall in mortality rates in under-developed countries has been brought about in part by the importation into those countries of western methods of hygiene, western

The Sociology of Population Control 71

methods of pest-control and western techniques of preventive medicine; it is largely due to the intervention of the advanced nations of the world that the present high growth rates in the under-developed countries now prevail and these countries have the right to look to the western world for assistance in overcoming the problems which have resulted. Moreover, one of the most effective means of reducing maternal and infant mortality in developing countries, and contributing even further to human betterment, would be through the widespread promotion and adoption of family planning amongst 'high risk' women. On this basis we should be no more reluctant to advocate family planning as a health measure than we are to promote maternal and child health services or immunization programmes. Secondly, it has been shown in large numbers of studies that women in under-developed countries *want* fewer children than they are accustomed to having; moreover, no major world religion presents obstacles to the acceptance of birth control methods comparable to those presented by the Catholic Church in Europe - perhaps the need for social engineering is not as great as is sometimes thought. Thirdly, and most importantly, the population problem is a global one; it is a problem of balancing finite world resources and limited mineral and agricultural wealth against a potentially infinite population growth rate. Indeed, in terms of the world ecology the slow population growth rate of the developed nations of the world poses a greater threat to the biosphere than the rapid growth of population in the under-developed countries. The population of the United Kingdom for example increases by less than 1000 additional people every day. In India the population increases by 50,000 people per day. But the more well to do inhabitant of the United Kingdom may consume up to 50 times as much as an Indian villager so that the drain on global resources presented by the current rate of population increase is of the same order of magnitude as that of India with a population seven times as large.

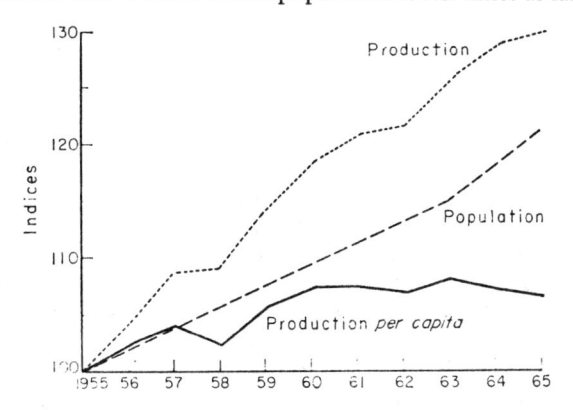

FIG. 1. World production and population rates 1955-65.

Figure 1 shows how on the world scale the rapid increase in population growth, during the late 1950s and early 1960s offset increased world population to give a static *per capita* production rate. What this diagram does not show and what is centrally important to the purpose of this paper, is the gap which exists between the developed countries and under-developed countries. The facts of the relationship between population growth and economic development cannot seriously be disputed. The under-developed countries of the world have birth rates of around 40 per 1000 of the population and GNPs of less than 500 dollars *per capita;* the developed nations have birth rates of 20 per 1000 of the population or below and GNPs *per capita* of more than 500 dollars.

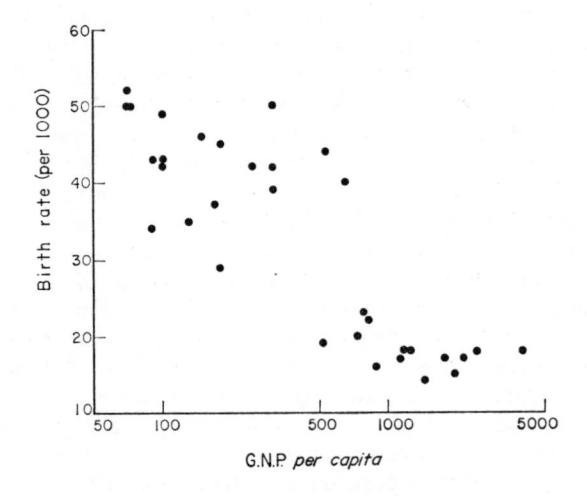

FIG. 2. Birth rates and GNP per head for 33 countries.

Figure 2 shows vividly the gap which divides these two sets of nations when all those countries in the world having populations of more than 15 million (and which together account for more than 85 per cent of the world's population) are plotted according to these two indices. The data on which this diagram is based are shown in Table 1, and this must be one of the most significant correlations to be found in the area of international development studies. What is not widely realized is that if the under-developed countries achieve an expansion of their GNP by an ambitious 6 per cent per annum, the criterion set by the Pearson Commission, the gap in *per capita* income between the rich and poor countries will continue to grow. At the moment the gap between the average of the two groups of countries is over 2000 dollars *per capita* per annum but by the end of the century it may be an embarrassing 7000 dollars *per capita* per annum.

The Sociology of Population Control 73

The implications of this change are alarming; already the United States, with 6 per cent of the world's population uses 40 per cent of the world's natural resources.

TABLE 1
Population, Birth Rate and GNP *per capita* of Largest 33 Countries

Country	Total population (1000s)	Birth rate per 1000	GNP *per capita* $
China	730,000	34	90
India	523,893	42	100
U.S.S.R.	237,798	17	1110
United States	201,152	18	3980
Pakistan	123,163	49	100
Indonesia	112,825	43	100
Japan	101,090	18	1190
Brazil	88,209	42	250
Nigeria	62,650	50	70
Germany (West)	60,165	15	1970
United Kingdom	55,283	17	1790
Italy	52,750	18	1230
France	49,920	17	2130
Mexico	47,627	44	530
Philippines	35,883	45	180
Thailand	33,693	46	150
Turkey	33,550	39	310
Spain	32,621	20	730
Poland	32,305	16	880
U.A.R.	31,693	37	170
Korea	30,470	29	180
Iran	27,150	50	310
Burma	26,353	50	70
Ethiopia	24,212	52	70
Argentina	23,617	22	820
Canada	20,772	18	2460
Yugoslavia	20,154	19	510
Colombia	20,043	42	310
South Africa	19,781	40	650
Rumania	19,721	23	780
Vietnam	17,414	35	130
Germany (East)	17,084	14	1430
Congo (Dem. Rep.)	16,730	43	90

Population growth inhibits development and modernization in a number of different ways. At its most basic level it means a sharing of available resources amongst an increased number of consumers in a way that nullifies any advance in economic output. One example which vividly illustrates this can be found in the building of the high Aswan dam in Egypt. This increased the cultivable area of the United Arab Republic by 40 per cent, yet between the time when the dam was planned and when Lake Nasser was filled up the population of the UAR had increased by precisely 40 per cent. A second case which is well documented is to be found in the Philippines. This is a country of 36 million people which is growing at the rate of 1 extra million every year. It is a rich country by the standards of the under-developed world, it has a high literacy rate and its GNP has grown by an astonishing 5.5 per cent per annum in the last decade. But while GNP increased by 88 per cent from 1955 to 1967 the *per capita* income only went up by 25 per cent. The labour force increased by 15 per cent, one third of whom are illiterate and there is already 11 per cent unemployment.

One of the greatest barriers to modernization is the shortage of investment capital. Population growth reduces the rate of increase in *per capita* funds available and is associated with diminishing *per capita* savings whilst at the same time increasing the need for savings. Moreover, in countries with high population growth the tendency will be for whatever capital is available to be invested in the construction of roads, bridges, schools and hospitals where capital costs are high and where marginal productivity is low. Enke (1966), in a cost-benefit analysis of family planning activities in India, has concluded that funds spent on birth control programmes in under-developed countries would be about 100 times more effective in raising *per capita* income than funds spent on conventional development projects.

A second prerequisite of development is the acquisition of high talent manpower both in the form of administrators, engineers, doctors and lawyers and in middle grade management. This requires not merely the provision of universities but the development of literacy at all levels of the population. There are numerous studies showing a statistical relationship between educational attainment and economic growth and one important incidental benefit which accrues from the raising of the educational level of a community is that the population is more receptive to the idea of fertility control (Berelson, 1969). Yet despite vast government expenditures on education in under-developed countries in the last two decades the number of adult illiterates in the world has increased due to population growth. If the number of children in the under-developed countries had remained at the 1950 level 82 per cent of those of primary school age would have been in full-time education by 1965 instead of the 54 per cent who actually achieved such places (Jones, 1971).

A third major necessity for modernization concerns the shift from a predominantly rural and agriculturally-based community to an urban and industrially-based society. Towns in Latin America are growing at 5 per cent a year in population. The geographical mobility which this implies has traditionally been associated with lower than average family size. On the other hand if the land reform needed to implement new and more productive methods of agriculture is to be achieved both urban and rural birth rates will have to be reduced. In India, for example, the average land holding is less than 2 acres per individual engaged in agriculture and this average would be severely reduced if the country were to attempt to continue to employ 70 per cent of its labour force in agriculture.

The choice now available to most under-developed countries does not lie between low population growth and high population growth but between high growth rates at best and crippling growth rates if no improvements in fertility control are brought about. Recent high birth rates in the under-developed world, together with low infant mortality rates, have resulted in a disproportionate concentration of population in the lower age groups. Whatever is done in the immediate future these people will grow up to become parents and for many years to come the population growth rate will remain high. Whether it will be contained depends upon improvements in family provision. Today the campaign for population control is going badly. In most countries with family planning programmes the number of acceptors being recruited rarely equals or exceeds the number of additional women who reach reproductive age each year. As a result of demographic changes in the last two decades, the population pyramids of most under-developed countries are grossly distorted and every year there are more young girls of 15 - 20 entering the fertile age group than there are women of 45 - 50 leaving it by the menopause or by death.

Contemporary Family Planning Programmes
In 1964 there were three countries with a government family planning policy in the world, by 1971 there were 26 including the majority of Asian countries and several African countries. In addition another 24 governments explicitly supported the work of voluntary family planning associations. Very significant sums of money are now being spent on family planning. India is spending 40 million dollars or 1.3 per cent of the national budget on family planning a sum equivalent to more than half the health budget. *Per capita* India is spending 7.7 cents, Pakistan 9.4 cents, Korea 19.4 cents and Jamaica 37.0 cents.

Local expenditures are being partially supported by overseas donor agencies. The World Bank plans to spend 150 million dollars in 5 years, USAID spends 100 million dollars annually, Sweden 10 million dollars, the UK 4 million dollars. Is this money sufficient, too much or too little?

The UN Fund for Population Activities thinks it is too little and calculates that at least 65 cents *per capita* is required annually to finance family planning programmes, that is something like 5 per cent of the national budget of a developing country and in some cases the sum will exceed the total health budget.

Well over 100 million dollars will be spent this year on family planning activities in under-developed countries. It is our contention that the family planning input which will be made available on this budget is in general ill-conceived and sociologically unrealistic. Most of the programmes provided might be compared to the arthritic belly dancer - more promising in outline than in performance.

With very few exceptions family planning programmes are conceived in terms of clinic services, provided within the context of public health services, staffed by doctors and offering predominantly female methods of contraception. This is true of governmental programmes, voluntary programmes and of the assistance provided by international agencies. The model on which such programmes are based is, of course, the family planning clinic movement of the developed countries.

The first timid reference to family planning in the World Health Organisation was made in a technical report (51) in 1952 when, writing on maternity care, a group of experts recommended 'guidance in parent-craft and in problems associated with infertility and family planning'. For many years no consensus of opinion was established in the UN or any specialized agency and the WHO outlook came to dominate international thinking. The WHO had accepted, without criticism, the premise that family planning is a clinic based activity in the same category as curative and preventive medicine. It has subsequently looked at large scale national family planning programmes, such as that of Pakistan, and made it a policy to attempt to bring these within the orbit of health services: 'the problem of family planning programmes having grown as separate campaigns and now calling attention to the need for their future integration, has been created mainly by the insufficient coverage of the population and geographical areas by the existing general health services of the respective countries ... once organized health services with sufficient coverage and capability are well established, the place of a separate campaign for tackling related problems becomes dubious and short-lived at best' (WHO, 1971).

Cultural Barriers to Birth Control Services

The near-universal acceptance of the idea that family planning should be provided within a public health context may be the greatest barrier to effective population control during the next decade. It is worthwhile to look at the emergence of the concept in the developed world as well as to question its validity as applied to contemporary under-developed countries.

The middle-classes who initiated the demographic decline in England did so without any vast apparatus of family planning clinics. It was not until 1921, when the major fall in the birth rate had taken place, that the first birth control clinics were set up in England and their ostensible purpose was to provide contraceptive services for precisely those sections of the population who could not obtain these on their own initiative. In this the earliest clinics were successful in that they attracted a large percentage of their clients from social classes IV and V. But as the family planning movement developed its clients came increasingly and disproportionately from the upper-middle and middle classes. The family planning clinic is thus an out of date and unsuccessful model; nor is there much evidence that, even amonst those it exists to serve, it is either an acceptable form of provision or an efficient one.

Complaints about poor advertising, inconvenient siting of clinics, inconvenient opening hours, delays and embarrassing examination and questioning are all common. Some criticism may be unfounded or exaggerated, but whether it is fact or myth that deters a potential user the result is the same. Economically the clinic system is very expensive. The logistic task of supplying contraceptive commodities to millions of users over several decades for each fertile couple is unlike that of other branches of established medical care. An analogy with preventive medical services is attractive but both literally and figuratively these latter are either one-shot affairs, such as immunization, or are conducted from some point remote from the user as with water purification, sewage disposal or the inspection of slaughterhouses. Contraceptive distribution is more similar to the provision of breakfast cereals - the commodities concerned are high volume, relatively low profit ones, a choice must be made from a restricted range of possibilities, they need to be widely known, readily available and are likely to be found in nearly all homes. Whatever the politico-economic philosophy of a country it is universally agreed that such materials are most efficiently distributed through a conventional marketing channel. It is notable that some of the most widely used pharmacological agents such as simple analgesics, cough mixtures and infant sedatives, as well as dangerous addictive drugs such as alcohol and nicotine, are distributed in this way. In sociological terms contraceptive distribution is truly one of paradox. For several methods outlets are controlled by a powerful and long established trade union - the medical profession - which until recently condemned all methods of family planning and many branches of which still refuse certain essential options. Constrained by restrictive practices, distribution is then administered by a large bureaucracy. For example, the Family Planning Association of Britain runs over 1000 clinics; it conducts over 5000 committee meetings a year and in 1970 it spent nearly £3 million but attracted only 237,547 new patients (1970-71). Similarly, a scheme of mobile family planning clinics in Kenya run by the IPPF has reached much less than 1 per cent of those in need.

Following the lead set by India in 1953, all the major under-developed countries of Asia, some of the most populous countries in Africa and a majority of the countries of Latin America have adopted national governmental population policies. Sometimes specific demographic targets have been set and without exception it has been assumed that the bulk of the population will turn to family planning clinics for contraceptive advice. In emulation of the domiciliary schemes set up in advanced countries some attempts have been made in recent years to carry family planning activities into the community and commonly this has been done by training field-workers to talk to individual fertile couples and to encourage them to visit clinics. Only in very few cases has any effort been made to provide these field-workers with contraceptives for distribution.

As with their western prototypes the family planning services that have been created have been dominated by the medical profession, have concentrated on female methods of contraception, have emphasised sophisticated techniques and for the most part have denied the place of sterilization and have condemned induced abortion. In India and Pakistan vasectomy has been widely used and a genuine initiative has been taken in trying to solve the difficult technical problem of making female sterilization available on a large scale. However, in most countries where there are large governmental family planning programmes, such as Indonesia and Egypt, sterilization has been implicitly or explicitly excluded.

Clinic services have operated mostly out of existing health service buildings. More rarely, purpose-designed units have been created, occasionally mobile units have been set up and one floating clinic has been donated to Pakistan. The case for family planning has been argued on the grounds of its contribution to maternal and child health. It has been maintained as an almost self-evident truth that contraceptives are medical drugs or procedures which require the advice and supervision of medical personnel. Within a generation the physician has undergone a remarkable reversal of attitude from being an opponent, or apathetic supporter, of birth control to attempting to create a closed shop of contraceptive techniques to such an extent that in many countries, ranging from the United Kingdom to Brazil, doctors have become unwilling to delegate even the simplest duty to their qualified medical assistants such as nurses or midwives. In many under-developed countries medical personnel are socially remote from the community they serve. Wealth, type of food, degree of literacy, means of transport, clothing and sometimes social custom and dialect may all emphasize the gap between those served and those providing the service. Unfortunately, there may also be additional factors which tend to widen, rather than bridge, the gap. The doctor, nurse or midwife may have been almost exclusively trained in hospital medicine and be ill-prepared to work in a village. Government salaries for doctors are commonly as low as £12 per month and for nurses and midwives they are even lower and if accommodation is provided free it is difficult to maintain a sufficient degree of idealism to voluntary work in the rural health service. Most medical personnel have their eyes firmly fixed on city employment where private practice is available to supplement low salaries and where life is less monotonous, social contacts more interesting and, in the case of female staff, marriage more likely. It is not surprising that many governments direct newly qualified personnel to work in the rural health services. Culturally isolated, young, medically inexperienced, forcibly exiled, sometimes over-worked, often in second-rate accommodation with poor equipment and with career goals elsewhere it is difficult to set about establishing the type of rapport with the community which would encourage timid individuals, only weakly motivated to control their fertility, to seek help.

The problem faced by under-developed countries in the provision of health services are qualitatively similar to those found in more developed societies. Most British doctors are as reluctant to work in Merthyr Tydfil as are Indian doctors to work in Uttar Pradesh. The trained Egyptian nurse who is tempted to Libya by the higher wages offered has her counterpart in the British nurse who emigrates to Canada or Australia. The emphasis on glamorous curative medicine in the urban hospital context at the expense of preventive rural health services which is common in many under-developed countries has its analogue in the western willingness to spend money on sophisticated techniques like renal transplantation whilst psychiatric and geriatric hospitals are starved of staff and money. Unfortunately poverty exacerbates a problem and a moderate deficiency in a rich country can become a total lack in a poor country.

Family planning, when provided through health facilities, is particularly sensitive to defects in service and the already difficult problems faced by under-developed countries become more serious still. Again, the problem is not peculiar to under-developed countries. The conscientious general practitioner in Britain usually provides more family planning advice than the lazy or uninterested; the woman who is kept waiting at a family planning clinic, who is asked embarrassing questions or is subjected to an uncomfortable pelvic examination is less likely than others to return. The factors which make these familiar difficulties worse in under-developed countries are that socio-economic pressures to control fertility are relatively weaker whilst certain other barriers, for example the reluctance of women to be examined by doctors - especially male doctors - are relatively stronger.

The People's Republic of China

In a speech before the Supreme State Conference in Peking on 27 February 1957, Chairman Mao, commenting on the 30 million births which take place every year in China said: 'This figure must also be of great concern to us all. I will quote two other figures. The increase in grain harvest for the last 2 years has been 10 million tons a year. This is barely sufficient to cover the needs of our growing population. The second figure concerns the problem of education. It is estimated that at present 40 per cent of our youth have not been placed in primary schools. Steps must, therefore, be taken to keep our population for a long time at a stable level, say of 600 million. A wide campaign of explanation and proper help must be undertaken to achieve this aim'.

In one sense Chairman Mao is the only national leader ever to advocate a policy of zero population growth. In another sense, the Maoist interpretation of Communism can be regarded as analogous to a religion and it may be said that Mao is the only Father of a church to speak out in favour of birth control. Of course, in practice the population of Mainland China cannot be stabilized for many decades, and there are difficulties common to all developing nations as Mao recognized in an interview in 1971. The American author Edgar Snow commented that there had been great changes in family planning in the previous 5 or 10 years. 'No, I have been taken in!' Mao is reported to have answered. In the countryside a woman still wanted to have boy children. If the first and second were girls, she would make another try. If the third one came and was still a girl, the mother would try again. Pretty soon there would be nine of them, the mother was already 45 or so, and she would finally decide to leave it at that. The attitude must be changed but it was taking time. Perhaps the same was true in the United States? In 1964, Chou En-Lai had expressed the real goal of the country which is to reduce the current growth rate to 1 per cent by AD 2000. Government zeal for family planning has waxed and waned slightly with the political changes that have taken place. It reached a low ebb in 1958 - 62 when, for example, some condom factories were closed for lack of demand. Currently, family planning appears to be given a good deal of priority.

The unique aspect of the Chinese programme is that, from a very early stage, it has encouraged all methods of fertility limitation, from endeavouring to raise the age of marriage, through the commercial distribution of contraceptives, to induced abortion. There has not been the emphasis on a particular method, or group of methods, that has often marred family planning programmes in other Asian countries. In the late 1950s a real effort was made to encourage the use of traditional, rural techniques of contraception. The swallowing of live tadpoles was given some publicity, but, unfortunately no indigenous method was found to be useful. The rhythm method has received some publicity and the commercial distribution of contraceptives is very much encouraged. It is the law that pharmacies, departmental stores, co-operative and trading companies must 'maintain reasonable stocks'. Machinery for the manufacture of condoms was imported from Japan in the 1950s. Foams, diaphragms and gels are available. An IUD programme began in 1958; a 22-tablet combined oral contraceptive is issued. In the rural communes near Peking it is claimed that 40 per cent of fertile women are using this method, but the extent of its distribution in the country as a whole is unknown. Vasectomy and tubal ligation are performed. Vasectomy is clinically simpler but tubal ligation has proved more popular. Sterilization is offered after one or two children.

China is the only nation which, as a political principle has made a genuine effort to raise the age of marriage with the overt intention of reducing the population growth rate. The minimum age of marriage was set at 20 for men and 18 for women soon after the Revolution. Proposals of 23 and 20 respectively from the National People's Consultative Conference were rejected in 1956, but an optional marriage age of 30 for men and 22 for women was recommended by the Party in 1963. Propaganda to this effect has been strong and practical provisions have been made, such as separate dormitories for the unmarried to live in.

The structure of society in Mainland China, with the commune as the basic unit of social organization, lends itself to enthusiastic family planning. In many ways, the cultural revolution, by reaching society and especially by weakening traditional bonds between the generations will further the changes necessary to achieve small families. Chairman Mao may be a rather Machiavellian Thomas Malthus.

In May 1957 the abortion law of China was reformed to permit termination of pregnancy in the first 3 months of gestation, providing the woman had not had a legal termination in the preceding year. Doctors protested at the liberality of this law and a few months later it was emphasized that abortion was mainly to be used for those who had suffered a failure with some reversible method of contraception. At least in the cities abortion now appears to be readily available and widely used. In Peking in 1964 a visitor observed a poster 'in praise of artificial termination of pregnancy'. The operation can cost 2 dollars (USA), or may be paid for by the husband's employer, or performed free for those who cannot afford it. In the first trimester out-patient techniques are often used; after 3 months of gestation the woman may stay in hospital 3 - 5 days. Following the operation the woman is eligible for 15 days leave from work which is a considerable benefit.

China is the home of the vacuum aspiration method of terminating pregnancy. As has been noted, the vacuum aspiration method has been carried to the rural areas by the ingenious use of a large bottle in which alcohol is burnt to create a partial vacuum or by using hand-operated pumps and hand-operated suction syringes. As was remarked in the *Chinese Journal of Gynaecology and Obstetrics* in 1966, 'this method of performing an abortion is simple, convenient and easy to control, it has the additional advantage - it can be taught quickly to lower level health personnel'. China has encouraged the development of a large core of para-medical workers, the so-called 'barefoot doctors'. These practitioners of medicine, have a simple training, work in the countryside, do antenatal care and obstetrics and are involved in family planning. By inference these people are also available to perform abortions. In addition, all physicians are required to spend 1 year in 3 working in rural areas. Abortion is said to be available in the 20,000 commune hospitals. It seems that the implementation of the family planning programmes at the rural level cannot be less and may be much greater than in India, Pakistan or Indonesia.

Edgar Snow saw two typical abortions performed in 1971. Acupuncture is used as anaesthesia but no doubt the effect is similar to the counselling used in some clinics in the USA. Although the women claimed to be eligible for 2 weeks paid leave, they went back to work the same afternoon. Except that one patient cheered herself with Mao's thought 'Fear neither hardship nor death', and that no fee was charged, the similarity in clinical procedure in Peking and New York is remarkable. Nation wide vital statistics are not available for China. However, very low birth rates are reported for particular rural communes and certain cities.

Conclusions

Sociologists and doctors need to join together to rethink the way in which the still too limited resources available for family planning can be invested to most effect. The model of free-standing, or health service-linked family planning clinics that has been transmitted from developed to under-developed countries has had its role in the provision of birth control to the community misinterpreted. Even if it had been or could become the major provider of services in rich countries the weaknesses of health-delivery systems together with the cultural discontinuities commonly found between medical personnel and those they serve, especially in rural areas, might well make such services inappropriate in poor countries.

Much greater use needs to be made of the social structures of communication, service and distribution already present in the community. Nearly all societies contain ideas concerning fertility limitation on to which new emphasis and concepts can be grafted. Traditional healers and midwives still play an important role in many societies, especially in relation to pregnancy and child birth and need to be brought into family planning programmes. A higher proportion of the population is engaged in retail distribution, usually of high volume/low profit-margin commodities, in under-developed than in developed countries and thus an efficient distributive network for contraceptives already exists and costs nothing to exploit beyond the cost of the contraceptives plus a suitable profit margin. It is too easily forgotton that the commercial channels of contraceptive distribution (often in the face of restrictive laws and an inability to advertise) are numerically more significant than professional family planning services (Black, 1972) and even in developing countries an estimated 40 per cent of contraceptives used come through commercial channels. In Britain condoms remain the commonest family planning method and barbers hold over 30 per cent of the retail outlet. This one salesforce probably helps to plan more families than specialized family planning clinics.

In order to achieve these ends medical practitioners and administrators will need to change their frame of reference. The supposed high standard of care of the individual patient achieved in the orthodox pattern of family planning clinic found in western countries has generated a tradition of clinical practice which is intolerant of conventional techniques of contraception and tends to overlook the need for abortion. Frequently it concentrates on remote medical contra-indications to the use of Pill and IUDs rather than on the overall problem of weighing the risks of a method with those of pregnancy or illegal abortion following its non-use. In the end, the system may leave those most in need unprotected. Key problems, such as the delegation of duties to para-medical personnel and the need for the free availability of oral contraceptives without medical supervision will remain controversial problems until there is a better dialogue between doctors and sociologists. In the development of that dialogue an understanding of the real as well as the easily visible pattern of birth control in western nations and its evaluation is essential.

References

Berelson, B. (1969). National family planning programmes: where we stand. In *Fertility and Family Planning: A World View,* edited by S.J. Behrman, L. Corsa and R. Freedman. Michigan: University of Michigan Press.
Black, R.T.L. (1972). A survey of contraceptive markets in four African countries. *Journal of Biosocial Science,* 4, 287-298.
Enke, S. (1966). The economic aspects of slowing population growth. *Economic Journal,* 76, 44-56.
Family Planning Association (1970-1971). *Annual Report,* p. 10.
Jones, G.W. (1971). Effect of population change on the attainment of educational goals. In *Rapid Population Growth: Consequences and Policy Implications,* edited by J. Revelle. Baltimore: Johns Hopkins Press.
Landstreet, Jr, B. (1971). Marxists. In *Ideology, Faith and Family Planning in Latin America,* edited by J.M. Stycos. New York: McGraw-Hill.
Lenin, V.I. (1913). *The Working Class and Neo-Malthusiansim.*
Stycos, J.M. (1971). *Ideology, Faith and Family Planning in Latin America.* New York: McGraw-Hill.
World Health Organisation (1971). Twenty-first session regional committee for the Eastern Mediterranean. WHO EM/RC21/*Technical Discussion,* 2, 20 August.

6
THEORIES OF MATE SELECTION

Bruce K. Eckland

This paper is devoted to a review and clarification of questions which both social and biological scientists might regard as crucial to an understanding of nonrandom mate selection. Owing to the numerous facets of the topic, the diverse nature of the criteria by which selection occurs, and the sharp differences in the scientific orientations of students who have directed their attention to the problem, it does not seem possible at this time to shape the apparent chaos into perfect, or even near-perfect, order and, out of this, develop a generalized theory of mate selection. Nevertheless, it is one of our objectives to systematize some of our thinking on the topic and consider certain gaps and weaknesses in our present theories and research.

Before embarking on this task, it would be proper to ask why the problem is worth investigating, a question which other speakers no doubt also will raise during the course of this conference. If the social and biological scientists had a better understanding of mate selection, what would happen to other parts of our knowledge or practice as a result? Despite the fact that our questions arise from quite different perspectives, there is at least one obvious point at which they cut across the various fields. This point is our common interest in the evolution of human societies, and assortative mating in this context is one of the important links between the physical and cultural components of man's evolution.

Looking first from the geneticists' side, at the core of the problem lies the whole issue of natural selection. Any divergence from perfect panmixia, i.e., random mating, splits the genetic composition of the human population into complex systems of subordinate populations. These may range from geographically isolated 'races' to socially isolated caste, ethnic, or economic groups. Regardless of the nature of the boundaries, each group is viewed as a biological entity, differing statistically from other groups with respect to certain genes. To the extent that different mating groups produce more or fewer children, 'natural' selection takes place.

In the absence of differential fertility, assortative mating alone does not alter the gene frequencies of the total population. Nevertheless, it *does* change the distribution and population variance of genes (Stern, 1960) and this, itself, is of considerable importance. Hirsch (1967), for example, has stated:

'As the social, ethnic, and economic barriers to education are removed throughout the world, and as the quality of education approaches a more uniformly high level of effectiveness, heredity may be expected to make an ever larger contribution to individual differences in intellectual functioning and consequently to success in our increasingly complex civilization. Universally compulsory education, improved methods of ability assessment and career counseling, and prolongation of the years of schooling further into the reproductive period of life can only increase the degree of positive assortative mating in our population. From a geneticist's point of view our attempt to create the great society might prove to be the greatest selective breeding experiment ever undertaken'(p. 128).

Long-term mate selection for educability or intelligence increases the proportion of relevant homozygous genotypes which over successive generations *tends* to produce a biotic model of class structure in which a child's educability and, therefore, future social status are genetically determined. Since these propositions hold whether or not everyone has the same number of children with exact replacement, assortative mating would seem to have consequences just as relevant as any other mechanisms involving the genetic character of human societies.

Also from the biological point of view, it is probable that assortative mating is becoming an increasingly important factor relative to others affecting the character of the gene pool. Infant mortality, for instance, does not appear to exert the same kind of selection pressure on the populations of Western societies today as it did a hundred, or even fifty, years ago. Likewise, accompanying the rise of mass education and spread of birth control information, fertility differentials appear to have narrowed markedly, especially in this country (Kirk, 1966). For example, the spread is not nearly as great is it once was between the number of children in lower and upper socio-economic families. It is not altogether clear, of course, just how the relaxation of selection pressures of this kind would, in the long run, affect future generations. Yet, assuming, as some have suggested, that these trends will continue, then a broader understanding of the nature and causes of mate selection may eventually become one of the outstanding objectives of population geneticists. One reason is that the more the assortative mating, the greater the rate of genetic selection. If nearly all members of a society reproduce and most reproduce about the same number of children, and these in turn live to reproduce, it might then be just as important to know who mates with whom as to know who reproduces and how much.

The interest of social scientists in mate selection has been more uneven and much more diffuse. Some anthropologists undoubtedly come closest to sharing the evolutionary perspective of geneticists, as indicated by their work in a variety of overlapping areas which deal in one way or another with mating, e.g., genetic drift, hybridization, and kinship systems. In contrast, sociologists have been less sensitive to genetic theories. We share with others an evolutionary approach, but one that rests almost wholly on social and cultural rather than physical processes. Nonetheless, mate selection lies at the core of a number of sociological problems. These range, for example, from studies of the manner in which class endogamy is perpetuated from one generation to the next to studies in which endogamy is conceived as a function of marital stability. While sociologists have helped to ascertain many facts as well as having developed a few quasi-theories about assortative mating, it is rather difficult when reviewing our literature on the subject to distinguish between that which is scientifically consequential and that which is scientifically trivial. The general orientation of social scientists, in any case, is far from trivial and can be used instructively in the region of mate selection and in ways heretofore neglected by population geneticists. Some of their 'theories' will be reviewed later in this paper.

Evolution in Parallel and Interaction

Differences in the basic theoretical orientations of the social and biological sciences with respect to human evolution and assortative mating perhaps can best be understood in terms of the set of diagrams that follow. Figure 1 illustrates the usual manner in which investigators in either field approach their subject matter. The course of human development is traced on separate but parallel tracks. Some textbooks and elementary courses in sociology begin with a brief treatment of genetics, but it is soon forgotten. In a like manner, students in a course in genetics are told that the expression of the genetic character of an individual depends largely on environmental influences, after which no further reference to environment seems to be necessary (Caspari, 1967).

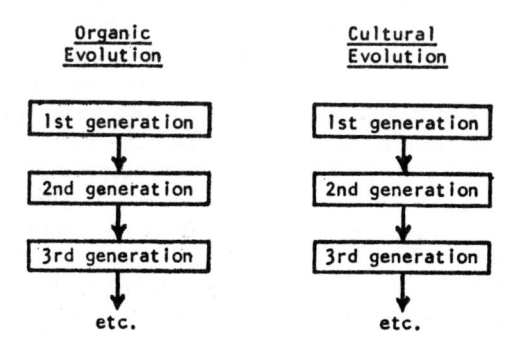

FIG. 1. Evolution in parallel

Evolution viewed in parallel has allowed each field to articulate its own theories and perspectives. Mate selection is only one case in point, but a good one. The anthropologist or sociologist typically begins with some universal statement to the effect that in no society is mate selection unregulated and then he may proceed to analyze the cultural controls that regulate the selection process. As he has defined his problem, there perhaps has been no need to consider physiological processes. The geneticist, on the other hand, typically introduces the topic with some statement about how mate selection alters the proportion of heterozygotes in the population (as we have done) and then proceeds to a discussion of allele frequencies or consanguinity. Because he is concerned almost exclusively with the nature of the genetic material, he does not care, for example, why tall people seem to prefer to marry tall people. I doubt that sociologists especially care either. There are, however, traits far more relevant than these, like education, which serve as a basis of assortative mating and to which sociologists have given considerable attention and the geneticists relatively little.

The gap about which I am speaking also can be illustrated by the manner in which some geneticists define assortative mating. To repeat a definition which appeared recently in the *Eugenics Quarterly*, assortative mating is 'the tendency of marriage partners to resemble one another as a result of preference or choice' (Post, 1965). The reference to individual 'preference or choice' illustrates one of the major weaknesses in the geneticist's understanding of the nature of culture and society. (It is not just this particular statement that is troublesome, but many others like it throughout the literature.)

Mate selection is *not* simply a matter of preference or choice. Despite the increased freedom and opportunities that young people have to select what they believe is the 'ideal' mate, there are a host of factors, many *well* beyond the control of the individual, which severely limit the number of eligible persons from which to choose. As unpalatable as this proposition may be, it rests on a rather large volume of data which suggests that the regulatory systems of society enforce in predictable ways a variety of norms and sometimes specific rules about who may marry whom. Perhaps the most important point I will have to make in this paper is that geneticists must begin to recast their assumptions about the nature of culture and society, just as sociologists must recast their thinking about genetics (Eckland, 1967).

Assuming that both geneticists and sociologists do reconsider their positions and assuming, too, that each discipline has a hold of some part of the truth, there still remains the unfilled gap in the kinds of knowledge needed to develop a set of interlocking theories between the social and biological sciences with regard to mate selection. I do not question that organic and cultural evolution can and, in many ways, must be studied as separate phenomena. The point is, however, that they do interact and this, too, should be studied; and to do so will require a much broader historical perspective than most geneticists and social scientists have exhibited up to now.

An interaction model of organic and cultural evolution must specify the precise nature of the relationships between the hereditary factors and environmental influences. Although certainly a very old idea, the notion of *interaction* has laid relatively dormant until recent years, probably largely due to the nature-nurture controversy and the racist arguments that covered most of the first half of the twentieth century. The expanded model in Figure 2 suggests a more elaborate system of causal paths along which there is continuous feedback between the genetic and cultural tracks from one generation to the next. As before, we are dealing with the processes by which generational replacement and change occur. However, in addition to the duplication of most genes and most cultural traits in each succeeding generation, new patterns invariably emerge through the interaction of heredity and environment. Briefly, and with no intent on my part to intimate either purpose or consciousness, (*a*) genes restrict the possible range of man's development and (*b*) within these limits he alters his environment or cultural arrangements in such ways as to change the frequencies or distribution of genes in the next generation which (*c*) enables him to carry out further changes.

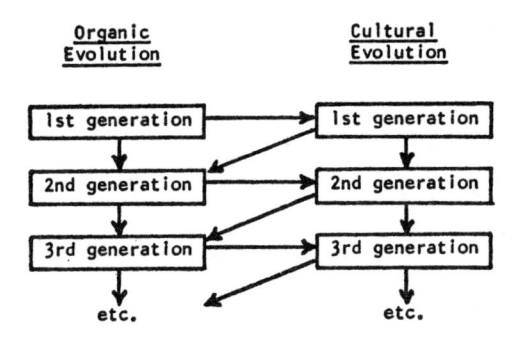

FIG. 2. Evolution in interaction

It is important to note here that the interaction of heredity and environment does not occur within the duration of a single generation, a point that social scientists, in particular, need to recognize. Holding for inspection a very short segment of the life span of a single cohort, as so often we do, it is not possible to observe, even to logically think about, heredity and environment in interaction. Within the span of one generation, the relationship appears only as a one-way process, with the genetic make-up of individuals determining the norms of reaction to the environment. The path from environment *back* to genetics which actually allows us to speak in terms of *interaction* appears only *between* generations, as in the above model. In other words, models of the sort abbreviated in Figure 3 do not fit reality. The cultural environment, of course, may have an immediate and direct effect upon an individual's endocrine system, as well as other physiological and morphological structures, but it cannot, as far as we know, alter his genes. Environment can only alter their phenotypic expression and, owing to selective mating, the genes of one's progeny in the next generation.

We have now moved into a position whereby we might raise two rather crucial questions regarding the search for significant variables in mate selection, that is, significant in the context of an interaction model. The first is: What genotypes have social definitions attached to their behavioral manifestations or, conversely, what physical, personality, and social traits depend on our genes? The answer requires determining how much, if any, of the variance of a particular trait is due to heredity (and how much to environment). For example, taking the operational definition of intelligence we now employ, if none of the variance can be attributed to genetic sources, then no matter how intense assortative mating is for intelligence, we most certainly would exclude it from any further consideration in our model. Objections sometimes have been raised against partitioning the variance on the grounds that there is a strong

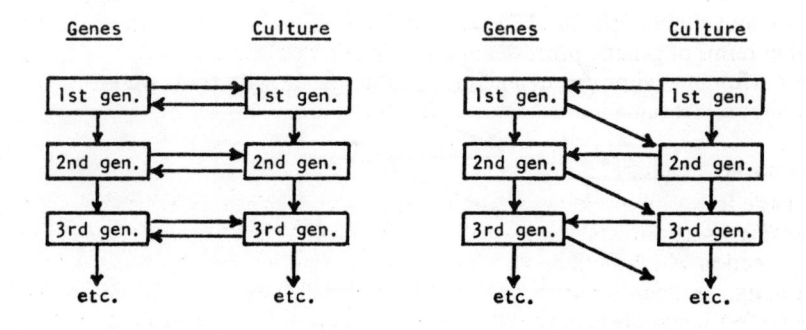

FIG. 3. False models

interaction component in the development of most traits. It will be recalled, however, that our general model permits no interaction of this form between heredity and environment in the development of the intelligence or any other phenotype of an *individual*. Every character is determined during the lifetime of that individual, with genotypes determining part of the course of development and not the other way around. There are other problems to be encountered in any analysis of variance which attempts to sort out the hereditary component, but this is not one of them.

The second question is: What criteria for mate selection are *functionally* relevant within a particular population at a particular time? This question, of course, raises some long-standing issues in genetics regarding the 'adaptive' quality of characteristics which are genetically variable. It appears, for example, that some traits like the O, A, B, and AB blood types for the most part are adaptively neutral or, at least, it is not known how they affect the biological or social fitness of their possessors in any significant way. Likewise, there are traits like eye color which apparently have no clear functional value and yet seem to be involved in the sorting which unites one mate with another. By this, I do not mean that the search for socially relevant traits in mate selection should be directed toward putting the science of genetics to the service of human welfare. Rather, it is my belief that the discovery of socially relevant biological dimensions of human variation is likely to be of the sort, such as intelligence, which may be treated simultaneously as Mendelian mechanisms in the reproductive process and as sorting and selecting mechanisms in the allocation of social status and in the maintenance of boundaries between social groups, the discovery of which may serve to further our general understanding of human evolution. Any delimiting, therefore, of the class of mate selection variables we eventually must take into account should deal, on the one hand, with traits which are understood in terms of genetic processes and partly in terms of social and other environmental processes and, on the other hand, with traits whose survival or social value is at least partly understood.

Notes on Terminology

Two basic forms of nonrandom mate selection are *assortative* mating and *inbreeding*. Assortative mating usually encompasses all character-specific mate selection which would not be expected to occur by chance. Inbreeding, on the other hand, encompasses all mating where departures from perfect panmixia involve the relatedness or ancestry of individuals. While some authors have used the terms in essentially this manner (e.g. Spuhler, 1962; Post, 1965), others have not (e.g. Allen, 1965; Warren, 1966). The latter have not restricted assortative mating to refer only to character-specific situations but have included inbreeding as one of its forms. Another variation is that some authors have used the labels *genotypic* assortative mating to refer to inbreeding and *phenotypic* assortative mating to refer to the nonrandom, character-specific form (e.g., Fuller and Thompson, 1960). Also, the terms *consanguine* and *conjugal* sometimes are used to make the same distinction.

Attention to the rules governing the selection of a spouse has led to another set of terms: the first, representing conformity to the norms, called *agathogamy;* the second, involving prohibited deviations from the norms, called *cacogamy* (Merton, 1964). *Incest*, a special case of inbreeding, involves prohibited deviations from the rules controlling matings between closely related persons and is also a special case of cacogamy since the latter includes other forms of socially disapproved matings as well, such as *mesalliance*, a marriage with one of an inferior position. Special cases of mesalliance are *hypergamy* to denote the pattern wherein the female marries upward into a higher social stratum (the male marries the one in the inferior position) and *hypogamy* wherein the female marries downward into a lower social stratum.

In common use are the more general terms *endogamy* and *exogamy* which refer to in-group marriages of almost any kind. Inbreeding is a special case of endogamy; *hybridization* and *admixture* are special cases of exogamy in which 'racial' features are the implied criteria. *Interbreeding* and *intermarriage* also have about the same meaning as above, except the latter term is more frequently used in reference to traits dealing with categories other than race, such as *interfaith* marriages. Miscegenation, another form of exogamy, is the term usually applied to interbreeding between white and Negro or other intergroup matings (legitimate and illegitimate) wherein the contractants have violated cultural proscriptions; and, in this respect, miscegenation is also a form of cacogamy, as well as a form of mesalliance.

Still another term commonly employed to describe assortative mating is *homogamy* which denotes something about the likeness or similarity of the married couples, with or without specific reference to any particular set of characteristics. Thus, one may speak in terms of racial homogamy or social homogamy or, simply, homogamous marriages. The antonym, *heterogamy*, is not widely used but could logically refer to mixed matings, the tendency toward random mating, or selection for 'dissimilar' traits. The latter, however, is more often called *negative* assortative mating; all other forms are called *positive* assortative mating.

The above discussion probably comes close to exhausting the arsenal of terms we employ. However, with few exceptions, the concepts which arise from their meaning do not appear to be especially useful for classifying mating patterns in such a manner as to provide a sound basis for bridging the gap between the organic and social models presented earlier. It is quite probable that not only do we need more knowledge of assortative mating upon which to base more generalized theories, but we very well might find it necessary either to develop a new set of concepts (and terms) or to undertake a major revision of those now used. At present, they are confusing and often redundant, many do not appear particularly relevant to our problem, and few perhaps mean the same thing

to both the geneticist and social scientist.
In the remainder of this paper, I shall review briefly some of the current theories of mate selection. By no means a complete review, I have neglected, for example, the very large body of work of anthropologists and population geneticists dealing with inbreeding. Studies of consanguineous marriages provide important information about genetic processes, such as the mutation load which is especially sensitive to inbreeding. Also reported in this literature, but not here, are a number of theories that attempt to explain the cultural development of kinship systems in which inbreeding is permitted or prescribed. However, most, although not all of this work tends to deal with small populations which have been isolated for many generations. It is not convenient for explaining assortative mating in large, relatively open, and highly mobile cultures. The following discussion, therefore, involves a search for those psychological and structural features which best show how assortative mating operates in contemporary societies.

Individualistic Theories

The disappearance of unilineal kinship systems in Western societies has led to a decline of kinship control over mate selection. The resulting freedom which young people now enjoy has brought about an enormously complex system. No doubt, the selection process actually begins long before the adolescent's first 'date'. Moreover, under conditions of serial monogamy where it is possible to have many wives but only one at a time, the process for some probably never ends. Determining the 'choice' are a myriad of emotional experiences and it is these experiences, along with a variety of subconscious drives and needs, upon which most psychological and other 'individualistic' theories are based.

The unconscious archetype
Some of the earliest and perhaps most radical theories of mate selection suggested that what guides a man to choose a woman (it was seldom thought to be the other way around) is instinct. Scholars believed that there must be for each particular man a particular women who, for reasons involving the survival of the species, corresponded most perfectly with him. A modern rendition of the same idea is Carl Jung's belief that falling in love is being caught by one's 'anima'. That is, every man inherits an anima which is an 'archetypal form' expressing a particular female image he carries within his genes. When the right woman comes along, the one who corresponds to the archetype, he instantly is 'seized' (Evans, 1964). However, no one, as far as we know, has actually discovered any pure biologically determined tendencies to assortative mating.

The parent image
A psychoanalytic view, based on the Oedipus configuration, has been that in terms of temperament and physical appearance one's ideal mate is a parent substitute. The boy, thus, seeks someone like his mother and the girl seeks someone like her father. While it admittedly would seem reasonable to expect parent images to either encourage or discourage a person marrying someone like his parent, no clear evidence has been produced to support the hypothesis. Sometimes striking resemblances between a man's wife and his mother, or a woman's husband and her father, have been noted. Apparently, however, these are only 'accidents', occurring hardly more frequently than expected by chance.

Like attracts like
Another generally unproven assumption, at least with respect to any well-known personality traits, involves the notion that 'likes attract'. Cattell and Nesselroade (1967) recently found significant correlations between husband and wife on a number of personality traits among both stably and unstably married couples. The correlations, moreover, were substantially higher (and more often in the predicted direction) among the 'normal' than among the unstably married couples. As the authors admit, however, it was not possible to determine whether the tendency of these couples to resemble each other was the basis for their initial attraction ('birds of a feather flock together') or whether the correlations were simply an outgrowth of the marital experience. Although the ordering of the variables is not clear, the evidence does tend to suggest that the stability of marriage and, thus the number of progeny of any particular set of parents, may depend to some extent on degrees of likeness.

The principle of complementary needs
Probably as old as any other is the notion that 'opposites attract'; for example, little men love big women, or a masochistic male desiring punishment seeks out a sadistic female who hungers to give it. Only in the past twenty years has a definitive theory along these lines been formulated and put to empirical test. This is Winch's theory of complementary needs which hypothesizes that each individual seeks that person who will provide him with maximum need gratification. The specific need pattern and personality of each partner will be 'complementary' (Winch, 1958). Accordingly, dominant women, for example, would tend to choose submissive men as mates rather than similarly dominant or aggressive ones. The results of a dozen or so investigations, however, are inconclusive, at best. More often than not, researchers have been unable to find a pattern of complementary differences. No less significant than other difficulties inherent in the problem is the discouraging fact that the correlation between what an individual thinks

is the personality of his mate and the actual personality of his mate is quite small (Udry, 1966). Nevertheless, the theory that either mate selection or marital stability involves an exchange of interdependent behaviors resulting from complementary rather than similar needs and personalities is a compelling idea and perhaps deserves more attention.

No firm conclusions can yet be reached about the reasons for similarity (or complementariness) or personality and physical traits in assortative mating. (Even the degree of association or disassociation on most personality characteristics is largely unkown.) To state that 'like attracts like' or 'opposites attract', we know are oversimplifications. Moreover, few attempts to provide the kinds of explanations we seek have thus far stood up to empirical tests.

Sociocultural Theories

In a very general way, social homogamy is a critical point in the integration or continuity of the family and other social institutions. It is a mechanism which serves to maintain the status quo and conserve traditional values and beliefs. And, because marriage itself is such a vital institution, it is not too difficult to understand why so many of the social characteristics which are important variables generally in society, such as race, religion, or class, are also the important variables in mate selection. Thus, most studies in the United States report a very high rate, over 99%, for racial endogamy, an overall rate perhaps as high as 90% for religious homogamy, and moderately high rates, 50% to 80% for class homogamy, the exact figures depending on the nature of the index used and the methods employed to calculate the rate.

One possible way of illustrating the conserving or maintenance function of social homogamy in mate selection is to try to visualize momentarily how a contemporary society would operate under conditions of *random* mating. Considering their proportions in the population, Negroes actually would be more likely to marry whites than other Negroes, Catholics more often than not would marry Protestants, and a college graduate would be more apt to marry a high school dropout than to marry another college graduate. In a like manner, about as often as not, dull would marry bright, old would marry young. Democrats would marry Republicans, and teetotalers would marry drinkers. What would be the end result of this kind of social heterogamy? A new melting pot, or chaos?

It seems that, in the absence of 'arranged marriages', a variety of controls govern mate selection and, in the process, substantially reduce the availability of certain individuals as potential mates. Many structures in society undoubtedly carry out these functions, sometimes in quite indirect ways, such as, the subtle manner in which the promotion of an 'organization man' may be based, in part, on how well his mate's characteristics meet the qualifications of a 'company wife'. Thus, despite the 'liberation' of mate selection and the romantic ideals of lovers who are convinced that social differences must not be allowed to stand in their way, probably one of the most important functions of both the elaborate 'rating and dating' complex and the ceremonial 'engagement' is to allow a society to make apparent who may 'marry upward' and under what conditions exogamy is permitted. We are referring here, then, not merely to a society's control over the orderly replacement of personnel, but to its integration and the transmission of culture as well.

Rather than reviewing any very well-formulated theories (since there may be none) in the remaining discussion, I have attempted to touch upon a fairly broad range of conditions under which homogamy, as a social fact, relates to other aspects of contemporary societies.

Propinquity and interaction
Whether we are speaking about place of residence, school, work, or such abstruse features of human ecology as the bus or streetcar routes along which people travel, propinquity obviously plays a major part in mate selection since, in nearly all cases, it is a precondition for engaging in interaction. (The mail-order bride, for instance, is one of several exceptions.) A person usually 'selects' a mate from the group of people he knows. Findings which illustrate the function of distance have been duplicated in dozens of studies. In Columbus, Ohio, it was once found that more than half of the adults who had been married in that city had actually lived within sixteen blocks of one another at the time of their first date (Clarke, 1952). Cherished notions about romantic love notwithstanding, the chances are about 50 - 50 that the 'one and only' lives within walking distance (Kephart, 1961).

As many authors have pointed out, people are not distributed through space in a random fashion. In fact, where people live, or work and play, corresponds so closely with one's social class (and race) that it is not quite clear whether propinquity, as a factor in mate selection, is simply a function of class endogamy or, the other way around, class endogamy is a function of propinquity. Ramsøy's (1966) recent attempt to resolve this issue, I want to note, misses the mark almost completely. Investigating over 5,000 couples living in Oslo, Norway, she concludes that propinquity and social homogamy are 'totally independent of one another' and, therefore, rejects the long-standing arguments that 'residential segregation of socio-economic and cultural groups in cities represents a kind of structural underpinning both to propinquity in mate selection and to homogamy'. More specifically, the author shows that 'couples who lived very near one another before marriage were no more likely to be of the same occupational status than couples who lived at opposite sides of the city'. This is astonishing, but misleading. The author equated the social status of the bride and, implicitly, her social class origin with *her* occupation at the time of marriage. No socio-economic index other than the bride's occupation unfortunately was known to the investigator and, thus, it was a convenient although poorly considered jump to make. To most sociologists, it should be a great surprise to find in any Western society, including Norway, that the occupations young women hold before marriage give a very clear indication of their social status, relative either to the occupational status of men they marry or to their own places of residence.

Exchange theory
An explanation often cited in the literature on mate selection, as well as in that on the more general topic of interpersonal attraction, deals in one form or another with the principle of exchange. A Marxian view, marriage is an exchange involving both the assets and liabilities which each partner brings to the relationship. Thus, a college-educated woman seldom brings any special earning power to the marriage, but rather she typically enters into contract with a male college graduate for whom her diploma is a social asset which may benefit his own career and possibly those of his children. In exchange, he offers her, with a fair degree of confidence, middle-class respectability. Norms of reciprocity might also help to explain the finding that most borderline mentally retarded women successfully marry and even, in some cases, marry upward, if they are physically attractive. This particular theory, however, has not been well-developed in regard to mate selection, despite its repeated usage. Also, it may be a more appropriate explanation of deviations from assortative mating or instances of negative mate selection than of positive selection.

Values and belief patterns
In contrast to the inconclusive evidence regarding assortative mating in terms of personality characteristics, numerous studies do indicate that married couples (and engaged couples) show far more consensus on various matters than do randomly matched couples. Even on some rather generalized values, as in the area of aesthetics or economics, social homogamy occurs. Apparently, our perception that other persons share with us the same or similar value orientations and beliefs facilitates considerably our attraction to them (Burgess and Wallin, 1943).

The importance of norms and values in mate selection, part of the social fabric of every society, also can be illustrated in a more direct way by looking at some of the specific sanctions that we pass along from generation to generation. Without really asking why, children quite routinely are brought up to believe that gentlemen prefer blondes (which may be only a myth perpetuated by the cosmetic industry), that girls should marry someone older rather than younger than themselves (which leaves most of them widows later on), and that a man should be at least a little taller than the woman whom he marries (which places the conspicuously tall girl at an enormous disadvantage). Simple folkways as such beliefs presently are, they nevertheless influence in predictable ways the 'choice' of many individuals.

Social stratification and class endogamy
We have already noted that the field of eligible mates is largely confined to the same social stratum to which an individual's family of orientation belongs. Social-class endogamy not only plays a significant part in the process of mate selection, it may also help to explain other forms of assortative mating. For example, part of the reason why marriage partners or engaged couples share many of the same values and beliefs no doubt is because they come from the same social backgrounds.

There are at least five explanations which can be offered for the persistence of class endogamy, each of which sounds reasonable enough and probably has a hold on some part of the truth.

First, simply to turn the next to last statement around, persons from the same class tend to marry *because* they share the same values (which reflect class differences) and not because they are otherwise aware or especially concerned about each other's background.

Second, during the period of dating and courtship most young people reside at the home of their parents. (Excluded here, of course, are the large minority in residential colleges and those who have left both school and home to take an apartment near their place of work.) The location of parental homes reflects the socio-economic status of the family and is the general basis for residential segregation. With respect to both within and between communities, the pattern of segregation places potential mates with different backgrounds at greater distances than those with similar backgrounds. Thus, to the extent that the function of distance (or propinquity) limits the field of eligibles, it also encourages class endogamy by restricting class exogamy.

Third, class endogamy in some cases is simply a function of the interlocking nature of class and ethnicity. A middle-class Negro, for example, probably is prevented from an exogamous marriage with a member of the upper-class not so much because class barriers block it but because he (or she) is Negro. The majority of the eligible mates in the class above are whites and, in this instance, what appears to be class endogamy is really racial endogamy.

Fourth, ascriptive norms of the family exert a great deal of pressure on persons, especially in the higher strata, to marry someone of their 'own kind', meaning the same social level. The pressures that parents exert in this regard sometimes are thought to have more than anything else to do with the process and certainly are visible at nearly every point at which young people come into meaningful contact with one another. Norms of kinship regarding the future status of a child may be involved, for example, in the parent's move to the right community, sending a child to prep school, or seeing that he gets into the proper college. Fifth, and an increasingly convincing argument, even as the structure of opportunities for social mobility open through direct competition within the educational system, class endogamy persists owing to the educational advantages (or disadvantages) accrued from one's family of orientation. Most colleges, whether commuter or residential, are matrimonial agencies. As suggested earlier, despite whatever else a woman may gain from her (or, more often, her parents') investment in higher education, the most important thing she can get out of college is the proper husband or at least the credentials that would increase her bargaining power in an exchange later on. Given the fact that men generally confer their status (whether achieved or ascribed) upon women and not the other way around (female proclamations to the contrary notwithstanding), marriage as a product of higher education has far more functional value for women than vocational or other more intrinsic rewards.

To carry this argument a bit further, access to college depends in large measure on the academic aptitude (or intelligence) of the applicants. Moreover, the hierarchical ordering of colleges which is based on this selectivity has led to a system of higher education which, in many ways, replicates the essential elements of the class structure. Differentiating those who go to college from those who do not, as well as where one goes to college, are *both* aptitude and social class. These two variables correspond so closely that despite the most stringent policies at some universities where academic aptitude and performance are the central criteria for admissions and where economic aid is no longer a major factor, students still come predominately from the higher socio-economic classes. For whatever the reason, genetic and environmental, this correspondence facilitates the intermarriage of individuals with similar social backgrounds, especially on American campuses where the sex ratio has been declining. It is interesting to note in this context that Warren's recent study of a representative sample of adults showed that roughly half of the similarity in class backgrounds of mates was due to assortative mating by education (Warren, 1966).

Ethnic solidarities
While intermarriage is both a cause and consequence in the assimilation of the descendants of different ethnic origin, various writers claim that the American 'melting pot' has failed to materialize. Religious and racial lines, in particular, are far from being obliterated. In fact, the very low frequency of exogamous marriages across these lines itself underscores the strength of the cleavages. Most authors also agree that nationality is not as binding as either race or religion as a factor in mate selection. Nation-

type solidarities are still found among some urban groups (Italian and Poles) and rural groups (Swedes and Finns), but our public school system and open class structure have softened considerably what were once rather rigid boundaries. There is some evidence, too, that religious cleavages have been softening somewhat, and perhaps are continuing to soften as the functions of this institution become increasingly secular and social-problem oriented. On the other hand, racial boundaries, from the view of mate selection, appear to be as binding today as at any previous point in history; at least I have found no evidence to the contrary. The gains that Negroes have made in the schools and at the polls during the past ten years apparently have not softened the color line with respect to intermarriage.

Explanations of racial endogamy in America, some of which would take us back several centuries in time are too varied to discuss here. It might be well to point out, however, that cultural and even legal prohibitions, probably have relatively little to do with the present low rate of interracial marriage. As one author has stated, 'the whole structure of social relationships between whites and Negroes in the United States has been organized in such a way as to prevent whites and Negroes from meeting, especially under circumstances which would lead to identifying each other as eligible partners . . . Under these circumstances, the few interracial marriages which do occur are the ones which need explaining' (Udry, 1966).

For the population geneticist too, it would seem that the deviant cases are the ones which require attention. Elsewhere I have suggested, for example, that genes associated with intelligence may simply drift across the white and Negro populations since it appears that only certain morphological features, like skin color, actually operate to maintain the color line (Eckland, 1967). In other words, if the skin of an individual with Negro ancestry is sufficiently light, he may 'pass' (with no strings attached) into the white population. Even just a lighter-than-average complexion 'for a Negro' probably enhances his chances of consummating what we socially define as an 'interracial'marriage. In neither the first or second case, however, is intelligence necessarily involved.

If intelligence *were* associated in any predictable way with racial exogamy, the drift would not be random and we would then have a number of interesting questions to raise. For instance, do only the lighter *and* brighter pass, and, if so, what effect, if any, would this be likely to have on the character of the Negro gene pool? What, too, is the character of the inflow of genes from the white population? We do know that the great majority of legally consummated interracial marriages involve Negro men and white women. Does this information provide any clues? And, what about the illegitimate progeny of white males and Negro prostitutes? How often are they placed for adoption in white households and with what consequences? Before taking any of these questions too seriously, we would want to have many more facts. For obvious reasons, our knowledge is extremely meager.

Precautionary Notes

In conclusion, five brief comments may be made upon the present state of research and theories of mate selection as revealed in the foregoing discussion.

First, there is a great deal of evidence of homogamous or assortative mating but relatively few theories to explain it and no satisfactory way of classifying its many forms.

Second, nearly all facts and theories regarding mate selection deal with engaged or married couples and hardly any attention has been given to illegitimacy (including adultery) and its relationship to assortative mating. It may be, such as in the case of miscegenation, that some of the most important aspects of mate selection occur outside the bonds of matrimony.

Third, our heavy emphasis upon courtship and marriage has obscured the fact that people often separate, divorce, and remarry. Mate selection may be a more or less continuous process for some individuals affecting the character of the progeny or each new set of partners.

Fourth, the relationships between fertility and assortative mating still must be specified. Are there, for example, any patterns of assortative mating on certain traits, like education, which affect the number of children a couple will have?

Fifth, most of the factors in mate selection appear to covary. We discussed some of the more obvious problems in this regard, such as the relationship between residential segregation (propinquity) and class endogamy. It would appear that much more work of this sort will need to be done.

In regard to the last point, it would also appear that it is precisely here that social scientists, and sociologists in particular, may best serve the needs of population geneticists. Through the application of causal (chain) models and multivariate techniques, it may eventually be possible to sort out the relevant from the irrelevant and to specify in fairly precise terms not only the distribution of assortative mating in the social structure with regard to any particular trait, but also the ordering of variables and processes which restrict the field of eligibles.

References

Allen, G. (1965). Random and nonrandom inbreeding. *Eugenics Quarterly*, 12, 181-198.

Burgess, E.W. and Wallin P. (1943). Homogamy in social characteristics. *American Journal of Sociology*, 49, 109-124.

Caspari, E. (1967). Genetic endowment and environment in the determination of human behavior: biological viewpoint. Paper read at the annual meeting of the American Educational Research Association, 17 February.

Cattell, R.B. and Nesselroade, J.R. (1967). 'Likeness' and 'completeness' theories examined by 16 personality factor measures on stably and unstably married couples. (Advanced Publication, No. 7). The Laboratory of Personality and Group Analysis, University of Illinois.

Clarke, A.C. (1952). An examination of the operation of residential propinquity as a factor in mate selection. *American Sociological Review*, 17, 17-22.

Eckland, B.K. (1967). Genetics and sociology: a reconsideration. *American Sociological Review*, 32, 173-194.

Evans, R.I. (1964). *Conversation with Carl Jung*. Princeton: Van Nostrand.

Fuller, J. and Thompson, W. (1960). *Behavior Genetics*. New York: Wiley.

Hirsch, J. (1967). Behavior-genetic or 'experimental' analysis: The challenge of science versus the lure of technology. *American Psychologist*, 22, 118-130.

Kephart, W.M. (1961). *The Family, Society and the Individual*. Boston: Houghton Mifflin.

Kirk, D. (1966). Demographic factors affecting the opportunity for natural selection in the United States. *Eugenics Quarterly*, 13, 270-273.

Merton, R. (1964). Intermarriage and the social structure: fact and theory, pp. 128-152. In *The Family: Its Structure and Functions*, edited by R.L. Coser. New York: St. Martin's.

Post, R.H. (Editor) (1965). Genetics and demography. *Eugenics Quarterly*, 12, 41-71.

Ramsøy, N.R. (1966). Assortative mating and the structure of cities. *American Sociological Review*, 51, 773-786.

Spuhler, J.N. (1962). Empirical studies on quantitative human genetics, pp. 241-252. In *The Use of Vital and Health Statistics for Genetics and Radiation Studies*, New York: United Nations and World Health Organization.

Stern, C. (1960). *Principles of Human Genetics*. San Francisco: W.H. Freeman.

Udry, J.R. (1966). *The Social Context of Marriage*. Philadelphia and New York: J.B. Lippincott.

Warren, B.L. (1966). A multiple variable approach to the assortative mating phenomenon. *Eugenics Quarterly*, 13, 285-290.

Winch, R. (1958). *Mate Selection*. London and New York: Harper & Row.

7
RACE: A POPULATION CONCEPT
William S. Laughlin

Human beings, like members of other species, are clustered into breeding groups. As a consequence the distribution of variation in the human species is clustered rather than randomly distributed. The basic groups, or breeding populations, are characterized in large part by the habit of mating within the populations in preference to mating outside the populations. If random breeding obtained for the entire species, that is, if any one person had an equal probability of mating with any other person in the world, there would, of course, be no groups. All groups within the human species are capable of exchanging genes. Mariners, missionaries, salesmen, and soldiers, as well as other migratory persons, have demonstrated the essential interfertility of all groups within our species, even those quite distantly removed from each other. Arctic Eskimos and African Negroes, Australian aborigines and Englishmen, American Indians and Frenchmen are known by their progeny to be mutually interfertile. Some mating always takes place between contiguous groups, even though discouraged by custom or law. Thus, taken altogether, the evidence for interbreeding between both remote and contiguous groups clearly proves that all humans constitute one single species. Further, there is no evidence that any human can interbreed with members of any other species, and this is reflected in the decided morphological gap between our species and all others. The common ancestry we share with the anthropoid apes is so remote that interbreeding is quite impossible and also no single group or division of the human species is tangibly closer to the anthropoid apes than others. The differences between groups reflect an old and successful system of evolution which has enabled our species to proliferate over the entire world without separating into new species.

Population Systems

The constituent populations of our species are of many dimensions, of different magnitudes, of varying antiquity and inclusiveness. There are five major continental divisions between whom there are substantial differences. However, the populations contained within each of these continental divisions differ greatly from each other. Blumenbach (1865) cited the five major divisions and these have been followed with minor innovations by researchers who have characterized the entire species (Boyd, 1950; Mourant, 1954; McArthur and Penrose, 1950; Howells, 1959; Coon, 1963).

The five continental divisions are the Europeans, Negroes, Mongoloids, American Indians, and Oceanic peoples. Within the European (Caucasoid or White) division the constituent populations such as Basques, Lapps, Icelanders, and Hindus differ so much from each other that the same growth standards or frequencies of blood groups would not fit all of them. These differences are commensurate with the fact that these groups have had little contact with each other for many centuries, for both geographical and cultural reasons. These populations in turn are composed of constituent groups that differ from each other. Reindeer Lapps and Coastal Lapps are different breeding isolates. Similarly, there are many Basque groups and they differ from each other, though not as much as Basques as a whole differ from Lapps as a whole. The smaller divisions are often termed breeding isolates, local races, or demes. The term *race* has been used for several levels of groups, from the smallest isolate or Mendelian population up through the continental divisions, and occasionally it has been used for the species as a whole. So far as zoological nomenclature is concerned races are subdivisions of species. However, there is no lower limit and without further specification the term race simply indicates a biologically perpetuating subdivision of the species.

Definitions of Race

Though many definitions of race are technically accurate, no one is sufficiently complete to adequately express all the component aspects without extensive explication. Boyd (1950) and many others have defined a race as a breeding population, or intrabreeding unit, which differs from all others in the frequency of one or more genes. Intrabreeding, not to be confused with inbreeding, calls attention to the fact that mate exchange commonly takes place within the population. All individuals within a breeding population are necessarily related to each other. The stipulation that a population differs from others in the frequency of one or more genes is unnecessary and somewhat extraneous. No two breeding populations are ever identical. Further, it is theoretically possible that two separate races might be identical in the frequencies of the genes for which they are studied yet differ in the network of genetic pathways underlying the frequencies. The habit of choosing mates within the group is the important behavior that defines a group. The physical characteristics are a consequence of the reproductive behavior. There is no gene for a group and no compelling external or internal force that holds it together.

A workable and economical definition is simply that races are groups between which restricted gene flow has taken place. This kind of definition is essentially the same as the first, focussing instead on the inhibitions to gene flow between groups. It has the value of indicating the continuity that exists between all groups within the species. It has only the drawback that it is non-pontifical and obvious.

If a stipulation such as 'uniqueness', 'distinctiveness', or magnitude of difference is included in a definition then the basic genetical fact of an interbreeding community is subjugated in favor of an historical fact. The longer two groups are isolated from each other the more they will differ. It is desirable to cope with the origins of differences, to intercept them at the moment a breeding community is established, as well as centuries later when sufficient differences have accumulated to draw the attention of even casual observers.

In order to call attention to certain aspects of races that are commonly overlooked, though perfectly well implied, I think the following definition also has utility as well as accuracy: A race is a cluster of genetic pathways whose intersections recombine molecular units of inheritance some of which develop into living organisms that reproduce. Too much attention has traditionally been given to the end products of the reproductive system, the traits of adult males and females most commonly used for morphological and serological sampling. At the same time the importance of the genealogical connections has been neglected. The genetic pathways, though invisible, are genuinely tangible in the sense that they can be assigned probability values and manipulated in a variety of ways. The degrees of relationship between individuals in a population can be computed, and it is necessary for individuals to be genetically related in order to be genetic members of a breeding population. The network of genetic pathways extends backward in time and outward between groups and therewith constitutes one of the real reasons for considering a population as a process.

Molecular materials are transmitted from parents to offspring, not traits. The final expression of a trait represents many biochemical steps and many complex interrelations. Recombination of genetic materials is crucial. Most variation is the result of recombination and enough variability exists to provide for future evolution without new or recurrent mutations (Crow, 1961, pp. 426-427). The living individuals of any race can express only a small fraction of the total variability which they carry. By the same token, any large population, Bushman, Basques, Lapps, or Icelanders, contains sufficient variability to recreate, with recombination and selection, the total range of variation for the entire species (Ginsburg and Laughlin, 1966).

The important fact is that races are populations, not individuals or types, and that there is a system of populations comprising the species. The population structures of species must be understood if the variation within the species is to be interpreted from a genetic, ecological, and evolutionary point of view (Mayr, 1963, p. 360, see Chapter 13, The Population Structure of Species; see also Grant, 1963, Chapter 12, Population Systems).

Races are populations and the cryptic variation carried in the population exceeds by several magnitudes the phenotypic or apparent variation which can be detected directly by caliper measurements, biochemical tests, or photographs. The anatomical and physiological characteristics of a race accessible to direct investigation are only a small part of the total variability available to succeeding generations of the same population. Measurement of the living adults and children is only a sample even though every living man, woman, and child is studied.

The crucial importance of the concept of population and of population thinking becomes obvious when it is appreciated that evolution takes place only in populations, not in individuals and not in higher systematic categories. Natural selection, the process which determines which individuals have a greater or lesser proportion of offspring that survive to reproduce in turn, operates only in populations. Basic genetic changes which take place in the individual, do not affect him. Rather, they can only be registered in the contribution he makes to his offspring. This has been most economically epitomized by G.G. Simpson (1964, p. 1535), 'Changes in individual expression - to put it figuratively, the way the message is read - do not affect the message itself. The necessary message - constructing feed-back - is not here but in a system of higher order: in the population and not the individual. It operates through natural selection, which operates in populations, just as populations are what really evolve'.

Defining Populations

Populations are processes, not states, in a very real sense. Any one study will sample the population at a particular point in time. The population is of course changing at the moment that it is being studied. Births and deaths and age changes in the living members continue without remission. This is micro-evolutionary change, but it contains the same processes that result in macro-evolutionary change which is simply long term evolution. Again, it is important to reiterate the basic fact that evolution only takes place in populations. Higher taxonomic categories and long term trends are the result of the action inside particular populations. If child growth is a research objective then the same individuals must be measured at intervals. Likewise, if secular changes are the major concern, then succeeding generations of the same population must be sampled.

Whether the populations studied are Lapps, Eskimos, Bushmen, Basques, Hutterites, or the people of Ann Arbor, Michigan, any individual from whom a specimen is taken or upon whom a measurement is made must be identified as a genetic member of the population, not a casual visitor. Thus, the first step consists of collecting genealogies and of verifying them. Any person who has given or received genetic material can be defined into the population to which his parents belong or to the two populations to which they individually belong if he is a hybrid offspring. The actual collection of genealogies can be done fairly quickly in a small isolate if it is confined to the individuals examined, but the collection of a full genealogy of even a small isolate is an extensive undertaking, especially if demographic data including age, birth order, and other variables are included. Various methods are available for the genetic analysis of metropolitan populations (Spuhler and Clark, 1961).

In short, a breeding group is defined as a group in which there is an actual exchange of genetic materials between individuals who thereby set up a cluster of related persons. In this sense, the cluster or race defines itself. The products of various unions result in individuals, some of whom live to reproductive age or beyond and who thus may return some genetic material to the population. In a small isolate everyone is related to each other. However, the relationship may be so remote that it cannot be traced by genealogical methods, and other methods must be employed to establish relationships between groups. Within a single breeding community there may be persons unrelated to those living there, and there will be a number who have one parent or grandparent from another group. Such persons have membership in more than one group and constitute a valuable group for studies of gene flow, the actual transmission of genetic material from one group to another.

Physical appearance or possession of particular genetic traits is not the basis for membership in a particular isolate or population, it is a consequence of such membership. Depending upon circumstances it may provide an excellent clue. If the investigator approaches the group with a preconceived notion of what the typical Eskimo or Basque looks like and an equally preconceived notion of how much an individual can depart from his ideal of a typical Eskimo, he may then reject individuals for the sample that do in fact have genetic membership. He will usually shorten the actual range of variation that exists in most human groups. Visual identification is not reliable until after the group has been characterized and then it may be of no use unless supported by machine analysis. People in contiguous groups tend to look like each other.

Characterization and Identification - Distinguished

The characterization or description of a group is a different process from the identification of single individuals. In forensic cases, or medicolegal cases a person (or skeleton) may be identified as that of a particular race, sex, and age. The ability to discriminate or identify an individual depends upon the degree of differentiation of the group to which it belongs. Identification, assignment, discrimination, or pigeonholing of individuals must follow after the pigeonholes have been constructed. In brief, identification refers to the assignment of individuals to groups, characterization refers to the description of the variation within a group, and classification refers to the arrangement of groups. Individuals cannot be classified, only population units can be classified.

Characterizing a Population

Any traits can be used to characterize a population and their selection depends upon the aims of the study. In general, populations differ in their genetic structure, (the degrees of relationship between the members, the members, the amount of inbreeding, etc.), in various demographic features (ratio of males to females, infant mortality, number of births per male or female, etc.), the genetic basis or mode of inheritance, and in the presence or absence and frequencies of various traits or characters. Any trait that varies between individuals within a population also varies between populations, though the interpopulation variation may be slight. Body size and proportions (stature, weight, relative length of trunk to legs), pigmentation of the hair, skin and eyes, hair form and distribution on the body, numbers of vertebrae, fingerprints, bone density, basal metabolic rate, sweating, fissural patterns on the chewing surfaces of the teeth, and blood groups are among those most commonly studied. Various chronic diseases, such as dislocated hips or imperfections of the spinal column are important traits whose epidemiology is being placed on a firm population basis (Neel, Shaw, and Schull, 1963). Diseases are extremely important because of their selective action and the fact that new methods are being developed for detection of the various host factors including inherited susceptibility to disease (Blumberg, 1961; Osborne, 1961).

The characterization of a group then consists of finding the distribution of variation within the group. This is accomplished by statistical methods, the construction of arithmetic means, and measures of dispersion for continuously varying traits such as stature or head size. For traits with discontinuous distribution, that is, where some individuals do and others do not display the trait in question, such as blood type B or Rhesus negative, percentages or proportions are used to describe their frequency.

Traits used in characterizing a population must have an appreciable element of heritability. However, they need not be under simple genetic control nor free of direct external modification. Many traits such as stature or weight are modified by external events in the life of the individual, notably nutrition and, in the case of weight, by work habits. Such traits have several pairs of genes involved in their inheritance in addition to many development factors leading to their expression at the time they are measured. Other traits, such as blood groups, have little or no modification with age, sex, diet, or habits. Nevertheless, their frequencies within a group may be seriously modified by the customary breeding habits of the people, by intrinsic factors such as incompatibilities between antigens and antibodies, and by the amount of mixture bringing different frequencies into the group. The adaptive value of most traits is not known and it is unsafe to assume that traits relatively unaffected by direct environmental modification are more stable or neutral in evolution.

Some behavioral traits have a simple mode of inheritance (relatively few biochemical steps between the gene and its expression), but most are obviously complex interactions depending upon sequence and timing in socialization of the individual. A syndrome, such as Mongolism (Down's syndrome), depends upon one additional chromosome where there should be only two, but there are important variations in frequency related to the age of the mother. Behavioral genetics has been a neglected field and little is known about the genetic factors for such traits as genius or intelligence generally. Twin studies prove a high component of heritability, but the mode of inheritance is not known. The difficulties of estimating genius in different cultures are presently insurmountable. Any discussion of traits, however, would be remiss in failing to carefully underline the fact that total behavior, and not just locomotor behavior, is crucial in the evolution of the human species (Mayr, 1963; Ginsburg, 1958).

Boundary-Maintaining Devices

In the early history of man geographic separation was a more important factor than it has been since the major increase in population, which began with the spread of neolithic food-producing economies some five thousand years BC. *Sinanthropus pekinensis,* the middle-Pleistocene fossil man of northern China, likely had no great problems in keeping out foreigners, for the nearest foreigners were too few and too distant to constitute a major threat to the integrity of his community. With increasing impingements between neighboring communities, attendant upon increase in population size and multiplication of groups, exclusion became a more obvious problem. A large share of the efforts of human groups goes into maintaining differentiation from other groups. A major function of culture is the maintenance of the integrity of groups, the mutual welfare of their members, whether tribal units or larger national groupings. The various kinship and mating rules common to all groups operate to obligate matings between members of groups and to minimize matings with nonmembers. Many other aspects of culture have important bearings on breeding behavior and thus many genetic consequences. The various mechanisms that are deliberately employed to maintain group boundaries, and the various practices that also serve this same function indirectly, are difficult to classify singly because of their complex interrelationships and because many are simply byproducts of internal social organization.

The most concrete and obvious devices for discouraging gene exchange are walls. The Great Wall of China, Hadrian's Wall in England, and the Pale which formerly surrounded Dublin are megaparietal versions of ghetto walls. Immigration barriers incorporated into law are equally effective though lacking in architectural magnificence. Whether membership is based upon kinship, or upon political citizenship, the distinction between members and nonmembers is always effectively made. Each cultural system limits participation in the culture to a well-recognized group by means of various techniques and ideologies. These include the preservation of territorial rights mentioned above, initiation rites, cleansing ceremonies, secret activities, privileged information, inheritance rights, and encouragement of self-defining concepts of ethnocentrism and religious beliefs which obligate marriage among the adherents of the religion. Linguistic communities, whether dialectical (mutually intelligible but distinctive) or of higher magnitude such as a language, are highly important in defining breeding communities and often denote relatively sharp lines of demarcation. Races such as Basques, Lapps, and Eskimos are neatly defined by their distinctive languages. Within each there are subdivisions which cohere with dialectical distinctions. Few outsiders ever learn to speak Basque or Eskimo, though members of these groups learn other languages quite easily. It is even rumored that children of these groups are born a year earlier than children of other linguistic stocks because of the additional time needed to learn their languages. Though there well may be no truth in this the general fact is that languages maximize intercourse among their speakers and inhibit intercourse between speakers of other languages. The generalization can be put in two forms, that people who marry each other tend to speak the same language, or that people who speak the same language tend to marry each other. It should be stressed that language and cultural ideas are not inherited genetically though learning ability is heritable to an important degree. Any human child can learn any language. The association between race and language, remarkably congruent in certain groups, is an indirect or historical association. As noted by Kroeber, 'Speech tends to be one of the most persistent population characters; and 'ethnic' boundaries are most often speech boundaries' (Kroeber, 1948, p. 221).

Mating rules are important to the internal structure of a culture as well as to its external boundaries and have much evolutionary significance as a consequence. The actual matings are of course more important than the rules for mating which often are ignored. The lack of conformity between actual behavior and ideal behavior in this respect is notable (Kunstadter *et al.*, 1963).

The most notable effect of mating rules is connected with inbreeding. All populations tend to be endogamous, to select their mates within the group, though they may be subdivided into exogamous divisions that depend upon other subdivisions for their mates. Endogamous groups often, but not always, encourage mating between close relatives, which is inbreeding.

Major physiographic features are always important in regulating contact between groups, even though they are not impenetrable. Deserts, oceans, and mountains can be crossed, but not as easily as crossing a street or visiting another village within the same community. Mountain ranges, fjords, glaciers, and various transitional zones between ecological areas are enormously important in understanding the distribution of people and the frequency of contacts between them. In each case the barriers are culturally interpreted. Use of the camel enables people to traverse deserts otherwise impassable, and use of boats may redefine a body of water into a well-traveled highway rather than a barrier, and the use of dogs and sleds among Arctic peoples, or the horse among Plains Indians vastly increased the range of their movements and the frequency of interaction between population units.

Caste differences may be fully as great as differences between geographically separate groups (Sanghvi, 1953). They illustrate quite uniquely the efficacy of cultural barriers to random mating between groups. Similarly, groups that are defined primarily on the basis of religion can become physically as distinctive as groups that are ecologically separated (Sachs and Bat-Miriam, 1957). Obviously several boundary maintaining devices operate in conjunction with each other though some factors may appear to be more prominent than others.

Other factors which serve as diffusion barriers consist of such things as the relative difference in population size between two contiguous groups. Large corporate units cannot be hybridized by smaller population units, but rather the large units dissipate or absorb smaller numbers of immigrants without leaving a trace in many cases. This has been important in the history of Japan (Suzuki, 1958). Still another category is that of population buffering by means of intervening populations. The effects of gene flow are diluted with each successive population unit that the genes are passed through, in the absence of maximizing agents such as a selective advantage.

In summary one might note that the great diversity within the human species is evidence that there are many effective boundary maintaining devices.

Intergradation Between Subspecies - Division

Since all races can exchange genes, and all do when the opportunity arises, there is much intergradation or overlap in the physical characteristics, though this is only one of several reasons. The taller American Indians such as Mohave have some members who are of the same stature as the much shorter Pueblo Indians. The overlap in measurements of size and form is common even for groups widely separated. This is not true for pigmentation and hair form. Widely separated groups may be sharply differentiated. The hair of all Eskimos is straight, and the head hair of all Bushmen is spirally tufted or kinky. No Northern Europeans are as heavily pigmented as Equatorial Negroes. Among serological traits there are a number of antigens that are absent in some groups and present in others. Many South American Indians are completely lacking in the antigens for blood groups A and B. The blood group Diego is common in South American Indians and completely absent in Europeans. More often the different races differ only in the frequency of genes for various blood groups, especially contiguous races, but this is by no means true for all the blood group genes. Combinations or patterns of traits vary so that contiguous groups, such as Japanese and Ainu, differ sharply from each other. American Indians are sharply differentiated from Mongoloids, such as the Aleuts and Eskimos, and Lapps are easily distinguished individually as well as corporately from surrounding Norwegians, Swedes, Finns, and Russians.

Two generalizations can be made that provide a general guide to appreciating the distribution of variation in relation to populations. Groups far removed from each other are most dissimilar and share the least affinity with each other. Similarity and affinity are closely related but not identical in all contexts. The second generalization is that intergradation in physical characteristics, or the absence of sharp lines, does not remove or nullify the existence of the populations. The fact that two groups are similar to each other does not mean that there is only one group instead of two. No two populations are ever identical, any more than two individuals are identical.

Mixture is one of the most important processes contributing to similarity between races. However, there are many other processes at work, some of which produce different results under different conditions. All races cannot mix with all other races in equal proportions. Differential degrees of mixture produce different results. Some groups live in areas where environmental stresses are more rigorous. There is for example no way that high altitude dwellers such as Andean Indians could escape the oxygen tension stresses of high altitude. Depending upon its history a particular race may have retained a greater proportion of genes from an earlier period. Differences in population size affect a number of evolutionary agencies and consequently abstract rates of change cannot be established. Intergradation between populations does not pose insurmountable problems in classification, if the populations have been established on a genetic basis.

Methods of Comparing Groups

The fact that different kinds of people live in different places has been known for several centuries. This fact, plus a knowledge of the genetics of variation does not automatically produce an understanding of the processes and patterns of human evolution, neither in general terms nor in the elucidation of the history of particular races. Comparisons between contemporaneous groups, and between successive groups in time, are essential components in the meaningful interpretation of both the processes and the trends in human evolution. There are many ways of comparing populations of which formal classifications are only one. The construction of a species standard within which each population can be compared is an efficient method of comparison; construction of clines or character gradients is still another useful method; and classification involving the estimation of biological distance (numerical taxonomy) between three or more groups constitutes a third major category of methods for handling variation between groups. It must be emphasized frequently that the quantification or description of degrees of similarity between races does not in itself explain how these came about. Differences and similarities must be described in objective and biologically meaningful ways. Such comparisons are an indispensable step to explaining the variations, but do not in themselves automatically provide an explanation.

Recognizing the unity of the human species, that no division has approached the boundary of speciation, and the corollary fact that no one division can serve as a norm for other divisions, it is interesting to know what the average value is for various measurements for the entire species. Thus, the average man is 165 cm tall, ranging from 121 cm to 199 cm as physiologically normal limits. Any particular population can be rated according to its divergence from such species standard values. The same standard frequencies have been computed for the major blood groups and provide an equally useful overview of the entire species and population divergence within it. The remarks of Penrose are relevant:

'Everyone is accustomed, quite erroneously, to regard the group from which he has originated as being the normal. Judged by world standards, his group is likely to be abnormal and he may have to fall back on the assumption that, though unusual, it may represent a specially desirable set of gene frequencies. He is perhaps justified only in inferring that his group has a genetic structure well suited in the past to its environment, else it would not have maintained itself' (Penrose, 1951, p.397).

Clinal Comparisons

Where a character varies over distance, from one geographical region to another, it is possible to trace the frequency of the character, for example, the frequency of blood group B, or the average value for a continuous trait such as stature or weight in each population unit of the region or areas under examination. The term 'cline' or 'gradient' refers to a single character that is being traced over distance, not to populations. A single population may participate in as many clines as it has characters which are found in other populations. A commonly cited example of a blood group cline is seen in the increase of blood group B proceeding from Western Europe into Central Asia. Geographical variation in stature and weight, in pigmentation, and in many other characters has been plotted for the world and a number of rules have been formulated to describe this variation. According to Bergman's rule the smaller sized geographical races within a species are found in the warmer parts of its continental distribution, and the larger races in the cooler parts. Within the New

World, for example, Central American Indians such as the Maya are small whereas North American Indians tend to be larger with increase in latitude.

Use of the term 'cline' and the study of gradation in measurable characters were originally proposed as an auxiliary taxonomic method to correct defects inherent in naming areal groups, in order to stress 'continuity and regularity of variation as against mere distinctness of groups' (Huxley, 1938, p. 219). Clines are generally considered to be the joint product of two opposing forces, selection and mixture. Selection tends to enhance the adaptation of a population to its local environment whereas gene flow or mixture tends to enhance similarities between populations. The explanation of clinal variation has tended to utilize correlations between characters and environment especially climate, nutrition, and disease, as evidence of adaptations, rather than as the beginning point for research to elucidate the relative contribution of the various factors that produce a trend in variation. Plausibility is often substituted for proof.

Classification

One way of comparing different populations is that of computing the relative degrees of similarity between three or more. The basic assumption underlying such comparisons is that similarity is a measure of relationship or affinity. It must be reiterated that formal classifications constitute only one aspect of the study of population units within the species. It is one method of studying the distribution of variation within the species and of following variation backward in time, of studying long term evolution, including the origins and affinities of various divisions. Formal classifications provide an objectivity that is seriously needed to correct many ancient and honored misconceptions concerning relationships of populations. The peculiar notions that Melanesians were significantly more similar and tangibly related to African Negroes, rather than to other Oceanic peoples, or that the Lapps were more similar to and therefore more closely related to Mongoloids rather than to other Europeans, are specimens of fallacious conclusions based upon causal inspection of physical data and preconceptions which are not supported when multivariate distance statistics or similar methods are employed.

Classification consists of the arrangement of groups. The term 'relational systematics' (Ginsburg and Laughlin, 1966) may be useful to emphasize the relational or arrangement nature of such operations. It is frequently confused with the enumeration or inventory of groups. The problem of arrangement remains, whether we choose to classify 10,000 small demes or five continental divisions. At the simplest level we may compare any three groups such as Icelanders, Southern Norwegians, and South African Bushmen. No single Bushman could be visually mistaken for either an Icelander or a Norwegian, and the formal examination of serological data, pigmentation, body measurements, hair form, and whatever other traits we wish to use will illustrate the fact that the two northern groups are more similar to each other than either is to the Bushman. We infer various things from this triangular comparison, one inference being that the Bushmen have been separated from the Scandinavians for a longer period of time than the two Scandinavian populations have been separated from each other. If we should take three neighborhoods or three village isolates on the island of Iceland we should have the same basic methodological problem, and if we chose to classify three genera, such as Paranthropus, Australopithecus, and Oreopithecus, we would still have the same basic problem in arrangement.

It is sometimes remarked that one of the problems facing the taxonomist is that there are no clear cut distinctions, no sharp lines, between populations. It is trivially obvious that populations within a species are not separated by sharp lines. This has been carefully noted from the time of Blumenbach (1795) through Darwin (Descent of Man, 1871) to the present. It is a consequence or a reflection of the fact that we are examining variation within a single species. The fact that two populations are extremely similar does not mean that there is only one population instead of two, if they have been genetically defined. A group that has recently fissioned from another group will obviously be quite similar to its parent population. It is, nevertheless, a distinguishable population if it constitutes a group in which the members habitually select most of their mates. Such small or newly formed groups are especially valuable for the study of the processes of population formation.

Conversely, if we choose to work with groups of higher taxonomic status, such as the three genera cited above, our problems in estimating relative degrees of similarity and of inferring affinity or phylogenetic relatedness remain as intransigent as before. No single skull of Oreopithecus, a Pliocene hominid, of Paranthropus, a lower Pleistocene Australopithecine, or of Australopithecus, a lower Pleistocene ancestor of man, could be mistaken for each other even by visual sorting. The absence of intergradation does not ameliorate or remove the problem of estimating their relationships. Paleontologists who are working with larger taxonomic groupings such as genera, or families, have quite as many troubles and literary altercations as anthropologists working inside our single species.

The labor involved in numerical classifications may be considerable (Rao, 1952; Sokal and Sneath, 1963; Spuhler, 1954; Campbell, 1963) and as with the construction of clines, or the comparison of populations with the species as a whole, the interpretation of the differences and similarities, and explanations are not automatically provided.

The purpose or purposes which provide the basis for a study provide the level of abstraction at which the researcher will operate. Thus, if we are interested in the effects of inbreeding and nutrition we shall find it necessary to study small groups such as immigrants from a Swiss valley who have moved to California. If we want to investigate the history of a stock that has congruence between linguistic, ecological, and genetical features such as the Eskimo, then we will compare all the village groups of Eskimos for which we can secure data. If we want to summarize for the world as a whole we may then resort to comparisons between the major continental areas. Our choice of population units is analogous to the contour interval used by surveyors and cartographers. A map of the world cannot show all the smaller variations that a soil map of a single country must show. Intervals of five or ten feet may be used for greater detail of small areas, and intervals of 500 or 1,000 feet for large continental areas. The comparisons we choose to make do not affect the existence of population units, they exist whether we choose to use them or not, whether we decide to give them formal taxonomic names or not.

Two examples may suffice here to illustrate the point that populations have a reality apart from the observer. At the lower level the Polar Eskimos, numbering originally some 250, may be cited as a population unit which can be decomposed into local demes but are a geographically delimited isolate in the extreme. These people thought they were the only people in the world when they were discovered and indeed they had probably been completely isolated for some two hundred years or more, a rare phenomenon in humans. If all isolates of this magnitude were listed for the world the number would run into the tens of thousands, yet they do exist and for some purposes they must be dealt with.

On the other hand we need to go back in time only 15,000 years to rid ourselves of any question concerning New World populations, for there were none. It would be entirely appropriate to summarize the major divisions of variation in the world into only three, if we confined ourselves to the world of 15,000 - 30,000 years ago. We should then have only Asiatic Mongoloids, Europeans, and Africans south of the Sahara. Actually there would have been as much diversity between the population units within these broad categories as there is today. However, we would not have to wonder about the position of the Oceanic peoples of Australia, Melanesia, Polynesia, and Micronesia - they did not exist. Now, whether American Indians should be classified as a separate race from their parental populations of Asia depends primarily upon whether you wish to emphasize origins or emphasize processes and the actual existence of these separate populations. The New World aborigines have had a separate evolutionary history for at least 11,000 years. Whether they are as distinct from Asiatics, as say Africans are from Europeans, is a separate question.

Viewed from the standpoint of biological evolution and of culture history, all human groups that have come into existence, for whatever reasons, are of value for studying the dynamics of race and culture, no matter how small they may actually be.

The Genetic Unity of the Species - Summary

The single human species is extremely diverse in many respects, and this diversity has been a major feature enabling the species to achieve its worldwide distribution and a high degree of control over nature and over the destiny of the species. This diversity, as well as the similarity, is seen in population units of various orders of magnitude ranging from small, local demes, breeds, neighborhoods, or local races through ever more inclusive groups, such as the continental divisions of mankind to the species as a whole. These population units, or races, have two points of critical significance for understanding man's place in nature. One point concerns the role they perform in the evolution of the species, and the other concerns how we apprehend the species, how we secure information about it. The first point may be epitomized for the moment with the observation that evolution only takes place in populations, not in individuals. The second point is based upon a sampling problem. We want to know and understand the evolution of the entire species. There is so much diversity that we cannot use one group as a standard for the species, neither is there any one race that can be omitted. The values for measurements of the body, for pigmentation, growth rates, or blood groups that are characteristic of any one population are not characteristic for other populations. We cannot predict from one population what other populations ought to be.

The next major idea concerns the uses of information about populations and this rests again upon the fact that breeding populations are the transactional units in which evolution is taking place, and evolution includes a multitude of phenomena ranging from disease susceptibility to gene frequency ratios, from infant mortality to hair form and behavior. Some of the information has significance for estimating affinities between groups, for racial history and for rates of evolution. However, the study of human populations, used synonymously here for races, involves much more than estimating affinities between peoples and making classifications. The genetic, morphological, ecological, and behavioral dynamics of a human population extend in many directions. In fact, the more that is known about the mechanics of population genetics, about the etiology and developmental phenomena of various traits, the better the applications that can be made to particular problems, such as those concerned with origins and affinities of human groups. Child growth is an enormously important area of interest. Information on child growth in different populations contributes to the understanding of child growth in any one population and for the species as a whole. The genetic basis of many traits, varies between different populations. Our understanding of what traits are, to what extent they are inherited, and the ways in which they are developed in their complex interactions with both the intrinsic and extrinsic environment can only be secured by population studies, ideally on all the populations of the world, and minimally on enough different populations to estimate the major parameters of the traits.

The most synoptic and grand problems can only be solved by studying particular characteristics of particular populations at a particular time. An over all charter for studying the entire human species is provided by the challenging question of what factors provide the cohesion that binds the species together. This has been phrased as a general problem by Mayr in his remark, 'The essential genetic unity of species cannot be doubted. Yet the mechanisms by which this unity is maintained are still largely unexplored' (Mayr, 1963, p. 523). We now know that there is but one human species, and we know a great deal about it, but we are only beginning to understand how the unity of our species has been maintained through thousands of years of adaptation to diverse areas encompassing the entire world.

The unity of the species does not rest exclusively upon admixture between races, though mixture is an important process that promotes similarity between those groups that mix by introducing the same traits into groups that did not previously have them and by equalizing their frequencies. Two other contributing categories to species unity are (1) common ancestors from which many traits held in common are retained, and (2) parallel evolution, the tendency of separate populations to evolve in the same direction owing to such things as a common starting point, the limit imposed upon possible new traits and recombinations based upon those already in hand, and similarities in selection pressures. Parallel evolution is a large and complex category which importantly includes variations in the basis of inheritance with similarity in the clinical or observational entities produced. There are alternate routes at the molecular, familial, and population level for adaptations which serve the same end. This has been an important trend in the primate order as a whole. The method of locomotion involving the use of the arms for swinging (brachiation) has arisen separately in Asia among the orangs and gibbons, in Africa among the chimpanzees and gorillas, and in South America among spider monkeys, woolly monkeys, and woolly spider monkeys. Races can and so exchange genes because they are capable of gene exchange, and previous or earlier gene exchange is one of the factors that has rendered them capable of such exchange. However, all three of the broad categories of shared inheritance, parallel evolution, and mixture are responsible for the maintenance of similarities between races and thus for the continued unity of our species.

It should further be noted that highly isolated divisions of the species have successfully solved their problem of survival, of biological perpetuation of themselves, and of communication. The fallacious belief that race mixture is a prerequisite of progress may be true for some small groups who are genuinely inbred and who have a significantly high frequency of disabling diseases as a consequence. However, populations in general carry an enormous amount of concealed genetic variability. This is adequate for the maintenance of genetic variability for future evolution for several hundreds of generations. If a major source of genetic variability, mutation, was stopped completely, neither the species as a whole nor its larger population units would be aware of it for thousands of years, except for reduced frequencies of some diseases such as hemophilia and muscular dystrophy (Crow, 1961). The rise of complex civilizations among the Maya and Incas of Central and South America, with no outside influence from Europe or from Asia, in a continent discovered and occupied by primitive hunters only 15,000 years ago, illustrates the enormous creativity potential in different pospulations.

References

Blumberg, B.S. (1961). Inherited susceptibility to disease. *Archives of Environmental Health,* 3, 612-636.
Blumenbach, J.F. (1865). On the natural variety of mankind. In *The Anthropological Treatises of Johann Friedrich Blumenbach.* London: Anthropological Society.
Boyd, W.C. (1950). *Genetics and the Races of Man.* Boston: D.C. Heath.
Campbell, B. (1963). Quantitative taxonomy and human evolution. In *Classification and Human Evolution,* edited by S.L. Washington. Viking Fund Publications in Anthropology, No. 37.
Coon, C.S. (1963). *The Origin of Races.* New York: A.A. Knopf.
Crow, J.F. (1961). Mechanisms and trends in human evolution. *Daedalus,* Summer, 416-431.
Ginsburg, B.E. (1958). Genetics as a tool in the study of behavior. *Perspectives in Biological Medicine,* 1, 397-424.
Ginsburg, B.E. and Laughlin, W.S. (1966). The multiple bases of human adaptability. *Eugenics Quarterly,* 13, 240-257.
Grant, V. (1963). *The Origin of Adaptations.* New York: Columbia University Press.
Howells, W. (1959). *Mankind in the Making.* New York: Doubleday.
Huxley, J.S. (1938). Clines: an auxiliary taxonomic principle. *Nature,* 142: 219.
Kroeber, A.L. (1948). *Anthropology.* New York: Harcourt, Brace.
Kunstadter, P., Buhler, R., Stephen, F.F. and Westoff, C.F. (1963). Demographic variability and preferential marriage patterns. *American Journal of Physical Anthropology,* 21, 575-589.
McArthur, M. and Penrose, L.S. (1950). World frequencies of the O, A, and B blood group genes. *Annals of Eugenics,* 15, 302-305.
Mayr, E. (1958). Behavior and systematics. In *Behavior and Evolution,* edited by A. Roe and G.G. Simpson. New Haven: Yale University Press.
Mayr, E. (1963). *Animal Species and Evolution.* Cambridge, Massachusetts: Harvard University Press.

Mourant, A.R. (1954). *The Distribution of the Human Blood Groups.* Oxford: Blackwell Scientific Publications.

Neel, J.V., Shaw, M.W. and Schull, W.J. (Editors) (1963). *Genetics and the Epidemiology Chronic Diseases.* Public Health Service Publication, No. 1163.

Osborne, R.H. (Editor) (1961). Genetic perspectives in disease resistance and susceptibility. *Annals of the New York Academy of Science,* 91.

Penrose, L.S. (1951). Genetics of the human race. In *Genetics in the Twentieth Century,* edited by L.C. Dunn. New York: Macmillan.

Rao, C.R. (1952). *Advanced Statistical Methods in Biometric Research.* New York: John Wiley & Sons.

Sachs, L. and Bat-Miriam, M. (1957). The genetics of Jewish populations, 1. Finger print patterns in Jewish populations in Israel. *American Journal of Human Genetics,* 9, 117-126.

Sanghvi, L.S. (1953). Comparison of genetical and morphological methods for a study of biological differences. *American Journal of Physical Anthropology,* 11, 385-404.

Simpson, G.G. (1964). Organisms and molecules in evolution. *Science,* 146, 1535-1538.

Sokal, R.R. and Sneath, P.H.A. (1963). *Principles of Numerical Taxonomy.* San Francisco: W.H. Freeman.

Spuhler, J.N. (1954). Sole problems in the physical anthropology of the American South-west. *American Anthropologist,* 56, 604-625.

Spuhler, J.N. and Clark, P.J. (1961). Migration into the human breeding population of Ann Arbor Michigan, 1900-1950. *Human Biology,* 33, 223-236.

Suzuki, H. (1958). *Changes in the Skull Features of the Japanese People from Ancient to Modern Times.* Selected Papers of the Fifth International Congress of Anthropological and Ethnological Sciences, pp. 717-724. Philadelphia: Pennsylvania Press.

8

HUMAN AND MEDICAL GENETICS: A SCIENTIFIC DISCIPLINE AND AN EXPANDING HORIZON

Arno G. Motulsky

I am deeply honored in receiving the Allan Award. I feel gratified to join the company of scientists such as Newton Morton, Oliver Smithies, James Neel, Vernon Ingram, Harry Harris, and Jérôme Lejeune whom this Society thought worthy of this Award. In considering my predecessors, I feel dwarfed by their achievements which have been so important in recent advances of human genetics. Nevertheless, I am grateful and delighted that you have seen fit to recognize my efforts.

I owe much to my teachers as summarized on the scientific pedigree (Fig. 1) and particularly to my colleagues in Seattle. Stanley Gartler exemplifies how a basic PhD geneticist uses clinical data for fundamental insights into genetic phenomena in man. Eloise Giblett's critical mind, no-nonsense attitude, and willingness to hear out and discuss ideas have been of great help. Over the years research fellows such as Philip Fialkow, George Fraser, and George Stamatoyannopoulos remained in or returned to Seattle and became independent and well-recognized scientists. A few years ago I was able to convince Akira Yoshida - an outstanding protein and enzyme chemist - that an appropriate field of action for men of his training might be *human* biochemical genetics. He joined our team, and his achievements in the delineation of the molecular lesions of the G6PD molecule are now well known. These people, our research associates Jean Bryant, Onchie Carino, and Amelia Schultz, and many others in the

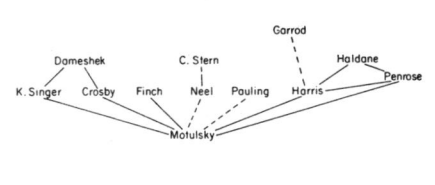

SCIENTIFIC PEDIGREE

FIG. 1. - The pedigree includes scientists with major impact on intellectual development. Dashed lines refer to men who have had such influence through ideas rather than by direct work in their laboratories. Dameshek, Stern, and Haldane are 'scientific grandfathers', respectively. (Dr Sturtevant first suggested and used such scientific pedigrees.)

Departments of Medicine, Genetics, Pediatrics, Pathology, Preventive Medicine, and Anthropology, as well as the many research fellows from this country and abroad, have made life in Seattle intellectually exciting. Any measure of success I owe to these associates.

The task facing the Allan Award winner in delivering a speech to this Society is difficult. No definite tradition regarding the nature of the address has yet been established. Current soul-searching and identity crises in academic circles make a survey of the current scene in human and medical genetics more appropriate than a purely scientific paper.

Current Status of Medical Genetics

The field of human and medical genetics lacks clear-cut demarcation. Unlike other fields, such as biochemistry, which are recognized as specific disciplines in medical schools or universities, medical or human genetics lacks independent status. In fact a similar situation exists in our parent field of genetics, which often is not represented independently but is found in various biology departments. Genetic concepts permeate many areas of basic biologic sciences and of clinical medicine. In addition, genetic ideas are being applied to sociology and other behavioral sciences. Since the field is relatively new, there is no uniformity in background and training among its practitioners. Some human geneticists are fundamental scientists who largely work in the laboratory; others are clinical investigators who work at the bench and with patients. Some are clinician scholars interested in the classification, description, and natural history of genetic diseases, and others are interested primarily in genetic counseling. Some human geneticists are explorers and spend their efforts in studying various exotic populations; others are mathematically inclined and devote their time to theoretical models. Still others with a similar background are more interested in experimental data and have become experts in computer application. Since genetics has become popular in medical schools, it is not uncommon to find physicians or other scientists with some cytogenetic training being considered as geneticists by their colleagues. In other medical schools, those who work on the biochemistry of the inborn errors of metabolism, which happen to be genetic in origin, have been designated the local geneticists. Our colleagues in basic genetics like to point out that the study of genetic diseases alone does not qualify a person as a geneticist. The lack of a broad genetic background among such scientists makes for a lopsided image of the field in some medical schools.

The number of medical schools who have divisions, departments, or units of medical or human genetics is not large. Geneticists are working in many places, ranging from PhDs in departments of anatomy, to serologists in blood banks, to physicians interested in genetic disease. PhD geneticists in college departments of biology continue to be a significant proportion of human geneticists, although this group has become proportionately smaller as the field has enlarged. This group works largely with classical, formal techniques. University presidents and deans who look at this heterogeneous group of individuals ranging widely in skill and talents find it difficult to see any clear patterns for the establishment of administrative units. In a few medical schools, departments of medical genetics have been established. In other schools, divisions of medical genetics have been created within departments of medicine and pediatrics and have a scope somewhat similar to that of independent departments. Departments, rather than divisions within departments, have the advantage of more solid local administrative support - an important feature in these days of diminishing outside grants.

Medical genetics in Europe has not reached institutional maturity either. Excellent centers exist, scattered in England, France, Germany, Holland, Switzerland, Italy, and the Scandinavian countries. Their organization differs considerably from country to country; recent development aiming at the establishment of human genetics institutes in most German medical faculties is of particular interest. One contrast between North America and Europe is the relative isolation of the various European university institutes. The easy cross-fertilization between basic scientists and clinicians and the mutual stimulation of scientists with different interests are often lacking. Ideally, a unit of human genetics should exist within a university where scientists interested in the fundamental aspects of biology and genetics can interact with those whose main concern is with human and medical application. Progress in the genetic aspects of the behavior and social sciences also appears favored by location of the biologic, medical, and social sciences on the same campus.

While the lack of a clear-cut delineation of medical genetics makes for slower institutional growth, this flexibility probably has some advantages. If a field becomes administratively rigid with well-defined boundaries, the advent of new scientific developments and directions may cause rapid obsolescence of its structures. We are all aware of this in certain areas in biology. Universities may thus become top-heavy with departments no longer relevant to the current state of science. Conversely, the newer fields will find it difficult to find funds and space. The Rockefeller University in New York solves this problem by building research units and laboratories around an outstanding investigator rather than having all scientific fields represented. This organization is one which universities cannot easily emulate because of their teaching and service obligations. The lack of a specific institutional base for medical genetics makes it more difficult for the less adventurous to seek a career in the field. Fewer workers consequently will devote their total energies to the area, since much genetic work will be on a part-time basis. Growth will be slower as compared with the potential that follows with full institutional recognition. Scientific advances in human genetics in the recent past argue that the lack of institutional units probably has not hampered progress. Yet, I believe that progress in the future requires a more solid foundation rather than the flexible and opportunistic organization seen heretofore.

Medical Genetics and Specialties in Medicine

Early interest in medical genetics in the United States often came from people with training in internal medicine rather than pediatrics. This is remarkable, since illnesses with genetic etiology are more frequently seen in children than in adults. However, the academic tradition in pediatrics was such that fewer pediatricians obtained their expertise in the area of genetic and developmental disorders. It is relatively recent that many academic pediatricians have become intensely concerned with genetic factors. The need for medical geneticists in departments of pediatrics is great and will continue for some time. My pediatrician friends tell me that pediatricians as a group are pragmatic in inclination, possibly explaining the earlier lack of interest in genetics when the field was largely theoretic. The division of patients by age groups in departments of internal medicine and pediatrics continues as a deterrent toward the best application of genetic research, teaching, and training in medical schools. Pediatricians usually do not examine adults; therefore, full family studies which include adults may not be prosecuted with the necessary vigor and care. Similarly, internists are neither trained in nor accustomed to examining children. Medical genetics cuts across all age groups and is involved in the biology and pathology of the gamete, embryo, fetus, newborn, child, adult, and aging individual. Medical geneticists are the generalists of academic medicine. Familiarity with the human organism in both childhood and adulthood is required, and training in both pediatrics and medicine is desirable for clinical geneticists. Furthermore, many genetic diseases are found in specialty areas such as ophthalmology, otolaryngology, dermatology, neurology, and psychiatry. Unlike the usual specialist, the medical geneticist needs to be acquainted with a large variety of conditions in different fields. This wide range of theoretical and clinical knowledge gives the field strength in that medical geneticists are more likely to see the 'forest from the individual trees'.

Status of Publications in Genetics

For a relatively small field which has not reached institutional recognition, the number of journals dealing with human genetics is remarkable. In September 1970 there are at least eight journals dealing with human and medical genetics alone. Two more journals deal with the social and eugenic implications of human genetics. Two more are concerned with human cytogenetics. In addition to the specific journals of human genetics, a considerable amount of material of interest to human geneticists appears in general journals such as *Science* and *Nature*, as well as in various pediatric, internal medicine, and medical specialty journals. Human geneticists, therefore, more so than many other specialists, have to keep up with a tremendous amount of literature. Although human geneticists as a group compare well with any other group of medical scientists, a considerable amount of trivial data finds its way into the different publications. Every editor is well aware that most rejected papers are ultimately published in other journals. The *American Journal of Human Genetics* rejects about 50% of submitted papers; many of these are published elsewhere later. It would be of interest for information specialists in association with experienced biomedical scientists to investigate the signal/noise ratio of publications in different fields of biology and medicine. How would our field compare with others?

Training of Human and Medical Geneticists

What type of people are being attracted into human and medical genetics at the present time? Some students are taking a basic science degree in genetics with a major in human genetics. The number of departments where such individuals can get strong PhD training in human genetics is small. Increase in manpower in this nonmedically trained group is an additional reason for the further establishment of human genetics units in the various universities. The best type of training requires that such departments are working in collaboration with the medical school. PhD candidates in human genetics need to develop experience in working with human material and need to become accustomed to collaborative relationships with physicians early in their training.

Most PhD students in genetics are not primarily interested in human genetics. Some of the brightest students are fascinated by molecular biology and are attracted to graduate schools where that work is done. With the progress of molecular genetics in the last 10 years and the availability of research and training grants, probably more students have been trained in these areas than can be absorbed by college faculties and research institutes. Consquently individuals already trained or still in training will have difficulty finding jobs consistent with their background. The potential surplus of such highly trained basic scientists may lead to a group of disgruntled men who will not use their full training. Medical schools and hospitals still suffer from a shortage of geneticists. The impact on human and medical genetics may be marked if a significant number of fundamentally trained individuals would shift emphasis from basic genetics to human genetics. Research in human genetics by such individuals is likely to yield high dividends. One of the obstacles to full implementation of such career shifts is a lack of background in *human* biology. It might be worthwhile to consider retraining schemes. Special training institutes and summer courses to acquaint PhD basic geneticists with human biology could be easy ways of solving this problem. The simplest way of acquiring training in human biology and pathology, however, is by attending a medical school.

Quite a few young physicians these days aspire to a career in medical genetics. Demand for trained individuals is still quite high. With the development of increased elective time, summer research projects, and PhD-MD type programs, many medical trainees have had significant exposure to research, often in medical genetics. In fact, because medical genetics attracts research-minded individuals, the number of trainees who have had previous research exposure is increasing.

Training in medical genetics ideally has three facets: (1) research work; (2) clinical work with genetic diseases, including genetic counseling; and (3) course work. Since most medical geneticists will be expected to teach, a strong background in the various aspects of general and human genetics is required. Ideally, training should prepare for the research problems of the future and requires an excellent background in genetics and molecular biology. A good knowledge of statistics is also desirable. Since most of these medical geneticists will ultimately be working in clinical departments, broad expertise in the many aspects of genetic disease is required. Such specialized knowledge can best be obtained by frequent exposure to a variety of genetic problems as they present in the clinic or hospital. Emphasis on laboratory research is considered important since the most significant advances in medical genetics are likely to come through the laboratory, and a large proportion of medical geneticists must contribute to that knowledge by research.

Some recent developments are disquieting. Young physicians in medical genetics - and this applies to other branches of medical research - become compartmentalized in their approach to patients on the one hand as compared with laboratory research on the other. Such individuals select research problems similar to those investigated by geneticists or biochemists with a PhD degree. A choice of problems identical with those pursued by basic scientists reflects a lack of imagination. Hopefully, MD investigators in clinical departments will acquire an excellent background in basic science and then concentrate on those experiments of nature we call 'disease'. The fundamental scientist is less likely to be aware of the myriad of problems posed by patients, and nontrivial problems of this nature do still exist. *Not* working on disease-related problems is a waste of years of medical training in most cases. If the clinical investigator will not work on clinically related problems, who will?

Working with human patients, families, and populations is logistically more difficult than setting up a bench experiment which can be started and often finished at a planned time. The ability to pursue patients and study subjects away from the hospital seems to go with certain temperaments. Some individuals never develop the inclination to do this type of work. The person who is committing himself to a career in medical genetics should realize that a large portion of his time will often be spent in such 'busy' work. While trained family workers can be helpful, much must be done by the investigator himself. Most physicians with the usual training expect the patient to come to the office or laboratory. It is common experience that important specimens will be missed in this manner and that the medical geneticist must actively pursue his patients and study subjects in the home.

Teaching of human genetics
Many, including nongeneticists, would agree that knowledge of the basic principles of genetics is desirable for the general public. Such an understanding is particularly worthwhile with the realization that social and behavioral differences between individuals may have a genetic basis. In addition, the possibility of biologic engineering even in its most benign aspects requires an informed citizenry before such procedures are instituted. Education in human genetics should start at the elementary school level. Such an approach requires that primary school teachers have a good foundation in human genetics which they could impart in simple ways to their students. High schools should see the offering of various courses in human biology with a strong emphasis on human genetics. Such courses also should be required in the nonacademic streams of high schools. Again, trained teachers are required. The initial emphasis, therefore, will need to be on college courses in human genetics. At the present time genetics is widely taught in colleges. However, many courses are given with the technical emphasis required by aspiring biologists or geneticists. Often the courses are not up-to-date. There is definite justification for college courses in *modern* human genetics to deal with the field in a less technical manner. Human genetics can be taught without reference to detailed DNA biochemistry or recombination mechanisms and other such phenomena. Courses dealing with the cultural and social aspects of human genetics are needed. The approach exemplified by Lerner's book, *Heredity, Evolution and Society*, shows that such courses are feasible. Student demand for relevance can be met by such courses. Many of us need to take more of an interest in this area of instruction.

Physicians have the greatest need to be informed, both in their technical role, because of the considerable frequency of genetic disease, and as citizens because they are likely to become initially involved in application of the more far-ranging schemes affecting reproduction and genetics. While medical schools generally recognize the need for instruction in human genetics, the reasons cited earlier make for an extremely variable pattern of courses.

Concepts and Methods in Human Genetics

Human and medical genetics has considerable appeal to those who are interested in the theoretical and intellectual basis of biology and medicine. The background and approach of human geneticists encourage a synthetic view of human biology and disease with potential insight into relationships which are not as apparent to other observers. Just as genetics provides the theoretical framework for biology, so does medical genetics provide much of this framework for medicine. The intellectual appeal of human genetics lies in its proven record in the generation of new concepts and hypotheses which have been heuristic and have led to new insights. Examples are the one-gene/one-protein hypothesis, the hypothesis of X-chromosome inactivation, the theory of XX/XY sex determination, the concepts of pharmacogenetics and genetic heterogeneity, and the theory of gene duplication. While most scientists do not consciously try to discover new concepts, they will usually search for hypotheses to explain poorly understood scattered phenomena. This observation appears particularly true in human genetics. The high frequency of broad generalized concepts in our field should continue to attract some of the most able young investigators. However, ideas alone are not sufficient. Ingenious mathematical and statistical techniques have been developed to extract a maximum of information from a minimum of often biased and skewed data. Furthermore, the field has a strong laboratory basis, and various laboratory methods have contributed significantly to its progress. Thus, the sex chromatin test led to a flurry of new discoveries. More followed when it became possible to examine human chromosomes directly. The recently introduced 'flashing Y technique' allows better studies dealing with the biology and pathology of the Y chromosome. The 'fingerprinting' and other methods of peptide analysis have given us new insights into the molecular mechanism of mutation. Electrophoresis, and particularly starch gel electrophoresis, has been an invaluable method in demonstrating the ubiquity of biochemical polymorphisms with many implications for population genetics. Simple screening tests make it possible to study enzyme deficiencies and enzyme aberrations in many subjects, providing material for our ultimate understanding of population structure. Somatic cell hybridization promises to make linkage studies simpler and offers insight into genetic control mechanisms. All of these techniques were not available 25 years ago. It is conceivable that methods analogous to those we use today may be hidden in departments of chemistry and physics only waiting to be transposed to our laboratories.

Lack of contact between different areas of science may lead to considerable retardation in knowledge. Cytogenetics was advanced among plant cytologists, yet a simple technique for the visualization of human chromosomes was not developed until the mid-1950s. The method could have been discovered some 35 - 40 years earlier. The reason for the gap was partially related to the lack of genetically trained investigators in medical schools and medical research institutes. Genetics as a science was developed largely in universities and agricultural institutions away from medical schools. While physicians were aware of the importance of hereditary factors, the lack of laboratory methods to demonstrate cytologic or biochemical effects of gene action and the lack of contact with geneticists discouraged human genetics research in the medical schools. Investigations in medical schools were carried out by those who dealt with disease phenotypes and simple traits in family groupings, such as by Dr William Allan whose memory is honored by this Award.

The usual approach in the investigation of disease is to reduce a complex process into its components. Such a procedure applies the various methods of basic science (physics, chemistry, structural biology, etc.) toward an analysis of the pathophysiology, biochemistry, and genetics of the disease process. In this approach, basic science concepts and methods which were developed in their own right are applied to elucidate abnormal function. The reverse process, that is, the discovery of basic scientific principles by the investigation of clinical phenomena, has occurred repeatedly in medical genetics recently. The XY and XX sex determination and the discovery of a single amino acid substitution as the cause of sickle-cell anemia have already been mentioned and are good examples. The existence of a single clone of protein-producing cells in multiple myloma in man and mouse has provided a rich source of material for the study of the molecular biology of antibodies. Demonstration of G6PD deficiency as the cause of drug-induced hemolytic anemia was followed by many different types of studies in clinical medicine, formal and development genetics, molecular pathology, embryology, population genetics, and anthropology. In fact, using hemoglobin and G6PD variants alone, an entire course of human genetics with all its principles could be taught.

Current Status of Areas in Human Genetics

Figure 2 attempts to indicate the current state of development of a variety of selected fields in the areas covered by medical genetics. The scale is arbitrary and one could argue about the estimates. There probably is little question that measured against the yardstick of ultimate and complete knowledge, the field of biochemical genetics is most advanced. However, even here large gaps remain. The redundancy of DNA in mammalian chromosomes is completely unexplained. The regulation of gene action in mammalian cells remains poorly understood. A tiny fraction of the total number of polymorphisms that must exist in man has been discovered. Many of these problems no longer are unique to human and medical genetics. It is likely that many answers to the questions posed will come from geneticists not necessarily identified with human genetics.

Human cytogenetics has made considerable progress since the first

Estimated extent of knowledge

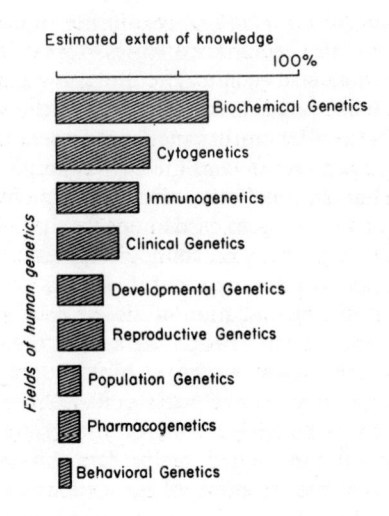

[Bar chart showing estimated knowledge (0 to 100%) across fields of human genetics:
- Biochemical Genetics
- Cytogenetics
- Immunogenetics
- Clinical Genetics
- Developmental Genetics
- Reproductive Genetics
- Population Genetics
- Pharmacogenetics
- Behavioral Genetics]

FIG. 2. - Estimated knowledge in 1970 compared with the ultimate and complete understanding of each field.

demonstration of the 46 chromosomes in 1956. Much progress has been a mop-up operation and has involved phenotype descriptions. However, we still have no good ways of identifying the individual human chromosomes. We still do not know the chromosomal location of most human genes. Normal mechanisms, such as pairing of homologous chromosomes and crossover, remain poorly understood. The etiology of the common chromosomal aberrations (such as the common trisomies) remains unknown, and the high frequency of chromosomal aberrations in our species is a riddle. The phenogenetics of the chromosomal errors is obscure. How does the addition of a single chromosome lead to complex malformations?

In immunogenetics, considerable progress has been made in understanding of the immunoglobulins, but the genetic basis of antibody variability still escapes us. Recent years have also seen the elucidation of gene action in the ABO blood group system. However, in most other blood groups we remain at the phenomenologic level with serologic descriptions, and little is known about the details underlying the genetic determinants. International collaboration has led to brilliant developments in histocompatibility testing, but the reason for the remarkable heterogeneity at the histocompatibility loci remains obscure.

In developmental genetics, the main problem remains that of gene control, that is, what makes genes turn on and off. What programs the development of the embryo? What is the significance of development genes such as fetal hemoglobin? How common are they? What is the genetic basis of birth defects? In clinical genetics, we understand the mechanisms of many autosomal recessive and X-linked recessive diseases and traits. However, gene action in the autosomal dominant diseases again is largely unknown. How does a mutation cause neurofibromatosis or polycystic kidneys? Many diseases such as diabetes, atherosclerosis, hypertension, and duodenal ulcer appear under polygenic determination. While the formal demonstration of such polygenic action is important as an initial approach, the ultimate understanding of the genetics of these disorders requires an analysis of the specific genes which comprise the different polygenic systems. We are almost completely in the dark regarding such genes. It is conceivable that many human polymorphisms may be components of polygenic systems making for resistance and susceptibility to some of the common diseases. At the present time we are largely in the descriptive phase of delineating the extent of polymorphisms in different populations. It is reasonably certain that chance alone cannot explain their existence. The possible selective factors causing this remarkable heterogeneity which is not confined to human populations remains unknown. More investigators are becoming concerned with human population structure, yet our understanding of the human gene pool remains rudimentary.

A poorly developed area of research in medical genetics might be termed 'clinical population genetics'. The term refers to the detailed study of patients and their families for a specified disease or symptom complex, such as has been done to some extent for deafness, blindness, mental retardation, etc. We lack data of the exact extent of the genetic determination in many disorders such as various endocrine disorders (e.g., hyperthyroidism or hyperparathyroidism) and many other diseases. A study of unselected consecutive patients using genetic, biochemical, and clinical methods is likely to yield considerable knowledge of potential benefit to patients and their families. Studies such as the natural history of polycystic kidneys done by Scandinavian investigators in the past are examples of this sort. However, since most clinicians are not oriented toward a population approach and since population geneticists usually are not clinicians, this field (with a few exceptions) has been rather undeveloped. While such work lacks the immediate excitement of some other areas in human genetics and takes a great deal of effort, it will provide the necessary background for much other work.

In behavioral genetics, few will deny that genes are active in the central nervous systems as in all other tissues, but the nature of that action remains entirely unknown. Some of our best-known colleagues in molecular biology have turned their attention to the investigation of behavioral phenomena in lower species. The genetic problems posed by *human* behavior are enormous and demand new approaches and insights.

We need more sociologists, anthropologists, psychologists, neurochemists, and neurophysiologists to obtain a rigorous background in human genetics as well as for human geneticists to get a better background in some of these areas. As Jim Neel has remarked, this area of research may be the most crucial one for survival of the human species. If we could learn more about the biologic basis of aggression, we might find means to control nuclear war with its potential destruction of Western civilization. Reprodductive genetics is another new area of recent interest to human geneticists which concerns genetic determinants of gamete formation, fertilization, and early development, and has some overlap with cytogenetics and developmental genetics. I did not use a separate category for formal genetics, but our modest knowledge of human linkage groups remains an important gap which needs filling.

Two types of technologic development promise many applications in human genetics - computer and automated laboratory techniques. Computers are making it possible now to digest large amounts of population data and deal with them in a variety of ways never before possible. For instance, we have collected laboratory and other demographic data on over 25,000 individuals in Greece in a study of malarial selection of various blood traits. Analysis of this material would be impossible without computers and remains a big 'headache' even with computers. As office terminals linked to computers with large capacities become available, this work should simplify in the future. Last year, a 17-year-old high school student in one week worked out and debugged a fairly complex program dealing with the establishment of a data bank of G6PD variants using a time-sharing computer. As young people are learning to work with computers as a natural extension of our modern environment, we can expect rapid progress in data utilization.

Computerized data records promise to be helpful in the orderly keeping of various genetic records. Using automated laboratory techniques, a variety of genetic and nongenetic traits will be screened at birth, in school, and before marriage. Hopefully, pattern-recognizing devices will do rapid chromosomal analyses; this material can be stored in computers as a permanent genetic and medical record of an individual. Information from doctors' offices and hospitals could tie in with such records so that every time an individual appears in a medical facility, a printout of previous data could be obtained. Along with these developments, we must learn to preserve the confidentiality of such records.

Recently a molecular biologist, Dr Gunther Stent, suggested that our society is coming close to the ultimate in possible knowledge in biology and other sciences, and that the intellectual excitement of the sort associated with the flowering of molecular biology no longer can be expected in the future. In looking at our abysmal ignorance concerning most of the phenomena of mammalian and human genetics as well as our lack of knowledge of the etiology of most genetic diseases, I cannot share Stent's pessimism (or some might call it optimism). While my vantage point point is considerably less lofty than that of Stent, I can foresee many exciting and unexpected discoveries of considerable intellectual excitement and potential significance in human and medical genetics for a long time to come. Having lived through most exciting times in biology, some of us have become pretty jaded. We get dispirited when progress in the laboratory slows and when the latest journal issue contains no really startling discoveries. (The contrast between the basic journals and those dealing with human genetics is often quite painful in this respect.) But exponential growth is unlikely to last in any field. We may be nearing an area where the 'hot' discoveries may slow down in our field. 'Homo scientificus' has existed for a very short time in human evolution. Hopefully, many generations of our descendants will follow, and the scientists of the future will want to and still need to make discoveries.

Status of Genetic Counseling

Genetic counseling is an important part of the activities in human genetics. As patients and their doctors are becoming increasingly aware of genetic factors in disease causation, more and more individuals will come to their medical advisers as well as to medical geneticists to ask about recurrence risks of diseases in their families. In most instances such advice can be given fairly securely, based on the principles of Mendelian inheritance or on empiric recurrence risks. As genetic education improves, most physicians will be able to perform genetic counseling for many diseases. Our nongeneticist medical colleagues soon will learn that there is no mystique about genetic counseling and will not need to refer these cases. In complex situations or obscure diseases, referrals to medical geneticists will continue, and we can be of real help. Since genetic advice requires accurate diagnosis, medically trained geneticists would appear to be the ideal genetic counselors.

The development of intrauterine diagnosis is giving an exciting new dimension to genetic counseling and allows definite rather than statistical diagnosis with selective abortion of affected fetuses. However, apart from the chromosomal aberrations, relatively few conditions can be diagnosed in this manner. The vast majority of diseases associated with structural protein abnormalities and/or dominant inheritance remain undiagnosable by this method. Similarly, all the common birth defects of complex etiology, such as cleft palate and CNS malformation, cannot be detected. In our excitement about a new method we should not lose a sense of proportion, particularly since the total impact of intrauterine diagnosis on public health is not very large today. However, techniques of fetal visualization and fetal biopsy may make it possible in the future to diagnose a variety of other conditions heretofore inaccessible to diagnosis.

The popularization of genetic counseling is bringing a new development. Responsible and well-informed healthy couples now sometimes appear before genetic counselors before marriage. These young people would like to know whether certain diseases could affect their children or simply want to be informed about the chances that their children will be healthy. They expect a genetic 'checkup' to give them this information. With better availability of screening for heterozygotes, we are entering a new area and may at least provide the rudiments of the desired genetic checkup. While at the present time we do not have sufficient knowledge or techniques to test for many heterozygote traits, some of us should get involved with the planning of premarital clinics for this type of counseling. If such units were established (and I do not advocate such centers for the immediate future), there would not be enough personnel in medical genetics available. Already, some colleges have foreseen the need for genetic counselors of paraprofessional training both for conventional needs and for the genetic counseling of the future. This development comes at a time when paramedical personnel are used much more extensively in all areas of medicine. Sarah Lawrence College in New York is pioneering in the establishment of curricula dealing with the biologic, social, and psychologic aspects of genetic counseling; graduates of the program could function effectively under the supervision of fully trained medical geneticists. This type of occupation should provide an important outlet for many young men and women who are attracted to service-oriented aspects of human genetics. At the present time there are few job outlets for these individuals.

Human Genetics and the Public

Since the large majority of the public is poorly educated in science, most people do not realize what scientists do. On the other hand, a field such as human genetics is of considerable interest to people since most parents see themselves in their children and are therefore interested in how heredity works. The advent of molecular biology, with resulting newspaper publicity on genetic engineering and the possibility of tailored genetic design, is bringing our field into the public domain. The public image of the 'mad scientist' manipulating human genes may be gaining strength along with occasional memories of a eugenic past which was tied up with an elitist and racist world view. The horrible excesses of Hitlerian Germany committed in the name of human genetics still are remembered by many. In general the swing from the purely social concerns of the early eugenicists to the entirely medically oriented preoccupation of recent decades has helped to make the field respectable in the eyes of the public. However, history repeats itself, and concern with the social and public issues of human genetics is again appearing.

It would be interesting for a social survey organization to canvass the attitudes of various groups in the population toward human genetics. Even with the negative feelings mentioned, I believe that the public expects more than we can deliver in the foreseeable future. The possibilities for genetic engineering are far from realized and will require considerably more work before we dare apply such techniques to human beings. It is important to emphasize this fact very forcefully.

In these days of diminishing research support, it is fashionable to point out that many scientific advances have taken place in the last two decades, and that a diminution of research support will prevent the solution of many important public health problems. While there is general merit in this argument, it is dangerous to promise breakthroughs if, in fact, such breakthroughs cannot be justified based on extrapolation of present knowledge. Most birth defects, as well as most common diseases such as atherosclerosis, hypertension, cancer, schizophrenia, and diabetes, do have genetic determinants. However, the nature of these genes is entirely unknown, and disease control for these disorders, based on genetic principles, is difficult to visualize within the present framework of our knowledge. I do not foresee genetic or environmental control of most of these diseases in the next 25 years. Promise of disease control by spokesmen for medical research has not yet led to differences in the frequency of birth defects or common diseases of middle age. Morbidity and mortality have not significantly decreased. It is, therefore, dangerous to tell the public that research in genetics is the panacea which will bring forward prevention and cures of many of our ills.

On the other hand we can point to many advances of practical significance: (1) we can detect chromosomal and biochemical disorders in utero allowing selective abortion of affected fetuses; (2) our understanding of the mechanisms of Rh hemolytic disease has led to preventive treatment by which this condition can be almost completely eliminated; (3) the development of histocompatibility testing now allows organ grafts with much less fear of rejection; (4) the development of simple screening tests to detect individuals susceptible to drug reactions allows prevention of such reactions; (5) the understanding of the genetics and pathophysiology in a variety of diseases allows preventive treatment of previously unsuspected affected patients - Wilson's disease and polyposis of the colon are examples; and (6) genetic counseling of the old-fashioned conventional type has many practical applications in preventing diseases within families. While the total public health impact of the examples cited may not be very large considering all diseases, other such discoveries are very likely to come from research in our field and other fields in the years to come. What we need, therefore, is continued orderly support of research in a variety of areas in genetics and elsewhere, since it is impossible to predict from which direction the practical advances will come.

Responsibilities Toward the Public

Most research scientists in the biomedical sciences are more interested in discovering new facts and concepts rather than in applying research findings to public health. This phenomenon is expected, since the research scientist, with a few exceptions, is more a man of thought or of action in the laboratory rather than a lobbyist in Congress, in the board rooms of government, or in the public sector. Consequently, most of us will turn to a new research problem rather than make sure that what had been found earlier is fully utilized. We expect various social agencies, including public health departments, or practising physicians to apply our research findings. With the rapid discovery of new findings, the required middlemen and social institutions often do not exist or cannot or will not act.

A good example is the neglect of implementation of the scientific findings in sickle-cell anemia. It has been known for the past 20 years that about 10% of the American black population are carriers of the sickling gene. Simple inexpensive tests to detect such carriers have been available for a similar period of time. The genetics of sickle-cell anemia is well defined, and we know that 25% among the offspring of two sickle-cell trait carriers will have a child affected with a disease requiring considerable medical attention throughout childhood and adolescence, usually resulting in premature death. About one in 400 black children in the United States will develop this disease. Compared with all other autosomal recessive disorders in this country, sickle-cell anemia has the highest frequency. Yet no public health agency spreads this information to the public at risk. Theoretically, it would be quite easy to test schoolchildren for the sickle trait and counsel the relevant population how to prevent this disease. Even parents who have a child with sickle-cell anemia often are not given the required advice to prevent a second affected child. The black community has only recently become aware of this problem and is urging various agencies to action. The sickle-cell anemia problem, unlike the problem of cancer of the lung induced by smoking, has no economic interests to make a preventive campaign so difficult. Admittedly, there are many practical and behavioral difficulties in a genetic counseling program based on the prevention of matings between heterozygotes. It is likely that testing of heterozygotes along with perfunctory counseling is not going to have much of an impact. However, if heterozygote testing is associated with an educational campaign in the schools and with propaganda through newspapers, magazines, radio, television, film strips, and movies, much more success could be expected. Such a campaign might not be inexpensive but certainly most of its techniques have been well developed by 'Madison Avenue'. Hopefully, in the not-too-distant future, intrauterine diagnosis of sickle-cell anemia may become possible. This approach, followed by selective abortion, would seem easier in the long run than one based on the avoidance of matings between heterozygotes or on complicated therapies of the disease, such as bone-marrow transplantation.

An interesting example of the interaction of science and society lies in the development of intrauterine diagnosis of genetic disease. This rather striking development is appealing and can be understood easily by the public. Science writers and writers for women's magazines have become interested, and many articles have appeared which cite the significance of this approach. At the same time, the necessary large-scale scientific facilities for testing of amniotic cells are not available, nor is the full fetal and maternal morbidity and mortality of this procedure entirely known. We face, therefore, a situation where the public and the medical profession demand a service which is only available in relatively few institutions. It can be expected that this demand will lead to the establishment of amniotic-cell testing by laboratories lacking the required scientific background. Fortunately, at the same time, competent laboratories will be forced to transform a research procedure into a service operation much more rapidly than without public demand. While the proliferation of poorly based facilities must be decried, strong public demand will help to get this procedure properly established in a much shorter period of time than if the process were left entirely to research scientists and to the medical profession.

Another aspect of applied research in human genetics needs comment. Since genes have a differential distribution in various populations, screening and population studies often need to be oriented toward a certain ethnic group or race. Testing for G6PD deficiency and sickle-cell trait has the highest yield in black populations and could hardly be justified in a Caucasian population in Seattle, for instance. Tay-Sachs disease occurs in Ashkenazic Jews with a fairly high frequency, and testing would not be warranted in other populations. The climate of the times in the black community is such that separatism is no longer considered undesirable by many black leaders. Screening for a genetic trait largely confined to blacks might be more acceptable now than it was in the past. Genetic public health measures in general will require better records of the population origin of individuals for appropriate screening. While such a procedure may be distasteful, the medical facts require such knowledge. Hopefully, physician and hospital records, as well as birth and marriage certificates, will begin such listings as ultimately will the census. To make such procedures more acceptable, public education will again be required.

Human geneticists must be in the forefront in exploring and explaining the true facts about race and the significance or lack of significance of racial differences. We are in the position to clearly point out when scientific data show unequivocable differences between races (e.g., the presence of the Diego factor among Oriental populations). But when differences in intelligence between populations are attributed to genetic factors, the lack of environmental equality and the remoteness of the measurement from relevant gene action should make us skeptical. However, an outright rejection of such suggestions is also not scientific even if such claims make us uncomfortable emotionally.

Research Support and Areas of Priority

Fairly clear signals have been given in Washington that the expansion of research activity which occurred at such a rapid rate in the past is coming to a standstill. At the same time, many authorities are becoming concerned about the delivery of health care. It would be a great tragedy if large proportions of the funds previously available for research now would be shifted to entirely applied areas. It may be worthwhile asking a broader question. Are there any principles which might be used in parcelling out the total funds available for research in all areas of science? At the present time no firm long-term guidelines appear to exist. Depending upon the existence of pressure groups pushing one or the other fields, funds have been allocated without any concern for the real priorities of the future. Politicians can only look as far as the next election and therefore have a short horizon. The most vocal pressure group with the most spectacular type of performance, for example the space program, may attract a very large slice of the funds but, in fact, may be least important if the real priorities were considered (i.e. the big problems of our planet: nuclear war and the population explosion). While too rigid planning might be distasteful and dangerous because the unexpected discovery from unexpected quarters could be overlooked, the time has come when each field of science needs to take stock of its current status followed by a 10-year extrapolation. With this information at hand, scientific statesmen with no axe to grind for any particular field need to sit down and divide the existing pie.

I believe that under such a plan, the field of human and medical genetics would do rather well. Population research would get a fairly high priority. The interface of population genetics and population growth is one that requires much further work. Similarly, the area of reproductive genetics has significant potential to develop new contraceptive agents based on sound genetic principles. The study of aggression needs high priority, and human behavioral geneticists will participate heavily in this approach. Three areas touching on both ecology and genetics carry exciting practical and theoretical possibilities for the future. The first deals with environmental agents, such as X rays, and particularly chemicals as mutagenic agents. While as geneticists we are primarily interested in germ cell damage, somatic cell damage leading to malignancies is an important danger which can be analyzed by a variety of techniques in somatic cell genetics. The second area of environmental-genetic research deals with the interaction of specific genotypes with particular environmental agents. Pharmacogenetics is a central component of this type of investigation. Another interesting example is represented by the hyperlipoproteinemias. Such disorders may cause no harm with relative undernutrition, but when present in modern Western societies with relative overnutrition, may result in public health impairment in the form of atherosclerosis. The third broad area of environmental-genetic research is the interaction of the long-term relationship of different genotypes to the environment. Most of our genetic diseases are deleterious and presumably are kept in the population by mutation pressure. In other cases, selection undoubtedly has made certain genes reach relatively high frequencies. The total impact of various selective agents on the human gene pool is hardly understood and requires considerably more work.

Our society provides a relatively large amount of money for research. Much research on the interaction of heredity and environment offers potentially visible payoff in the near future. While research on diseases and traits that cannot be prevented should be done to discover basic principles and ultimate management, it will be easier to obtain funds for research on diseases which have a higher probability for prevention or treatment. We cannot all remain in ivory towers and disclaim public responsibility for the work we are doing. In each individual case a decision must be made whether to remain in the ivory tower (and I feel strongly that quite a few of us should remain) or whether to turn to some of the more applied areas. Unfortunately, the availability of funds rather than a conscious decision will have a strong influence on future direction for many of us.

In summary, we can take pride in the strength and promise of our field. Human genetics already has illuminated many aspects of human health, disease, and behavior and is likely to continue to do so in the future. Human geneticists have the potential to contribute to the most urgent problems facing human survival: the prevention of nuclear war and the curbing of the population explosion. The human brain is the most precious possession of our species. To understand and control its workings remains our greatest challenge. I am sufficiently optimistic to believe that our scientific successors, be it in 1, 10, or 100 generations, will ultimately achieve this task. Once that goal has been reached, human culture - as the highest achievement of evolution - will flourish as never before. Men, women, and children all over the world will then be able to live a truly *human* existence in peace and in health. As human geneticists we may consider ourselves privileged to contribute to this vision.

9

ASSUMPTION AND FACT IN ANTHROPOLOGICAL GENETICS

D.F. Roberts

No one will deny the great stimulus that the development of the science of genetics gave to physical anthropology. The theme of this lecture is the potential debt in the reverse direction. I hope to show that the physical anthropologist is a partner without whom field genetic data cannot be fully interpreted by the geneticist, a partner moreover who on his own account is able to make appreciable contributions to general genetic theory. This does not refer to the several cases where the inheritance of a character, rare or absent in European populations, is elucidated through studies in other populations where it is more frequent, nor to the now classic case of the abnormal haemoglobins, where an anthropological phase of study proved to be the commencement of a chain of investigations that gave new impetus to the polymorphic concept. Instead I have in mind population genetics, where the investigator of human populations has at his disposal a wealth of information - and for purpose of the present discussion I refer particularly to demographic, i.e. numerical, information - that is not available for any other free-living species. In its absence, geneticists have used a number of assumptions, which have been translated direct into human genetics. It is the purpose of this lecture to examine the validity of some of these assumptions and of others occasionally met in the anthropological literature.

Fate of New Mutant Genes

The simplest, perhaps, is a fundamental assumption concerning the rate of loss or survival of new mutants. In the case of a new mutant a of a normal allele A, present in an adult heterozygote who mates with a normal homozygote, the probability that the mutant will not be present in the next generation is 1 if the mating is infertile, 0.5 if it produces one child, 0.0625 if there are four children, and 0.000244 if there are twelve offspring. The probability of loss of new mutants in a population depends then on its pattern of fertility, as well as on whether it is numerically stable, expanding or contracting. It was Fisher (1930) who originally demonstrated that in a stable population there was a high probability that a new mutant would become extinct, no matter whether it was neutral or slightly beneficial, within a few generations of its origin - >75 per cent in six generations. The probabilities he calculated are well known. For these he assumed, drawing from his experience at Rothamsted, that the distribution of family size in a population approximated a Poisson series. This assumption, valid in a botanical context, Haldane (1939) pointed out might not hold for human populations.

A few years ago I instituted investigations to examine this assumption in various human groups, collecting data to examine the form of the distribution curve of numbers of women by the number of their offspring who survived. To the distribution shown in a sample of elderly women in Ngara, Tanganyika (Fig. 1), which may be taken as representative, was

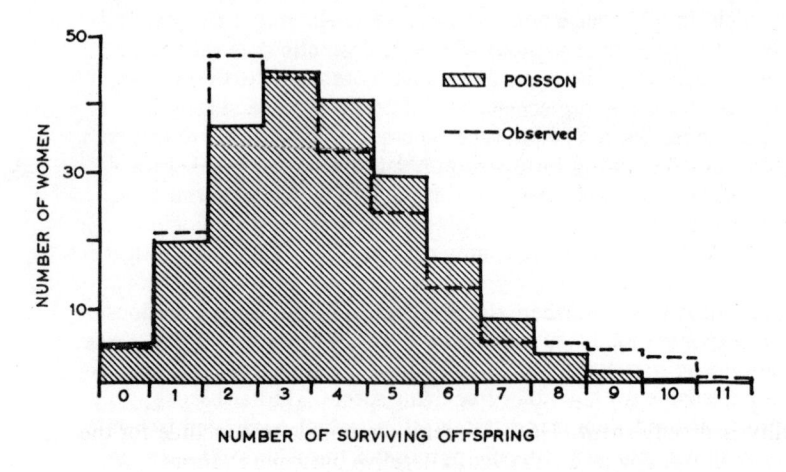

FIG. 1

fitted a Poisson distribution of the same mean; this departs highly significantly ($\chi^2 = 19.56$, 8 d.f. significant at 0.02) from the observed distribution, which has by comparison considerable over-dispersion. On the other hand a negative binomial (fitted by the Greenwood and Yule method) gives a better fit, which though not good, does not depart significantly from the observed ($\chi^2 = 12.55$, 9 d.f. not significant). Clearly in this case the assumption does not hold. Similar findings emerge from a Greek island sample (Fig. 2). Brass (1958) showed that the distribution of the number of births per woman in four East African populations could be described by a negative binomial, and Kojima and Kelleher (1962) for the number of births in the United States population also showed a better fit of a negative binomial than a Poisson. Neither of these represents survivors to adulthood which is the essential consideration; while for the latter it may be assumed that this is approximated by the number of births; this is not a reasonable assumption for 'underdeveloped' populations. Our own Ngara figures do not of course yet represent the

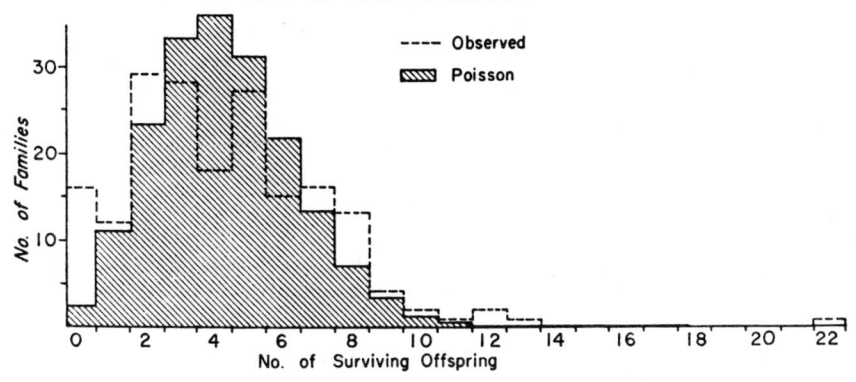

DISTRIBUTION OF NOS. OF SURVIVING OFFSPRING IN UNIONS OF MORE THAN 25 YEARS DURATION

FIG. 2

number of survivors to reproductive age, but most of those listed as survivors are now adult - out of 785, only two are below the age of three years, another twelve below six years, another twenty-four below ten years, and forty-four below fifteen years - so that the force of infant and child mortality is already spent. Hence it seems reasonable to conclude for the time being that survivor distribution is negative binomial in form.

The implications of this on the probable fate of new mutants are straightforward. To take a simple example: in the present Ngara data with a negative binomial distribution of survivors, the probability of loss of a new mutant in a single generation is 0.185; were the distribution Poisson, but of the same mean, the corresponding probability would be 0.161. Generalizing, the probability of survival is smaller than in the case of a Poisson distribution of the same mean, by an amount depending on the variance (Kojima and Kelleher, 1962). If the variance is twice the mean, the probability of survival of a mutant is about two-thirds that calculated under a Poisson distribution. Thus as the breeding habits of man's earliest ancestors became less and less prodigal of offspring, so it became more difficult for them to retain neutral and slightly favourable new mutants in their genepool. For their retention one has to look at the factor of increasing population sizes, and particularly expansion over successive generations.

The Sewall Wright Models

Let us now turn to the Sewall Wright models of gene frequency change, the island model and the distance model (Wright, 1943; 1946); the former was of course initially derived to deal with experimental populations, for which purpose it is highly useful since in the laboratory the assumptions necessary to its application can be thoroughly controlled, while the latter was an attempt to extend it to the conditions obtaining in wild populations. It is curious how little attention has been given to examining the assumptions implicit in applying these to natural populations. In the distance model, Cavalli Sforza (1958) has questioned the normality of the curve of parent/offspring distances. On the basis of 8,665 matings in northern Italy, he finds this curve to be leptocurtic, more so than for say insect distributions; he examined the ratio of the number of matings at a given distance to the number of persons living at that distance and found a good fit to the curve $e^{-k\sqrt{}}$ (distance) ; he also obtained a good fit, except at at longer distances, with the gravitational model, where the probability of marriage is directly proportional to the number of people living in a village at a given distance, and inversely proportional to the square of the distance. My Dinka and Shilluk data are also highly leptocurtic on account of the high proportion of individuals who remain in the village in which they themselves were born. It seems however that the assumption of a normal distribution of parental distance is probably not very critical; the wording of Wright's papers, and his model of gametic dispersal by a single sex, indicate this, but this is a point which requires following up.

The assumption in the distance model that the variance of the grandparental birth-place distance is twice that of the parents from the place of birth of offspring can be examined from the Dinka data, as in the following table:

Variances of	E W co-ordinate	N S co-ordinate
grandfather	15.92 miles	34.61 miles
grandmother	84.80 miles	289.39 miles
father	10.21 miles	19.47 miles
mother	122.32 miles	225.24 miles
pooled grandparents	50.14 miles	161.36 miles
pooled parents	65.97 miles	123.30 miles

These figures show that although there is some approach to the condition in the male ancestors, the assumption does not hold in the maternal. Similarly there are data illuminating the assumption that the mean distance of the grandparental birth-places is $\sqrt{2}$ that of the parental birth-places relative to that of the child:

Mean distance along	father	mother	grandfather	grandmother	
N S co-ordinate	0.83	9.3	1.25	10.4	miles
E W co-ordinate	0.82	8.0	1.20	6.5	miles

Again the assumption is fairly close for the male but not for the female ancestors. The reasons include perhaps the limit to the distance that can be covered in search of a wife, and the necessity to maintain social links in marriage. The net effect of these departures from the assumed condition, some of which are taken into account in Wright's (1951) published variants of the basic model, is to slightly increase the rate of random loss and fixation of genes. In passing, from such demographic data may be obtained not only the average distance of gene flow per generation but also its direction; in the Dinka, this movement was about a mile and a half per generation in a direction a little to the west of north in the area sampled.

A fundamental assumption in the Sewall Wright models of population genetics is that the 'islands' in the island model, and the 'neighbourhoods' in the distance model, are of uniform size. This blatantly disagrees with the human situation. Now it is a curious fact that whereas we know quite a lot about the total size of large population units, which have been used to good effect, e.g. in Birdsell's (1953) analyses of tribal density and environment, we know next to nothing of numerical variation in the size of the social subdivisions of such units. For whatever unit is taken as the 'island', it must be related to some socially accepted division within the population as a whole, whether it is territorial, e.g. village or community, or social, e.g. clan. An obvious first step is to try to establish within a population the form of the distribution of identifiable units. Such studies have been made in other populations occurring in nature - we know the form of the distribution of the number of lice per head on Hindu prisoners in jail, of isopods under boards, of ticks on individual sheep, of mites on rats, of beetleaf hopper and wireworm in communities in a field - but there is very little for human populations. Many years ago Auerbach (1913) discovered that the size of cities in a nation when plotted on double log paper against their numerical rank falls on a straight line, a relationship which Lotka (1925, 1941) pointed out was of wide application in other fields, e.g. Pareto's law of the frequency distribution of incomes, Willis's theory of age and area as applied to the frequency of biological genera and species. Statistically this proceeding is unhappy on account of the high degree of intrinsic correlation between the two variables, and moreover it does not hold for the examples analysed below. It is much more useful to apply a straightforward curve fitting approach, examining the goodness of fit of various distributions.

Of the distributions that have been proposed to describe community size in other organisms, it was early shown that the Poisson distribution was inadequate; more often than not there is over-dispersion, the variance being significantly larger than the mean. A class of distributions was evolved called (after Polya) contagious, in which the presence of one organism within a territorial unit increases the chance of others being there. Of these the most relevant to the present analysis is the Neyman type A contagious distribution (two parameter), of which I have used the truncated form to allow for the fact that there can be no community with zero inhabitants, fitting it by the Douglas method; in devising this, Neyman assumed an initial population in which groups are randomly dispersed within Poisson limits, but then individuals moved out independently from each territory but at a rate too slow to equalize the distribution over the entire range. A different type of relevant distribution is the negative binomial, again unimodal; this is an extension of the Poisson series, but in which the population mean (the expected value of each cell) is not constant but varies continuously in a distribution proportional to that of χ^2; again I have used a truncated form. A third distribution, shown to be relevant in studies of other organisms, is Fisher's logarithmic distribution; this is an extension of the negative binomial where the over-dispersion is increased and the zero category omitted. These three types of distribution were selected as being the most likely of those in the literature to suit the human situation, and they have been fitted to some of the populations for whom I have data.

The Shilluk (Pumphrey, 1941) are a homogeneous polity, embodying various component social units which are recognized by their own names, and of the territorially identifiable units there are the homestead (*gol*), hamlet (*pac*), and settlement (*podh*). Figure 3 shows the observed distribution of the number of settlements by size, together with the curves expected if the three selected distributions are fitted. Whereas the departures of the observed from the Neyman A and the negative binomial are highly significant as 0.1 per cent and 1 per cent respectively (χ^2 = 41.64 with 14 degrees of freedom, and 28.00 with 10 degrees of freedom), there is no significant departure from the lognormal distribution (χ^2 = 8.53 with 11 degrees of freedom). Tests for the normality of the transformed data show that g_1 and g_2 are not significant (g_1 = 0.4451 ± S E 0.2557; g_2 = 0.191 ± 0.483) though there is a slight tendency towards positive skewness.

At a quite different cultural level are the Hausa-speaking communities in northern Nigeria. In Kankiya district, Katsina Province, to which the next analysis refers, the settlements are composed predominantly of Habe cultivators, a politically dominant minority of settled Fulani, and here and there families of other groups who regard themselves as distinct from these. Administration is stabilized under the native authority through districts divided into village areas, and each village area comprises a number of hamlets, territorially distinct. The distribution of hamlet sizes in Kankiya district (Fig. 4) compared with the same three types of distribution as in the case of the Shilluk shows the same results, significant departures from

Departure from	Shilluk	Hausa
Lognormal	x^2 8.53 [11 d.f.] not significant	8.57 [12 d.f.] n.s.
Neyman A	41.64 [14 d.f.] significant at 0.001	14.09 [5 d.f.] significant at 0.02
negative binomial	28.00 [10 d.f.] significant at 0.01	14.01 [6 d.f.] significant at 0.05

negative binomial and Neyman A curves, but no appreciable deviation from the lognormal curve, and again the last is slightly but not significantly positively skewed. The χ^2 values are shown in the table.

I suspect that here we may have a fundamental generalization, relating to human community size within a population, which may be of some value in general anthropology in that comparison of such distribution curves may provide a way of summarizing the overall effects of ecology, technology and social structure, at least in so far as they affect population aggregations; its importance may indeed be greater (as Birdsell (1962) has suggested to me) as a consideration in problems of designed culture change in backward nations. But for the moment, as regards population genetics, it should now be possible to reformulate Sewall Wright's mathematical model of gene frequency change taking into account the logarithmic form of the variation in 'island' size. This I have not yet had time to do, but preliminary calculations suggest that its effect will be to increase the probability of random loss or fixation of genes beyond that given by the existing model.

Drift in an Isolate

There is one application of the island model, in which the assumption of uniformity of island size is valid. The dispersion by drift of gene frequencies at one locus among islands in whom the original frequency was the same is the most generally known application. It is less well known that the same model may be applied to consider the dispersion of allele frequencies at a number of different (unlinked) loci within one island provided they were all of the same initial frequency; in this latter situation of course the population size is identical for all loci. In such a single isolated population, it is often assumed that observed aberrant gene frequencies must be due to drift if selection can be excluded. That this assumption is not justified can be well illustrated by an example that has come to be widely quoted as almost a classic case of genetic drift in man.

Glass *et al.* (1952) published demographic and gene frequency data on a religious isolate in the United States, the Dunker community in Franklin County, Pennsylvania. The sect was established in 1708, near Krefeld, in the Rhineland, and in 1719 there was a migration of 28 persons to Germantown, Pennsylvania, where they were later joined by

148　　　　　　　　　　　*D.F. Roberts*

many others. In 1881 the sect split, a minority retaining its original practices, amongst which was that of marrying amongst themselves and dressing distinctively, but it does not maintain separate schools nor does its way of life differ appreciably from that of other Americans of the same localities. Thus this isolate has been in existence in America for over

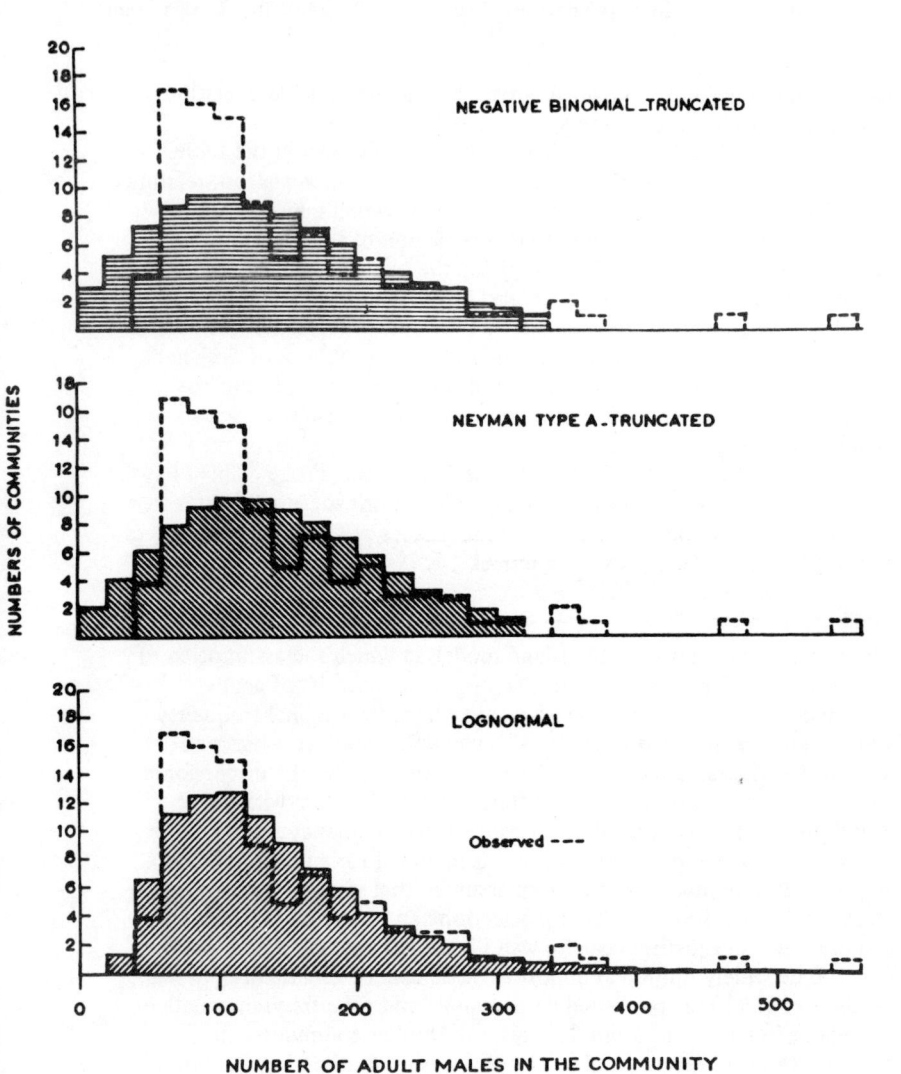

FIG. 3.

FIG. 4

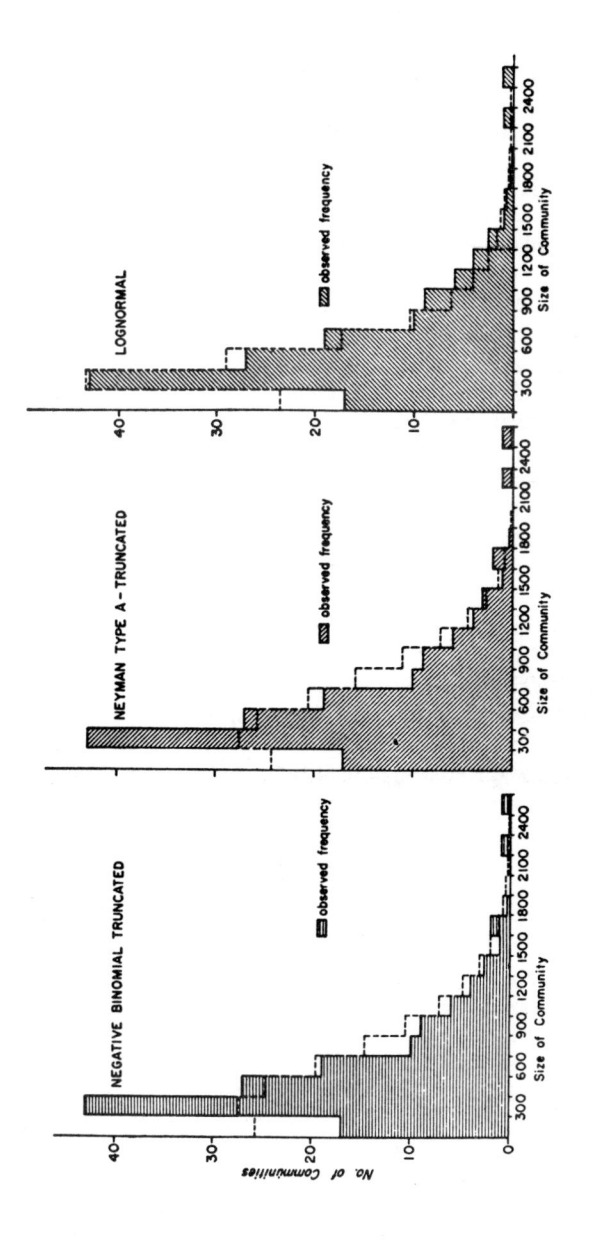

two centuries, with a drastic reduction in the size of the mating group some eighty years ago. The community in Franklin County now comprises some twenty extended families, about 298 adults and children over three years of age and about 350 when others are included who though not members of the sect themselves, are the children of members. To calculate the size of the isolate, Glass found that the average age of mothers at the birth of their children is twenty-six years, of fathers is thirty years, so that twenty-eight years was taken as the length of a generation. Persons within the isolate now aged under twenty-eight had ninety parents also belonging to the isolate. Glass did not take into account other factors, e.g. differential fertility, which would have slightly altered the effective size of the population but we will accept his figures. He then obtained genetic information from 265 individuals, of whom 231 came within the strict definition of the isolate, so that his sampling was 77 per cent complete. He examined records of marriages to discover the direction and amount of gene flow, finding that the frequency of endogamous marriage had remained constant over the past three generations while the maximum gene flow into the isolate was about 22 per cent. In the other direction there had been considerable loss of individuals from the isolate, probably about one-quarter of adults each generation, and such loss had not been random on account of the tendency for the emigration of family units. Comparison of the gene frequencies of the isolate with those from West Germany and from a control series from the USA showed highly significant differences in ABO frequencies of the Dunker from both - B had practically disappeared and A was more frequent, highly significant increase in M gene frequency, but no significant difference in Rh frequencies; in other characters the isolate differed significantly from American white in the frequency of mid-digital hair, the frequency of attached ear-lobes, but not in the frequency of distal hyperextensibility of the thumb. Glass argued that in view of the similarity of living conditions of the isolate and the surrounding other American population, there was likely to be no difference in selection intensities between the two, therefore any differences observable between the isolate and its surrounds in a direction away from that of the original German population, must be due to drift. In a later paper Glass (1956) pointed out that it may be objected that one could not distinguish genetic drift over successional generations from the effect of a unique sampling that provided a very few genotypes in the progenitors of the isolate. He therefore examined frequency differences between generations in the isolate. He found that whereas ABO groups were stable between generations, the MN frequencies for example showed highly significant differences which were attributed to drifting. That no such exaggerated fluctuations appear in successive generations of large populations, though minor fluctuations do, is well established, e.g. by Boorman (1950), Bryce et al. (1950) and Race and Sanger (1962).

Anthropological Genetics 151

What Glass did not consider was the likelihood of his results. Thus between the first and second generations the frequency of gene M changed from 0.550 to 0.685, a difference of + 0.135. The drift variance - and by drift is meant the random variation in gene frequency due to sampling in the transmission of gametes from one generation to the next - of all gene frequencies initially 0.550 in an isolate of size 90 in the next generation is

$$\sigma_q^2 = \frac{q(1-q)}{2N} = 0.0011375.$$

But on account of immigration from the surrounding population with the same frequency of the alleles, this variance is reduced to $(1 - m)^2 \sigma^2 q$; the drift variance then would be 0.0008366 if immigration were 22 per cent, or 0.001114 if immigration were 10 per cent, and the corresponding s.d.s. 0.02892 and 0.03338 respectively. A difference in one generation of the magnitude of 0.135 is 4.67 or 4.04 times these s.d.s.; both highly remote probabilities. If the generation difference of 0.135 stems from a misprint and the real figure is 0.108, then this is 3.73 or 3.24 times these s.d.s., again representing remote probabilities. In fact, an acceptable probability, say 1 in 20, for this amount of drift increase to have occurred in a single generation would necessitate the effective population size to have been as low as twenty-five were there 22 per cent immigration or thirty-three were there 10 per cent immigration. Glass was either extremely fortunate in having hit upon this locus in those he studied, or else some explanation other than drift must be invoked for the change, and the most likely appears to be emigration of the N bearing families.

Local Variation in Selection

The Wright models envisage local variations in selection pressures so that 'islands' or 'neighbourhoods' are exposed to different intensities. That such local differences exist in human populations can be well shown by one category of demographic information not yet mentioned in this discussion, that relating to rates of mortality or morbidity or immunity. Suppose for purposes of argument that tuberculosis is a selective element of significance, against which some genotypes are better protected than others. During the course of the Katsina field investigations, the opportunity was taken of examining tuberculosis immunity status by Heaf testing using purified protein derivative. Altogether 2,003 subjects were tested, but nearly half (933) failed to return on the appointed day for the reaction to be read, so that results for only 1,070 are available. In three villages it was necessary for the reactions to be read by a technician, whose classification of the intensity of reaction subsequently proved to be different from mine, so these results are excluded; thus all the reactions dealt with here were read by myself and inter-observer error eliminated. Now there is some doubt as to the meaning attaching to positive Heaf tests; there is some relationship with leprosy, whose incidence is high in this area, and also with sensitization to mycobacteria of the Phlei type such as could be brought about through grass abrasions of unprotected legs, so that the distribution of slight positive (+) reactions should be discounted. Heaf reactions of ++ and stronger, which may be taken to indicate tuberculosis-immune status, show quite a clear geographical pattern in their frequency in adults, a statistically significant cline of diminishing frequency as one moves away from Katsina city. Thus in Katsina the frequency is 38 per cent; in villages eight to twelve miles distant from the city it is 29 per cent; in villages up to twenty miles

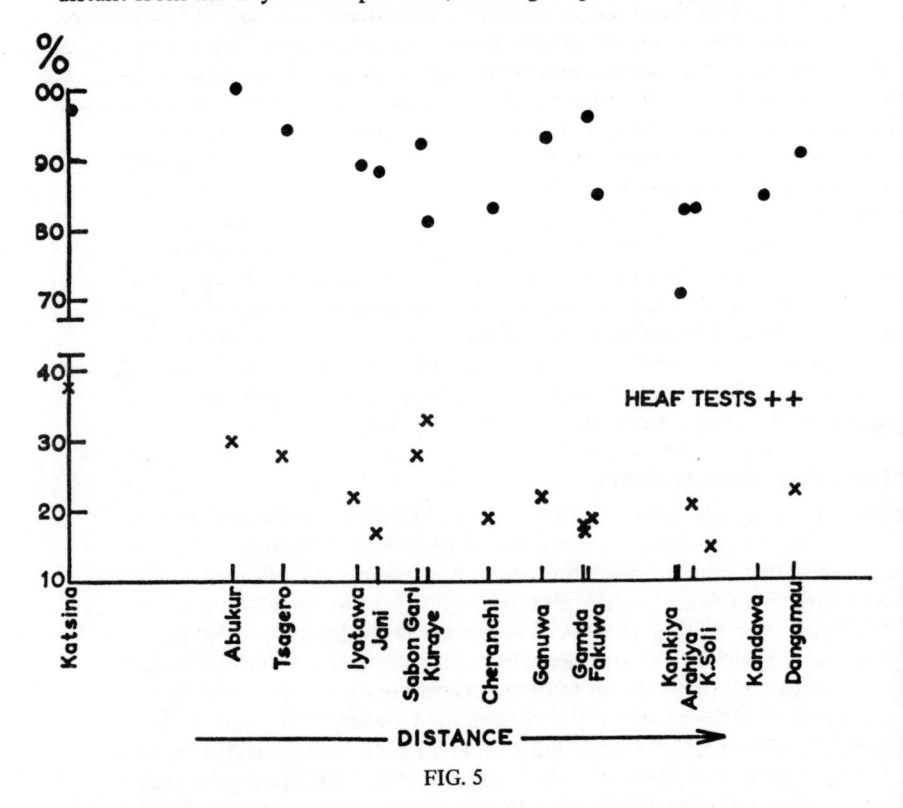

FIG. 5

distant it is 24 per cent; and at greater distances the frequency settles down to a general level of 21 per cent. (A similar cline is shown in the distribution of all positive reactions.) In children the increasing frequency of ++ reactions with age (0 in the age group under 5; 5.4 per cent in those aged 5 - 9; 5.3 per cent in the age group 10 - 14; and 13.2 per cent in those aged 15 - 19) necessitated age subdivision of the sample; the age groups were then numerically inadequate to show confirmatory clines, but the results suggested that in the more remote rural groups the ++ frequencies were attained at later ages.

The cline of diminishing frequency of immunity outwards from the urban to the rural areas suggests differential contact with the disease, heaviest in the city, least in the open remoter villages. If this disease should be a selective agent - I do not say it is, but it may well be - then different selection pressures would be set up within this population. Instead of this indirect argument through immunity status, one can take a more direct example, of parasite infestation (Collard, 1962). During this survey specimens of urines and stools were collected for analysis at Kankiya rural health centre. From 728 subjects examined, it is clear that there is pronounced variation in the frequency of bilharzia (*Schistosoma haematobium*) infection, not in a regular gradient, but irregularly from village to village (Fig. 6), probably related to the distribution of the open ponds, by no means clean, whose water is used for a variety of purposes. Similar local variation occurs in ancylostomiasis (788 individuals examined).

There emerge two points from this discussion. First in the diseases examined the population is shown to be far from homogeneous in exposure to them; they may or may not exert some selective influence, but even if they do not it seems reasonable to expect that other diseases which are selectively important may show similar patterns of heterogeneity. Secondly, and this I want to stress, such variations in exposure may occur on a far more local scale than is generally envisaged - the whole area covered in this survey was only about forty miles by twenty miles. Such local variations, moreover, are not restricted to 'underdeveloped' populations; in countries such as the United Kingdom where registration statistics are good, mortality from specific causes can be examined and the patterns shown by some diseases indicate similar local variation - e.g. cancer of the stomach, bronchitis - with age-standardized mortality rates varying threefold over distances of a few dozen miles (Howe, 1963).

Thus the territory of a population may be divided by its disease distribution into a number of local niches, each exerting its characteristic combination of selective pressures, and so making for local diversification of gene frequencies but countered by migration etc., as envisaged in the Wright models. In a static population with no migration between niches the resultant pattern of gene frequencies, as Levins (1962) has shown, may either consist of a succession of clines or of a number of sharply demarcated pockets, depending on whether the population's tolerance for environmental diversity is large relative to the niche differences or vice versa.

SCHISTOSOMA HAEMATOBIUM

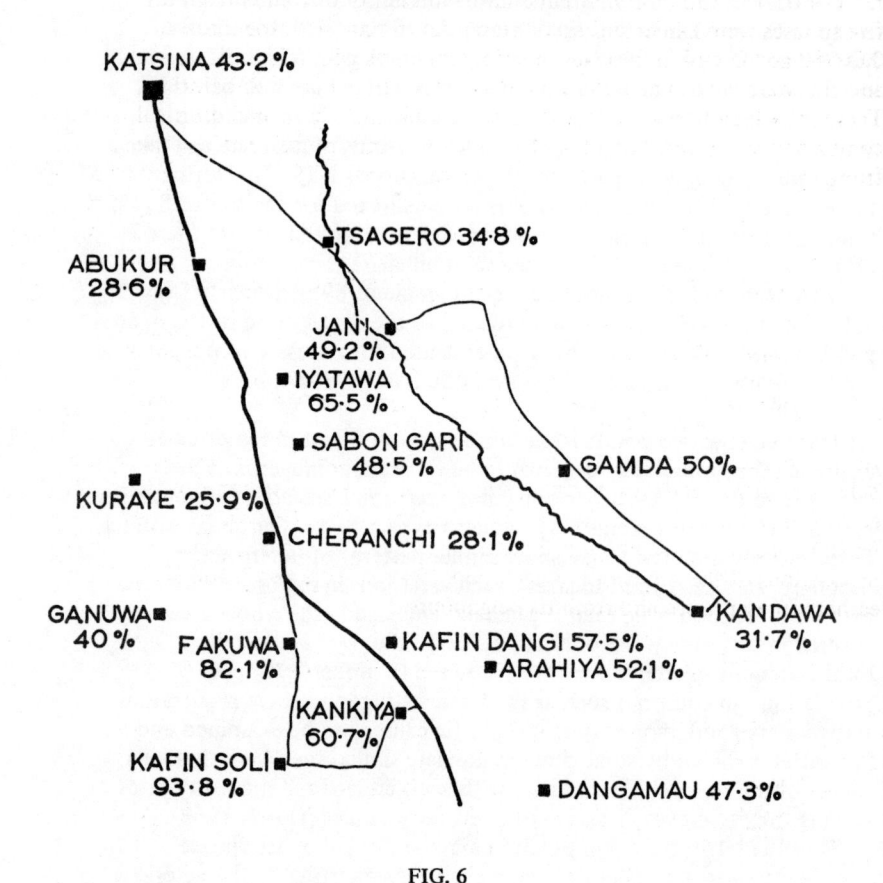

KATSINA 43·2%
TSAGERO 34·8%
ABUKUR 28·6%
JAN'I 49·2%
IYATAWA 65·5%
SABON GARI 48·5%
GAMDA 50%
KURAYE 25·9%
CHERANCHI 28·1%
GANUWA 40%
FAKUWA 82·1%
KAFIN DANGI 57·5%
KANDAWA 31·7%
ARAHIYA 52·1%
KANKIYA 60·7%
KAFIN SOLI 93·8%
DANGAMAU 47·3%

FIG. 6

Intermixture

There are many other assumptions in the Sewall Wright models, either in the theory or in past applications of them, that may be profitably examined in the light of human demographic data. Instead, however, let us turn to some others of general type, and first those relating to intermixture. The effects on gene frequency of massive population mixture are obvious. It is perhaps sometimes forgotten how extensive are the

Anthropological Genetics 155

cumulative effects of *slight* but continued intermixture. This can be shown from the Nilotic work. Observations were made on the incidence of intermarriage among the northern Nilotic populations. In 288 marriages in Dinka villages, whose progeny would eventually come to be regarded as Dinka, eight spouses were Nuer and five were Shilluk, giving gene flow rates of 0.01389 and 0.00868; in Shilluk villages, out of 255 marriages, five spouses were Dinka and none were Nuer, giving gene flow rates of 0.00980 and 0; and in 200 Nuer matings, one was with a Shilluk woman and five were with Dinka, the gene flow rates being 0.0025 and 0.0125. These rates may be set out in the form of a table, the principal diagonal comprising the proportion of spouses each recipient population receives from itself.

Gene flow rates

Recipient population	Donating population		
	Nuer	Dinka	Shilluk
Nuer	0.9850	0.0125	0.0025
Dinka	0.0138	0.9775	0.0087
Shilluk	0	0.0098	0.9902

At first glance these gene flow rates are very slight, four out of the six being less than 1 per cent, and one might be tempted to assume that their genetic effect is slight. But let us consider their cumulative effect if they remain constant for say twenty generations. The table shows what proportions of the gene pool of each population are derived from its earlier representative and from its neighbours.

Accumulated admixture after twenty generations

Recipient population	Donating population		
	Nuer	Dinka	Shilluk
Nuer	0.7637	0.1810	0.0553
Dinka	0.1961	0.6693	0.1346
Shilluk	0.0195	0.1465	0.8340

Now twenty generations is a very short time in human evolutionary history, but even in this short period and with these low intermixture rates per generation, the gene pool of the Dinka say is seen to derive only two-thirds of its genes from the earlier Dinka population, and one-third from the other two populations. 'Ancestral' is a word that clearly needs applying with care to human populations.

Using such data on rates of intermarriage we can calculate how gene frequencies change under intermixture; and of course if we know the gene frequencies we can calculate the amount of admixture that has occurred. Now an assumption frequently met with in race mixture studies is that one particular allele may be used as a marker of the presence or absence of some component population. Thus in Dr Pollitzer's recent study (unpublished) of the Catawba Indians of Rock Hill, South Carolina, it was found for example that the Rh combination cDe is absent among them. This at first sight would perhaps suggest that they have no Negro admixture, since this combination is present at high frequency in the American Negro deriving from that in African populations, and is rare or absent in the European and American Indian respectively. Suppose however we calculate the amounts of admixture by our least squares method (Roberts and Hiorns, 1962) which considers simultaneously a number of different alleles and which can be applied no matter how many populations are intermixing: in this case if we use Pollitzer's data on eleven alleles, R^o Fy^a R' r m O A R^2 S P_1 Jk^a, then the present Catawba frequencies, if brought about by intermixture alone, represent a Negro component of 6.03 per cent. The calculated admixture gives an expected frequency of cDe of 0.047, a frequency low enough in a small population for drift to have led to the loss of the combination within a few generations. This example shows that reliance on a single allele is not always justified; all allele frequencies are subject to sampling error, both in sampling and in drift between generations. By using a number of loci in such calculations, these errors tend to cancel each other out.

Homogeneity of Populations

There is a general assumption that we all make from time to time, usually for convenience, when we refer say to the gene frequencies of 'the Dinka', 'the Lapps'; in so doing we imply that the gene frequencies throughout a population are homogeneous, though the Wright models and our earlier discussion have warned us that the possibility is very real of local variation in gene frequency occasioned by differential selection or perhaps drift, quite apart from those variations due to pockets of colonization by immigrant groups, and the continued existence of pockets of relict populations. By using the simplest of demographic information, that relating subjects to locality and community, the existence of local variation at the ABO locus was demonstrated in a very unexpected region in the classic study of Fraser Roberts (1953) in north-eastern England, and the few local studies that have since been made have proved profitable - of the ABO frequencies in Wales (Watkin, 1956) and glucose-6-phosphate dehydrogenase deficiency in Sardinia (Motulsky and Campbell-Kraut, 1961). That these reports of local variation are not rare 'isolated' instances and that the phenomenon is more widespread, is shown by several recent investigations. The small Greek island of Tinos covers only some seventy-five square miles, much of its area is inhospitable mountain, and settlement occurs in fairly distinct clusters. On the basis of these, the island was divided into five regions and the ABO blood groups were examined in approximately a 7 per cent sample of the total population. Differences in blood group frequency among the regions were highly significant statistically (Roberts et al., 1965). This local variation was related to the marriage pattern, there being very little gene flow between the rural areas - and incidentally this was not due to the direct effects of geographical barriers. Similar local variation in ABO frequencies was found in the island of Gran Canaria in the Canaries (Roberts et al., 1966), and has been reported in northern Italy (Cavalli-Sforza, 1963).

What of other genetically determined characters? Consider our preliminary analysis (Roberts and Coope, 1963) of fingerprints of a sample of some 500 children, of whom at least one parent was born locally, who live in the Vale of the White Horse and on the Berkshire Heights, i.e. that part of Berkshire north of the chalk downs. The area as a whole is predominantly rural, but there are in the north-east of it three urban areas (1) the western suburbs of Oxford, (2) the administrative centre and industrial town of Abingdon, (3) the industrial community of Didcot, centred on the railway industry. Comparing first, in the eastern part of this area, the urban centres with the rural districts surrounding them, as regards the distributions of total ridge counts in the two sexes. The standard deviations in the rural districts are 41.61 for males and 43.30 for females, whereas in the urban areas the standard deviations are respectively 54.07 and 48.53. In both sexes there is a clear tendency for the children living in towns to have greater variability in total ridge counts than children living in the immediate surrounding areas; this tendency attains statistical significance in males and is in the same direction in females. Since the urban populations contain a higher proportion of 'immigrants' from other parts of England than does the rural, this finding points to the existence of regional and local variation in Britain. Secondly, it is clear from this finding that the inclusion of results on urban populations may obscure any underlying geographical pattern that may exist in the more stable rural population. Dividing our rural results into two areas, an eastern and a western, by a line running south-east through Kingston Bagpuize, the distribution curves show a marked shift in position, indicating differences in mean ridge counts. These are lower in the western area in both sexes, 111.7 and 104.6 in males and females respectively, by comparison with 141.0 in males and 129.0 in females in the eastern rural area. This drop is significant at the 5 per cent level in males, and is in the same direction in females. It is of relevance perhaps that Dr Kopec's (unpublished) analysis of ABO blood group data indicates a change in frequencies along a line not far to the east of our own dividing line. In view of the relatively small number of subjects so far analysed and the relatively small geographical area so far covered, that either of the dermatoglyphic findings attains a level of statistical significance is encouraging. Both are compatible with the present thesis that in populations that have not yet succumbed to the twentieth-century urge to high mobility, genetic variation may be more local than is generally envisaged.

Conclusion

In drawing together these examples, it has been my object to demonstrate to you how useful demographic data can be in population genetics, data which many a cultural anthropologist is in a position to collect but does not do so because he doesn't appreciate their usefulness, data which many a geneticist requires but does not have - simple data such as are used here, on fertility variations, mating distances, intermarriage rates, size of populations and component units, population density, the numbers of parents and sex ratios in communities, data on who dies and at what approximate age, and at a more complex level who suffers or dies from what ailments. The examples I have used are by no means exhaustive, and others will be found elsewhere.(Roberts, 1963), e.g. how the action of natural selection may be traced and at what age it is effective (Roberts and Boyo, 1962) by observing at what ages which children die, how to partition natural selection into components due to differential fertility and mortality (Crow, 1958; Spuhler, 1961), how the extent of random drift per generation can be calculated (Lasker, 1954; Roberts, 1956a, b), and how all these can be used to test hypotheses of the cultural anthropologist about population origins (Roberts, 1962).

Nor have I exhausted by any means the numerous assumptions that are made daily in population genetics, assumptions that populations are of infinite size, that random mating occurs, that gene and genotype frequencies are in Hardy-Weinberg equilibrium, that all polymorphisms are balanced . . . . But there, perhaps in the examination of these and their implications I have sketched some of the next twenty years' work in anthropological genetics.

References

Auerbach, F. (1913). Das Gesetz der Bevölkerungskonzentration. *Petermanns Geographische Mitteilungen*, 59, 74.
Birdsell, J.B. (1953). Some environmental and cultural factors influencing the structuring of Australian aboriginal populations. *American Naturalist*, 87, 171.
Boorman, K.E. (1950). An analysis of the blood types and clinical condition of 2,000 consecutive mothers and their infants. *Annals of Eugenics*, 15, 120-134.
Brass, W. (1958). The distribution of births in human populations. *Population Studies*, 12, 51-72.
Bryce, L.M., Jacobowicz, R., McArthur, N. and Penrose, L.S. (1950). Blood group frequencies in a mother and infant sample of the Australian population. *Annals of Eugenics*, 15, 271-275.

Cavalli-Sforza, L.L. (1958). Some data on the genetic structure of human populations. *Proceedings of the Tenth International Congress on Genetics*, 1, 389-407. Toronto: University of Toronto Press.

Cavalli-Sforza, L.L. (1963). Genetic drift for blood groups. In *The Genetics of Migrant and Isolate Populations*, edited by E. Goldschmidt. Baltimore: Williams & Wilkins.

Collard, P. (1962). A sample survey to estimate the prevalence of certain communicable diseases in Katsina province, Nigeria. *West African Medical Journal*, 11, 3.

Crow, J.F. (1958). Some possibilities for measuring selection intensities in man. *Human Biology*, 30, 1-13.

Fisher, R.A. (1930). *The Genetical Theory of Natural Selection*. London: Oxford University Press.

Glass, B. (1956). On the evidence of random genetic drift in human populations. *American Journal of Physical Anthropology*, 14, 541.

Glass, B., Sacks, M.S., Jahn, E.F. and Hess, C. (1952). Genetic drift in a religious isolate. *American Naturalist*, 86, 145-159.

Haldane, J.B.S. (1939). The equilibrium between mutation and random extinction. *Annals of Eugenics*, 9, 400-405.

Howe, G.M. (1963). *A National Atlas of Disease Mortality in the United Kingdom*. London: Royal Geographical Society.

Kojima, K. and Kelleher, T.M. (1962). Survival of mutant genes. *American Naturalist*, 96, 329-346.

Lasker, G.W. (1954). Human evolution in contemporary communities. *Southwestern Journal of Anthropology*, 10, 353.

Levins, R. (1962). Theory of fitness in a heterogeneous environment: 1. The fitness set and adaptive function. *American Naturalist*, 96, 361.

Lotka, A.J. (1925). *Elements of Physical Biology*. Baltimore: Williams & Wilkins.

Lotka, A.J. (1941). The law of urban concentration. *Science*, 94, 164.

Motulsky, A.G. and Campbell-Kraut, J.M. (1961). Population genetics of G6PD deficiency of the red cell. In *Conference of Genetic Polymorphisms and Geographic Variations in Disease*, edited by B.S. Blumberg. New York: Grune & Stratton.

Pumphrey, M.E.C. (1941). The Shilluk tribe. *Sudan Notes and Records*, 24, 7.

Race, R.R. and Sanger, R. (1962). *Blood Groups in Man*. Fourth edition. Oxford: Blackwell Scientific Press.

Roberts, D.F. (1956a). A demographic study of a Dinka village. *Human Biology*, 28, 323-349.

Roberts, D.F. (1956b). Some genetic implications of Nilotic demography. *Acta Genetica et Statistica Medica* (Basel), 6, 446-452.

Roberts, D.F. (1962). Serology and the history of the northern Nilotes. *Journal of African History*, 3, 301.

Roberts, D.F. (1963). Genetical demography. In a discussion on demography, edited by P.B. Medawar and D.V. Glass. *Proceedings of the Royal Society, B*. 159, 122.

Roberts, D.F. and Boyo, A.E. (1962). Abnormal haemoglobins in childhood among the Yoruba. *Human Biology*, 34, 20-37.

Roberts, D.F. and Coope, E. (1963). A preliminary report on local dermatoglyphic variation in the Oxford region. *Proceedings of the International Conference on Genetics*. The Hague.

Roberts, D.F., Evans, M., Ikin, E. and Mourant, A.E. (1966). Blood groups and the affinities of the Canary Islanders. *Man*, 1, 512.

Roberts, D.F. and Hiorns, R.W. (1962). The dynamics of racial intermixture. *American Journal of Human Genetics*, 14, 261-277.

Roberts, D.F., Luttrell, V. and Pasternak-Slater, C. (1965). Genetics and geography in Tinos: a study of the influence of geographical barriers. *Eugenics Review*, 56, 185-193.

Roberts, J.A.F. (1953). An analysis of the blood group records of the north of England. *Heredity*, 7, 361-388.

Spuhler, J.N. (1961). The scope of natural selection in man. In *Genetic Selection in Man: Third Macy Conference on Genetics*, edited by W.J. Schull. Ann Arbor: University of Michigan Press.

Watkin, I.M. (1956). ABO blood groups and racial characteristics in rural Wales. *Heredity*, 10, 161-193.

Wright, S. (1943). Isolation by distance. *Genetics*, 28, 114-128.

Wright, S. (1946). Isolation by distance under diverse systems of mating. *Genetics*, 31, 39-59.

Wright, S. (1951). The genetical structure of populations. *Annals of Eugenics*, 15, 323-354.

10

RACE, ETHNIC GROUP, AND DISEASE

Albert Damon

The associations between disease and racial or ethnic group concern a variety of scientists and administrators. The practising physician can use such information in the diagnosis and treatment of disease; the public health official, in planning programs which aim to detect, prevent, or eradicate disease, as well as in allocating scarce and costly health resources like doctors, nurses, educators, clinics, and hospitals. The epidemiologist uses such data to help explain the distribution and determinants of disease frequency, thereby suggesting leads for the laboratory scientist's investigation of the causes of disease. The demographer uses knowledge of the racial distribution of disease to help explain distinctive patterns of population structure or of vital statistics.

Among basic scientists, the geneticist deals with the mechanisms and mode of transmission of hereditary disease within populations and with the differing gene frequencies among populations separated in time, place, and origin. The anthropologist tries to account for such population differences in terms of the origin, evolution, distribution, and differing environments - natural, biological, and cultural - of the populations concerned. Disease is a major selective factor in human evolution, and its present distribution affords clues to the past history and future course of mankind.

The difference between the approaches of the basic and the applied human biologist is that the former attempts to explain human variation. He regards the manifestations of human diversity as the dependent variable - dependent on climate, habitat, migration, inbreeding, and genetic mechanisms. The applied scientist, on the other hand, takes the manifestations of human variability as given - that is, as the independent variable - and tries to turn these biological differences to practical ends, such as finding, treating, and preventing disease.

Before presenting the associations between race and disease, let us define some terms. The science of the distribution and determinants of disease in man is epidemiology, an applied biomedical discipline which has recently expanded its scope from infectious diseases ('epidemics') to the chronic, noninfectious disorders of multiple or uncertain etiology which now account for most of the disability and deaths in advanced societies. Examples are coronary heart disease, hypertension, cancer, 'strokes', arthritis, peptic ulcer, and mental illness.

As in other observational sciences, the first step in epidemiologic method (MacMahon et al., 1960) is description. The prevalence of disease is charted in respect to time, place, and person. The personal or 'host' characteristics most relevant to disease frequency are age, sex, and race. Of secondary importance, on the whole, are other biological traits like physical constitution, birth order and maternal age, and socioeconomic traits like income, occupation, and marital status. Sometimes, as for single-gene disorders like hemophilia, genetic constitution is of prime importance.

From his initial description the epidemiologist frames hypotheses to account for the observed distributions. He then tests these hypotheses by specifically designed quantitative, analytic studies, still observational in method. If his hypothesis survives analytic test, his final step is to clinch the proof by experiment - as, for example, in fluoridating water supplies to reduce caries frequency.

It can be seen that clinical medicine, pathology, physical anthropology, and demography all contribute to descriptive epidemiology. Our concern here is with the personal characteristic of race - a concept of physical anthropology - in its association with disease, as defined clinically and pathologically. We shall summarize the evidence briefly and then discuss possible explanations. Fortunately the only strong emotion aroused by this aspect of race is humanitarian, to prevent or relieve suffering, so that we need not plead to justify the research or debate the ethics of examining the evidence.

Definition of Race and Ethnic Group

For descriptive purposes, the epidemiologist analyzes disease rates among groups of persons who are more homogeneous than the general population, whether this relative homogeneity has been derived biologically or culturally. The word 'relative' should be stressed, both because human beings and human groups, like all living things, are innately variable and because no group is completely isolated from outside influence. *A biologically* distinct group can be termed a race or population. Such a group, as a result of past breeding patterns, has a 'relatively' large percentage of genes in common. The great preponderance of human genes are, of course, shared by all men. A racial group may vary in number from a few hundred to a few hundred million, and in residential area, whether of origin or of current residence, from local to geographic to continental in size (Garn, 1965).

A racial group may, and in fact often does, have distinguishing physical features - like skin color, hair form, and facial conformation - as well as distinctive aggregates of genes ('genotype') and of traits ('phenotype') determined by laboratory test but not externally apparent. Examples of such cryptic genetic traits are blood groups, hemoglobin variants, blood cell and serum enzymes, and ability to taste phenylthiocarbamide.

A *culturally* distinct group is an ethnic group. Frequently the two kinds of homogeneity, biological and cultural, overlap or coincide, as in the case of most primitive tribes or of linguistic, religious, or colored minorities in a city or country, provided only that the members of the group share a common ancestry. For many practical purposes then, including epidemiologic description, it may not matter *how* a particular group under study became distinctive, nor the precise proportion of biology and culture in its present distinctiveness. The Boston Irish, Italian, Jewish, Armenian, and Negro communities, for example, are distinctive both biologically and culturally; they are racial as well as ethnic groupings.

Biological and cultural similarity can reinforce one another. On the one hand, distinctive physical features make it easy for society to practice or enforce certain breeding patterns, as intermarriage or interbreeding between white persons and Negroes is now forbidden in South Africa. On the other hand, distinctive cultural practices like religion may isolate breeding populations more or less completely, as in the case of the Jews for many centuries, or small contemporary groups like the Amish, Dunkers, and Hutterites. Whatever has caused or continues to maintain a group in relative isolation, social or biological, the net result is a group with more genes or social practices, or both, in common than the population at large.

It is important to distinguish between biological and cultural homogeneity in investigating the cause of disease or in attempting prevention. In the case of genetic diseases occurring mainly or exclusively among groups which may be both racial and ethnic, it would be fruitless to seek explanation in terms of current cultural practices. Whatever the cultural or environmental factors at the origin of or contributing to the persistence of the hemoglobin S (sickle-cell) mutation among African Negroes or Tay-Sachs disease (infantile amaurotic idiocy) among Jews, the current bearers of these genes are defined biologically, not culturally. On the other hand, one should not ascribe differences in disease frequency to racial or biological homogeneity unless cultural and environmental factors can be ruled out. For all human diseases, both heredity and environment are involved, the relative proportions varying from one disease, population, and person to another.

Race and Disease

For a general picture let us first examine racial differences in disease within a single country, the United States. Here, medical diagnosis and population coverage, though by no means perfect, are more uniform for the various racial and ethnic subgroups than would be the case in international comparisons. There are three major indices of health or disease status for a population or group: mortality as reflected by death certification, examination of a representative sample, and morbidity (illness) as measured by household or hospital surveys. We shall consider only the first two, since hospital records and household interviews correspond poorly with the true medical status of a population.

Mortality in the United States. In the 1960 census, Whites made up 88.6% of the population of 179,326,000, and Nonwhites 11.4%. The Nonwhites were 92% Negro, 2.6% American Indian, 2.3% Japanese, 1.2% Chinese, 0.9% Filipino, and 1.1% all others. Needless to say, the 'Whites' were also ethnically and biologically diverse, as will be discussed below. Mortality rates for Whites and Nonwhites in 1900 and 1965 appear in Table 1. In both years the Nonwhite death rates exceeded those for Whites. Despite the great reduction in death rates since 1900, 60% among Whites and 63% among Nonwhites, the relative proportions (adjusted for age) have moved only slightly toward equality. A further breakdown by age, omitted here, shows 1965 mortality rates for Nonwhites higher at all ages except 75 and over.

DEATH RATES FOR WHITES AND NONWHITES
IN THE UNITED STATES, 1900 AND 1965

(Annual rates per 1,000 population in specified group)

| YEAR | MORTALITY RATES |||| Rate in whites as percentage of rate in nonwhites ||
| | White || Nonwhite || ||
	Unadjusted	Adjusted*	Unadjusted	Adjusted*	Unadjusted	Adjusted*
1900	17.0	17.6	25.0	27.8	68	63
1965	9.4	7.1	9.6	10.3	98	69

* Adjusted to the age distribution of the total US population in 1940, to take account of age differences and changes in the White and Nonwhite populations

TABLE 1

More informative is the comparison of death rates by cause, set out in Table 2. On the whole, the White rates exceeded Nonwhite rates in the

DEATH RATES FROM SELECTED CAUSES FOR WHITES
AND NONWHITES IN THE UNITED STATES, 1965
(Per 100,000 population in specified group)

CAUSE	MORTALITY RATES White	MORTALITY RATES Nonwhite	Rate in whites as percentage of rate in nonwhites
Suicide	11.9	5.0	238
Leukemia	7.4	4.1	180
Arteriosclerotic heart disease	303.8	175.8	173
Urinary cancer	7.5	4.6	163
Lymphosarcoma	8.1	5.1	159
Breast cancer	14.6	9.5	154
Peptic ulcer	5.6	3.8	147
Respiratory cancer	27.7	20.6	134
Digestive cancer	49.6	41.8	119
Motor vehicle accidents	25.3	25.8	98
Vascular lesions of the central nervous system	102.3	114.7	89
Genital cancer	20.5	23.3	88
Cirrhosis of liver	12.5	14.6	86
Diabetes mellitus	16.7	20.1	83
Accidents, other than motor vehicle	28.9	41.2	70
Pneumonia	28.9	44.2	65
Hypertensive heart disease	24.7	55.3	45
Tuberculosis	3.4	9.3	37
Syphilis	1.0	2.8	36
Homicide	3.0	24.6	12

TABLE 2

chronic, noninfectious, and 'degenerative' diseases, with the major exceptions of diabetes, hypertension, and 'strokes' (vascular lesions of the central nervous system), which are associated with hypertension. The Nonwhites, on the other hand, had higher death rates for infectious diseases and genital cancer. With the sole exception of genital cancer, White cancer rates were higher. Among subcategories of cancer not shown in Table 2, White death rates were four to five times higher than Nonwhite rates for testicular and skin cancer, roughly equal for prostatic and endometrial cancer, but only 50% and 67% as high as Nonwhite rates

for cervical and penile cancer, respectively.
National Health Examination Survey. Data from this Survey, conducted between 1962 and 1964 on 6,672 adults aged 18 to 79 years and representing the civilian, non-institutionalized population of the United States, can tell only about common morbid conditions. One would hardly expect such a small sample to contain many persons with cancer, for example. For the same reason - small numbers in the total sample - the Nonwhites were virtually all Negroes.

The major findings relevant to race and disease are these. White and Negro rates were similar for coronary heart disease, rheumatoid arthritis, and osteoarthritis. Negro rates were significantly higher for hypertension; for hypertensive heart disease, both absolutely and as a percentage of those with hypertension; and for syphilis as indicated by positive serological test. Negroes had superior hearing and (uncorrected) visual acuity, for both near and distant vision. Negroes had higher mean blood pressure levels, both systolic and diastolic, than Whites. Negro men had higher blood glucose and lower cholesterol levels than White men. Negroes of both sexes had only two-thirds as many decayed, missing, and filled teeth as Whites, even among persons of the same income or education. On the other hand, Negroes had one and a half times the periodontal (gum) disease of Whites.

Special surveys. Data for other Nonwhites in the United States are sparse, being confined, among American Indians as a whole, to infectious diseases and accidents, both of which show higher than national rates (Wagner and Rabeau, 1964), or to surveys of specific conditions. For example, osteoarthritis is relatively frequent among Blackfoot and Pima Indians; diabetes, among the Papago; and gallbladder disease, trachoma, and congenitally dislocated hips among Southwestern Indians in general. On the other hand, Southwestern Indians have relatively little duodenal ulcer (Sievers and Marquis, 1962) despite a high percentage of Indians (83% or more) with blood group O, which is associated with duodenal ulcer among Caucasians, Japanese, and Nigerians.

On Hawaii, persons of pure or predominantly Polynesian ancestry have strikingly high rates of diabetes (Sloan, 1963). For coronary heart disease, their rates exceed those among Caucasians, Filipinos, and Japanese living in Hawaii (Moellering and Bassett, 1967). Rates were higher for pure Hawaiians than for part Hawaiians. Among men with coronary heart disease, Hawaiians were three times as likely to die from the acute episode as Japanese, and pure Hawaiians were more likely to die than part Hawaiians.

Chinese and Japanese in the United States show some distinctive patterns, particularly in respect to cancer. Among both groups, death rates for prostatic cancer and breast cancer are much lower than for the White population, and the rates for digestive cancer (esophagus, stomach, and liver) much higher. The Japanese have unusually high rates for esophageal and stomach cancer as do the Chinese for nasopharyngeal and liver cancer (Smith, 1956a, b). In both groups, chronic lymphatic leukemia is about half as common as among the White population (Shimkin and Loveland, 1961).

The number of such comparisons could be greatly extended, within other countries having distinctive racial and ethnic groups, such as South Africa and Israel, as well as in the United States. Tables 3 and 4, the former and part of the latter from McKusick (1967), summarize the associations between race or ethnic group and disease for simply-inherited disorders (Table 3) and for disorders of complex genetics or in which genetic factors are unproved (Table 4). On the whole, the single-gene disorders are extremely rare compared to those of multiple causation, which constitute the major burden of disease in developed countries. In Table 4 we have attempted to include only confirmed associations, omitting curiosities and single reports, however intriguing (e.g. Kudo, 1968).

Discussion

What use can we make of the clear associations between racial or ethnic group and disease presented so far? The practical scientist can, as mentioned, apply them immediately to the detection, diagnosis, and treatment of disease. A given expenditure of resources will find, cure, and prevent more cervical cancer, syphilis, and tuberculosis among Nonwhites in the United States than among Whites, for example. In clinical medicine, fever, abdominal pain, and leucocytosis may have different implications in a Northern European (a 'surgical' condition like appendicitis or cholecystitis), a Mediterranean (favism, glucose-6-phosphate dehydrogenase deficiency, or familial Mediterranean fever), and a Negro (possible sickling crisis). In the two last cases, the patient may be spared needless surgical exploration if the physician is aware of the ethnic and racial associations of disease.

Much more difficult is explaining the associations. Toward this end we shall follow the useful checklist of MacMahon et al. (1960):

1. Errors of measurement.
2. Differences between groups with respect to more directly associated demographic variables.
3. Differences in environment.
4. Differences in bodily constitution.
5. Differences in genetic constitution.

Errors of measurement, the first item, means that racial or ethnic distributions of disease are liable to distortion due to inadequate diagnosis, differential access to and utilization of medical facilities, and lack of

RACIAL AND ETHNIC DISEASE: SIMPLY INHERITED DISORDERS*

Ethnic Group	Relatively high frequency	Relatively low frequency
Ashkenazic Jews	Abetalipoproteinemia Bloom's disease Dystonia musculorum deformans Factor XI (PTA) deficiency Familial dysautonomia Gaucher's disease Niemann-Pick disease Pentosuria Spongy degeneration of brain Stub thumbs Tay-Sachs disease	Phenylketonuria
Mediterranean peoples (Greeks, Italians, Sephardic Jews)	Familial Mediterranean fever G-6-PD deficiency, Mediterranean type Thalassemia (mainly β)	Cystic fibrosis
Africans	G-6-PD deficiency, African type Hemoglobinopathies, esp. Hb S, Hb C, α and β thal, persistent Hb F	Cystic fibrosis Hemophilia Phenylketonuria Wilson's disease
Japanese (Koreans)	Acatalasia Dyschromatosis universalis hereditaria Oguchi's disease	
Chinese	α thalassemia G-6-PD deficiency, Chinese type	
Armenians	Familial Mediterranean fever	

* Data from McKusick, 1967. For references on individual conditions, see McKusick, 1966.

TABLE 3

precision in estimating populations at risk. Transient residence and low utilization of medical facilities, even within the same medical care plans, are more common among Nonwhites than among Whites in the United States. Jews, on the other hand, make maximum use of medical facilities in comparison with other White subgroups. As for diagnosis, skin rashes or

RACIAL AND ETHNIC DISEASE: MULTIFACTORIAL DISORDERS WITH A COMPLEX OR UNPROVED GENETIC COMPONENT*

Ethnic group	High frequency	Low frequency
Ashkenazic Jews	Buerger's disease Diabetes mellitus Hypercholesterolemia Hyperuricemia Kaposi's sarcoma Leukemia Pemphigus vulgaris Polycythemia vera Ulcerative colitis and regional enteritis	Alcoholism Cervical cancer Pyloric stenosis Tuberculosis
Sephardic Jews	Cystic disease of lung	
Northern Europeans	Pernicious anemia	
Irish	Major CNS malformations (anencephaly, encephalocele)	
Chinese	Nasopharyngeal cancer Trophoblastic disease	Chronic lymphatic leukemia Prostatic cancer
Japanese	Cerbrovascular accidents Cleft lip-palate Gastric cancer Trophoblastic disease	Acne vulgaris Breast cancer Chronic lymphatic leukemia Congenital hip disease Otosclerosis Prostatic cancer
Filipinos (US only)	Hyperuricemia	
Polynesians (Hawaiians)	Clubfoot Coronary heart disease Diabetes mellitus	
Africans	Ainhum Cervical cancer Esophageal cancer Hypertension Polydactyly Prehelical fissure Sarcoidosis Systemic lupus erythematosus	Arteriosclerosis Congenital hip disease Gallstones Major CNS malformations (anencephaly, encephalocele)

RACIAL AND ETHNIC DISEASE: MULTIFACTORIAL DISORDERS
WITH A COMPLEX OR UNPROVED GENETIC COMPONENT*

Ethnic group	High frequency	Low frequency
Africans cont'd.	Tuberculosis Uterine fibroids	Multiple sclerosis Osteoporosis and fracture of hip and spine Otosclerosis Pediculosis capitis Polycythemia vera Psoriasis Pyloric stenosis Skin cancer
American Indian	Congenital dislocation of hip Gallbladder disease Rheumatoid arthritis Tuberculosis	Duodenal ulcer
Icelanders	Glaucoma	
Eskimos	Otitis, deafness Salivary gland tumors	

* Enlarged from Damon, 1962, and McKusick, 1967.

TABLE 4

skin cancer might be harder to diagnose among Nonwhites than among Whites. Not only have such errors been considered before entering the diseases in Tables 3 and 4, but the internal evidence of the tables - one or another group higher for some diseases, lower for others - shows that no such simple explanation can account for the associations observed.

Differences between groups with respect to more directly associated variables. Some reported differences between groups may reflect differences in age, sex, or socioeconomic status rather than differential disease susceptibility. When disease rates are compared for Whites and Nonwhites of similar age, sex, and socioeconomic status - in respect to occupation, residence, education, income and the like - and when the differences persist, they cannot be attributed to these demographic variables. Such is the case for many of the disorders in Tables 3 and 4.

Differences in environment. Apart from the demographic variables associated with socioeconomic status just mentioned, there are many finer differences in customs and way of life. Dietary habits, use of tobacco and alcohol, amount of physical exertion, age at first intercourse or at marriage, number of children, contraceptive and infant feeding practices differ from one group to another and doubtless underlie many ethnic differences in disease.

The relative contributions of heredity and environment to such differences can be assessed epidemiologically in two ways: by studying disease rates among migrants - that is, the same breeding group in different environments - and among members of different racial or ethnic groups in the 'same' environment. (The quotation marks indicate that the microenvironment of an ethnic group need not be identical to that of its neighbor in the same geographic or macro-environment.) For example, rates of stomach cancer are higher for Japanese living in the United States than for American Whites. But rates for Japanese living in Hawaii exceed those for Japanese in the mainland United States, while rates for Japanese living in Japan are highest of all. Among the Japanese living in Hawaii, rates of stomach cancer are higher for those born in Japan than for those born in Hawaii. A similar situation holds for nasopharyngeal cancer among Chinese in California. Thus, the causal factors must be associated with a way of life that changes with migration, whether or not a minor genetic factor may also be involved.

On the other hand, Negroes of West African origin have higher blood pressure and more hypertensive disease than Whites in a variety of environments in the Caribbean, Panama, and the United States (summarized by Phillips and Burch, 1960; Florey and Cuadrado, 1968). This consistency in various environments argues for heredity.

An example of the comparison of different breeding populations in the 'same' environment would be the Hawaiian studies of coronary heart disease already cited (Moellering and Bassett, 1967), showing marked differences among men of pure Hawaiian, part Hawaiian, and Japanese descent. Unfortunately, one cannot be sure how similar their living habits were.

Differences in body constitution. This topic brings us closer to the biological associations of interest to the anthropologist and geneticist. A few examples must suffice. Melanin protects against sunlight, accounting for the much lower rates of skin cancer among pigmented groups. The Negro ectoderm responds to injury with excessive connective tissue to form keloids, or raised scars. Connective tissue from Caucasians, Negroes, Eskimos, and American Indians is reported to differ in amount and composition (Boucek *et al.*, 1958).

The increased density of Negro bone (Trotter *et al.*, 1960) may in part account for the relatively low frequency of spine and hip fractures among elderly Negroes (Bollet *et al.*, 1965; Moldawer *et al.*, 1965). On the other hand, despite the reduced bone density of Orientals, presumed to be genetic (Garn et al., 1964), Wong (1965) reported lower rates of forearm fractures among Chinese and Malays in Singapore than among Swedes in Sweden. Negroes have markedly lower frequencies of Legg-Perthes disease, an osteochondrosis of the femoral head affecting mainly young males, than do Caucasions. American Indians, who may also have lower frequencies of Legg-Perthes disease, are much more susceptible to congenital dislocation of the hip than Whites, whereas Negroes are markedly less so. Anatomical differences in the shape of the acetabulum have been adduced in explanation.

The nasal index, breadth/length, varies with humidity and inversely with latitude (Weiner, 1964). The long, narrow nose of Eskimos is not wholly successful as an adaptation to a cold, dry environment. This may explain in part their frequent upper respiratory infections, leading to draining ears and deafness (Brody and McAlister, 1965), in contrast to Africans and Malayans.

The rarity of pediculosis capitis (head lice) among Negroes is unexplained but may relate to some characteristic of the scalp or hair.

A physiological characteristic which varies among breeding populations is the level of immunity against micro-organisms. Lacking previous exposure, some groups are extremely susceptible to diseases which are mild in other populations. Fatal epidemics of measles and upper respiratory infections among Eskimos and Melanesians, smallpox among American Indians, and susceptibility to tuberculosis among all of these groups as well as Negroes, have been well documented. On the other hand, Ashkenazic Jews are relatively resistant to tuberculosis, presumably because they have lived for centuries under crowded conditions where only the resistant survived. Negroes appear relatively resistant to vivax malaria, for similar selective reasons (Bruce-Chwatt, 1967).

Research into the disease and immunological status of the few remaining isolates, unexposed to the larger culture, can contribute greatly to our understanding of disease as a selective factor in evolution, the history and geography of disease, and our knowledge of human origins and distribution (Hackett, 1963; Hudson, 1963, 1965; World Health Organization, 1968).

One way to demonstrate the reality of racial differences in physiological and biochemical functions, some of which underlie differences in disease frequency and severity, is by a list, as in Table 5. Further research will undoubtedly disclose many more racial differences than appear in this partial list. Race is clearly more than skin deep. In fact, the validity of the classical scheme of human races, described morphologically by early anthropologists and subsequently confirmed on serological grounds, is independently substantiated by physiological and pathological evidence. Some of the three-way distributions, as for bone density, twinning, and possibly blood pressure, are particularly striking.

Race, Ethnic Group, and Disease

SOME RACIAL DIFFERENCES IN PHYSIOLOGY AND BIOCHEMISTRY

In relation to Caucasoid norms

TRAIT	Negroids	Mongoloids (Orientals)
Birth:		
weight	−	−
skeletal maturation	+	
dental maturation	+	
neurological maturation	+	
Neonatal motor development	+	
Acuity, auditory and visual	+	
Blood pressure	+	−
Bone density	+	−
Color blindness	−	−
Corneal arcus	+	
Fibrinolysin activity	+	
Isoniazid inactivation		+
Keloid formation	+	
Lactase dificiency (adult)	+	+
Pulmonary function	−	
Serum globulins	+	
Skin resistance, electrical	+	
Tasting, phenylthiocarbamide	+	+
Twinning, dizygotic	+	−

TABLE 5

Differences in genetic constitution. Such differences determine many of the bodily characteristics just mentioned, such as skin color or bone density. For only a few of the single-gene disorders in Table 3 is there evidence for heterozygote advantage, the mechanism usually postulated for the persistence of such deleterious genes in numbers beyond those expected from mutation - that is, as 'balanced polymorphisms'. Hemoglobin S has been shown to confer resistance to falciparum malaria in heterozygotes. The same is strongly suspected but not yet fully established for other abnormal hemoglobins, for glucose-6-phosphate dehydrogenase deficiency, and for thalassemia. Increased fertility, another aspect of heterozygote advantage besides resistance to disease, has been reported for carriers of cystic fibrosis (Knudson *et al.*, 1967), and suggested, together with improved survival, for heterozygote carriers of Tay-Sachs disease

(Myrianthopoulos and Aronson, 1966).

But with almost 30% of human genetic loci estimated to be polymorphic, and with most of these probably 'relics' of previous selective crises (Bodmer, 1968), we have a long way to go in accounting for them all and probably never can.

The genetic component is overwhelming in the single-gene disorders. In the multi-causal disorders, environmental factors tend to dominate the genetic ones. There is little doubt, for example, that alcoholism, tuberculosis, and cervical cancer are largely environmental in origin. But even for tuberculosis, an infectious disease most common in low-income, crowded communities, several twin studies - the latest by Harvald and Hauge (1965) - have shown a genetic substrate, and the disease is much more frequent and severe among Negroes than among White persons, independent of childhood infection (Lurie, 1964). Incidentally, it should be noted that diseases with a genetic component need not be associated with race - for example, peptic ulcer (Damon and Polednak, 1967).

Diseases which change in frequency or manifestation over periods too short for genetic influences (mutation, selection, gene flow, drift) to operate must be mainly environmental in origin. Examples relevant here are the decline in mortality from hypertension and cervical cancer, and the oscillations in leukemia rates in the United States during the last thirty to forty years.

In connection with the genetic influences just noted, McKusick (1967) points out that no racial or ethnic differences in mutation rates have been found and the gene flow as well as mutation could account for the occasional occurrence of (say) cystic fibrosis in an American Negro.

A further difficulty in assessing the genetic component in the multifactorial diseases in Table 4 is that the genetic component is polygenic rather tha monogenic, as in the simply-inherited disorders of Table 3. Variability in both the genetic and the environmental determinants of disease means that one cannot expect associations to hold or to be equally strong among all populations at all times or in the same population at different times and in different places. Research among racially mixed populations, as well as among the isolates, the migrants and the different sedentary groups living in the same environment already discussed should help to settle these questions.

References

Bodmer, W.F. (1968). Demographic approaches to the measurement of differential selection in human populations. *Proceedings of the National Academy of Sciences,* 59, 690-699.
Bollet, A.J., Engh, G. and Parson, W. (1965). Epidemiology of osteoporosis. *Archives of Internal Medicine,* 116, 191-194.

Boucek, R.J., Noble, N.L., Kao, K.T. and Elden, H.R. (1958). The effects of age, sex, and race upon the acetic acid fractions of collagen (human biopsy-connective tissue). *Journal of Gerontology*, 13, 2-9.

Brody, J.A., and McAlister, R. (1965). Draining ears and deafness among Alaskan Eskimos. *Archives of Otolaryngology*, 81, 29-33.

Bruce-Chwatt, L.J. (1967). Malaria: In *Textbook of Medicine*, edited by P.B. Beeson and W. McDermott. Philadelphia: Saunders.

Damon, A. (1962). Some host factors in disease: sex, race, ethnic group, and body form. *Journal of the National Medical Association*, 54, 424-431.

Damon, A. and Polednak, A. P. (1967). Constitution, genetics, and body form in peptic ulcer: a review. *Journal of Chronic Diseases*, 20, 787-802.

Florey, C. du V. and Cuadrado, R.R. (1968). Blood pressure in native Cape Verdeans and in Cape Verdean immigrants and their descendants living in New England. *Human Biology*, 40, 189-211.

Garn, S.M. (1965). *Human Races*. Second edition. Springfield, Illinois: Thomas.

Garn, S.M., Pao, E.M. and Rihl, M.E. (1964). Compact bone in Chinese and Japanese. *Science*, 143, 1439-1440.

Hackett, C.J. (1963). On the origin of the human treponematoses. *Bulletin of the World Health Organization*, 29, 7-41.

Harvald, B. and Hauge, H.M. (1965). Hereditary factors elucidated by twin studies. In *Genetics and the Epidemiology of Chronic Diseases*. edited by J.V. Neel, M.J. Shaw and W.J. Shull. Washington: US Public Health Service Publication No. 1163.

Hudson, E.H. (1963). Treponematosis and anthropology. *Annals of Internal Medicine*, 58, 1037-1048.

Hudson, E.H. (1965). Treponematosis and man's social evolution. *American Anthropologist*, 67, 885-901.

Knudson, A.G., Wayne, L. and Hallett, W.Y. (1967). On the selective advantage of cystic fibrosis heterozygotes. *American Journal of Human Genetics*, 19, 388-392.

Kudo, T. (1968). Spontaneous occlusion of the circle of Willis. A disease apparently confined to Japanese. *Neurology*, 18, 485-496.

Lurie, M.B. (1964). *Resistance to Tuberculosis*. Cambridge, Mass.: Harvard University Press.

McKusick, V.A. (1966). *Mendelian Inheritance in Man*. Catalogue of Autosomal Dominant, Autosomal Recessive, and X-Linked Phenotypes. Baltimore: John Hopkins Press.

McKusick, V.A. (1967). The ethnic distribution of disease in the United States. *Journal of Chronic Diseases*, 20, 115-118.

MacMahon, B., Pugh, T.F. and Ibsen, J. (1960). *Epidemiologic Methods*. Boston: Little & Brown.

Moellering, R.C. and Bassett, D.R. (1967). Myocardial infaction in Hawaiian and Japanese males on Oahu - a review of 505 cases occurring between 1955 and 1964. *Journal of Chronic Diseases*. 20, 89-101.

Moldawer, M., Zimmerman, S.J. and Collins, L.C. (1965). Incidence of osteoporosis in elderly whites and elderly Negroes. *Journal of the American Medical Association*, 194, 855-862.

Myrianthopoulos, N.C. and Aronson, S.M. (1966). Population dynamics of Tay-Sachs disease, 1. Reproductive fitness and selection. *American Journal of Human Genetics*, 18, 313-327.

Phillips, J.H. and Burch, G.E. (1960). A review of cardiovascular diseases in the white and Negro races. *Medicine*, 39, 241-288.

Shimkin, M.B., Loveland, D.B. (1961). A note on mortality from lymphatic leukemia in oriental populations in the United States. *Blood*, 17, 763-766.

Sievers, M.L. and Marquis, J.R. (1962). Duodenal ulcer among Southwestern American Indians. *Gastroenterology*, 42, 566-569.
Sloan, N.R. (1963). Ethnic distribution of diabetes mellitus in Hawaii. *Journal of the American Medical Association*, 183, 419-424.
Smith, R.L. (1956a). Recorded and expected mortality among the Japanese of the United States and Hawaii, with special reference to cancer. *Journal of the National Cancer Institute*, 17, 459-473.
Smith, R.L. (1956b). Recorded and expected mortality among the Chinese of Hawaii and the United States, with special reference to cancer. *Journal of the National Cancer Institute*, 17, 667-676.
Trotter, M., Broman, G.E. and Peterson, R.R. (1960). Densities of bones of white and Negro skeletons. *Journal of Bone and Joint Surgery*, 42-A, 50-58.
Wagner, C.J. and Rabeau, E.S. (1964). Indian poverty and Indian health. *Health, Education and Welfare Indicators*, March, 24-44.
Weiner, J.S. (1964). Climatic adaptation. In *Human Biology*, edited by G.A. Harrison, J.S. Weiner, J.M. Tanner and N.A. Barnicot. New York and London: Oxford University Press.
Wong, P.C.N. (1965). Epidemiology of fractures of the forearm among the major racial groups in Singapore. *Acta Orthopaedica Scandinavica*, 36, 168-178.
World Health Organization (1968). *Research on Human Population Genetics*. Technical Report 387. Geneva: WHO.

11

SPINA BIFIDA AND ANENCEPHALY: A PROBLEM IN GENETIC-ENVIRONMENTAL INTERACTION

C.O. Carter

Anencephaly and spina bifida cystica are, in terms of public health, the most important congenital malformations in Britain and especially in the north and west of Britain. They both arise as failures of closure of the neural tube. This tube originates as a flat and thickened plate of ectoderm, the medullary plate, along the back of the embryo which infolds by the formations of medullary ridges on either side. The ridges grow round and back to form a medullary tube enclosing the spinal canal. This medullary tube differentiates into the brain and spinal cord. The formation of the tube is almost complete by the end of the third week after conception. Failure of closure at the head end is followed by failure of formation of the vertex of the skull and by incomplete formation and degeneration of the cerebral lobes of the brain; the basal parts of the brain then lie exposed on the surface. This condition is called anencephaly and is not compatible with more than a few hours of post-natal life. Anencephalics are usually stillborn, but about 1 in 10 are registered as liveborn and then as infant deaths.

Failure of closure of the cervical, thoracic or lumbar parts of the neural tube is followed by failure of closure of the posterior part of the vertebral arches and spines. This leaves the incompletely folded part of the spinal cord exposed or covered only by a cystic swelling limited behind by a thin membrane. The condition is called spina bifida cystica (hereinafter called 'spina bifida') and about 1 in 5 patients are stillborn. Of those liveborn the great majority until recently died in infancy either from infection, or from a blockage of the passage of cerebrospinal fluid out of the skull down the spinal cord, which led to progressive enlargement of the skull (hydrocephalus) and raised pressure within the skull with damage to the brain. In recent years the prognosis in infancy has greatly improved because of advances in surgical techniques. In particular the practice of early closure of the lesion on the back by drawing skin over it prevents infection, and the development of special valves permits the drainage of cerebrospinal fluid from within the brain to the circulatory system (usually the right ventricle of the heart) and prevents the development of hydrocephalus. As a result of these procedures some 60 - 80% of liveborn children with spina bifida may be expected to survive instead of less than 20%. The majority of such survivors, however, will require major orthopaedic and genito-urinary surgery to attempt to compensate for partial or complete paralysis of leg muscles and of the bladder. It is very difficult to know in advance which patients will do well and so the attempt is usually made to treat all patients. In some instances there is complete failure of closure of the neural tube, causing both anencephaly and a complete spina bifida along the length of the spinal canal.

The incidence of anencephaly in England and Wales has been about 2 per thousand total births, the figures for still- and livebirths combined falling from 2.2 in 1961 to 1.8 in 1966 and the stillbirth rate from anencephaly falling from 2.0 to 1.6 (Registrar General's Statistical Review: Part 1, Medical). At a time when the stillbirth rate is about 16 per thousand this means that about 1 in 8 of all stillbirths are due to this condition. The patients with spina bifida, about 2.4 per thousand total births, account for about 1 in 25 stillbirths and also until recently for about 1 in 8 of all infant deaths. With the new treatments these patients will contribute fewer infant deaths, but will demand formidable efforts from the medical and educational services to minimize their handicaps. The incidence of spina bifida, however, is less well established in Britain on a national scale than that of anencephaly. The system of voluntary notification of malformations is as yet by no means complete. Special studies, however, indicate that there are about 20% more births with spina bifida than with anencephaly. The incidence of spina bifida is often underestimated because in public records many instances of hydrocephalus secondary to spina bifida are classified as 'hydrocephalus'. True primary congenital hydrocephalus is a rare and non-homogeneous group of malformations, not related to neural tube malformations in either genetic or epidemiological characteristics.

Prevention of this group of malformations is self-evidently highly desirable. It is only likely to be possible when the causative factors are fully worked out. In the following sections of this article some of the clues to aetiology are discussed. It is already apparent that the problem is one of complex genetic - environmental interaction - very much a biosocial problem.

Regional Variation in Incidence in Britain

One lead to the aetiology is given by the striking regional variations in incidence of neural tube malformations. Within Britain it has long been known that both anencephaly and spina bifida are more common in Ireland and to a lesser degree in Scotland than in south-east England. Since 1961 the causes of stillbirth have been statutorily recorded in England and Wales (they have long been recorded in Scotland) and this has shown the regional pattern for anencephaly clearly in the Registrar General's Annual Statistical Review (Part 1, Medical). The areas of highest incidence are Wales and the North West region, and the incidence falls progressively as one moves south and east across Britain. The lowest incidence is found in East Anglia and the South East region. Thus for 1963 - 66 inclusive the incidence of anencephalic stillbirths in the hospital regions of Britain was: Wales 2.7, Liverpool 2.4, Manchester 2.2, Newcastle 2.1, Sheffield 1.8, Leeds 1.7, Birmingham 1.7, South West 1.7, contrasting with 1.5 for Oxford, 1.6 for Wessex, 1.4 for East Anglia and 1.2, 1.2, 1.4 and 1.2 for the four Metropolitan regions. Over the same period the figure for Scotland was 2.8. In Scotland the trend by the north-south axis is reversed in that the incidence is lower north of the line joining the Firths of Clyde and Tay. The pattern of incidence is shown in Figure 1. For Wales and Scotland the incidence is twice that in the south-east of England. Other data indicate that the incidence in both the north

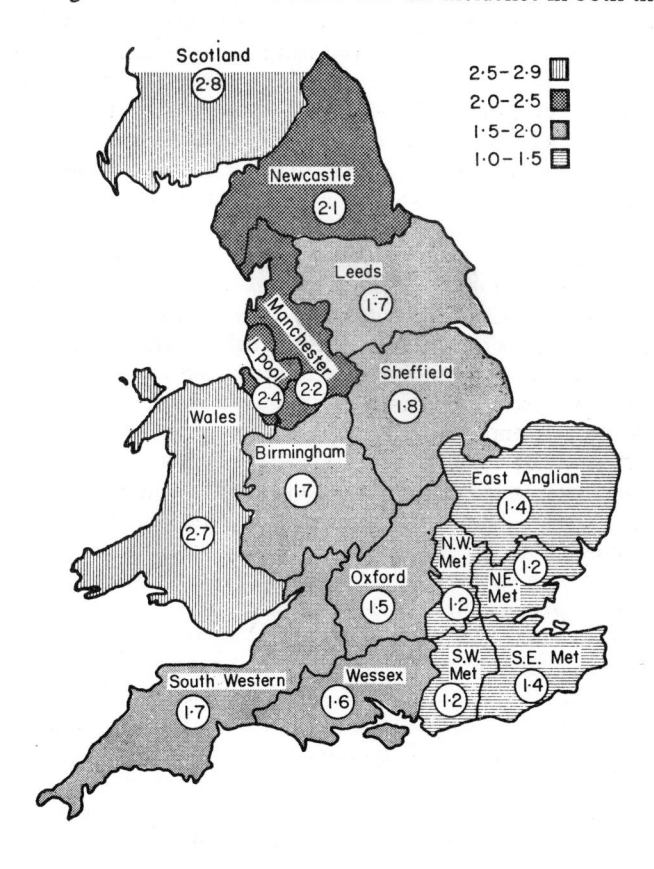

FIGURE 1. Anencephalic stillbirths by regional hospital areas.

and the south of Ireland is as high or higher than that in Wales or Scotland. The incidence of spina bifida is less accurately known from registration data, but is known from special studies to show a variation within Britain paralleling that of anencephaly.

World-wide Regional Variation
Some years ago Penrose (1957) assembled much of the information then available on the world incidence of anencephaly. Most of these data relate to hospital births, which are known to be unrepresentative since anencephaly often causes obstetric complications (hydramnios and failure of engagement of the head) which lead to selective admission to hospital. However, the data available made clear the relatively high incidence in Ireland and north-west Britain compared with south-east England, but also made clear that there was a marked further fall in incidence once one moved across the Channel. Most incidences in European hospitals are less than half that in south-east England, being only of the order of 0.5 - 0.75 per thousand. Data from Japan and Hong Kong indicate that the Japanese and Chinese incidence was also probably about 0.5 - 0.75 per thousand and data from South Africa indicate that the incidence in Negroes was lower still.

The world-wide geographical distribution is now better documented as a result of the survey reported on behalf of the World Health Organization by Stevenson *et al.* (1966). The survey was based on reports from twenty-four large hospital maternity units from sixteen countries including in north-western Europe, Belfast; south-western Europe, Madrid; in eastern Europe, Czechoslovakia, Ljubljana and Zagreb; in South Africa, Johannesburg (Whites), Pretoria (Bantu) and Cape Town (Cape coloured); in India, Calcutta and Bombay; in East Asia, Singapore, Kuala Lumpur, Hong Kong and Manila; in Australia, Melbourne; in Central America, Mexico and Panama; and in South America, Sao Paulo, Santiago, Bogota and Medelin. Belfast expectedly had the highest incidences; after standardization for maternal age these were (including encephalocoele with spina bifida) 4.5 for spina bifida, 4.5 for anencephaly and 1.2 labelled as hydrocephalus - but it must be remembered that these are figures for hospitals with some selective admission. The only centre with an incidence approaching Belfast was Alexandria in Egypt with 3.8 for anencephaly, 3.1 for spina bifida and 2.0 for hydrocephalus. Most other centres tended to have a relatively low incidence with figures of 0.3 - 1.0 for anencephaly and 0.3 - 1.5 for spina bifida. In Bombay the incidence was relatively high, 1.9 for anencephaly and 1.1 for spina bifida, and a special enquiry from Amritsar (the Sikh capital) showed an incidence of anencephaly of 4.0 per thousand. This survey then produced evidence of two areas of high incidence outside Britain and British descended populations, namely Alexandria in Egypt and Amritsar in the Punjab. It is of much interest to know the limits of these newly found areas of high incidence. Constant regional variations within a country similar to that in Britain have been reported only from the USA and Canada (Hewitt, 1965). In both countries there is a steady fall as one passes across the country from the Atlantic to the Pacific provinces.

The Effect of Migration

Regional variation of this kind could have several explanations. It might be essentially due to the genetic differences between peoples. With Britain, for example, the regional variation parallels that of Celtic place names and the incidence of the gene for O red blood cell antigen. It might be due to differences in soil and climate; the high incidence areas in Britain are in the geologically older highland area. It might be due to social differences; areas of high incidence are also areas of relatively high overall infant mortality, which is rightly regarded as a good index of social standards.

Some help in distinguishing genetic and environmental causes of racial variations might be expected from the study of migrants. Present indications are that migrants retain the incidences of the areas from which they came. The high incidence in Sikhs was first noted not in the Punjab, but in Singapore (Searle, 1959). The Indians in Fiji have a higher incidence of anencephaly than the Melanesians (MacDonald, quoted by Stevenson *et al.*, 1966), Negroes or part Negroes have a lower incidence than Whites in both the USA (Alter, 1962) and South Africa, the American Indians in British Columbia have a lower incidence than the Whites (Miller, 1964). Preliminary reports for immigrants to Britain (Leck, 1968) indicate that Indians and Pakistanis (mostly from the Punjab and including many Sikhs) have an incidence as high as that of native Englishmen, while West Indians (Negro and part Negro) have an appreciably lower incidence than the Whites. The incidence in North American cities is to some extent explicable in racial terms. Here, since nearly all births are in hospital, hospital incidences are representative of those of the general population. In Boston with a high proportion of Irish descent the incidence of anencephaly was 2.3 per thousand; it was 1.9 in Rhode Island; 2.1 in Montreal, but only 0.6 in Rochester with a large Scandinavian element (references given in Penrose, 1957). A special study (Naggan and MacMahon, 1967) in Boston showed a relatively high rate when either parent was of Irish descent and higher still when the mother had been born in Ireland, although even then the rate was probably lower than that in Ireland itself. Overall the implication is that racial differences persist after migration. A possible exception is provided by Australia, which both in the World Health Organization survey and in special studies (Collman and Stoller, 1962) appears to have an unusually low incidence of neural tube malformations (0.7 for anencephaly, 0.6 for spina bifida and

0.6 for hydrocephaly). This cannot be accounted for by the 'new Australians' from Europe, and suggests a real reduction even if the migration from Britain to Australia was, as is probably the case, predominantly from the south-east. In contrast there is the interesting suggestion from Hawaii that the incidence of neural tube malformations in the Japanese there is higher than that in Japan (Morton *et al.*, 1966).

Where racial differences do persist after migration this suggests that geographical factors, for example hours of sunlight, cannot be important, but does not necessarily exclude cultural and dietary environmental factors, since these may be retained for a generation or more. It is difficult, however, to regard the low racial incidence in Negroes apparently maintained in such different cultures as South African, West Indian and North American as anything but genetically determined.

Family Studies

Evidence of the importance of genetic factors is supplied by the sex ratio; there is a small excess of females in the case of spina bifida (sex ratio is about 0.8) and a large excess with anencephaly (the sex ratio in England and Wales is about 0.4). Curiously enough, this female excess with anencephaly is not seen in Negroes (Gittelsohn and Milham, 1965).

Evidence of genetic factors in aetiology is also given by family studies. Good twin studies are unfortunately not available. The high early mortality of those affected made it difficult to blood group both twins before death. Blood grouping of cord blood taken at delivery has not been advanced on any substantial scale. Notable individual case reports have appeared, for example monozygotic triplets all with anencephaly (Scott and Patterson, 1966); but there are also several case reports of only one of a pair of monozygotic co-twins being affected, clearly indicating that the aetiology of nueral tube malformations is not wholly genetic. From New York (Gittelsohn and Milham, 1965) quoted figures indicating that 24 of 126 like sex co-twins and only 4 of 53 unlike sex co-twins of patients with major central nervous system malformations were also affected with such malformations, suggesting but not proving that a higher proportion of monozygotic co-twins are also affected.

Family studies are limited by the high mortality which hitherto has made it possible to estimate the proportion affected of only one type of first degree relative, namely brothers and sisters; few patients have yet had children, and parents of patients are inevitably almost all unaffected. Furthermore, deaths from neural tube malformations will not always be widely known within a family. A mother herself is not always told that a particular stillborn child had anencephaly or spina bifida. It is not difficult to check all a mother's births against hospital and local authority records, but it is a formidable undertaking to check all children born to husband's sisters and sisters-in-law. Family studies show, at least for brothers and sisters, that the proportion affected with neural tube malformations is some seven times higher than the proportion in the general population. The findings in three British surveys from Birmingham (Record and McKeown, 1950), Southampton (Williamson, 1965) and South Wales (Carter *et al.*, 1968) are summarized in Table 1.

	Index patients	Population incidence (%)	Sibs affected with CNS malformations %		Relative to population incidence
Birmingham (Record & McKeown, 1950) (subsequent sibs to index patients only)	Spina bifida Anencephaly	0.30 0.20	8 in 209) 3.83 5 in 194) 2.56 13 in 403	3.23	x6.5
Southampton (Williamson, 1965) (all sibs)	Spina bifida Anencephaly	0.32 0.19	7 in 119) 5.89 2 in 41) 4.89 9 in 160	5.63	x11.0
South Wales	Spina bifida Anencephaly	0.41 0.35	52 in 854) 29 in 709) 6.09 81 in 1563	5.18	x6.8

TABLE 1. Studies of incidence in general population and proportion of sibs affected in Britain.

Two studies from the United States (MacMahon *et al.*, 1953; Milham, 1962) have given similar proportions.

A familial concentration of this kind could be due to the genetic resemblance of brothers and sisters (who on average have half their genes in common) or to common environment, or to both. Common family environment in the usual sense could hardly account for the findings, but common persistent intrauterine environment provided by the mother (this could depend in part on the mother's genotype) could well account for a sib resemblance of this degree. For common congenital malformations for which information is available on children as well as sibs of index patients, for example cleft lip and palate, talipes equinovarus, certain congenital malformations of the heart and pyloric stenosis, a major influence of common intrauterine environment may be excluded, since the incidence in children is as high as the incidence in brothers and sisters. There is also a raised incidence of these malformations, though to a lesser degree, in nephews and nieces and in first cousins. However, such maternal influence cannot be excluded at present in the case of neural tube malformations, and some support for the hypothesis that the maternal rather than the foetal genotype is important is given by the finding that there is very probably a raised incidence in mothers' sisters' children (Hindse-Nielsen, 1938; Williamson, 1965; Carter and Roberts, 1967; Carter et al., 1968). Whereas the higher reported incidence in maternal cousins as a group may be due to incomplete information about the father's side of the family, the higher reported incidence in mother's sister's than mother's brother's children suggests a real difference. Data on half-brothers and -sisters would be most valuable in assessing intrauterine effects, but no large series are available.

Another indication of genetic influence is provided by parental consanguinity. Most of the family studies show a small increase, about two-fold, in parental consanguinity. More direct evidence for the importance of consanguinity comes from the World Health Organization survey (Stevenson et al., 1966). In Alexandria the frequency of neural tube defects of all types was 14.2 per thousand among the offspring of first cousin or more closely related parents and 5.7 per thousand among the offspring of unrelated marriages. A similar effect of parental consanguinity was seen in Bombay. Consanguinity effects of this order are to be expected in areas of high population incidence with either recessive or polygenic inheritance (Newcombe, 1964).

The evidence for genetic factors in the aetiology of these neural tube malformations needs supplementing by much further study: of twins, of half-sibs, of first cousins, of the offspring of racially mixed marriages according to whether the husband or wife comes from a group with a high incidence. It is also important that risks to sibs should be established in areas of low population incidence.

Maternal Age and Birth Order

Among the factors of obstetric interest there is an effect of both parity and mother's age on the incidence of neural tube malformations. In all studies of neural tube malformations there is an excess of first-born. For anencephalic stillbirths, an excess of first-born and also of those born at late birth orders can clearly be seen in England and Wales where the average rates for 1962 - 66 inclusive are 2.0 for first-born, 1.4 for second, 1.5 for third, 1.9 for fourth and 2.0 for fifth and about 2.2 for sixth and later births. In addition an effect of early and of late maternal age is seen in most studies. The rates of anencephaly for England and Wales for 1962 - 66 inclusive were 2.2 for maternal age less than 20, 1.8 for age 20 - 24, 1.6 for age 25 - 29, 1.6 for age 30 - 34, 2.0 for age 35 - 39, 2.0 for age 40 - 44 (and 2.7 for age over 45, though the numbers here are small). There is no suggestion of any independent paternal age effect. The effects of birth order and maternal age cannot be separated on the date given by the Registrar General. In the South Wales survey (Carter *et al.*, 1968) standardization for maternal age leaves little late birth order effect for anencephaly and spina bifida. However, the late birth and maternal age factors were independent in the Birmingham survey (Record and McKeown, 1949), in a New York survey (Gittelsohn and Milham, 1965) and in the special tabulation of the anencephaly data for Scotland (Record, 1961). The Scottish findings are shown in Table 2.

No. of previous children	Maternal age (years)				
	Under 20	20-	25-	30-	35 and over
0	3.6	3.1	2.6	2.9	3.0
1	-	2.1	2.0	2.3	2.1
2	-	1.7	2.3	2.9	3.5
3 and 4	-	-	2.7	3.0	3.8
5 and over	-	-	-	3.0	4.9

TABLE 2. Anencephalic stillbirth rates standardized for social class.

Such maternal age and birth order effects are usually interpreted as due to environmental influences. It is certainly difficult to visualize any genetic correlation with birth order. Increasing maternal age is known to be associated with a marked increase of chromosomal non-disjunction, and so with the incidence of conditions such as mongolism. Increased paternal age is known to be associated with an increased incidence of mutation on at least some gene loci, for example the mutations responsible for classical achondroplasia and Apert's syndrome. In the case of the neural tube malformations, however, where neither chromosomal non-disjunctions nor gene mutation appear to be concerned, maternal age effects may reasonably be supposed to indicate the effect of environmental influences.

Secular Changes and Seasonal Changes

The incidence of neural tube malformations shows consistent trends for years at a time. For example, in Birmingham the incidence fell from 1940 to 1949 (Leck, 1966); Edwards (1958), however, noted that the anencephalic stillbirth date for Scotland shows no considerable variation. Further, the sustained decrease in Birmingham from 1940 to 1949 was followed by a steady rise until 1957 when it started to fall again from 1958 to 1965 (Leck, 1966). In South Wales (Laurence *et al.*, 1968a) there was no significant change from 1957 to 1966.

An effect of season of birth, and by implication of season of conception, was seen constantly in the earlier Scottish anencephalic data (Edwards, 1958; Leck and Record, 1966) and in data from Birmingham. The excess was for 'winter' (October - March) births implying an excess in March - July conceptions, since the average gestation period of anencephalics is about 8 months. Some more recent studies have shown little seasonal effect (Smithells *et al.*, 1964) and negative findings have been reported from France (Frézal *et al.*, 1964). The South Wales survey gave a different seasonal incidence with an unusally low rate for conceptions from April to June (Laurence *et al.*, 1968b). In Scotland in more recent years, 1959 - 63, the seasonal difference has disappeared and was much reduced in Birmingham. In England and Wales seasonal variation has also been inconsistent. A winter excess of anencephalic stillbirths was seen in 1961, 1963 and 1964, but not in 1962 (Leck and Record, 1966). A similar excess was seen in 1965, but not in 1966 (Registrar General's Statistical Review of England and Wales).

Such secular and seasonal variations suggest at first sight an influence of infection, but no consistent associations with particular evidence has been found. Coffey and Jessop (1959) found an association of influenza A and anencephaly, but this has not been found in other studies.

Social Class

The Scottish anencephaly data and other studies constantly show a marked effect of social class (Edwards, 1958). For example, in Scotland for 1950 - 56 the rate per thousand total births was found to be 2.1 for fathers in Social Class I, 3.0 in Class II, 4.4 in Class III, 4.8 in Class IV and 5.5 in Class V. In the South Wales survey (Laurence *et al.*, 1968b) with a more homogeneous population the expected class effect was less marked but still present.

It is difficult not to attribute such social class effects to environmental factors. A genetic correlation, however, is possible not so much with racial groups (the social class effect was seen in the Boston study, Naggan and MacMahon, 1967, within the Irish group), but with factors that make for social mobility such as intelligence and, to a lesser degree, stature.

Conclusions

The clues given above are intriguing, but as yet provide no complete picture of the aetiology of neural tube malformations; some of the implications have been discussed above. There is good evidence for the importance of genetic factors, both from the racial variation and the raised incidence in brothers and sisters of patients. These genetic factors are not microscopically visible chromosomal abnormalities and they are probably not mutant genes of large effect; they are probably polygenic, though it may be that not many gene loci are involved. These genes could be those of the foetus itself, controlling its own development, but could also be genes of the mother affecting the intrauterine environment she provides for the foetus. An indication of the possible importance of the maternal genotype is given by the raised incidence in mothers' sisters' children. Evidence for the importance of the foetal genotype is provided by the effect of parental consanguinity, for example in the data from Alexandria. It is unfortunate that more data are not available on the incidence in maternal as compared with paternal half-sibs of patients and on the relative incidence in the two types of White - Negro or Indian - Negro crosses, since these would reveal any purely maternal influences.

There is also good evidence of the importance of environmental factors from maternal age and birth order effects, from the rather variable secular and seasonal differences, and especially from social class effects. No single environmental agent, however, is suggested by these effects, and it may well be that the environmental contributing factors, like the genetic, are multiple. The maternal age and birth order effects are perhaps rather non-specific, maternal age of 20 - 25 and second and third birth order is associated with low stillbirth and infant mortality rates, even if neural tube malformations are excluded. The social class effects would in pre-war years have suggested that nutritional differences were important. Such differences have now largely disappeared in Britain except among children in large families. There are, for example, little social class differences now in the age of menarche (Douglas, 1964). If, however, it was the mother's nutrition in infancy which was important, then nutritional differences by social class of the decade 1935 - 45 may well have been important.

The time has now come, perhaps, for a more direct attack on the possible genetic and environmental influences. Experimental work on animals is not always relevant to human teratology. However, such studies (Giroud, 1960) have shown that two consistent methods, among others, of producing such malformations in rodents is the production of folic-acid deficiency in the mother animal and the administration of excess vitamin A. That folic acid may be important in man is indicated by one or two instances where women have taken aminopterin (a folic acid antagonist) as an abortifacient early in pregnancy and this has been followed by the birth of a child with a neural tube malformation (Thiersch, 1960). Mechanisms of this kind could be both genetic and environmental. Deficiencies or excess of metabolites such as folic acid or vitamin A could be produced either by anomalies of dietary intake or by inborn errors of metabolism of the ingested vitamins.

Acknowledgments

I am much indebted to Dr K.M. Laurence, who planned and directed the South Wales survey, for much helpful discussion on the findings of the survey. I am indebted to Dr R. Record and the Editors of the *British Journal of Preventive and Social Medicine* for permission to reproduce Table 2.

References

Alter, M. (1962). Anencephalus, hydrocephalus and spina bifida. *Archives of Neurology, Chicago*, 7, 411.

Carter, C.O., David, P.A. and Laurence, K.M. (1968). A family study of major central nervous system malformations in South Wales. *Journal of Medical Genetics*, 5, 81.

Carter, C.O. and Roberts, J.A.F. (1967). The risk of recurrence after two children with central nervous system malformations. *Lancet*, i, 306.

Coffey, V.P. and Jessop, W.J.E. (1959). Maternal influenza and congenital deformities. A follow-up study. *Lancet*, i, 748.

Collman, R.D. and Stoller, A. (1962). Epidemiology of congenital anomalies of the central nervous system with special reference to patterns in the State of Victoria, Australia. *Journal of Mental Deficiency Research*, 6, 22.

Douglas, J.W.B. (1964). *The Home and the School*. London: MacGibbon & Kee.

Edwards, J.H. (1958). Congenital malformations of the central nervous system in Scotland. *British Journal of Preventive and Social Medicine*, 12, 115.

Frézal, J., Kelley, J., Guillemot, M.L. and Lamy, M. (1964). Anencephaly in France. *American Journal of Human Genetics*, 16, 336.

Giroud, A. (1960). In *CIBA Foundation Symposium on Congenital Malformations*, edited by G.E.W. Wolstenholme and C.M. O'Connor. London: Churchill.

Gittelsohn, A.M. and Milham, S. (1965). In *Genetics and the Epidemiology of Chronic Diseases*, J.V. Neel, M.J. Shaw and W.J. Shull. Washington: US Public Health Service Publication No. 1163.

Hewitt, D. (1965). In *Genetics and the Epidemiology of Chronic Diseases*, edited by J.V. Neel, M.J. Shaw and W.J. Shull. Washington: US Public Health Service Publication No. 1163.

Hindse-Nielsen, S. (1938). Spina bifida - prognosis; heredity; a clinical study. *Acta Schirurgica Scandinavica*, 80, 525.

Laurence, K.M., Carter, C.O. and David, P.A. (1968a). The major central nervous system malformations in South Wales. I. *British Journal of Preventive and Social Medicine*, 22, 146.

Laurence, K.M., Carter, C.O. and David, P.A. (1968b). The major central nervous system malformations in South Wales. II. *British Journal of Preventive and Social Medicine*, 22, 212.

Leck, I. (1966). Change in the incidence of neural tube defects. *Lancet*, ii, 791.

Leck, I. (1968). Ethnic differences in the incidence of malformations. *British Journal of Preventive and Social Medicine*, 22, 114.

Leck, I. and Record, R.G. (1966). Seasonal incidence of anencephalus. *British Journal of Preventive and Social Medicine*, 20, 67.

MacMahon, B., Pugh, T.F. and Ingalls, T.H. (1953). Anencephalus, spina bifida and hydrocephalus. Incidence related to sex, race and season of birth, and incidence in siblings. *British Journal of Preventive and Social Medicine*, 7, 211.

Milham, S. (1962). Increased incidence of anencephalus and spina bifida in siblings of affected cases. *Science*, 138, 593.

Miller, J.R. (1964). In *Second International Conference on Congenital Malformations*, edited by M. Fishbein. New York: International Medical Congress Limited.

Morton, N.F., Chung, C.S. and Mi, W.P. (1966). *Genetics of Interracial Crosses in Hawaii*. Basel: Karger.

Naggan, L. and MacMahon, B. (1967). Ethnic differences in prevalence of anencephaly and spina bifida in Boston, Massachusetts. *New England Journal of Medicine*, 277, 119.

Newcombe, H. (1964). In *Second International Conference on Congenital Malformations*, edited by M. Fishbein. New York: International Medical Congress Limited.

Penrose, L.S. (1957). Genetics of anencephaly. *Journal of Mental Deficiency Research*, 1, 4.

Record, R.G. (1961). Anencephalus in Scotland. *British Journal of Preventive and Social Medicine*, 15, 93.

Record, R.G. and McKeown, T. (1949). Congenital malformations of the central nervous system. I. A survey of 930 cases. *British Journal of Preventive and Social Medicine*, 3, 183.

Record, R.G. and McKeown, T. (1950). Congenital malformations of the central nervous system. III. Risks of malformations in sibs of malformed individuals. *British Journal of Preventive and Social Medicine*, 15, 93.

Registrar General's Statistical Review of England and Wales (1966). Part I. *Tables, Medical*. London: HMSO.

Scott, J.M. and Patterson, L. (1966). Monozygous anencephalic triplets - a case report. *Journal of Obstetrics and Gynaecology of the British Commonwealth*, 73, 147.

Searle, A.G. (1959). The incidence of anencephaly in a polytypic population. *Annals of Human Genetics*, 23, 279.

Smithells, R.W., Chinn, E.R. and Franklin, D. (1964). Anencephaly in Liverpool. *Developmental Medicine and Child Neurology*, 6, 231.

Stevenson, A.C., Johnston, H.A., Stewart, M.I.P. and Golding, D.R. (1966). Congenital malformations. *Bulletin of the World Health Organization*, 34 (Suppl.).

Thiersch, J.B. (1960). Discussion following paper by M.M. Nelson. In *CIBA Foundation Symposium on Congenital Malformations*, edited by G.E.W. Wolstenholme and C.M. O'Connor. London: Churchill.

Williamson, E.M. (1965). Incidence and family aggregation of major congenital malformations of the central nervous system. *Journal of Medical Genetics*, 2, 161.

12
THOUGHT AND THE BRAIN*

O.L. Zangwill

I regret that not even the title of this Address is original. I have borrowed it from that of an old book by Henri Piéron called *Le Cerveau et la Pensée* (1923). In this book, the author's aim was to link, as and where possible, such knowledge as we have in psychology with what is known about the structure and functions of the brain. To his task, Piéron brought much erudition and a biological outlook not always so clearly in evidence today. In particular, he thought proper to adduce evidence not only from anatomy and physiology but also from clinical neurology, a field of medicine only too seldom represented in contemporary psychological texts. If I have purloined his title, it is because my own work over the years owes much to Piéron's example and reflects in considerable measure his own approach to psychological issues.

Lest some of you may think that I am a 'reductionist', as contemporary idiom has it, i.e. that my aim is to explain - or explain away - psychological phenomena in terms of physics and chemistry, I must hasten to say that nothing is further from my intention. You will hear nothing from me about nervous impulses or receptive fields, about transmitter substances or molecular models of memory, important as all of these may ultimately prove for explanation in psychology. My interest lies wholly within the traditional field of psychology, in human experience and human behaviour, and more especially in the ways in which study of the effects of brain injury may throw light upon their nature. Indeed the only real difference between my approach and that of those, such as John Cohen, who advocate a specifically humanistic psychology (Cohen, 1970), is that I prefer to think of man's humanity as vested in his bodily structure and function, not least, in the activities of his brain.

I. Fechner and Psychophysics

As a Professor of Experimental Psychology, it is perhaps only proper that I should begin by paying tribute to the man who is generally accepted as the founder of my discipline. I refer of course to Gustav Theodor Fechner, the 'father of experimental psychology', whose famous book *Elemente der Psychophysik* appeared in 1860. Fechner is remembered

---
* Presidential Address to the British Psychological Society delivered at Nottingham on 5 April 1975.

today almost exclusively for his psychophysical law, which inspired what William James so slightingly dismissed as 'that dreadful literature' (James, 1890, 1, p. 549). But James had in mind only what Fechner himself termed *outer psychophysics,* namely, the correlation of sensory magnitude with the intensity of physical stimulus. But this, Fechner thought, was only the first step. Much more important, he believed, was what he called *inner psychophysics,* the correlation of subjective magnitude with the intensity of the central excitatory process. He thought that inner psychophysics would ultimately make possible a quantitative treatment not only of sensation but also of images, affects and indeed states of consciousness generally. Although techniques appropriate to such study were not available in Fechner's time and are indeed only in their infancy today, it is at least clear that, for him psychophysics would eventually evolve into psychophysiology and that the whole idea of experimental psychology implied a close and essential concern for the cerebral basis of mind.

Although Fechner did not take his idea of inner psychophysics very far, much of what he wrote was strikingly in advance of its time. For example, he made much play with the notion of a limen of consciousness, which might be affected both by sleep and wakefulness as well as by shifts of attention, voluntary or involuntary. This notion has been adequately expounded by Boring (1929) and I shall not consider it further here. I would however like to say something about Fechner's general ideas on consciousness which as I have suggested elsewhere (Zangwill, 1974) have surprising relevance to modern work.

Much influenced by the French physiologist Flourens, and anticipating Lashley over half a century later, Fechner placed great stress on the equipotentiality of the cerebral cortex. Consciousness he regarded essentially as an attribute of the cerebral hemispheres, although insisting that not all parts of them are of equivalent importance for mental life. Above all, he contended that continuity of anatomical structure is an essential condition of the unity of consciousness, a thesis later developed by the Germany philosopher, Eduard von Hartmann (1931). This led Fechner to consider closely the issues raised by the brain's duplex structure. If, he argued, it were possible to divide the brain longitudinally in the mid-line - an experiment which, incidentally, he considered impossible to achieve - something like the duplication of a human being would be brought about. 'The two cerebral hemispheres', he wrote,, 'while beginning with the same moods, predispositions, knowledge and memories, indeed the same consciousness generally, will thereafter develop differently according to the external relations into which each will enter' (1860, 2, p. 537). In short, splitting the brain will divide the stream of consciousness.

Hardly surprisingly, Fechner's position found its opponents, among them a once famous founder-member of this Society, William McDougall. In his *Body and Mind* (1911), McDougall came out strongly against the view that the unity of consciousness is conditional upon the continuity of nervous structure. In this connexion, the late Sir Cyril Burt has related that McDougall more than once tried to bargain with the great Sherrington that if ever he (McDougall) should be smitten by an incurable disease, Sherrington should cut through his corpus callosum, that massive band of nerve fibres uniting the two hemispheres. 'If the physiologists are right', said McDougall, 'the result should be split personality. If I am right, my consciousness should remain a unitary consciousness.' And this, Burt comments, he seemed to regard as the most convincing evidence of something like a soul!

II. The Split-Brain Experiment

As we now know, the experiment thought by Fechner to be impossible and by McDougall to be practicable only in the case of a scientific martyr, is now a recognized neurosurgical procedure. I should, however, make clear that this drastic operation is carried out only in cases of severe and intractable epilepsy that have failed to respond to anticonvulsant medication. Known as commissurotomy, the operation was introduced by van Wagenen and Akelaitis in the early 'forties and revived in the 'sixties by Philip Vogel and Joseph Bogen, of the California College of Medicine. Roger Sperry, a distinguished psychologist and the first to develop experimental split-brain surgery in animals, was quick to see the gain to science from careful psychological study of individuals who had undergone this operation. At his kind invitation, I was privileged to spend some time in his Department at the California Institute of Technology five years ago and to gain first-hand experience of split-brain patients and their investigation.

I would like to say a little about the work of Sperry and his associates, which I regard as of first-rate importance. What are the effects of brain bisection upon psychological capacity? Does the operation really produce a doubling of the human being, as prophesied by Fechner? Or does consciousness remain unitary, as McDougall contended? At first blush, the advantage might appear definitely to lie with McDougall. Neither Akelaitis, nor after him Bogen and Sperry, could detect any gross change in intellect, personality or general behaviour of the split-brain patient after recovery from the immediate effects of the operation. So in spite of brain bisection, it would seem that the person remains unitary.

But this is not the whole story. Using techniques of a simplicity bordering upon the brilliant, Sperry and his co-workers have been able to show beyond reasonable doubt that each hemisphere of the brain may under appropriate circumstances operate independently of its fellow (see, for example, Sperry *et al.*, 1969). For example, if the eyes are closed an object actively explored by the left hand is not recognized by the right hand and vice versa. And similarly, the picture of an object exposed in the left half-field of vision is not recognized when re-exposed in the right half-field. These perceptual and discriminative tasks are carried out unilaterally and there is no apparent transfer of information between the hemispheres. There is even evidence that the two hemispheres may carry out concurrent tasks, such as copying designs flashed simultaneously to the two visual half-fields, without mutual awareness of each other's activity. Under conditions of unilateral input, therefore, each hemisphere functions as an independent processor, producing results reminiscent of the behaviour of two separate individuals. In Sperry's words, 'each hemisphere . . . seems to have its own conscious sphere for sensation, perception and other mental activities and the whole realm of gnostic activity of the one is cut off from the corresponding experience of the other hemisphere' (Sperry et al., 1969).

Thus Fechner, too, has been proved right: Duplex conscious activity of the two hemispheres can result from callosal section. One must, however, remember that Fechner was writing before Broca and others had established that the two hemispheres appear to differ with regard to the representation of language. This asymmetry in the control of speech, originally established on the basis of clinical study, is beautifully illustrated in Sperry's work (Gazzaniga and Sperry, 1967). It is found that objects explored by active touch, or pictures or words exposed in the visual half-fields, can be named or described only when explored by the right hand or exposed in the right half-field. That is to say, expressive speech appears to be the prerogative of the left cerebral hemisphere. Although the right hemisphere does appear to possess limited powers of comprehension, its expressive capacities are extraordinarily limited. This is probably due to the left hemisphere possessing a virtual monopoly in control of the motor systems involved in linguistic expression, whether by speech or writing.

It has been argued by some critics, most notably Sir John Eccles (1965; 1973), that duplex processing does not necessarily imply duplex consciousness. Eccles has repeatedly stated that he regards the right hemisphere as a computer and its activities as devoid of consciousness. He argues first, that consciousness cannot be assumed in the absence of some form of symbolic communication; and secondly, that there is no evidence to suggest that the right hemisphere can, in and by itself, initiate voluntary activity. I have taken issue with Eccles elsewhere (Zangwill, 1974) and do not wish to repeat my arguments here. I may, however, perhaps remind you that it is possible for an adult to survive the loss of his entire left hemisphere without any apparent change in his level of consciousness. A patient that I was once able to study by courtesy of Dr Aaron Smith (1966; 1972), whose left hemisphere had been totally excised on account of an extensive and fast-growing cerebral tumour, was alert, co-operative, and fully responsive to all around him. In spite of severe aphasia, he could understand a good deal of what was said to him and was even able to sing a little! Emotional frustration was forcibly expressed by constant bad language. This patient was quite able to initiate voluntary movement of the non-paralysed parts of his body and even able to achieve a low-average score on a diagrammatic intelligence test. In view of facts of this kind, as well as the evidence assembled by Sperry and his co-workers as to the concurrence of unrelated perceptual events in the two disconnected hemispheres (Levy *et al.*, 1972), I think we can accept Fechner's argument that consciousness is linked with the waking activity of either or both cerebral hemispheres and that its unity normally depends upon the structural link between them. Eccles' argument, like that of McDougall, is little more than a desperate rearguard action to safeguard the existence and indivisibility of the soul.

III. Cerebral Dominance

I would now like to consider in rather more detail the implications of asymmetry in cerebral hemisphere function for issues in general psychology, with special reference to the differential effects of unilateral cerebral lesions. Traditionally, it has been supposed that one hemisphere, as a rule the left but occasionally the right, 'takes the lead' in the acquisition of language and manipulative skill. In consequence, aphasia and kindred disorders of speech are widely thought to result from lesions of the hemisphere contralateral to the preferred hand. This general relation between speech and handedness is crystallized in the phrase *cerebral dominance.*

A good deal of my own work over the years has been concerned with this question of cerebral dominance and its relation to handedness (Zangwill, 1960*a*; 1964*a*). While the correlation between right-handedness and left-brainedness (i.e. aphasia resulting from lesions of the left hemisphere) has not been seriously questioned, my own work and that of many others has cast considerable doubt upon the complementary correlation between left-handedness and right-brainedness (cf. Humphrey and Zangwill, 1952; Ettlinger *et al.*, 1956; Zangwill, 1960*a*). Indeed a majority of left-handers or those with mixed patterns of lateral preferences appear to develop aphasia from lesions not of the right hemisphere but of the left hemisphere. None the less, aphasia from lesions of the right hemisphere does appear to be more common among left-handers than among right-handers, suggesting that there is indeed some relation, if an obscure one, between handedness and the acquisition of speech. We are at present collecting information about aphasia from right-sided lesions as it presents in both right- and left-handed individuals which it is hoped may throw further light on this vexed problem.

Apart from handedness, however, there does seem to be evidence that the left hemisphere has particular relevance to the initiation of voluntary activity. Although it would be naive to try to locate the Will in either hemisphere, there seems little doubt that purposive motor activity proceeds for the most part under left hemisphere control. Indeed this is probably the reason why the general behaviour of the split-brain patient differs so little from that of the normal individual. It is also noteworthy that difficulty in demonstrating the use of common objects, which neurologists describe as *ideational apraxia* (Zangwill, 1960b), appears to be a syndrome of the dominant cerebral hemisphere. It may indeed be that cerebral dominance evolved in the first place in connexion with tool-using and manipulative skill and only secondarily in relation to the evolution of language.

Until recently, it was widely accepted that, apart from language, equivalent lesions of the two hemispheres produce identical patterns of disability. Here again, some of my own work has suggested that lesions of the right, or minor, hemisphere may give rise to psychological deficits rather different from those associated with comparable lesions of the dominant hemisphere. Paterson and I first stumbled on this possibility in our work on brain injuries during the last war (Paterson and Zangwill, 1944), though we did not at first perceive its full implications. By and large, posterior lesions of the right hemisphere are prone to give rise to striking disorders in visuo-spatial perception and in the execution of constructional tasks under visual control. These are both more marked, and qualitatively different from, somewhat similar perceptual deficits arising from lesions of the left hemisphere. In the first place, neglect of the left-hand side of visual space is often extremely prominent. And in the second place, there is a noteworthy failure in the analysis of spatial relationships, leading to gross breakdown on simple tests of copying, drawing and assembling mosaics (McFie *et al.*, 1950; Ettlinger *et al.*, 1956). In the case of left hemisphere lesions, on the other hand, difficulties on such tasks tend to arise from deficits in form or colour perception, from loss of knowledge or manual skill, and may involve a general defect in abstraction (McFie and Zangwill, 1960).

These observations have been greatly strengthened by the outcome of split-brain studies. Bogen, in particular, has reported that, at all events in the earlier post-operative stages, the patient cannot write with his left hand, as might indeed be expected, but neither can he draw nor copy with his right. For example, even though right-handed, the patient makes a much better shot at drawing a cube with his left hand than with his right (Bogen and Gazzaniga, 1965). Further, careful experiments by Levy *et al.*, (1972) have shown that if displays such as photographs of human faces or other complicated designs difficult to specify in words are shown to both hemispheres simultaneously and the patient required to respond by pointing to its duplicate in a multiple-choice array, the split-brain subject shows a marked predilection to react to the right hemisphere input. It is only if a verbal response is demanded that there is a shift to left hemisphere control. Moreover, the efficiency of visual discrimination is greater when input is processed by the right hemisphere than by the left. Unless verbal coding is essential, therefore, it seems likely that the right hemisphere typically takes the lead in processing complex visual information.

Even more interesting, perhaps, is the suggestion by Levy-Agresti and Sperry (1968) that the two hemispheres exhibit a characteristic difference in approach to visual tasks. In the case of the left hemisphere, the subject proceeds by sequential analysis of key features and makes obvious use of verbal coding. In the case of the right hemisphere, on the other hand, he proceeds by global impression displaying what used to be called synthetic rather than analytical perception. I suggested in my Sir Frederic Bartlett lecture three years ago (Zangwill, 1972) that these differences in strategy parallel closely those drawn by Bartlett (1932) between the vocalizer and the visualizer. Bartlett pointed out that, in remembering, vocalizers tend to rely largely on verbal analysis and are better than visualizers at retaining an order of presentation. Visualizers, on the other hand, tend to recall in more direct and pictorial a manner and make little use of verbal coding. From the point of view of accuracy, fortunately, neither method seems greatly superior to the other.

Vision is not the only sense which appears to bear a special relation to the activities of the right hemisphere. In her work at the Montreal Neurological Institute, Brenda Milner (1962) has reported significantly greater impairment in certain psycho-acoustic tasks, in particular the perception of tonal quality and pattern, in patients with right-sided than in those with left-sided temporal lobe excisions. In trained musicians, too, there is evidence to suggest that disorders of musical appreciation and performance occur surprisingly often with right-sided cerebral lesions. It seems possible therefore that the right hemisphere has a special role to play in a number of human accomplishments that do not call for linguistic sophistication.

In this brief and summary account of interhemispheric relations and cerebral dominance, I have limited myself almost exclusively to clinical studies as it is in these that my experience principally lies. I need not remind you, however, of the many and ingenious attempts that have been made in recent years to study these issues using experimental techniques such as dichotic listening and the differential measurement of perceptual efficiency in the right and left half-fields of vision (cf. Blakemore *et al.*, 1972). These studies have in general borne out the findings of clinical observation and are helping us to understand their nature; not least, the role of each hemisphere respectively in directing and sustaining attention. Mention, too, should be made of attempts to study hemispheric asymmetries by means of physiological techniques, such as electroencephalography. In spite of the many hazards that enter into such experiments and the wide range of individual differences in results, we see in such work a promise that Fechner's inner psychophysics may yet become a reality.

IV. Thought and Language

So far, we have considered relatively low-level psychological performance, e.g. perception, discrimination and motor skill, in relation to the duplex organization of the brain. But what of the higher mental processes? What of intelligence, problem-solving and thought? Here, too, I think an approach from the neurological standpoint is not without its promise. Let us consider first the activities of the left hemisphere which, as we have seen, are closely related to the acquisition and use of language and which many people have supposed to bear an important relation to conceptual thought.

In the study of aphasia, there has been a good deal of disagreement as to whether intellectual capacity is or is not primarily affected. As we know, most aphasics are capable of exercising adequate judgement in practical matters, and, as Weisenberg and McBride (1935) were the first to demonstrate, intelligence as measured by appropriate non-verbal methods may remain at a relatively high level. None the less, I do not think it possible to maintain that in aphasia only language is impaired; thinking, too, is appreciably affected. For example, aphasic patients are apt to experience great difficulty in what I have called the understanding and explanation of overall meaning (Zangwill, 1964b). If, for example, a patient whose speech disorder is only minimal is asked to explain, say, a simple proverb, he will frequently repeat it over and over again and evidently accepts it as entirely familiar. Yet he finds himself totally unable to find other words in which to express its meaning. Other patients, particularly those with left frontal lobe lesions, find difficulty in initiating conversation and seem to lack verbal fluency, not only in retrieval of words but of ideas as well. This Alexander Luria (1968) has described as 'dynamic aphasia'. I have noticed that such patients often do very badly on Liam Hudson's tests of divergent thinking (Hudson, 1966), suggesting that the patient's thought has become more stereotyped, less productive and less original. Such limitations in thought are seldom seen with lesions of the right hemisphere, suggesting that the left is specialized not only for language in the narrower sense, but also for those thought processes which find expression in linguistic form (Zangwill, 1966).

This conclusion is borne out, to some extent at least, by studies of recovery from aphasia in intelligent and well-educated subjects. Elvin and Oldfield (1951), for example, charted the progress of a university history student rendered dysphasic by a war wound of the brain. They analysed in great detail a series of tutorial essays covering the whole period of this student's university career. By and large, consistent progress was made in both form and content. First, words, and in particular prepositions, were increasingly less often misused. Secondly, 'over-general' words, e.g. 'things', gradually dropped out and expression became progressively more precise. And thirdly, the capacity to express ideas clearly and logically improved continuously. Whereas at first ideas were often 'telescoped' and the subject was apt unwittingly to change his viewpoint in expounding his argument, his later essays were well organized in content and satisfactory in style. Although it is difficult to disentangle the effects of education from those of natural recovery, it certainly appeared that in this young man improvement in formal composition proceeded *pari passu* with improvement in the organization and logical structure of his thinking.

Not surprisingly, the effects of aphasia on creative writing are catastrophic. Baudelaire is a characteristic example. Whereas several painters and even a few composers have been able to continue their work in spite of strokes causing serious damage to the left hemisphere, I know of no case of a writer similarly fortunate. Indeed, at a more mundane level, the after-effects of aphasia are always more serious for people such as secretaries and journalists than for those whose occupations are primarily technical. The indispensable instrument of the writer is not so much the pen as the left cerebral hemisphere.

V. Visual Thinking

What of the right cerebral hemisphere? I have already pointed out that lesions of its posterior portions are apt to produce marked defects in visuo-motor skill. In attenuated form, such defects may persist indefinitely, as Freda Newcombe (1969) has shown in a careful follow-up study of patients with circumscribed war wounds of the brain. But right hemisphere lesions may do more than impair perception; they may, if less constantly, produce appreciable handicap in visual recognition, particularly of faces and places, and in visual memory. Some patients report that their visual imagery has become faint and sketchy and others remark that they have ceased to dream (Humphrey and Zangwill, 1951). Even the illusion of *déjà vu* seems to bear a statistically significant relation to epileptogenic lesions of the right temporal lobe (Cole and Zangwill, 1963).

There is thus *prima facie* evidence that the right hemisphere has an important part to play in what might loosely be called visual thinking. The impoverishment of visual imagery and the cessation of dreaming suggest, perhaps, a deficiency in the kind of thinking commonly described as imagination or fantasy and regarded by Freud as the primary process of thought, closely related to unconscious activity. But visual thinking is also involved in many high-level conscious activities, as, for example, the soluuon of diagrammatic intelligence tests. Although Newcombe was unable to ascertain any significant difference in score on Raven's Matrices as between men who had sustained unilateral lesions of either the right or the left hemisphere, many other studies have given evidence of a singificant inferiority of the right-hemisphere cases (Piercy and Smyth, 1962). It is also of some interest to note that, in Aaron Smith's studies of hemispherectomy, all three of his patients with right-sided hemisphere excision performed excessively poorly on this test. Only the patient with a left hemisphere excision managed to achieve a score within the low average range.

At the risk of being somewhat speculative, I have often been led to wonder whether, in the kind of problem-solving which proceeds by what used to be called insight, the right hemisphere may not play a predominant role. This kind of thinking has no need of language, as Köhler (1925) so brilliantly demonstrated in his early work on the mentality of apes. As you will remember, the problems he set his chimpanzees were essentially visual problems, using tools and overcoming obstacles, in which what he described as a restructuring of the field was essential to their solution. In spite of Washoe and other recent stars of the primate firmament, would it be wholly facile to suppose that the chimpanzee has in effect two right hemispheres?

In man, the development of propositional language renders the kind of thinking exemplified by Köhler's apes difficult to demonstrate, except perhaps in the split-brain patient. None the less, insight is not a bad way of describing what goes on when one suddenly sees the point of a humorous drawing or political cartoon. It also describes well the solution of puzzle-pictures, such as the 'Horse-and-Rider' problem used by Bartlett (1957) as an example of one-step problem-solving.

In this connexion, I may add that Bartlett himself called attention to the somewhat idiosyncratic thinking of creative artists, apparently so different from the 'closed system' variety of thinking characteristic of scientists and logicians and so favourite a subject of study in the psychological laboratory. 'There have indeed', wrote Barlett, 'been persons who apparently wish to maintain that certain sorts of artists, especially those whose proper medium is colour, forms, shape and tone - painters and musicians - do not think at all' (1957, p. 187). Perhaps it would be fairer to say that artists and musicians think, but that their thinking differs in important respects from that of the scientist or engineer.

Can neurology throw any light on this matter? As I have said, the painter, unlike the writer or poet, is often able to maintain his work at a high level in spite of severe aphasia, often complicated by an enforced change of handedness. This might suggest that the right hemisphere is critically implicated in artistic endeavour. On the other hand, the effect of a right hemisphere lesion on the work of professional artists does not appear anything like as crippling as one might have anticipated. Professor Richard Jung, of Freiburg, who has made a special study of painters who have sustained right-sided strokes, notes only a striking and on occasion persistent neglect of the right half of the canvas - that is to say, of the part of the painting to the artist's left. There may also be certain changes in technique and manner of execution, probably in part compensatory (cf. Gardner, 1975). It would seem, therefore, that the right hemisphere is by no means as vital to artistic expression as is the left to literary creation.

One recent author, Robert Ornstein (1972), has made large claims on behalf of the right hemisphere as the seat of intuition as opposed to analytical thought. He claims that Western culture, with its stress on logic and literacy, has done much to damp down a whole world of intuitive and mystical experience.

While I am fully prepared to admit, with Ornstein, that the disconnected right hemisphere of the split-brain patient reacts to visual input in a global, quasi-intuitive manner, and even that the right hemisphere of a normal individual may well be the leading hemisphere in visual and spatial thinking, I can see no reason to link the activities of this hemisphere in any exclusive way with the manifestations of transcendental meditation or other altered states of consciousness. While it is of course possible that the right hemisphere is specially concerned in such activities, it is equally concerned in such typical manifestations of Western culture as the reading of maps and circuit diagrams, the design of architectural plans and the lay-out of aircraft instrument panels. Let us, therefore, be wary of an updated phrenology that seeks to provide a scientific justification for some, to me at least, irrational and disturbing trends in modern thought. Albeit mute, the right hemisphere is neither less nor more rational than its articulate fellow.

VI. Developmental Disorders

The differences between the effects of right and left hemisphere lesions in the adult find a certain parallel in the developmental handicaps not uncommonly encountered in schoolchildren. On the one hand, we see children with marked and often rather selective backwardness in learning to read and spell. Such children, who are often referred to as dyslexic, have as a rule been rather slow in learning to talk and tend to score very much more poorly on verbal than on non-verbal intelligence tests. On the other hand, we have children whose level of verbal ability is consistently superior to the non-verbal and who show marked disability in spatial perception and manipulative skill. One inquiry which we undertook in Cambridge schools some years ago (Brenner *et al.*, 1967), and in which over 800 children were tested, disclosed that roughly 3 per cent of the children gave evidence of a discrepancy of at least two S.D.s between their scores on a visual - spatial test battery and on a standard verbal intelligence test. Such children are typically awkward and clumsy and often in trouble on this account. Their mothers tell one that they were slow to learn to do up buttons or tie their shoelaces. At school, their handwriting is badly formed and uneven and their sums poorly set out, leading to frequent mistakes in simple arithmetic. They draw badly and are abysmally poor at such activities as carpentry or needlework. Worst of all for schoolboy prestige, they are singularly inept at ball games.

I do not wish to suggest that these patterns necessarily result from brain injury, though in some cases they evidently do. Even in the latter, however, we do not necessarily find that the pattern of disability corresponds strictly to a lesion of one or other hemisphere. The plasticity of the child's brain, and the fact that the brain damage was sustained before linguistic or visuo-motor skills had been acquired, renders the position very different from what is found in the brain-injured adult.

Perhaps I should say a word or two more about dyslexia, if only in view of the controversy which any mention of this term is liable to arouse. In the first place, it is important to bear in mind that, even in cases in which no definite evidence of brain damage can be elicited, the difficulties often resemble closely what is found in organic conditions (cf. Critchley, 1964). For example, these children have obvious difficulty in retaining serial order, a factor which, when taken together with poor rote learning, evidently contributes to the quite excessive difficulty in learning to spell (Doehring, 1968). In the second place, a family history of language backwardness is not uncommon, as also a familial history of left-handedness (Zangwill, 1960a). These factors, together with the tendency to reversals in reading and spelling, and sometimes to right-to-left ocular scanning (Blakemore and Zangwill, 1972), make one wonder whether a constitutional failure to establish cerebral dominance may not play some part in the condition. Whatever its ultimate nature, however, I would plead in the strongest terms that developmental disorders be approached within the general framework of paediatric neurology and genetics and that their existence, even when relatively mild, be taken seriously by psychologists, especially those whose special concern lies in education. There is no truth in the innuendo that dyslexia is a 'middle class disease', a mere name thought up by ambitious parents to disguise the stupidity or indolence of their offspring. Dyslexia may affect children, above all boys, of all classes and all levels of intelligence. It merits understanding and compassion, and above all research into its causes and remedial management at home and at school.

VII. Is There a Take-Over?

Is an approach to psychology such as I have outlined in the best interests of the subject? Do we really need to consider the brain in our attempts to explain human behaviour? These are questions which have long proved controversial. G.F. Stout reminded us in the first chapter of his *Manual of Psychology* that, had it not been for the anatomists, 'Conscious individuals might have thought, felt, willed and known about themselves without ever supposing that they had brains at all' (Stout, 1924, p. 17). In this, if only in this, Freud might well have agreed with him. Although everyone today knows that he has a brain, and few would deny that it has something to do with how he thinks, feels, wills and knows about himself, psychologists still disagree as to the relevance of physiology to their subject.

This rather central issue has recently been brought to the fore by Dr R.B. Joynson, a distinguished member of the Psychology Department at Nottingham University. In two papers published in our *Bulletin* (Joynson, 1970; 1972), followed by a short book (Joynson, 1974), this author has expressed his concern about a number of trends in contemporary psychology, not least the tendency to seek a coalescence between neurology and psychology, as advocated by the late Karl Lashley (1941) and echoed on occasion by myself. Although Joynson has no wish to deny that the relations between neurology and psychology should be close, he considers that it behoves those who are keen to foster it to provide a clear and positive indication of the role of psychology in any such alliance. 'In particular', he asks, 'does Zangwill have any workable conception of a psychological explanation as something in any way different from a physiological explanation?' Unless he does, Joynson concludes, the conception of a unified scientific discipline appears no more than a means of concealing the disappearance of psychology.

I am no philosopher and have no wish to get embroiled with the mind-body problem. But Joynson has offered a clear challenge and it is incumbent upon me to try to meet it. First, I should like to say what I understand by a physiological explanation: It is an explanation put forward by physiologists, whose discipline is traditionally concerned with the physical activities of the body. In so far as it has concerned itself with the nervous system, it has, in my view quite properly, resolutely set its face against explanation in terms of vital forces or psychical powers. In this connexion, one must bear in mind that the concept of a 'spinal cord soul' persisted right up to the end of the last century and that the notion of 'higher brain centres', which still finds a place in physiological texts, is an odd amalgam of physiological and psychological thinking (Zangwill, 1971). Given this background, it is hardly surprising that modern physiologists have adopted Cartesian dualism as their working philosophy and have been wary of dabbling in the realm of mind.

But today there are signs that the scene is changing. No longer do neurophysiologists confine their studies to the intimate biophysics of nervous transmission or to the electrical activities of single units. In studies of the central nervous system, more particularly those concerned with the functions of the hypothalamus, the limbic system and the cerebral cortex, the neurophysiologist is becoming increasingly involved in behavioural issues. And far from displacing the psychologist, he is increasingly welcomed as an essential partner. The psychologist brings to neurobiology not only the techniques of comparative psychology but also a body of thinking concerned with the nature of appetite, emotion, motivation and learning with which the physiologist is in general ill acquainted. Indeed there are already signs that theory in neurobiology is becoming a great deal more sophisticated than it once was and increasingly ready to embody what have traditionally been viewed as psychological modes of explanation.

I thus came to Joynson's central question. Do I have any workable conception of a psychological explanation as something in any way different from a physiological explanation? My answer can only be that I regard a psychological explanation as one which purports to account for the behaviour of an organism as a whole in its transactions with the environment. As I see it, the central nervous system is organized on a hierarchical basis and no clear-cut distinction can be drawn between those of its activities which are associated with consciousness and those which are not. Reflex adjustments merge into habitual reactions; habitual reactions into motor skills; motor skills into productive thinking. Psychology, moreover, unlike physiology, is intimately concerned with the issues of development. As J.B. Watson once put it: 'The physiologist *qua* physiologist knows nothing of the total situations in the daily life of an individual that shape his action and conduct. He may teach us all there is to know about the mechanism of stepping, but it is not his task to determine whether man walks before he crawls' (Watson, 1929, p. 20).

As I see it, then, a psychological explanation is one concerned with the development, organization and control of human behaviour. It should proceed - and here I believe I follow Fechner - in a manner consistent with our knowledge of the body and brain and loyal to the methods of the natural sciences. If so envisaged, I have no fear of that breakdown of modern psychology which Joynson so gloomily prognosticates. Let me end by citing the three closing words of Kenneth Craik's brilliant essay on *The Nature of Explanation* (1943), written in the darkest days of the last war when very much more than psychology seemed in imminent danger of dissolution. 'And so', wrote Craik, '*tentare*'.

References

Bartlett, F.C. (1932). *Remembering.* London: Cambridge University Press.
Bartlett, F.C. (1957). *Thinking: An Experimental and Social Study.* London: Allen & Unwin.
Blakemore, C.B., Iversen, S.D. and Zangwill, O.L. (1972). Brain functions. *Annual Review of Psychology,* 23, 413-456.
Blakemore, C.B. and Zangwill, O.L. (1972). Dyslexia: reversal of eye movements during reading. *Neuropsychologia,* 10, 371-373.
Bogen, J.E. and Gazzaniga, M.S. (1965). Cerebral commissurotomy in man: minor hemisphere dominance for certain spatial functions. *Journal of Neurosurgery,* 23, 394-399.
Boring, E.G. (1929). *A History of Experimental Psychology.* New York: Century.
Brenner, N.W., Gillman, S., Farrell, M. and Zangwill, O.L. (1967). Visuo-motor disability in schoolchildren. *British Medical Journal,* iv, 259-262.
Cohen, J. (1970). *Homo Psychologicus.* London: Allen & Unwin.
Cole, M. and Zangwill, O.L. (1963). Déjà vu in temporal lobe epilepsy. *Journal of Neurology, Neurosurgery and Psychiatry,* 26, 37.
Craik, K.J.W. (1943). *The Nature of Explanation.* London: Cambridge University Press.
Critchley, M. (1964). *Developmental Dyslexia.* London: Heinemann.
Doehring, D.G. (1968). *Patterns of Impairment in Specific Reading Disability.* Bloomington: Indiana University Press.
Eccles, J.C. (1965). *The Brain and the Unity of Conscious Experience.* Nineteenth Eddington Memorial Lecture. London: Cambridge University Press.
Eccles, J.C. (1973). *The Understanding of the Brain.* New York: McGraw-Hill.
Elvin, M.B. and Oldfield, R.C. (1951). Disabilities and progress of a dysphasic university student. *Journal of Neurology, Neurosurgery and Psychiatry,* 14, 118-128.
Ettlinger, G., Jackson, C.V. and Zangwill, O.L. (1956). Cerebral dominance in sinistrals. *Brain,* 79, 569-588.
Ettlinger, G., Warrington, E. and Zangwill, O.L. (1956). A further study of visual-spatial agnosia. *Brain,* 80, 335-361.
Fechner, G.T. (1860). *Elemente der Psychophysik,* Vol. 2. Leipzig: Breitkopf & Härtel.
Gardner, H. (1975). *The Shattered Mind: The Person after Brain Damage.* New York: Alfred A. Knopf.
Gazzaniga, M.S. and Sperry, R.W. (1967). Language after section of the cerebral commissures. *Brain,* 90, 131-148.
Hartmann, E. von (1931) *Philosophy of the Unconscious: Speculative Results According to the Inductive Method of Physical Science.* London: Kegan Paul, Trench & Trubner.
Hudson, L. (1966). *Contrary Imaginations.* London: Methuen.
Humphrey, M.E. and Zangwill, O.L. (1951). Cessation of dreaming after brain injury. *Journal of Neurology, Neurosurgery and Psychiatry,* 14, 322-325.
Humphrey, M.E. and Zangwill, O.L. (1952). Dysplasia in left-handed patients with unilateral brain lesions. *Journal of Neurology, Neurosurgery and Psychiatry,* 15, 184-193.
James, W. (1890). *Principles of Psychology,* Vol. 2. London: Macmillan.
Joynson, R.B. (1970). The breakdown of modern psychology. *Bulletin of the British Psychological Society,* 23, 261-269.
Joynson, R.B. (1972). The return of mind. *Bulletin of the British Psychological Society,* 25, 1-10.

Joynson, R.B. (1974). *Psychology and Common Sense*. London: Routledge & Kegan Paul.
Köhler, W. (1925). *The Mentality of Apes*. Translated by E. Winter. New York: Harcourt Brace.
Lashley, K.S. (1941). Coalescence of neurology and psychology. *Proceedings of the American Philosophical Society*, 84, 461-470.
Levy-Agresti, J. and Sperry, R.W. (1968). Differential perceptual capacities in major and minor hemispheres. *Proceedings of the National Academy of Sciences, U.S.A.*, 61, 1151.
Levy, J., Trevarthen, C. and Sperry, R.W. (1972). Perception of bilateral chimeric figures following hemispheric deconnection. *Brain*, 95, 61-78.
Lauria, A.R. (1968). The mechanism of 'dynamic aphasia'. *Foundations of Language*, 4, 296-307.
McDougall, W. (1911). *Body and Mind*. London: Methuen.
McFie, J., Piercy, M.F. and Zangwill, O.L. (1950). Visual-spatial agnosia associated with lesions of the right cerebral hemisphere. *Brain*, 73, 167-190.
McFie, J. and Zangwill, O.L. (1960). Visuo-constructive disorders associated with lesions of the left parietal lobe. *Brain*, 83, 243-260.
Milner, B. (1962). Laterality effects in audition. In *Interhemispheric Relations and Cerebral Dominance*, edited by V.B. Mountcastle. Baltimore: Johns Hopkins Press, pp. 177-195.
Newcombe, F. (1969). *Missile Wounds of the Brain: A Study of Psychological Deficits*. London: Oxford University Press.
Ornstein, R. (1972). *The Psychology of Consciousness*. San Francisco: W.H. Freeman.
Paterson, A. and Zangwill, O.L. (1944). Disorders of visual perception associated with lesions of the right cerebral hemisphere. *Brain*, 67, 331-358.
Piercy, M.F. and Smyth, V.O.G. (1962). Right hemisphere dominance for certain non-verbal intellectual skills. *Brain*, 85, 775-790.
Piéron, H. (1923). *Le Cerveau et la Pensée*. Translated by C.K. Ogden. *Thought and the Brain*. 1927. London: Kegan Paul, Trench & Trubner.
Smith, A. (1966). Speech and other functions after left (dominant) hemispherectomy. *Journal of Neurology, Neurosurgery and Psychiatry*, 29, 467-471.
Smith, A. (1972). Dominant and non-dominant hemispherectomy. In *Drugs, Development and Cerebral Function*, edited by W.L. Smith. Springfield, Illinois: Thomas.
Sperry, R.W., Gazzaniga, M.S. and Bogen, J.E. (1969). Interhemispheric relationships: the neocortical syndromes and hemisphere disconnection. In *Handbook of Clinical Neurology*, Vol. 4, edited by P.H. Vinken and G.W. Bruyn. Amsterdam: North Holland.
Stout, G.F. (1924). *A Manual of Psychology*. Third edition. London: University Tutorial Press.
Watson, J.B. (1929). *Psychology from the Standpoint of a Behaviorist*. Third edition, revised. Philadelphia: Lippincott.
Weisenberg, T and McBridge, K.E. (1935). *Aphasia: A Clinical and Psychological Study*. New York: The Commonwealth Fund.
Zangwill, O.L. (1960a). *Cerebral Dominance and its Relation to Psychological Function*. Henderson Trust Lecture No. 19. Edinburgh: Oliver & Boyd.
Zangwill, O.L. (1960b). Le problème d'apraxie idéatoire. *Revue Neurologique*, 102, 596-603.
Zangwill, O.L. (1961). Asymmetry of cerebral hemisphere function. In *Scientific Aspects of Neurology*, edited by H. Garland, pp. 51-62. Edinburgh: Livingstone.

Zangwill, O.L. (1964a). The current status of cerebral dominance. *Proceedings of the Association of Research into Nervous and Mental Diseases,* **42**, 103-118.
Zangwill, O.L. (1964b). Intelligence in aphasia. In *Disorders of Language,* edited by A.V.S. de Reuck and M. O'Connor, pp. 261-274. London: Churchill.
Zangwill, O.L. (1966). Psychological deficits associated with frontal lobe lesions. *International Journal of Neurology,* **2**, 395-402.
Zangwill, O.L. (1971). Diagram-makers old and new. *Totus Homo, Rome,* **3**, 53-58.
Zangwill, O.L. (1972). 'Remembering' re-visited. Third Sir Frederic Bartlett Lecture. *Quarterly Journal of Experimental Psychology,* **24**, 123-138.
Zangwill, O.L. (1974). Consciousness and the cerebral hemisphere. In *Hemisphere Function in the Human Brain,* edited by S.J. Dimond and J.G. Beaumont, pp. 264-278. London: Elek Scientific Books.

13

GENETICS AND EDUCABILITY*

J.M. Thoday

Everyone is educable; the blind can be taught to read, the deaf can be taught to speak, those without legs can be taught to walk. Everyone can profit from an education appropriate to his needs, and, in so far as we are able, we should be giving everyone such an education. These things are axiomatic. But they do not in any way imply that each of us could profit equally from the same given educational environment, for we are all different, each of us is unique genetically, as well as in environmental history. Hence, our needs may differ.

It is my contention that we shall not approach the ideal of giving each an education appropriate to his needs unless we frankly recognize that there are important genetic as well as environmental causes of human variety, and frankly discuss the implications of this genetic variety in relation to our concepts of the various functions of the educational process.

This I propose to try to do, briefly, in this paper, in which though it is in no way intended to be a black paper, I shall try to call spades spades whenever the facts or logic seem to me to require this, and I shall not mind if I offend some of those whose minds are for any reason closed on unresolved issues.

First, I must say something about the meaning of statements about people. We make such statements in reference to particular attributes of people, which are therefore always abstractions, and such statements are always comparative. The statement 'This man is tall' is an abstraction in that it refers only to the man's stature. It is comparative in that it says nothing about the man's stature except that it is greater than that of some other man or men. We often confuse ourselves about this by using words like 'tallness', 'intelligence', 'character' or 'trait' which tend to seduce us into thinking we are saying something about the character of a man in isolation. But whatever we say about a man is in fact a comparative statement expressing his differences from some other men (or women), unless our statement refers to some attributes of all men, in which case our statement is comparing men with apes or monkeys, fish, broad beans or pebbles on the beach.

* Paper read at the 21st anniversary meeting of the Institute of Biology, 31 March 1971.

Statements about the genetic or environmental causes of human attributes, such as stature or educability, are therefore statements about the causes of differences between individuals or groups of individuals. They are not statements about those individuals or groups themselves in isolation.

Further we should realize that, however resounding they may seem, and however politically effective they may be, most statements about *everyone* are not only abstractions but are also trivial. I begin with such a trivial statement 'Everyone is educable'. All it means, of course, is that you can teach everyone something, which is just as true of dogs or squids or flatworms. Everyone *is* educable. But the problems we have to face arise from the fact that in particular respects people differ in their educability.

Second, I must say something about causes of variation in educability and spell out as best I can the meaning and use of that grossly misunderstood concept 'heritability'.

When a new human being starts existence as a zygote it has a range of potentialities determined by its unique set of genes. It also already has a unique environment, which is provided by its mother and is affected by its mother's unique genotype and unique history. By the time it is born, a child will have been affected by that environment so that differences between individuals at birth are not only a consequence of genetic variation, but may have been contributed to by environmental factors, some of them themselves genetic, others determined by the mother's reaction to her conditions perhaps even long before the child itself was conceived.

I am surprised how seldom one comes across clear recognition of this, for there is no formal objection to the argument that differential nutritional conditions in different socio-economic groups in the 1930s may have affected, say, the IQs of the descendants of these people now.

However, such formal arguments are of use only for political or heuristic purposes. Humans like other animals are homeostatic, and can in some measure compensate for the consequences of early disturbances of development especially if conditions improve later. Such formal statements are therefore statements only of what *might be* the causes of things. Truly informative statements have to be quantitative, assessing the *relative* effects of different causes. It is for this reason that the concept 'heritability' is of importance to the present topic, for a heritability estimate is a statement about the relative importance of two sets of causes of variation in the circumstances in which that estimate was obtained.

Heritability estimates for human variables in particular populations may be obtained in many ways, from correlations with degree of biological relationship compared with the theoretical genetic correlations, from twin studies, from studies of adopted children, studies of children reared in orphanages, and so on. The derivation of such estimates, and the limitations and assumptions involved in each kind of estimate are complex matters, which I do not propose to consider, except to point out that there must be general agreement between the estimates derived from independent means if we are to place any weight on these estimates.

We must, however, consider much more carefully what a heritability estimate means when we have obtained one. It is here that there is much confusion.

I will discuss the meaning of heritability in relation to the psychometric variable 'performance in IQ tests' without for the moment considering the relevance of IQ score to educability, because IQ has been extensively studied and there is general agreement that, in the European and white American populations in which those studies have been made, the heritability of IQ variation is very high, of the order of 70% or so.

Now such an estimate only means that in the population studied, averaged over all the individuals studied, the environmental differences that actually affected the population account for about 30% of the variety in the population, the remainder being accounted for by the relevant genetic variety in that population.

Such an estimate, therefore, says nothing about any particular individuals in that population, says nothing about any other populations, and says nothing about the relevance of genetic or environmental differences in the causation of differences between that population and any other, as for example between racial groups. Furthermore, the same level of heritability can result from environmental factors of large effect that act upon a small proportion of the population or from the action of a large number of factors each of small effect, provided that unfavourable factors affecting the lower half of the distribution are more or less balanced by favourable factors affecting the upper half, for otherwise the distribution would not be approximately symmetrical. (This is true even if the symmetry of the distribution is mathematically imposed by scaling, because the genetic or environmental effects measured are effects on the relevant scale.)

Thus quite a high heritability is perfectly consistent with the concept that some individuals have been affected by distinctly unfavourable environments. A high heritability does not tell us that environmental modifications could have little effect on individual phenotypes.

What then does heritability tell us?

The measure was first invented to enable the prediction of responses to natural or artificial selection in animal and plant breeding. Though this sort of prediction must concern us with respect to the consequences for future generations of correlations between fertility and measures related to educability, the use of heritability for this purpose is of marginal concern to the present topic.

Heritability estimates, however, have something to tell us about the consequences that might result from manipulation of environmental factors that now affect our population. To illustrate this I have drawn up two tables showing what we might expect if we were able to manipulate environments - (1) so as to give everyone the most favourable of *present environments*, from this (and only this) point of view, or (2) so as to provide compensating environments such that those now most favoured would be given the least favourable and those now most deprived would be given the most favourable of the *present environments*.

In looking at these figures we should bear in mind that the best estimates of IQ heritability we have, which are for European and American white populations *and these only*, are around 0.7 or 70%, or 80% if we correct for measurement error.

Effect that the most favourable existing environments would have had on the IQ means of samples whose present IQ is given, with different heritabilities

Heritability %	\multicolumn{7}{c}{Present IQ}
	70	80	90	100	110	120	130
100	70	80	90	100	110	120	130
80	82	90	98	106	114	122	130
50	100	105	110	115	120	125	130
20	118	120	122	124	126	128	130
0	130	130	130	130	130	130	130

TABLE 1

Effect of compensating environments with varying present heritabilities

Heritability %	\multicolumn{7}{c}{Present IQ}
	70	80	90	100	110	120	130
100	70	80	90	100	110	120	130
80	82	88	94	100	106	112	118
50	100	100	100	100	100	100	100
20	118	112	106	100	94	88	82
0	130	120	110	100	90	80	70

TABLE 2

The tables assume that environmental and genetic deviations are correlated. The results differ considerably from those to be read from the relevant distributions given by Jensen (1969).

These two tables are not to be regarded as anything but grossly oversimplified models which ignore important possibilities. But I hope they serve to illustrate two basic points. First, unless heritability is virtually 100%, improving the environment by manipulating the features that at present vary can have important effects. Second, fully compensating environments would only have egalitarian consequences if heritability were exactly 50%, and then, of course, they would ensure that there would be no individuals with high IQs, which I doubt would be desirable.

The tables do not illustrate other points.

First, even if heritability is 100% *new* environmental factors may be found that are effective. This is obvious, for heritability only measures the relation between existing genetic and existing environmental variance. It tells us nothing about the possible effects of new environments. Thus the finding that heritability of IQ is high has no implications whatever concerning the possibility of boosting the attributes that are measured by IQ tests through the use of new techniques, educational and otherwise. This points to possible sources of failure of 'head start' programmes which tended merely to use old techniques on new people.

Second, the tables ignore the possibility of genotype - environment interaction (see Thoday, 1965). There is genotype - environment interaction if a given genetic difference differs in its effect in different environments. The most recent available analysis of IQ data (Jinks and Fulker, 1970) suggests that genotype - environment interaction components of IQ variance are small. But for two reasons this does not mean that such interaction components are small for educability. For one thing IQ is only a partial measure of particular kinds of educability. For another the techniques for detecting such interaction will only detect some rather systematic kinds of interaction. Practising educationalists of course are well aware of individual interaction with educational processes especially in respect to the fact that some children will progress faster if pushed harder, whereas others will progress slower or even regress. Some need to be pushed. Others need *not* to be pushed.

Third, is a point that needs repeating again and again. Heritability estimates cannot be applied to populations different from those from which they were obtained. Neither can heritability estimates obtained from within populations be applied to between-population differences.

Thus if we take the pair of populations whose IQ differences are most extensively discussed, US Negroes and US Whites, the high heritability of IQ in US Whites tells us nothing about its heritability in US Negroes. Neither does it tell us anything about the causes of the difference in average IQ between these two populations.

Incidentally, on the same grounds, such knowledge of American Negroes as we have must not be applied to Africans. Extrapolation from one Negro population to another is as unjustifiable as any other assumption about people made on the basis of their racial classification rather than their individual attributes.

Such extrapolations from population to population are illegitimate because the gene frequencies of the population may differ and the environments, cultural and physical, differ. We are nevertheless very prone to make such extrapolations. A nice illustration of their dangers is provided by the XYY sex chromosome situation. As everyone knows by now, XYY males have been found in higher frequency in British maximum security prisons than in samples of male children. There is some doubt about the statistical validity of this finding, but, if it finally proves sound, it implies that our XYY males have a slightly higher probability of behaving in such a way that they end up in such prisons. Some might express this in a general sense by saying that XYYs tend to criminal behaviour. But of course this statement *must* be qualified by specification of its limitation to the particular social environment in which the finding has been made. If this qualified statement proves true our educational system needs altering so that special conditions are created for XYY individuals to ensure that they are less at risk.

I said a moment ago that knowledge of the heritability of a variable within a population can tell us nothing about the differences between populations. And I have spelt out elsewhere (Thoday, 1969) the reasons that make it clear that when the populations differ in obvious visible racial attributes such as skin colour as for most US Negroes and Whites, present techniques make it impossible to discover whether the average difference between the populations in a behaviour variable is all genetic or all cultural or any mixture of the two. We must face up to the implications of our ignorance in this respect.

The implication of this ignorance is that we must *not* implement policies whose justification derives solely from one extreme hypothesis unless it is clear that if that hypothesis is wrong there will not be harmful effects. It is for this reason that I and those who think like me get disturbed at the frequency with which discussions of educational policy with respect to race and class differences are based on extreme environmentalist assumptions.

I take an extreme example from the writings of the sociologists Davis and Havighurst, who wrote (1948) 'any difference between the average response of different cultural groups to a mental problem may be attributed to their unlike cultures. Therefore, all problems that show socio-economic differences in performance should be ruled out of the tests as unfair'.

Genetics and Educability 215

Now I will leave aside the matter that fairness and unfairness is not an attribute of tests themselves but of the uses to which test results are put. The quotation makes two points. It is the first of these that seems to me to have dangerous implications.

It is of course true that differences between average responses of different cultural groups *may* be attributed to their unlike cultures. But it is equally true that such differences *may* be attributed to differing gene frequencies.

As I have already pointed out, with respect to ethnic groups we cannot know how much either is true. With respect to socio-economic groups we do not know, though the correlation of IQ and social mobility (Gibson, 1970) must lead us to expect some part to be genetic (see Thoday and Gibson, 1970).

Let us then ask what the consequences of extreme environmentalist assumptions might be if it so happened that these assumptions are wrong.

Extreme environmentalist assumptions lead to the concept that it is unfair if different groups prove to have different average success in any educational process, and hence lead to pressure that the educational system be so geared that each cultural group becomes represented according to its proportionate numbers whether in grammar schools, universities, or among first, second and third classes in degree examinations in any subject. Such pressures are already with us and are reported to be very strong in some American universities.

Supposing, however, that part of the difference between some cultural groups in particular aspects of educability are in fact genetic, this sort of treatment can only ultimately mean that the standard of performance required of different groups will come to differ. Then we are taking an enormous risk because employers will rapidly discover that, for example, a first class degree held by a member of one group is worth less or more than that held by a member of another group. Members of the group whose degrees thus become to be held in low esteem will have had aspirations raised that must inevitably lead to disappointment and even to an acuter sense of injustice than we have known before. And these aspirations will have been raised and disappointed, not because of the merits of the individual himself, but because once again the individual has been treated in a particular way because of his membership of a race or class.

Thus the extreme environmentalist assumption provides no solution to class or race problems unless that assumption be wholly and exclusively true, and if it be not true it is likely to exacerbate those very problems it is designed to deal with.

I am of course aware that many of those who hold extreme environmentalist assumptions argue that it is legitimate to hold them as true unless and until others prove that they are untrue. This is of course an old technique, to which Herbert Spencer drew attention in 1852 when he wrote '... the majority of men who are born to a given belief ... demand the most rigorous proof of any adverse belief, but assume that their own needs none'. I would merely point out that this attitude can provide no excuse for those who take it, if the policies they promote prove to have the unfortunate consequences to which I have drawn attention.

In concluding this section on the meaning and limitations of heritability estimates, I want to make it quite clear that nothing I have said should be construed as an argument against attempts to improve the environment, educational or otherwise, of cultural groups who live in conditions we have reason to believe may be disadvantageous. Such attempts should of course be made. But they should not be made on the basis of *a priori* assumptions that will provoke disappointment and the sense of injustice if the attempts are not 100% successful. Within any group there is a wide variety of potential talents and a great deal of this variety is genetic. But we have no reason to believe that all groups have precisely the same distribution of such talents. At the same time we have every reason to believe that all groups overlap in their distributions of such talents. For example 30% of US Negroes perform better than the average US White in IQ tests. The wide distribution of talents within groups means that our basic aim must be to promote the development of the talents of individuals regardless of the groups from which those individuals come. It is individual variation not group differences in educability we must concentrate on. Our educational system must be geared to the concept of unique individuals with unique needs, and with unique capacities to contribute to society.

Let us now turn to individual variation and forget group comparisons. With respect to difference between individuals, the relevance of genetics to educability depends both upon the meanings we attach to educability and upon the degree to which relevant aspects of educability are influenced by genetic variety.

Obviously neither of these can be discussed without consideration of the manifold functions of education. Yet far too often we see such discussions almost confined to consideration of ability as measured by tests of IQ type. The variation in abilities that are assessed by IQ type tests is of course of great importance. But we have known that there are other variables also of importance ever since, in his critical investigations of Californian school children, Terman (1947) demonstrated that, within the high IQ sample he followed up, the 25% who performed least well by the criteria he used did not differ in mean IQ from the 25% who achieved most. We will never reach a situation in which we can make reasonable prediction of success in the educational process, or, even more important, predictions of the kind of education that is likely to be most profitable for a given individual, until we cease so much to rely on a single dimension such as IQ tests provide. We need to seek the widest battery of metrics that do not correlate with, or show the minimum correlation with, results of IQ tests.

Over-reliance on tests of ability of the IQ type has been ubiquitous. An example is provided by Floud and Halsey's (1957) demonstration that our process of educational selection led to lower socio-economic groups being under-represented in grammar schools or Universities in relation to their ability. But the authors' only measure of ability was IQ so that their argument involves the implict assumption that IQ tests measure *all* the variation in ability that is relevant to such education. IQ plays its part in these discussions because IQ variation is important. It has been extensively studied. We know a good deal about its correlation with educational achievement as defined in particular ways. We know it is correlated with social mobility, and we know it has very high heritability in some populations. But IQ should never be treated as a complete measure of educability. We must not neglect other aspects of educability, some of which of course will also be influenced by genetic variation. IQ is not even a complete measure of variation of *academic* ability, so that over-concentration on IQ would not be justified even if we were to regard promotion of academics as the sole function of the total educational process, which I suppose no one does. Our knowledge of the limitations of IQ tests should long ago have led us to extensive application of other tests whose results show the minimum correlation with IQ, with the aim of discovering how we can best advise and educate particular individuals according to their particular individual needs and abilities.

Education which begins at birth has a number of ends, all of which have to be compromised because they are not wholly compatible with one another. These aims of education may be divided into two groups, those concerning the needs of the individual and those concerning the needs of society. Individuals vary in their capacity to respond to different modes of education in respect to all these aims.

Individuals have to be taught and vary in capacity to learn:
1. to look after themselves;
2. to get on with others who are different from themselves;
3. to acquire those skills that will maximize their potential contribution to society and hence their success in life;
4. to acquire appreciation of those of the good things of life that will make life rewarding for *them*;
5. to develop their peculiar individual creativities;
6. to develop their critical faculties as far as possible so that their gullibility or exploitability may be minimized.

Society needs:
1. individuals who can look after themselves;
2. individuals that can live with one another, which of course requires that the individuals recognize that others may have different needs;
3. individuals with vocational skills in frequencies proportional to the needs of the existing social system;
4. the transmission of tradition so that the society may have continuity over time, and may profit from the accumulated experience of earlier generations;
5. individuals of critical and creative ability so that society may change, and tradition shall not become a dead hand on change. Such critical ability must be such that it is able to distinguish between traditions that are sound and should be preserved and traditions that are ill founded and needing change. Change merely for the sake of change is not our need.

Not everyone can fulfil all these educational needs in equal measure, and it seems to me that our attitude to all these functions of the educational process must be affected by recognition that we are dealing with unique individuals with unique needs and unique capacities to contribute to society. Furthermore, it is only when we recognize this uniqueness of individuals that we are brought face to face with a fundamental dilemma of society and of the educational system that fits people to society.

Many of the needs of individuals I have mentioned are compatible with the needs of society. But the need of individuals to be given the maximum chance to develop their own particular potentialities and the need that individuals with vocational skills shall be produced in proportion to the requirements of the social system are clearly incompatible to some degree.

If we allow ourselves to forget that the individual's need, what will be the best life for a particular individual, is an intrinsic property of that individual as well as of the society in which he has to live, and to some extent is an intrinsic genetic property of that individual, then we can too easily seduce ourselves into thinking that the needs of society are wholly compatible with the needs of individuals. But if we think these needs *are* wholly compatible, we will inevitably force individuals into occupations which will not suit them.

We may illustrate this concept of varying individual needs by a close analogy. Different people have different visual needs, the differences being in part genetic. Some are blind, some are long-sighted, some myopic, some astigmatic, and the degrees of myopia, etcetera vary from individual to individual. We can meet some of these needs by providing different glasses for different individuals. We would not meet them if we insisted that everyone needed the same kind of glasses. To insist that everyone has the same educational needs is comparable to insisting that they all need the same glasses.

We do not at present know as much about individual variety of educational need as we do about visual needs. But unless we recognize that individual needs vary we will never discover how to meet the variety of need.

Recognition of the basic genetic individuality of people is thus a prerequisite for a just educational system and for a just social system. As that famous Marxist geneticist, J.B.S. Haldane, expressed it: 'That society enjoys the greatest amount of liberty in which the greatest number of human genotypes can develop their peculiar abilities'. I would only add 'and satisfy their peculiar needs'.

Such a society will never be approached if we deny the relevance of genetic variation in education.

References

Davis, W.A. and Havighurst, R.J. (1948). The measurement of mental systems (can intelligence be measured?) *Scientific Monthly,* 66, 301-316.
Floud, J. and Halsey, A.H. (1957). Intelligence tests, social class and selection for schools. *British Journal of Sociology,* 8, 33-39.
Gibson, J.B. (1970). Biological aspects of a high socio-economic group.
1. IQ education and social mobility. *Journal of Biosocial Science,* 2, 1-16.
Jensen, A. (1969). How much can we boost IQ and scholastic achievement? *Harvard Educational Review,* 39, 1-123.
Jinks, J.L. and Fulker, D.W. (1970). Comparison of the biometrical genetical, MAVA, and classical approaches to the analysis of human behaviour. *Psychological Bulletin,* 73, 311-349.
Otis, A.S. (1949). Comments and criticism: can intelligence be measured? (A reply to Davis and Havighurst). *Scientific Monthly,* 67, 312-313.
Terman, L.M. (1947). *Psychological Approaches to the Biography of Genius.* Occasional Papers on Eugenics: 4. London: Hamish Hamilton.
Thoday, J.M. (1965). Geneticism and environmentalism. In *Biological Aspects of Social Problems,* edited by J.E. Meade and A.S. Parkes. Pp. 92-106. Edinburgh: Oliver & Boyd.
Thoday, J.M. (1969). Limitations of genetic comparisons of populations. *Journal of Biosocial Science,* Suppl. 1, 3-14.
Thoday, J.M. and Gibson, J.B. (1970). Environmental and genetical contributions to class difference: a model experiment. *Science,* 167, 990-992.

14

THE BIOLOGICAL BASIS OF CRIMINAL BEHAVIOUR*

H.J. Eysenck

Around the turn of the century the famous Italian anthropologist Cesare Lombroso published a book entitled *Il Reo Nato* (The Born Criminal) in which he put forward his view that criminals are born and not made; that they inherit a disposition towards crime; and that they can be recognised by certain physical characteristics or 'stigmata'. This view became very popular and aroused a great deal of discussion and interest, but when other research workers failed to discover any undue excess of stigmata among prisoners in England, Germany, France and elsewhere the whole theory fell into disrepute. Strictly speaking what had been disproved was merely the theory linking criminal conduct with certain bodily characteristics, but even in science there is such a thing as guilt by association and it was widely believed that the whole theory of constitutional determinants of criminality had been disproved.

At the same time psychoanalytic theories began to extend to the field of criminology, and research began to centre on environmental variables such as broken homes, parental discipline, the quality of the home, sibling relations, toilet training, weaning and other similar hypothetical causes of criminality. The quality of much of this research was not very high but nevertheless a number of suggestive relationships were found. However, the causal interpretation of these relationships implied a fatal ambiguity. Let us suppose that we study the family background of a thousand criminals and a thousand law abiding citizens, equated exactly for sex, age, social class, education, intelligence and other important variables, and suppose further that we find broken homes to be much more characteristic of the background of our criminals than of our honest citizens. It is customary to interpret this by saying that broken homes cause criminal behaviour, but this does not, of course, follow. It could equally well be that genetic factors handed on by the parents to the children cause both the breaking up of the home and also the criminal behaviour of the children. This is an important consideration. It is not always realised by investigators in the social sciences that we have no reliable methods for implicating environmental variables in the causation

* Presidential Address delivered to Section J (Psychology) on August 28, 1964, at the Southampton Meeting of the British Association.

of human actions, and all the researches interpreted as showing environmental causation can with ease be reinterpreted to show the influence of constitutional factors. Science cannot be built on the shifting quicksands of arbitrary assumptions.

Fortunately the position is different on the constitutional side. Here we do have methods of investigation which enable us with considerable assurance to determine the influence of constitutional and hereditary factors, and it is with investigations of this kind that I shall be concerned in this paper. In stressing genetic factors I am merely trying to restore a balance that has been seriously disturbed by the unqualified stress on environmental factors so characteristic of the last fifty years. I have no wish to rule out environmental factors as unimportant, irrelevant or immaterial; clearly, all human behaviour is powerfully influenced by heredity *and* environment, and to deny the importance of either is to step outside the bounds of scientific realism. Nevertheless, the stress has been so much on environment that a brief appreciation of the biological side seems to be in order, and if I seem to disregard environmental influences in this paper, this is done only because of pressure of space and because so many other sources are available which discuss these influences in great detail.

The proper scientific study of constitutional factors in crime began with a German professor, Johannes Lange, who published a survey of his investigations in 1928 under the title *Crime as Destiny*. In this book, which created a sensation when it was published, he demonstrated that criminal behaviour was very powerfully based on genetic factors and that environmental influences were relatively weak. His method of proof was based on the so-called twin method, first suggested by Sir Francis Galton, a cousin of Charles Darwin. As is well known, there are two kinds of twins, identical or monozygotic, and fraternal or dizygotic. Identical twins come from a single sperm; the ovum divides into two after impregnation and thus two individuals develop who are identical with respect to heredity. In the case of fraternal twins two ova are fertilised by two sperms, and the resulting individuals are no more alike genetically than are siblings born in the ordinary way. Identical twins are always of the same sex, fraternal twins are equally frequently identical or different with regard to sex. The diagnosis of monozygosity or dizygosity can be made with very high accuracy by studying physical characteristics such as blood groups, finger prints and so forth; when these are congruent probability is high that the twins are identical, whereas when they are different it is practically certain that the twins are not identical but fraternal.

The use of the twin method for the study of the relative importance of heredity and environment is based on the following consideration. Suppose that individual differences in a trait or an ability are determined entirely by heredity. In that case identical twins would be completely alike in their scores on a perfectly reliable measure of that trait or ability, whereas fraternal twins would be very much less alike as they share only 50 per cent identical heredity. At the other extreme consider a trait or an ability, individual differences in which are caused entirely by environmental factors. Here the similarity between identical twins should be no greater than that between fraternal twins because although the former are more alike genetically, genetic factors play no part in the traits or abilities considered. Similar considerations apply where both heredity and environment are concerned in different degrees in the causation of individual differences, and we can say quite generally that the more alike identical twins are as compared with fraternal twins with respect to a given trait or ability, the greater is the influence of genetic factors on the causation of individual differences in that trait or ability.

Lange used this method in the following manner. He would locate criminals in Bavarian prisons whose records showed that they had a twin of the same sex. He would then search out the twin and determine whether he or she was concordant (i.e. had also committed a crime) or was discordant (i.e. had not committed a crime). If there were constitutional causes for criminal behaviour then identical twins should be concordant more frequently than fraternal twins. Lange located thirteen pairs of identical twins, of whom ten were concordant, and seventeen pairs of fraternal twins of whom only two were concordant. These figures strongly suggest the overwhelming importance of genetic causes.

Even more impressive perhaps than these figures are the case histories published by Lange in which he shows not only that identical twins tend to commit crimes, but that the crimes tend to be very similar, even when the twins were brought up separately and did not know of each other's criminal propensities. Altogether Lange's book was so persuasive, and its theortetical importance so clear, that many other investigators in Germany, the United States and elsewhere repeated his studies. Table 1 shows the results; I have added to the figures for adult criminals those for juvenile delinquents, childhood behaviour disorders and also for homosexuality and alcoholism, which although not crimes in some countries are often associated with criminality. All in all these figures bear out Lange's main contention, although they are perhaps not quite as striking as were his data. They show that criminal behaviour is concordant over twice as frequently in identical as in fraternal twins, and that consequently heredity must be accorded a prominent place in its causation.

But there is one very powerful argument against Lange's theory. This argument relates to the fact that it is very difficult to demonstrate any feasible mechanism for the inheritance of criminality. What is meant is essentially this. We can conceive of nervous structures of various types as being inherited through the ordinary process of Mendelian genetics, even though our understanding of these processes is incomplete. But how can we imagine that some kind of psychological or social or even ethical propensity such as criminality can be inherited? What kind of structure can be imagined to underlie such a type of conduct? After all, criminality is a social concept, not a biological one.

Concordance of Identical and Fraternal Twins Respectively for Various Types of Criminal, Antisocial, and Asocial Behaviour

	Number of twin pairs	Identical	Fraternal	Proportion concordant Identical	Fraternal
Adult crime	225	107	118	71	34
Juvenile delinquency	67	42	25	85	75
Childhood behaviour disorder	107	47	60	87	43
Homosexuality	63	37	26	100	12
Alcoholism	82	26	56	65	30

TABLE 1

Let us begin to answer this objection by considering the question of whether the criminals in our prisons are characterised by a special type of personality. Before we can answer this question let us very briefly consider the description of the normal personality current at the moment. Figure 1 shows in diagrammatic form the ancient doctrine of the four temperaments - choleric, melancholic, phlegmatic and sanguine. This doctrine, which we owe to Hippocrates and Galen, is illustrated on the inside of the figure; on the outside we have the results of modern investigations by means of the statistical analysis of ratings, questionnaires and objective tests. It will be seen that a description of much of human conduct can be given in terms of two major dimensions or axes, one of which we may call 'emotionality' or 'neuroticism', going from the stable to the unstable type of personality; the other may be called extraversion as opposed to introversion using terms familiar for hundreds of years to European psychologists and lately popularised by Jung. The exact meaning of these terms can be apprehended by looking at the traits most closely associated with them. Thus the unstable person is moody, touchy, anxious, restless, rigid, etc. while the stable person is calm, carefree, reliable, even-tempered and lively. Similarly the introvert is reserved, thoughtful, unsociable, passive, quiet and careful, whereas the extravert

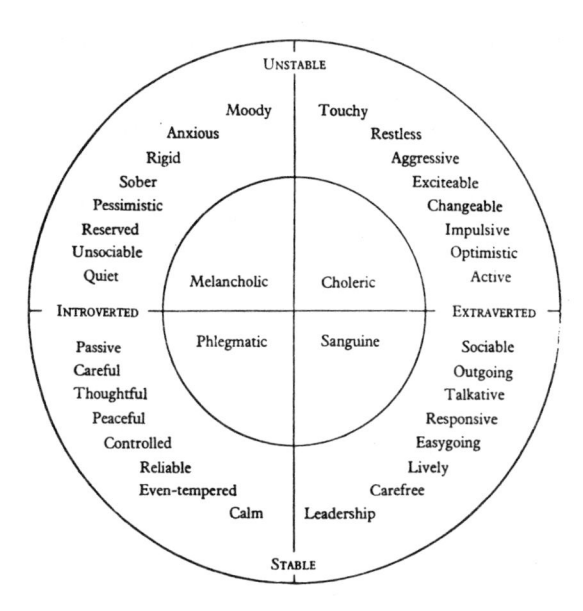

FIGURE 1. Diagrammatic model of personality organisation. In the centre are given the four ancient 'temperaments'; on the outer ring are shown the results of large numbers of modern experimental and statistical investigations into the relationships obtaining between traits.

is sociable, active, out-going, impulsive, talkative and optimistic. We can measure these two dimensions most easily by means of personality questionnaires, provided that our subjects have no reason to try and disguise their responses in some way. Thus in research enquiries, questionnaires have been found to be both reliable and valid; from the point of view of selection procedures, however, where people are motivated to try and give as good an account of themselves as possible, questionnaires are almost entirely useless.

Where in this picture would we expect our criminals to come? Let me say briefly at this point that from theoretical considerations it was predicted that criminals would have a personality make-up putting them in the *choleric* quadrant, as compared with the neurotics in our mental hospitals who would be likely to fall in the *melancholic* quadrant. Before discussing the reasons for this hypothesis, let us consider some evidence to see whether the hypothesis is in fact true. Figure 2 shows the results of several investigations carried out on thousands of prisoners and

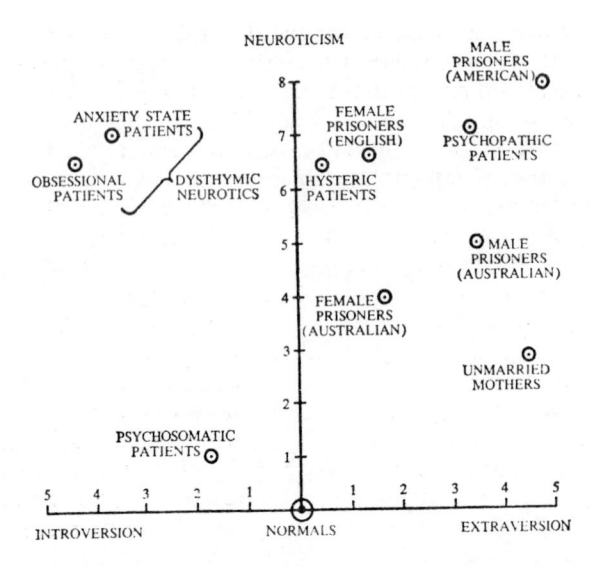

FIGURE 2. Diagram showing the position of various neurotic and criminal groups with respect to neuroticism or emotionality and extraversion-introversion. The diagram is derived from many empirical studies and shows that, essentially, neurotics are introverted, criminals extraverted, and that both groups have high scores on emotionality or neuroticism.

neurotics. It will be seen that, as predicted, our neurotic groups are high on introversion and neuroticism, i.e. are indeed located in the melancholic quadrant, while our criminals are high on extraversion and neuroticism, i.e. are indeed located in the choleric quadrant. It will also be noted that psychopathic patients can be found in the choleric quadrant together with the prisoners, and it is this group that may present us with a clue to the genetic basis of criminality.

We may get some notion of what the term 'psychopath', means when we realise that it is often used interchangeably with the term 'moral imbecile'. The Californian psychologist, H.G. Gough, has given a summary of the characteristics of the psychopath. According to him, psychopaths are characterised by an over-evaluation of immediate goals as opposed to remote or deferred ones; unconcern over the rights and privileges of others when recognising that they could interfere with personal satisfaction in any way; impulsive behaviour, or apparent incongruity between the strength of the stimulus and the magnitude of the behavioural response; inability to form deep or persistent attachments to other persons; poor judgment and planning in attaining defined goals;

apparent lack of anxiety and distress over social maladjustment and unwillingness or inability to consider maladjustment as such; a tendency to project blame on to others and to take no responsibility for failures; meaningless prevarication, often about trivial matters in situations where detection is inevitable; almost complete lack of dependability and of willingness to assume responsibility; and finally, emotional poverty. The psychopath, it will be seen, behaves in many ways like a criminal although it would be quite wrong to identify the two; not all psychopaths are criminals and not all criminals are psychopaths. Nevertheless, if we could understand why the psychopath behaves as he does we might have an important clue as to the reasons for the behaviour of the criminal.

Actually this problem is wrongly put. After all, does not the psychopath behave in what we might call a perfectly 'natural' way? Are not our young children psychopaths in pretty much the same way - selfish, egotistical, cruel, without thought of consequences, living for the moment and without guilt or shame? The proper question surely is - why are we not all behaving like psychopaths and criminals, take what we want when we want it and to Hell with the consequences? The answer is usually given that it is the policeman on the beat and the judge in his court who keep us in order, but while there is some truth in this it would certainly not be correct to say that we behave in a lawful manner because of some calculus of hedonistic consequences. The probability of being caught for any but the most clumsy crime is so small that on a rational basis most people would probably be well advised to go in for a life of crime; on balance it would probably pay them much better than what they are doing at the moment. Napoleon pointed out that you can do everything with bayonets except sit on them, and in the same way the law and the police would be powerless if the whole population were determined to get what they wanted regardless of the rules and restrictions of society.

Religious people have proposed an alternative theory which is much closer to the facts. They say that we refrain from criminal activities not because we fear the punishment but because our conscience will not let us act in this fashion. This is true as far as it goes but it does not go far enough: as a scientific theory it fails to give us any clues as to the nature and origin of this conscience. It is here that modern learning theory enables us to supply the answer. Putting it quite briefly and bluntly we may say *that conscience is a conditioned reflex.* This statement may require some amplification.

It is widely known how the great Russian psychologist I.P. Pavlov demonstrated the process of conditioning. Having shown that a buzzer would not produce salivation in a dog he would then pair the buzzer a number of times with the presentation of meat, which invariably provoked salivation in the hungry dog. After some twenty pairings the dog would salivate to the buzzer alone without the presentation of food.

Pavlov thus demonstrated a method for producing a neural association in the brain between the conditioned stimulus (the buzzer) and the unconditioned stimulus (the meat), so that from then on the conditioned stimulus would acquire the response-producing qualities of the unconditioned stimulus. He went on from there to discover the major laws governing the process of conditioning, of extinction, generalisation, inhibition, and so forth, but we need not follow him there. Let us consider rather how this process may affect the growth of conscience.

First we must distinguish conditioning from learning. The laws of learning or problem solving state simply that, in general, those activities which are pleasurable and which are rewarded will be learned, whereas activities which are not pleasurable and are not rewarded will not be learned. This account of learning is entirely rational from the hedonistic point of view; it proceeds essentially by trial and error, and may benefit from teaching.

Conditioning, on the other hand, does not proceed by trial and error but through association by contiguity. What is acquired by conditioning is usually not so much a specific response as *an emotion*. It is interesting to note that this distinction between learning and conditioning corresponds rather well to a very profound physiological differentiation within the nervous system. We have, first of all, the central nervous system, which mediates essentially the reception of incoming impulses which transmit sensory information, and which is also concerned with outgoing impulses which activate the skeletal muscles, sometimes called the striped muscles from their striated appearance. It is this system which is essentially involved in *learning*. We also have, however, the autonomic nervous system, which is concerned with the glands and the smooth, or involuntary muscles. It is this latter system which is primarily involved in *conditioning*. On the whole, we may further say that the activity of the central nervous system tends to be voluntary; that of the autonomic nervous system, involuntary. Psychoanalysts, too, have recognised the existence of these two systems. Trial-and-error learning is very similar to what Freud has called the 'pleasure principle', whereas conditioning is more closely related to the 'reality principle'; in other words, as Mowrer has put it,

> 'Living organisms acquire conditioned responses or emotions not because it is pleasant to do so but because it is *realistic*. It is certainly not pleasant to be afraid, for example, but it is often very helpful, from the standpoint of personal survival. At the same time, it is biologically useful for living organisms to be able to learn those responses which reduce their drives, regardless of whether these drives be primary (as in the case of hunger) or secondary (as in the case of fear); but it apparently is quite necessary that the neural mechanism which mediates this kind of learning be different from the mechanism whereby emotional, or 'attitudinal' learning comes about.'

Consider the case of the very young child. He has to learn a great number of different things, by means of trial-and-error. As we have pointed out before, there is no real difficulty in accounting for this, because all correct responses tend to be rewarded immediately and incorrect ones, not being rewarded, will tend to drop out; gradually his performance will improve, and he will learn whatever he wishes to. But there are also many other behaviour patterns which he has to acquire, not so much because he wants to, but because society insists that he should. He has to keep clean, he has to learn to use the toilet, he has to refrain from overt aggressive and sexual behaviour, and so on. The list of these socially required activities is almost endless. Clearly, learning, as defined earlier, does not come in to this very much, because the child is not usually rewarded for carrying out these activities; quite the contrary. He is rewarded, in a sense for not carrying them out, because in any case carrying them out is what he wishes to do. If somebody annoys him, he wants to punch him in the nose; if he feels like it, he wants to defecate and urinate wherever he happens to be without interrupting his game to go to the toilet. In other words, reinforcement follows immediately upon his disregard of these social mores, the patterns of behaviour which are desirable from the point of view of society. How, then, can the individual ever become socialised?

Suppose now that our little boy misbehaves. Immediately his mother will give him a smack, or stand him in the corner, or send him off to his room, or inflict one of the many punishments which have become customary with parents over the centuries. In this case, the particular asocial or antisocial activity in which he has been indulging is immediately followed by a strong, pain-producing stimulus. The conditioned stimulus is the particular kind of activity in which the child has been indulging; the unconditioned stimulus is the slap, or whatever constitutes the punishment in this case, and the response is the pain and fear produced in the young child. In this situation we would expect conditioning to take place, so that from then on this particular type of activity would be followed by a conditioned fear response. After a few repetitions, this fear response should be sufficiently strong to keep the child from indulging in that type of activity again.

There are, of course, many such activities which are punished; exactly the same situation hardly ever recurs twice. Nevertheless we would expect a fairly general reaction of fear and autonomic 'unpleasure' to become associated with all antisocial activities, because of the process of stimulus generalisation well known from the laboratory. In fact, stimulus generalisation would be expected to be enhanced considerably by the process of 'naming', which parents usually indulge in. Every time the little child misbehaves, its misbehaviour is labelled 'bad', 'naughty', 'wicked', or whatever the term chosen by the parents might be.

Through this verbal labelling the child is helped in the generalisation process and finally groups all these activities together by association as being potentially dangerous, punishment-producing, and particularly as being productive of conditioned anxiety and fear responses. Thus our little child grows up, gradually acquiring a repertoire of conditioned fear responses to a wide set of different behaviour patterns, all of which have one thing in common - that they are disapproved by parents and teachers, siblings and peers, and that they have, in the past, frequently been associated with punishment and, therefore, with the consequent autonomic upheaval. As 'burnt child shuns fire', so punished child shuns wickedness.

What will happen when the child is in a situation where temptation is strong to do one of these forbidden things? The answer is, of course, that he will tend to go and do it. But as he approaches the object arousing temptation, there should also be a strong upsurge of the conditioned emotional reaction, the fear or anxiety which has become conditioned to his approach to such an object under such circumstances. The strength of this fear-anxiety reaction should be sufficient to deter him from pursuing his antisocial activities any further. If it is indeed strong enough, then he will desist; if it is not, he will carry on, in spite of the increasing strength of the fear-anxiety responses. It will be seen, therefore, that whether he does or does not behave in a socially approved manner depends essentially on the strength of the temptation and on the strength of the conditioned avoidance reaction which has been built into him, as it were, through a process of training or conditioning.

It is possible to demonstrate the actual process of conditioning in the animal laboratory. Consider the case of the pike and the minnows. If a ravenous pike is introduced into a large tank full of minnows he will immediately dash across and gobble them up. Suppose now that we wish to introduce into the pike's conscience a notion that minnows are taboo. How would we set about this? We simply introduce plate glass between two parts of the tank, confining the minnows on the one side and putting the pike in on the other side. The pike will immediately rush across to the other side and bump its nose against the plate glass. Thus the conditioned stimulus (the sight of the minnows) is followed by the unconditioned stimulus (the painful collision with the glass plate) producing the pain-fear-anxiety reaction in the fish. After many repetitions of this association the glass plate may be removed and the pike will be seen to swim around among the minnows without attacking them. Thus may the experimental psychologist make the lamb lie down with the lion!

Or consider some experiments with puppies. The animals, two days hungry, are brought one at a time into a room furnished only with a chair and two dishes, one filled with boiled horsemeat, much liked by the puppies, the other full of a much less well liked commercial dog food (as advertised on television). The puppies usually make straight for the horsemeat, but as they touch it they are swatted by the experimenter, who is sitting on the chair, with a rolled-up newspaper in his hand. If one gentle blow is not enough then the puppy is swatted again and again until he finally gives up his attempts to eat the horsemeat and turns to the commercial dog food, which he can eat without being swatted.

When the puppies had firmly learned the taboo on horsemeat after several days' training the temptation phase began with the experimentalist absent from the room. Again the choice had to be made between a dish of boiled horsemeat and a few pellets of dog food. The puppies soon gobbled up the dog food and then began to react to the large dish of horsemeat. Some puppies would circle the dish over and over again. Some puppies walked around the room with their eyes towards the wall, not looking at the dish. Other puppies got down on their bellies and slowly crawled forward, barking and whining. There was a large range of variability in the emotional behaviour of the puppies in the presence of the tabooed horsemeat. Resistance to temptation was measured as the number of seconds or minutes which passed before the subject ate the tabooed food.

The puppies were allowed half an hour a day in the experimental room. If they did not eat the horsemeat by that time, they were brought back to their home cages, were not fed, and, a day later, were introduced again into the experimental room. This continued until the puppy finally violated the taboo and ate the horsemeat, or until he had fasted so long that he had to be fed in his cage, in order to keep him alive.

There was a very great range of resistance to temptation. The shortest period of time it took a puppy to overcome his training and eat the horsemeat was six minutes, and the longest period of time was sixteen days without eating, after which time the experiment had to be stopped and the puppy fed in his home cage. This great range of variability made it possible to test the influence of various experimental conditions on the growth of conscience in these puppies. For instance, it was shown that when the puppies were hand-fed throughout their early life by the experimenter, then they developed a conscience much more strongly than did other animals which had been machine-fed. This may suggest by analogy the importance of close family relations as relevant to successful conditioning.

It will be seen that we have psychopathic puppies contravening our 'law' without putting up much of a resistance, and we have very law abiding puppies who would rather die than violate the taboo. It is interesting to note that this very strong 'conscience' was created by a few swattings with a rolled-up newspaper which would certainly not have been very painful to the animals, and that in spite of this very gentle training the effects were such as to make the animal prefer death by starvation to going counter to the 'conscience' thus created. Could there be a moral hidden in the results of these experiments, which incidentally have been extended to young children in recent years with similar results?

What is responsible for the difference between the psychopathic and the law abiding puppies? It clearly cannot be anything in the nature of the environment because they were all brought up in exactly the same way under closely controlled conditions. The reason, it may be surmised, lies in the very marked individual differences in conditionability already remarked upon by Pavlov in his early work. It has frequently been shown that animals, and humans also, differ profoundly in the speed with which conditioned reflexes are formed, the strength of the reflexes so produced and their resistance to extinction. Some animals and people are readily conditionable in the sense that they form conditioned responses quickly, strongly and lastingly, while others at the opposite extreme can be conditioned only with difficulty. It seems reasonable to suggest that the psychopathic puppies were those whose nervous system was congenitally predisposed to develop conditioned responses slowly and poorly, whereas the law abiding puppies were endowed with a nervous system which could be conditioned strongly and with ease. If this is not an absurd suggestion then we may perhaps wonder whether in human beings too it may not be possible that the psychopath, the criminal and perhaps the extravert generally is characterised by poor conditionability, while the neurotic, the law abiding citizen and the introvert generally may be characterised by easy conditionability.

Consider first of all the differences between extraverts and introverts. We know from twin studies that this personality dimension has a strong basis in heredity and it had been hypothesised that the agent responsible for the transliteration of the genetic component into behaviour was indeed the conditioned response. Figure 3 shows some data on human conditioning collected in my department by Dr C. Franks. It will be seen from the figure that at all stages introverts condition twice as strongly as extraverts and many other investigators have since duplicated these findings. When we turn to the difference between neurotics (melancholics) and psychopaths (cholerics) we find that here, too, a number of studies support our hypothesis. Lykken and Spence in America, Tong and Franks in this country, and Shagass and Kerenyi in Canada have all produced data in agreement with our hypothesis. It would seem, therefore, that we may have discovered here the link between behaviour patterns on the one hand and constitutional factors on the other. What is inherited is a predisposition on the part of the nervous system to mediate the establishment of conditioned responses well or poorly; this, as it were, is the genotypic aspect of criminality. Individuals

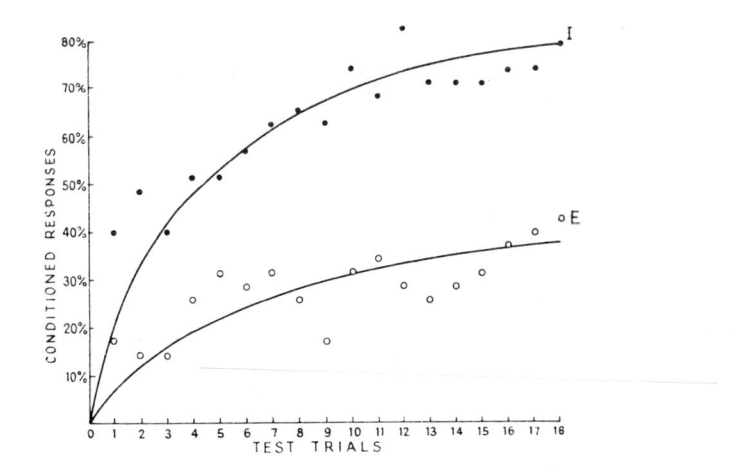

FIGURE 3. Results of an experiment in which introverted and extraverted subjects respectively were conditioned to respond with an eyeblink to a tone delivered over earphones. It will be seen that the introverted group at all stages showed twice as many conditioned responses as did the extraverted group.

so endowed genetically then interact with an environment which produces conditioned and unconditioned stimuli in a fashion probably not too far removed from randomness, and these stimuli imposed on a nervous system of a particular kind then produce the phenotypic behaviour we encounter in everyday life. It will be clear that this hypothesis leaves room for environmental factors to enter as the actual application of conditioned and unconditioned stimuli by parents, teachers, siblings, and others must play an important part in our general theory.

It will be seen that our theory accounts not only for criminal behaviour but also for neurotic behaviour. The typical neurotic conditions only too well the fears and anxieties of everyday life and attaches them to what are really harmless and neutral stimuli. It is his ready conditionability which, while keeping him out of the clutches of the law, makes him prey to anxiety, obsessions, depression and the many other inappropriate emotional reactions so characteristic of neurotic patients in our hospitals. Too much conditioning can be fatal as too little; as in so many other things it is safest not to be at either extreme of this continuum, and of course the majority of people condition adequately but not too strongly, thus avoiding the fate of being either criminal or neurotic.

We have said very little about the role of emotionality in all this. Yet it will be remembered from our first figure that both cholerics and melancholics are characterised by a high degree of emotionality or instability, while our phlegmatics and sanguines, although they might be equally extraverted or introverted, were stable and subject neither to undue neurotic nor criminal activities. Here too we are dealing with an innate difference between people, related largely to the activity of the autonomic nervous system, which, it will be remembered, is closely related to the expression of the emotions. In some people the autonomic system, and the emotions aroused through it, are produced very quickly, strongly and lastingly; people of this kind are thus predisposed to overemotional, unstable conduct. At the other extreme we have people whose emotions are difficult to arouse, are not very strong, and do not last for very long periods of time. In between of course, we have the great majority of the population, the arousal of whose emotions is intermediate between these two extremes. Emotionality like extraversion-introversion is thus linked with our nervous structure, and as several experimental twin studies have shown, there is a very firm hereditary basis for this trait also.

We may now ask ourselves how emotionality interacts with extraversion-introversion to produce criminal and neurotic behaviour patterns. The answer in brief is that emotion, particularly strong emotion, acts as a drive. In other words, our habit systems require activation before they issue in behaviour; the greater the drive or motivation under which we are working the stronger will be the expression of these habit systems in actual conduct. In the unstable, emotional person there is, in addition to all the other drives and sources of motivation which we all share, the very powerful additional drive of strong autonomic, emotional reaction, and this increases and exaggerates the habit patterns laid down by training and teaching. Emotion, one might say, acts very much as a supercharger does in a car; by forcibly blowing the air-petrol mixture into the cylinder it produces an explosive charge much stronger than would be possible with the ordinary system of carburation. It is the addition of this explosive element to high degrees of extraversion or introversion which is responsible for criminal and neurotic behaviour. Criminals and neurotics are doubly predisposed by genetic factors; they condition too well or too poorly, and the resultant habit systems are boosted by their inherited strong emotions to produce the violent reactions leading them into prison or mental hospital.

What I have said so far can, of course, be generalised beyond the field of legal crime. The predisposition towards impulsive, unethical, antisocial activities leads extraverts to have more accidents at work and in the home, to have illegitimate children more frequently and commit a greater number of traffic offences and have more traffic accidents. They also suffer from enuresis (bed-wetting) more frequently! All these are minor violations of the moral code of our society, not usually punishable by law but they are of a piece with the personality make-up of the typical criminal. Indeed there is considerable evidence that known criminals commit a far greater number of traffic offences and have more serious accidents than do non-criminal citizens. There is also very strong evidence to show that criminals suffer from enuresis to quite an exceptional extent!

The biological causation of criminal acitivities is apparent in their genetic determination; to this extent then Cesare Lombroso was right. Is there anything to take the place of his stigmata, i.e. some type of bodily configuration which might characterise our criminal as compared with the rest of the population? There is good evidence that extraverts, as compared with introverts, tend to be of a more stocky, broad type of body build, while introverts tend to be lean and narrow-chested. We would accordingly expect criminals to be stocky in body build rather than lean, and Sheldon in America and Gibbens in this country have furnished ample evidence to show that there is indeed quite a marked tendency along these lines. This tendency even extends to the physique of drivers involved in accidents, and in one study at least it was found that accident-prone miners tended to be more stocky in body-build than accident-free miners. Even here then Lombroso was at least in part right; criminals can be distinguished from the rest of the population on the basis of physical signs, although it should be added that these are not the signs he suggested and that the relationship with criminality is much too low to be of any practical value.

If we are willing to grant that there is some substance in the system of ideas I have been discussing here, can we suggest any way of improving our current methods of dealing with criminals? The answer surely must be that almost any change would be for the better. To say that our present methods are primitive is to understate the case; we are still doing today what the Assyrians, Carthaginians and Romans did two and three thousand years ago. We avenge but we do not reclaim; instead of conditioning prisoners to the acquisition of a conscience and training them in those attitudes and social skills required to keep them out of prison we train them in humiliation, degradation and vice. To do all this and to bewail the sad effects of increasing criminality and recidivism indicates a certain rather curious thought-splitting on the part of society, an impossible desire to have your cake and eat it too.

At the bottom of all our errors lies probably a fundamental psychological fallacy. We think that punishment deters, and we go on to imagine that the more severe the punishment the greater the deterrence. This is not always true. The statistical study of the effects of increasing the severity of punishment, as by corporal punishment, death penalty, etc. is in complete accord with experimental laboratory studies in showing that the effects of punishment are extremely variable, very difficult to predict and often contrary to expectation. Severe punishment heightens the prisoners' emotionality to a very considerable degree and this 'booster' action may combine with the existing systems of habits to make these more rigid and difficult to eliminate. These facts have been demonstrated so often as to constitute a psychological truism, yet the only action most people can think of when confronted with an increase in crime is to call for greater severity of punishment, i.e. precisely the remedy least likely to succeed and most likely to make matters worse.

What then would the psychologist suggest? He would suggest in the first place, the adoption of a therapeutic rather than a penal attitude, i.e. the adoption as his main aim of the *cure* of the criminal rather than his *punishment*. To do this requires that the process of conditioning which clearly did not go far enough in the past should be recognised and brought to a successful conclusion. Such a process would, of course, have to be adapted to the circumstances of each case; we would require to know the degree of conditionability of each criminal, as well as gain some knowledge of the past history of social conditioning which he has undergone. It would require considerable research, both in the laboratory and in actual prison conditions to work out the most appropriate methods of doing this, but learning theory is far enough advanced to suggest plausible and worthwhile methods for at least our first attempts along these lines.

It is clear that introverted and extraverted criminals would require rather different types of treatment, and there is already some experimental evidence from California that matching the right treatment to the personality of the offender gives significantly better results than treating everyone alike. However, the majority of offenders will always be extraverted and with an innate deficit as far as conditionability is concerned; how can we hope to achieve anything by trying to condition the adolescent or the adult when we have failed to condition the child, and when this failure was due to genetic rather than to environmental causes? The answer, fortunately, is relatively simple. It is possible to change a person's position on the extravert-introvert continuum by means of drugs. Stimulant drugs such as nicotine or caffeine have an introverting effect; depressant drugs such as alcohol have an extraverting effect. If, therefore, we wish to use our conditioning procedure to affect strongly extraverted people who lack to a greater or lesser degree the faculty of being easily conditioned, then we will simply have to shift them along the continuum by daily doses of a stimulant drug such as amphetamine. There is ample evidence from the literature that the effects are quick, beneficial and drastic. Figure 4 shows the results of one such experiment in which groups of criminals were rated for their behaviour in a kind of Borstal in America. There were three groups of criminals, receiving respectively no drug at all, dummy tablets (placebos), and increasing doses of amphetamine. The results show clearly that at the beginning of the experiment all groups improved a little, probably due to the novelty of the experimental procedure and the general interest aroused in it. But after a while the no-drug group and the dummy tablet group both went back to their original level, while the amphetamine group continued to improve to the end of the experiment. This is only one of many similar experiments demonstrating the efficiency of drug treatment, and there is additional evidence to show that extraverts are exceptionally tolerant of stimulant drugs and that if given under medical supervision these are not habit forming. No attempt was made in these studies to combine the drug administration with a properly planned system of conditioning; it may be surmised that the combination would have very much greater effects than one or the other taken by itself.

At the moment many people are worried about the increase in criminality but do not know what can be done about it. There are two opposing groups who claim to know. Some call for greater severity, more punitive measures, the bringing back of the cat and so forth, all measures the cruelty of which is only exceeded by their inefficiency. Others call for a psychiatric understanding of criminals, their psychoanalytic treatment and quite generally the application of psychotherapeutic measures. These proposals, while humane, are based on unproven theories,

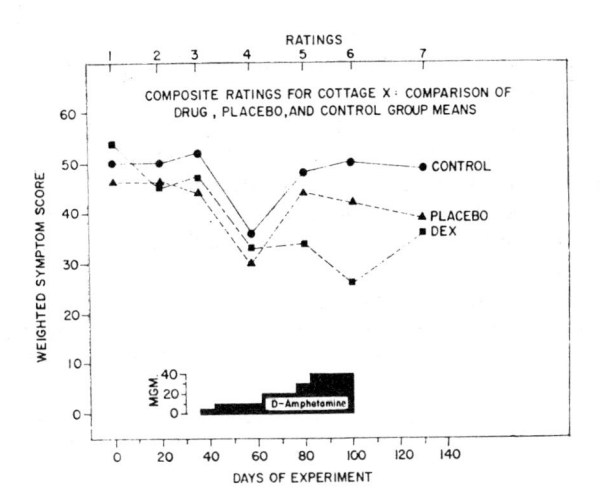

FIGURE 4. Results of an experiment showing a reduction in behaviour problems (weighted symptom score) of three groups of criminals given respectively no-drugs, placebo or D-amphetamine in increasing doses; it will be seen that the only group showing prolonged beneficial effects was the drug group.

and the evidence as far as it goes suggests that these measures would be no more efficacious than those suggested by the first group. Perhaps a brief example may illustrate the difference of the suggestions here made from those currently advocated.

As our trial case let us consider enuresis, which, as we have seen before, is often the accompaniment of criminal mentality. Here, too, we have many worried parents, not knowing what to do with a child who wets his bed; here, too, we have one group attempting to beat the nonsense out of the child, with the effect that the trouble is stamped in all the more firmly, and another group who send the child to the psychoanalyst with effects scarcely more promising. What is the answer given by experimental psychology? According to conditioning theory the child has failed to connect the conditioned stimulus, i.e. the swelling of the bladder, with the appropriate response, waking up and going to the toilet; this failure is presumably due to the fact that the child is innately predisposed to form conditioned responses poorly and with difficulty. What is needed accordingly is neither punishment nor psychoanalysis; it is a simple training along conditioning lines. Accordingly we make the child sleep on a blanket containing electrodes that are connected to a battery and a bell; whenever the child begins to urinate in his sleep the bell rings and wakes him up before he has a chance to produce more than a few drops. By thus introducing artificially an unconditioned stimulus (the bell) into the situation and by pairing it with the enlargement of the bladder we condition the child to respond with waking up to the conditioned stimulus, thus curing the bed-wetting. When this method was introduced many years ago by Mowrer he claimed 100 per cent success, and although the rate has been slightly lower in the many investigations carried out since there can be no doubt that the method is far superior to any other currently in use. It not only cures the symptom but it also eliminates all the worries and anxieties attaching to it, as well as doing away with the family quarrels so often resulting from the symptom. Furthermore, counter to what some people had feared, there is no evidence that other symptoms may arise to take the place of the one that has been eliminated. In the rare cases where the method runs into difficulties it has been shown that the administration of stimulant drugs, by shifting the child's personality towards introversion and greater conditionability, produces a rapid cure in conjunction with the bell and blanket.

Although psychologists, therefore, recognise the biological nature of the defect in the case of the enuretic child there is no 'therapeutic nihilism'; once we have pin-pointed the precise deficit involved we can aid nature by arranging a programme of conditioning, and if need be by improving the conditionability of the patient by means of drugs. Thus enuresis in miniature presents an outline of what the psychologist would suggest should be done in the case of criminality as a whole. We must cease to govern our behaviour by irrational impulses more appropriate to bygone ages, or by superstitious ultra-modern beliefs lacking in evidence, and rely rather on scientific experimentation and well documented facts.

References

As the necessary documentation for this paper would be too lengthy to make its inclusion feasible, the reader is referred to *Crime and Personality* by H.J. Eysenck (Routledge and Kegan Paul, 1964,) which includes a full bibliography.

15

FUNCTIONALIST INTERPRETATIONS OF PRIMITIVE WARFARE

C.R. Hallpike

Warfare has never received the attention from anthropologists which is its due. One can only suppose that its obvious characteristics of death, chaos, and destruction are a theoretical embarrassment to a discipline which has tended to believe that human societies are functionally integrated systems, well adapted to their environments. It is perhaps not surprising, therefore, that when anthropologists have had to explain warfare, they have expended considerable ingenuity in demonstrating that, contrary to appearances, warfare may indeed be socially beneficial. I have elsewhere (Hallpike, 1972: 331) described this belief as similar to the assertion that dry-rot is structurally beneficial to a house because it induces the owner to repair it. It is therefore the object of this article to examine the validity of functionalist explanations of primitive warfare.

The functionalist analysis of warfare has been given new prominence by the work of ecological theorists such as Vayda. Vayda defines the 'function' of anything as 'the contribution that it makes to keeping or restoring some property or variable of a system within a certain range of states or values' (Vayda, 1968a: 102). Collins amplifies the nature of what he calls functional systems as follows 'A functional system is characterized by what are known, in popular engineering terminology, as "feedback" mechanisms' (Collins, 1965: 273). And he goes on to say that 'Biological phenomena, of course, abound in systems that exemplify relations such as those described above' (Collins, 1965: 273) and he lists the temperature-maintaining system of the human body, and the systems which maintain the blood-sugar level, and the red blood cell level. Vayda and Leeds, moreover, in their preface to the book in which Collins's paper appears talk of the 'possibility and also the fruitfulness of functionalist analyses concerned not only with the interrelation of sociological variables but also with the operation of mechanisms maintaining environmental variables at values *conducive to the survival or expansion of human populations*' (Leeds and Vayda, 1965: iv; my emphasis).

So far, then, this seems to be the traditional functionalist recipe for the explanation of cultural traits, but which includes the extra item of 'environmental variables'. It turns out, however, that this new type of functionalism claims that it is not really trying to explain the existence of traits such as warfare at all, but merely how, having come into existence, they operate. 'In short, functional analysis as here conceived explains behaviour, or the operation of systems, not the presence of traits' (Collins, 1965: 277) and he continues 'For example, although Sweet is certainly concerned to provide an accurate description of the Bedouin institution of camel raiding, she makes no effort to explain its presence in the Bedouin cultural repertory' (Collins, 1965: 277). Vayda has also stated that in his view the purpose of functional analysis is not to explain the presence of traits, but to show how systems work, e.g. in his Foreword to Rappaport's *Pigs for the ancestors* he states that the object of the analysis is a 'demonstration of how things work rather than an explanation of why they exist or how they have come to be' (Vayda, 1968b: x).

The kind of functionalist analysis proposed by Vayda and the other ecological functionalists seems therefore to be trapped between two equally uncomfortable alternatives. The first is to analyse the actual working of interrelated systems of variables within a society, without any claim that this either explains their existence, or has any predictive value about their possible development. This procedure, while no doubt of academic interest to cybernetic specialists will be, in relation to our primary task of explaining social institutions, pretty trivial stuff even though it will be immune to the usual arguments against functionalism. The other alternative is to take the view that these functional systems are indeed likely to be relevant to the survival of societies, because the mechanisms concerned maintain 'environmental variables at values conducive to the survival or expansion of human populations'. Once it is conceded, however, that functional systems such as warfare have environmental consequences relevant to the society's survival, it is obvious that natural selection may be responsible for their presence. If this is so, then the ecological theorists will be able to claim that their analyses *do* have explanatory power but their claims will then become vulnerable to the usual arguments against functionalism. In this article I have therefore thought it profitable to see whether it can be shown that the kinds of ecological effects claimed by Vayda do in fact result from warfare, and, if so, if these consequences have any capacity to explain warfare.

Our enquiry is further confused by the ambiguity which sometimes exists between the concepts of 'function' and 'adaptation'. Ideally, we might be inclined to distinguish a 'functional' custom as one which helped to maintain some system of relationships within a society, and an 'adaptive' custom as one which contributed to the survival of the society in its natural or human environments. Thus, a custom which was functional, in so far as it contributed to the maintenance of a system of relationships within a society, could also be maladaptive, and contrarily, an adaptive custom might be dysfunctional. A good example of the contribution of warfare to the maintenance of a social system is provided by Krapf-Askari's analysis of the Nzakara, the immediate neighbours of the Azande. Here warfare was the source of female captives, given as wives by the ruling clan to maintain its dominant position.

'The Bandia [the ruling clan], having entered Nzakara society as a small group of foreign conquerors, felt the need on the morrow of their conquest to reward the southern clans who had supported them in their campaigns, as well to make themselves popular with the bulk of the population. (Dampièrre E. de, 1967, p.294). In order to do this, they took over the old lineage head's role of wife-givers: not wife-givers to their own Bandia clan alone, but to the population at large . . . For, in their new role of universal wife-givers, the Bandia of course needed very much larger 'hands' of women than the old lineage heads had done. The solution was to acquire women elsewhere by capture (Dampièrre, p.294); and Dampièrre notes that commoner Nzakara appear to have fulfilled their military obligations willingly enough: the supply of wives depended on the frequency and success of raids on neighbouring people . . . Once instituted, the system became self perpetuating: . . .' (Krapf-Askari, 1972: 26-7).

Whether such warfare could meaningfully be said to be adaptive for Nzakara society as such is another matter, however.

In the course of this article it will therefore be necessary to use the word 'function' in a very general sense, to include the notions of 'beneficial' and 'adaptive'.

Functional theories of warfare make some or all of the following assumptions about human society and its relations with the natural and the human environments.

1. Societies are unambiguously definable in extent.
2. They are integrated systems which have needs or basic conditions for successful functioning, and these can be objectively specified so that one can define the minimum requirements of social harmony.
3. Societies compete with one another, and with the natural environment.
4. There will thus be a tendency for every society to be in a state of adaptation to its natural and human environment.

Let us consider these assumptions in turn. First of all, is it true that societies are unambiguously definable in extent? (We may refer to this as 'the Boundary Problem').

To define a 'society' is very much harder than defining the rabbit population of a particular warren - and even biologists, if I am correct, have problems in specifying the particular animal populations they are studying. My recent fieldwork among the Tauade of Papua showed clearly that while they spoke mutually intelligible dialects of the same language, had similar social organisation, and had most customs in common, they did not thereby feel any special unity against other groups with different languages and customs, such as the Fuyughe and Kunimaipa, and never faced these groups collectively in battle. Indeed, on the borders of these groups much peaceful intermarriage and social intercourse took place. In such a situation one local group overlaps another in composition of members, and this next group overlaps another, and so on, so that a chaining effect is produced, and over distance the nature of the society slowly changes in language and customs so that it has no clear boundary. In what respect therefore are we justified in calling the Tauade speakers a 'society'? In so far as there is high mobility between each local tribe (numbering about 150 - 250 on average) and its neighbours, much intermarriage between these local tribes, and many mutual invitations to dances and feasts, we would immediately be inclined to say that they did form a society, even though it is fuzzy about the edges. But this does not imply that inter-tribal relations were traditionally friendly. Warfare was endemic, alliances fluctuated between friendship and enmity, and cannibalism and mutilation were favourite devices for dishonouring the bodies of enemy dead. If we are to accept that a normal state of friendship between groups defines them as a single society, then clearly the Tauade do not constitute a single society. Yet among the Tauade even tribes are split by violence and disputes, which sometimes have a higher incidence *within* tribes than between them. Nor are they in any way unique; they are comparable to the Nuer, Somali, and many other peoples whose feuding and internal violence is described in the literature. In such situations, therefore, we must either conclude that they have no society, or that they have a very anarchical one, which besides being anarchical, has no clear boundaries, either in terms of social interaction, or on the ground.

It is the vague and anarchical character of societies such as the Tauade which provides fertile ground for one of the most common, and most specious, devices in functionalist analyses of warfare. Such arguments depend upon the arbitrary selection of a particular organisational level, or group, in the society, with reference to which warfare or any other practice can then be said to be functional. By shifting one's definition of the group for which violence is said to be advantageous to suit the case, one can, of course, always prove that it is advantageous for someone, ending with the extreme case of the functional value of murder for the killer, because it removes his inner tensions, and makes him feel that he is a fine fellow.

Chagnon's hypothesis on the functional features of Yanomamö warfare is a good example of this ambiguity in the definition of the group for whom warfare is advantageous:

> 'The hypothesis I put forward here is that a militant ideology and the warfare it entails function to preserve the sovereignty of independent villages in a milieu of chronic warfare' (Chagnon, 1967: 112).

Yet it is plain from his ethnographic description of the Yanamamö (Chagnon, 1967; 1968) that social interaction takes place between a *number* of autonomous villages, and that there are forms of alliance varying from trade, to feasting, the exchange of women and the giving of refuge to allies worsted in battle, and that the villages are all integral parts of a larger social system. Moreover, even the autonomous villages can split (or 'fission', as Chagnon inelegantly terms it) and that if one of the groups so produced is too small to be viable by itself (below about forty individuals) it will have to take refuge with a host group, and will lose its autonomy permanently. Thus, while it can be argued that it is adaptive for any *one* village to engage in warfare, and be generally ferocious, in a situation where everyone else is equally ferocious, it does not follow that it is adaptive for that *group* of villages to engage in constant raiding and feuding among themselves - they would be much better off in terms of material prosperity if they lived at peace. Chagnon's hypothesis is therefore only plausible because of the conceptual sleight-of-hand which persuades us that the real group for which the behaviour pattern in question is adaptive is the village, when it is plain that Yanomamö village is part of a larger society for whom warfare can no more be claimed to be adaptive than it can for the Tauade. His hypothesis is also entirely circular, and amounts to no more than the statement that a military ideology functions to maintain warfare, which functions to maintain a militant ideology; but that is by the way!

The Yanomamö, like the Tauade, and other acephalous societies, engage in warfare because among other reasons they cannot stop, not because they necessarily as a culture derive any benefit from fighting. In the absence of any central authority they are condemned to fight for ever, other conditions remaining the same, since for any one group to cease defending itself would be suicidal. In some cases of this type the people have no real desire to continue fighting, and may welcome outside pacification. We should recognise that there are likely to be many situations, not necessarily involving warfare, where the society in question is caught in a vicious circle - as we may be in the circle of economic growth - and that, while the society may not be wiped out, the institution may be perpetuated because there is no way to stop it, not because it is performing some vital function for that society.

It seems to me therefore that the conceptual difficulties involved in the definition of the boundaries of a particular society, and the consequent latitude for anthropologists to choose whatever group in society suits their theory as the reference group lie at the root of many bogus functionalist arguments.

Let us now consider the assumption that societies are integrated systems which have needs, which can be objectively defined so that one can specify the minimum criteria of social harmony. In the first place, we should note that the concept of social harmony, or social cohesion, is frequently confused with that of equilibrium. It is perfectly proper for us, as anthropologists, to have measures of social harmony - such as rates for homicide, fist fights, exchanges of verbal abuse and so on - and to apply these to any society we choose. We may then conclude that the Tauade are very anarchical or socially disharmonious, but this does not imply that their society is not in equilibrium, since the people themselves may accept this level of violence as normal, and make no effort to reduce it. When anthropologists talk about the function of a custom in maintaining social cohesion or harmony, therefore, what they should often be saying is that it helps to maintain equilibrium, which is a very different thing. Vengeance is the principal means of maintaining equilibrium between Tauade tribes, but by its very nature it produces *disharmony*. There is, of course, no such quality as 'social harmony' in the abstract, in the sense of fixed characteristics of social interaction which are necessary for the existence of all societies, analogous to the health of a biological organism.

As we shall see, it is the absence of any universally valid criteria of the 'health' or, conversely, the anomie of societies in general which allows anthropologists in many cases to invent their own ideas of the needs of any particular society, in the satisfaction of which needs a particular institution is then said to be functional.

For example, it is sometimes argued that warfare satisfies economic needs. A very clear statement of this point of view is made by Newcomb (1950). He defines war as:

> 'A type of armed conflict between societies, meeting in competition for anything which is valued by the groups involved, usually consisting of territory or certain products of this territory, such as good hunting grounds, oil-producing or agricultural lands . . The particular forms which war may take are of course varied, but warfare everywhere and at all times is alike in one respect; it is motivated by economic need, and the biological competition of societies, real or imagined, basic or otherwise [whatever that may mean]' (Newcombe, 1950: 317-18).

Now the claim that all warfare is always motivated by economic need is, in terms of the consensus of ethnographic facts, merely ridiculous, and needs no special refutation here. It turns out, however, that what

Newcomb means by 'motivated' is not what most people would take the word to mean. For he is following the lead of Leslie White, whom he quotes as saying 'Warfare is a struggle between systems, not individuals. Its explanation is therefore social or cultural, not psychological' (White, 1947: 691). In this way Newcomb can dismiss all the evidence of ethnographers of Plains Indian warfare upon the reasons why the Indians valued warfare so highly, on the grounds that:

> 'The motivation of the individual is not the cause of warfare, it is rather the method by which a cultural irritation or need is satisfied' (Newcomb, 1958: 320).

One feels inclined to ask at this point if a culture can scratch itself. He and White are both in a philosophical muddle, which leads them to suppose that a social system can have needs, motives and frustrations unknown to its members. When Newcomb claims therefore that 'all warfare is economically motivated', he means that the motives of real people are irrelevant, and that warfare is:

> 'a function of socio-cultural systems, and individuals are . . . no more than the means through which these systems attain their ends' (Newcombe, 1950: 317) and,
>
> '. . . it does not matter for what reason the individual thinks he is fighting, and dying, as long as he is satisfying the needs and imperatives of his culture' (Newcomb, 1950: 329).

In objecting to the type of theory which Newcomb is advancing, one would not wish to deny that cultures may have a cognitive orientation which the people themselves are unable to articulate, or that processes of institutional logic may operate in ways that the members of society do not understand. But to claim that a culture is an integrated kind of Being with distinct needs which have to be satisfied is to indulge in fantasy.

Newcomb argues that the introduction of the horse in north America made possible a highly specialised nomadic hunting culture dependent on the bison herds. As he correctly observes, this kind of specialisation has disadvantages as well as advantages, for when the herds were exhausted the cultures based on them collapsed also. It should be noted that a contributory factor to this process was the extreme improvidence of the Indians in their consumption of the bison and deer, since they would only eat the best cuts of fat and meat, and left the rest to rot, so that two or three days after a very successful hunt all the edible meat would be gone, and the Indians had to start hunting again. We are not told if this obviously maladaptive behaviour was the fault of the culture! But before the herds were exhausted, when contact was first made with European settlers in the region of the Great Lakes, some Indian tribes acquired firearms. In fights over hunting grounds population pressures were set up towards the south and west, in which displaced tribes pushed out their neighbours. This apparently set up a chain reaction in which warfare was greatly exacerbated in the continuing struggle over hunting grounds.

But, even, if we accept this general picture of Plains Indians warfare as true (and I am not sufficiently familiar with the ethnography to dispute its accuracy) Newcomb's conclusions do not follow. For example, he refers to a series of battles between the Chippewa and the Sioux in the seventeenth and eighteenth centuries, ending with the battle of Cross Lake in 1800, and comments:

> 'These were not boyish raids for adventure or glory; they constituted serious warfare, fought by men defending their homes and families against invaders seeking to escape from their own ravaged and overrun homes to the east' (Newcomb, 1950: 323).

It seems implausible, however, that people in such a situation *would* have thought that they were only having boyish games for fun and adventure, not realising that their hunting grounds were being taken, and that their homes were being destroyed around them. To suggest that only the culture was aware of these profound economic truths, while individuals went their deluded way pursuing honour and glory, is a parody of social analysis.

While it seems that here, despite Newcomb's claims that only cultural needs were involved, individuals often did fight in terms of genuine human needs, ecological theorists talk in terms of the needs or characteristics of ecosystems which are unlikely to have much relevance to actual human behaviour. For example, Vayda argues that warfare may have the function, among others, of

> 'the spacing out of relatively stable populations within finite territories ... and the prevention of population increase so great as to lead to an over-exploitation and deterioration of resources' (Vayda, 1961 : 347)

But there are many cases where the inhabitants of a territory *have* degraded it and caused its resources to deteriorate, at every level of civilisation. The Tauade did it to their forest cover, and much of the Aibala valley is now sterile grassland. In the United States in the nineteenth century the passenger pigeon and the bison were exterminated, and the dust bowl of Oklahoma was created.

Not only may a population ruin their environment, they may be quite indifferent to the consequence, either thinking that they will be able to move elsewhere, or that they will be able to put things right, or that it will only become a problem long after they are dead. Consequently, the statement that such-and-such a practice has certain beneficial ecological consequences will not explain this practice if the people are ignorant of or indifferent to these results, and in such cases will have no predictive value concerning the people's future behaviour. There is no particular reason to assume that ecological benefits - if they are benefits - such as the spacing out of population are due to anything other than chance. Vayda's attempt to show that warfare among the Marings of the Madang and Western Highlands Districts of New Guinea might have the function of maintaining the existing level of population in relation to land resources is not even supported by his own data. He writes:

'... the available evidence gives no indication that the offences had a cumulative effect in provoking war or that their commission correlated with the pressure of particular Maring groups upon their land' (Vayda, 1971: 4), and

'The fact is, however, that when we were doing our field work in the 1960's we could find no clear evidence of such [population] pressure anywhere in the Maring region except in the Kauwatyi and Kundagai territory, where there were tracts of permanent grassland and degraded secondary forest' (Vayda, 1971: 20).

Nor do we find that there was any significant relationship between aggression and land shortage, according to Vayda himself:

'Some of the smallest Simbai Valley clan populations, living at the edge of a vast expanse of unoccupied forest extending eastwards along the Bismarck Range, fought as often as did some of the large clan cluster populations of the Central Maring area, where there are not only higher population densities, but also such other indications of greater pressure on resources as shorter fallow periods for garden plots ... ' (Vayda, 1971: 6).

When people were actually driven out of their territory, the casualties do not seem to have been very heavy:

'When some 300 Tyenda were routed following the Kauwatyi's surprise raid, 14 Tyenda men, 6 women and 3 children were killed. The 600 Manamban lost only 8 men and 3 women in the course of being routed by the combined forces of the Kauwatyi and Tukemenga (although there had been 20 other Manamban deaths at the fight ground previously). If these figures indicate the heaviest mortality suffered in Maring wars, it may be questioned whether routs in general were effective in decisively affecting the capacity of groups to defend and use land' (Vayda. 1971: 13).

Nor does the normal result of routing appear to have been generally to deprive the losers of their territory more than temporarily at most:

'I have accounts of 21 routs. In seven of these the groups did not even leave their own territory and took refuge in portions of it at some distance from the borderlands where the enemy had engaged them. Among the 14 other cases the members of some routed groups fled across the Bismarck Range or the major rivers, but there were others when they remained closer and indeed, sometimes continued to maintain a claim to their territory by going to it for food' (Vayda, 1971: 13).

In 13 of these 14 cases, the defeated groups returned to their territory. The only group which failed to do so was the now extinct Woraiu:

'that had been living on the south side of the Jimi River, where it had been attacked by an alliance of the Mindyi and Kumom clans' (Vayda, 1971: 11).

When some groups returned to their territory after being routed, they re-established their prosperity, made appropriate sacrifices to the ancestor spirits, and they replanted the boundary stakes to signify that they would not relinquish any land. Not all groups did this, and by not replanting the stakes would leave some territory vacant to be annexed. It is significant that Vayda adds, however, 'Informants stated this as a possibility, but were unable to cite any recent examples' (Vayda, 1971: 17). They did cite, however, a gift of land by the Tyenda to their allies the Bokapai and Tsuwenkai of about 30 - 40 per cent of Tyenda land. But this was clearly not the result of conquest, and the circumstances suggest that it was land which the donors felt able to part with.

Vayda summarises the facts of land redistribution as follows 'The fact remains that most groups in recent decades have held on to their own lands after warfare' (Vayda, 1971: 19). It also seems to have been the case that the majority of fights, of differing degrees of severity, led to peace without any territorial conquest at all (Vayda, 1971: 19-20). The obvious fact that warfare among the Maring patently did not have any noticeable effect in redistributing land drives Vayda to state that even so, their system of warfare might have had such effects if things had been different!

'In other words, even if territorial conquests had been only an infrequent rather than a regular aftermath of Maring warfare for a considerable time, the warfare remained the kind that could, through an already institutionalized systematic process, lead again to the adjustment of man/resource ratios whenever demographic and ecological conditions changed sufficiently to make it appropriate for this to happen' (Vayda, 1971: 22-3).

And he appends the note 'When, if ever, such conditions obtained throughout the Maring area is problematic.' All that Vayda establishes in this paper is that in some cases warfare may be the means by which groups which are short of primary forest for new gardens may acquire other people's. No one would suggest that, in some cases, people may not fight over land, or anything else which they fancy and which is in short supply, but this does not explain why the Marings fought.

When one reads such vain attempts to explain primitive warfare by appeals to its ecological effects or functions, one realises that 'function' has frequently the covert significance of 'What a twentieth-century materialist rationalist intellectual from Europe or America thinks is sensible allocation of labour and resources'. When such a person encounters primitive societies, he is baffled by their indifference to *his* criteria of what is sensible, and therefore casts about for some hidden reason which will be the *real* explanation for their behaviour. This is especially likely to be the case with that form of behaviour which particularly horrifies intellectuals - warfare. In consequence, many such functionalist explanations of warfare have a strongly ethnocentric bias.

A good example of this ethnocentricism can be found in Rappaport's *Pigs for the ancestors*. After a detailed analysis of the amount of energy which the Tsembaga expend in pig rearing, compared with the energy which is obtained from eating them, he remarks:

'We could only be mystified by a prolonged and laborious procedure, such as Tsembaga pig raising, which resulted in the return of somewhat less energy than was actually invested' (Rappaport, 1968: 63).

By parity of reasoning, one can imagine an ethnographer being puzzled by the fact that the members of the Bongo-Bongo tribe have sexual intercourse 271 times for each pregnancy, an obvious disparity of energy expenditure in relation to the benefits accruing to the group by the possible acquisition of a new member. 'Obviously,' he will conclude, 'this mysterious behaviour can be explained only when we realise that the function of sexual intercourse is the strengthening of the marital bond, and hence group solidarity in general.' In fact, it will come as no surprise to anyone who understands human beings to be told that people copulate because they think it is pleasant; if intercourse were as disagreeable as being poked in the eye with a burnt stick we should have much less of it, whatever its putative consequences for social solidarity.

Because sexual gratification, love of prestige and power over others, and envy of those who have these advantages, are some of the strongest forces in human nature, men enjoy killing other men. The human race has evolved few more definitive means of proving one's superiority over an enemy than by battering him to death and eating him, or by burning his habitation, ravaging his crops and raping his wife. The tortuous explanations advanced by academics for the prevalence of violence in primitive societies in some cases disclose their lack of knowledge of human nature.

Another familiar functionalist argument, which has more plausibility than the ecological variety which we have just considered, is that warfare is beneficial because it reinforces the solidarity of the group. Camilla Wedgwood (1930) proposes an argument of this type. She prefaces analysis with a classic statement of the functionalist position.

> 'The more we study the culture of people both 'savage' and 'civilised', the more it becomes apparent that no social institution comes into being and continues to flourish unless it has a definite function to fulfil in the culture of which it forms a part. This is as true of war as of any other institution, and, though the immediate causes of war are diverse and there are different forms which it may take, yet, as I hope to show from the following analysis of warfare in Melanesia, one of its constant functions is to strenthen the bonds of union between individuals of the fighting community and make them increasingly conscious that they are members of the same unit' (Wedgwood, 1930: 6).

In dealing with the conflict between groups which are normally friendly, such as different clans within the same tribe, for example, she argues that where a member of one clan violates a rule of conduct:

> 'the loyalty of his fellow clansmen to the community as a whole demands that they look askance at him; their loyalty to him as a member of their clan demands that they put themselves for his sake in opposition to the rest of the community. The social structure of Melanesia is for the most part one in which the clan is all important, a man's loyalty to his clan must outweigh other loyalties, and the recognized practice of clansmen joining in defence of a fellow member serves to reaffirm and thereby strengthen the bonds which exist between them. At the same time, in order that such conflicts, while strengthening the clan, may not prove disruptive to the larger unit, these are regulated and controlled, and no acts of vindictive hostility such as cannibalism are permitted. The wider unity is never lost sight of, while the strength of the bonds of kinship is intensified' (Wedgwood, 1930: 32).

Now, on the surface, all this looks very plausible, until, that is, we stop and think for a minute, and ask ourselves if such societies, based upon strong clans which nevertheless owe allegiance to a wider society, need necessarily have organised themselves in the way that Wedgwood describes. The answer is clearly 'No'. There are many instances in the ethnographic literature of similar societies which have developed forms of mediation to settle conflicts between component groups, and where, indeed, individuals who risk plunging the clan or comparable group into unwanted warfare may be disciplined by their fellow group members. The Konso of Ethiopia, for example, told me that before the Amhara conquest, if a man from one town stole a goat, say, from a man of another town, the injured party could usually obtain redress from the offending town. The elders would oblige the thief to pay compensation, and would not consider themselves obliged to go to war just to defend one of their number who had done wrong.

While it cannot be disputed that warfare does indeed strengthen the internal solidarity of the group which engages in it, it does not follow, as we have seen, that the whole society is so strengthened. It is all very well for Wedgwood to insist that 'the wider unity is never lost sight of', but it is hard to see that the total society is actually *strengthened* by the fact that the clans restrain themselves from eating each other! (Wedgwood has here reversed the true explanation for the prohibition on cannibalism, which is that because the people feel that they are really members of the same society, they feel repugnance at the idea of eating each other, which is usually reserved for true enemies.)

Wedgwood has in fact committed the basic error of assuming that 'whatever is, is necessary', rather than the result of a local concatenation of circumstances which are the product of a particular culture, and not of the working of some universal law.

Wedgwood also argues that warfare is functional because it dissipates the anger of the group:

'Wars were not undertaken without some cause, such as murder, by physical or magical means, insult to an important person, damage to gardens etc. They were in fact entered upon when the community had in some way suffered and needed some other people on whom to vent its anger for the injury which it had received. The expression of this anger, in fighting, relieved it; the discomfort and irritation which was disquieting the community was brought to an end, and thus a sense of well-being was restored' (Wedgwood, 1930: 33).

While it is true that such provocations are frequently the cause of warfare in primitive societies, as they were among the Tauade, to identify a cause is not to demonstrate a function, either for the immediate group or for the larger society. Undoubtedly, after killing one of the members of the tribe responsible for such a provocation, the victorious group would feel a sense of well-being, but it was likely to be short-lived, and replaced by a very different sense when the other group raided them in turn, killed their pigs, burnt their houses, ravaged their gardens, took away a few corpses to eat, and perhaps even drove them temporarily out of their land altogether! In the war 'game' which the Tauade played with each other, their obsession with vengeance merely meant that *everyone* was angry *all* the time.

Vayda advances a somewhat similar theory, and believes that primitive warfare may be functional in the regulation of what he calls 'sociopolitical variables'.

'We can say that the hypothesis is that when some such variable as the number, frequency, or magnitude of the offences committed against a group exceeds a certain value, then the group goes to war, and thereafter, at least temporarily, the number, frequency or magnitude of offences committed declines' (Vayda, 1967b: 135).

But, as in the case of Wedgwood's theory, Vayda's hypothesis is inherently incapable of explaining warfare when vengeance is the norm. Among the Tauade, a tribe which provoked another would not be chastened by the retaliation into offending no more, but, on the contrary, would be infused with rage and hatred, and meditate on the first opportunity for 'pay-back'. Not would strict reciprocity be observed, and if they could kill several people for one of their own, so much the better.

A more sophisticated theory of conflict argues that there is a general tendency in society for cross-cutting ties both to produce disputes and violence, but also to bring about their resolution and the re-establishment of social cohesion. This type of theory is, of course, closely associated with the work of Gluckman. The basic theme of Gluckman's theory of social conflict is that:

'... men quarrel in terms of certain of their customary allegiances, but are restrained from violence through other conflicting allegiances which are also enjoined on them by custom. The result is that conflicts in one set of relationships over a wide range of society or through a longer period of time, lead to the re-establishment of social cohesion' (Gluckman, 1963: 2) and

'The critical results of their [anthropologists'] analysis is to show that these societies are so organized into a series of groups and relationships, that people who are friends on one basis are enemies on another' (Gluckman, 1963: 4).

As an example of such a process he quotes Colson's study of the Tonga of Northern Rhodesia. In this case, a man of clan A kills a man of clan B. The two clans break off relations, and apparently in days before colonial rule the men of B residing in A's territory would flee home, and *vice versa*. Women of clan A married to men of B are threatened and insulted by men of B, which upsets their husbands, and disposes them to accept the compensation which is offered through the offices of affines of both clans, and peace is made.

Now, as Gluckman says, this is a very generally valid principle of human relations, which has long been recognised by many scholars, and with which no-one who has reflected at all on human society would wish to disagree. The objection which one would wish to make is that Gluckman seems to think that it is a universal law of human society, instead of simply a special case. Indeed, his whole book *Custom and conflict in Africa* is organised around the theme that cross-cutting ties, while dividing men, ultimately bind them together. Yet his examples are not really paradigmatic, but only illustrative.

In the case of the Konso, they have evolved a group of autonomous towns numbering about 1,500 souls on average which, apart from very small clusters of two to three towns, which I call nuclear alliances, have almost no cross-cutting ties. The result has been, predictably, chronic warfare, which even the regional peacemakers and priests have been largely powerless to prevent. It is therefore quite possible for societies to exist where cross-cutting ties are largely inoperative, where political anarchy is the result, and yet where life goes on from one generation to another in a perfectly viable manner.

It might be objected, however, that even if such societies as the Konso exist, at least they show that the absence of cross-cutting ties will produce large amounts of conflict which are difficult to resolve, and that this at least negatively validates Gluckman's thesis. This is true enough. But as in the case of the Tauade it is possible to show that the multiplicity of cross-cutting ties in certain conditions can actually *maximise* conflict.

A possible relationship between tribes in a society similar to the Tauade can be shown diagrammatically, as in figure 1 (in the diagram, broken lines denote hostility, connected lines denote friendship). Tribes I, II and III are each divided into kin groups (reckoned cognatically) designated by a letter. A man in kin group D has relatives in groups G and J. Let us suppose that a man of B kills a person of G. Now this man of D may be very angry and upset about this, so he kills a person of B in vengeance. He may then be under threat of retaliation in his own tribe I, but because B have relations in E of II, the man of D may be able to flee to his relatives of J in III.

In other words, because tribes are fragmented within themselves into kin groups, which are too loose to provide effective control over their members' acts, yet in terms of which vengeance is taken, and because these kin groups spill over into other tribes, a killing of a person in another tribe by a man in one's own tribe may be revenged *within* the tribe of the killer, and the retaliator has also the chance to use other kin ties to find refuge in a third tribe. It is the capacity of men to flee to relatives in other tribes which undoubtedly contributed to the high rate of homicide among the Tauade. In the tribe where I lived during field work, the homicide rate over a fifty-year period was of the order of 1/180 *per annum*.

Since it is an ill wind that blows nobody good, functionalists are almost always able to show that everything which people do has some advantageous aspects for someone, so that diametrically opposite situations will be described as 'adaptively - or functionally - advantageous'.

For example, if a group of tribes habitually lives at peace, it will be shown that there are certain conditions which make this possible, whose function will then have been demonstrated to contribute to the maintenance of peace. But, should the tribes concerned habitually have lived in a state of chronic anarchy and violence, the functionalist is not discouraged. He may either say that each tribe is a separate society, and that warfare contributes to the solidarity of each so-called society, or, that it eliminates weaklings and contributes to the vigour of the group, besides keeping down the surplus population, and supplying protein if they are cannibals. Some good examples of this kind of intellectual juggling can be found in Vayda's analysis of Maori and Iban warfare.

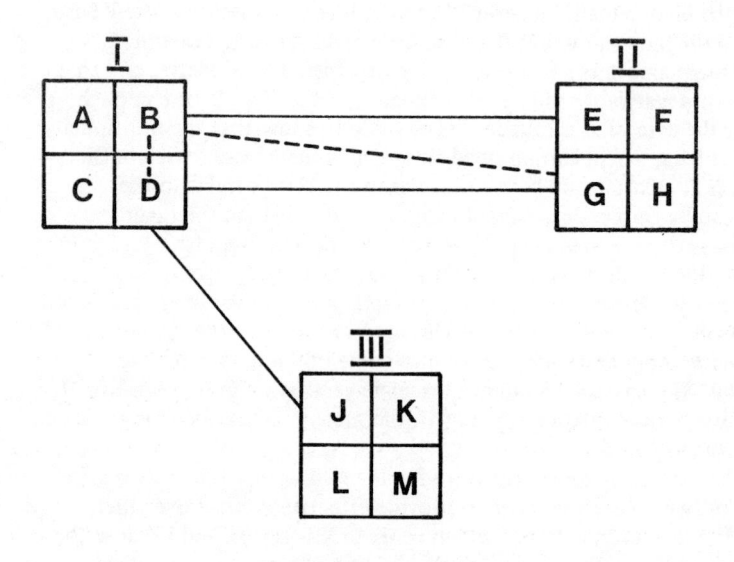

FIGURE 1

In his paper on Maori warfare, he again advances the hypothesis that their warfare was a mechanism for the distribution of the population, this time throughout the New Zealand environment. Apparently tribes preferred to take other tribes' land which had previously been cleared, rather than clear the primary forest themselves.

> 'It now becomes clear what were the viable alternatives confronting such a group [which had exhausted its existing cleared land]. It could undertake either to expand into the virgin rain-forest or to get previously used land from other groups. Because the labor involved in clearing the primary forest was so great, the preferred alternative probably was to get previously

used land from other groups - by force if necessary. If the time and effort required for either clearing virgin land in order to make room for cultivation or breaking ground for the first time in order to dig fern root were considerably more than were necessary for the operations of both conquest and the preparation of previously used land, it follows that conquests would have added more efficiently to the prospects of particular groups than would peaceful dispersion' (Vayda, 1967a: 377).

This argument is a complete fallacy, since it purports to compare, under the heading 'effort' things which are incommensurable - the quantity of energy expended in clearing primary forest, and the lives lost and serious injuries received in the process of conquering some other tribe's land. Since these two items cannot be compared, it is meaningless to talk of the relative efficiency of either possible solutions to this problem. Vayda continues that the end process would have been that if the survivors of the defeated group persisted as a group, they might

'invade the territory of some even weaker group, and this latter group might be driven off to yet other land - probably to virgin forest which the group would then have no option but to clear. In any case, an end result would be the occupation and exploiting of previously unexploited (or under exploited) land, and, in all likelihood, an increase in the extent of New Zealand's area covered by second growth rather than by virgin forest' (Vayda, 1967a: 378).

If we accept this argument as valid it is hard to reconcile it with another argument, which Vayda makes about Iban warfare and its ecological consequences, based on Freeman's ethnographic data. Freeman states that the Iban, unlike the Maori, prefer to cultivate virgin forest, but Vayda is apparently sceptical of his claims in this respect:

'However, as Freeman (1955: pp. 111, 115, 117-18) himself makes clear, the preference for virgin forest was neither so general nor so intense as to induce them to allow second growth to revert to climax vegetation. Leach (1950: p. 89) writing of Sarawak, has stated that in 'most normal circumstances the total amount of virgin jungle cleared in any one year is almost infinitesimal', and it seems warranted to conclude that the relative ease of clearing second growth may well have been a factor in the Iban taking previously farmed land from other groups at times rather than expanding into virgin territory' (Vayda, 1961: 354).

Vayda clearly implies that Freeman has exaggerated the Iban preference for virgin forest, and by the quotation from Leach suggests that even if such a preference exists, its effects have been minimal. Freeman's own account makes it clear, however, that Vayda's interpretation of Iban agriculture is quite untenable, and has seriously misrepresented the facts.

'To the Iban virgin jungle is the most highly valued of all resources: by felling it rights over land are acquired, and if weather conditions be favourable, virgin land yields crops of exceptional abundance for two years in succession. The 'rich, untouched vegetation' of the Baleh was, to the Iban, the most inviting of prizes, and desire to exploit it was the over-ruling incentive of their advance and an important motive in prompting their fierce attacks on alien tribes that stood in the way. Head-hunting and a craving for virgin land went hand in hand. During the past eighty years, hundreds of thousands of acres have been felled and farmed, so that today aerial photographs of the Baleh show complex mosaics in which remaining enclaves of virgin forest are surrounded and interspersed with secondary jungle at many different stages of regeneration' (Freeman, 1955: 111).

And he elaborates,

'By felling virgin forest a family obtains rights of ownership over land, rights of usufruct over the secondary jungle which in due course springs up: and by Iban *adat* these rights are permanently vested in the family and its heirs for as long as they care to exercise them' (1955: 115).

And he also points out:

'... weed control is one of the major difficulties with which Iban farmers have to cope. [And] One of the great advantages of farming virgin land is that weeds are few and fairly easy to control' (1955: 128).

White Vayda has obviously misrepresented Freeman's material, his argument about the Iban preference for virgin forest is still illuminating for our purposes.

'This preference is also something that may have promoted peace within the Iban tribes - by virtue of stimulating the younger and hardier people to settle the more recently pioneered areas and not to vie unduly for land in the old areas. It should be noted also that for the younger and hardier people the virgin forest may have seemed more attractive because of the greater possibilities for the collection of jungle produce' (Vayda, 1961: 354).

We have here then two societies of expanding swidden agriculturalists, Maori and Iban, one of which seems to have had a preference for taking other people's secondary growth land, instead of cultivating virgin forest, with much warfare as a result, while the Iban had the opposite practice. In the case of the Maoris Vayda argues that:

'it seems reasonable to identify the conquests [those which were followed by land redistribution] as an agency whereby more and more of the New Zealand environment was settled and exploited by the Maori people' (Vayda, 1967a: 378).

In the case of the Iban he argues that the more intensive use of land is functional because it produces peace, which entirely reverses the first argument! This is a good case of being able to prove that everything is functional, by pointing out the beneficial consequences of some form of behaviour, which is not difficult and then concluding that the causes of this are functional. It would surely have been equally beneficial for the Maori to have had a preference for cultivating virgin forest, since it would have toughened them physically and been good for their characters, and reduced the level of violence.

The functionalist illusion that if an institution exists it does so because it plays some essential part in maintaining the social system, and is therefore necessary, is similar to the fallacy that every historical event could only have occurred in the way that it actually did. We may call this the fallacy of hindsight. As we all know, the remarkable fact about victims of this fallacy is that the confidence of their demonstrations of inevitability after the event is only equalled by their incapacity to predict those same consequences before they have taken place. The conviction which demonstrations of historical inevitability carry derives in large measure from a general tendency to ignore other possibilities which were never realised. Similarly, much of the superficial conviction which functionalist arguments possess derives, as I pointed out earlier, from a failure to consider alternative possibilities open to a society. For example, if we consider the case of social adaptation to the environment, a particular environment may facilitate some kinds of institution, render others more difficult, and still others impossible, but there must be few if any environments which *demand* one and one only adaptation in the form of a particular social or technological institution. Since there are, therefore, in practice always several alternative possibilities open to a society in its organisational and technological response to a particular environment, to say that the possibility actually followed is adaptive is not to say that no other forms of adaptation were possible.

For example, the Tauade prefer leisure to work, and their dependence on root crops as opposed to grain gives them more opportunity for leisure than the Konso have, depending as they do on millet, barley, wheat and maize. Nor do the Tauade choose to live permanently in large villages, which are certainly quite feasible for them in ecological terms. They prefer to consume pork in the 'irrational' manner of periodic orgies of gluttony - a mode of consumption which minimises the benefits of available protein. These feasts are held in order to give renown to the hosts. The Tauade also have an extreme, one might say obsessive, aversion to animal and human faeces, unlike the Konso who use both for manure. In exactly the same environment it would be possible to fence the pigs, and so prevent their excessive ravages of the gardens, to use their dung in combination with human faeces and vegetable compost as manure to allow more permanent gardens, to consume pigs in smaller numbers more frequently and to conserve their meat by smoking to ensure a more regular and efficient intake of protein, and to live in large settlements. The second mode of livelihood would require harder work, less leisure, more planning and an attitude to feasts different from their present one, but to describe it as more adaptive than their present agricultural system would be mistaken; it would simply be differently adaptive. Because the Tauade are able to maintain what to them is a satisfactory level of subsistence by their traditional methods of raising and consuming pigs and cultivating their gardens, and because, objectively speaking, they do not suffer nutritional or other physical harmful effects, we should conclude that, in relation to their physical environment, their mode of livelihood is adaptively neutral.

Finally, let us consider the common functionalist assumption that societies are in competition with one another, and that as a result of natural selection we find that the winners in this process are the societies which are best adapted to their natural and human environments. Newcomb writes, for example:

> 'an analogy might be drawn here between a living organism and a sociocultural system, both of which must struggle against environmental forces and against their fellow organisms' (Newcomb, 1950: 317).

and more recently Carneiro has expressed the same belief with specific emphasis on the role of warfare in the competition of societies:

> 'When societies fight, the cultural equivalent of natural selection comes into play ... As societies compete, the less well adapted tend to fall by the wayside, leaving outstanding those best able to withstand the competition... Cultural selection, which operates even on traits of little or no adaptive value, acts with special intensity on traits directly concerned with survival. And since there is generally no greater challenge to a society's existence than war, it is here that we find selection operating most rigorously' (Carneiro, 1970: xii).

This type of reasoning is vulnerable to two objections. The first is that it may not be possible to define the competing groups, as we saw earlier. The second is that no state of true competition, as opposed to violence, may really exist at all in such situations. Among the Tauade, no tribe normally has anything that any other tribe needs, though no one is of course averse to stealing a pig or two, or a woman, if she is willing. The tribe among whom I lived possessed an area of salt grass, which is now no longer used because of the introduction of European salt. It is significant that in the past there was apparently no fighting over this much desired and valuable commodity. My informants told me that people from other tribes would come and give pork, or some other esteemed valuable, in exchange for access to this salt grass. It was also told that another tribe, the Laitate, who used to have no pandanus trees before they moved to new land, and took some of the trees of another tribe, had the custom for a long time of trading with pork for the nuts with other tribes. There are many examples in the ethnographic literature of economic disparities which are settled by trade and not warfare. My informants also told me that only one of their clans, the Karuai, was autochthonous, and that the others had come later, bringing pigs and sweet potatoes, which the Karuai have never seen before, and in exchange for these eagerly accepted innovations allowed the newcomers to settle among them. It is obvious that social change among the Tauade is now, and has been, the result of diffusion and trade, and not of competition, and the Tauade are in no way unique in New Guinea, or anywhere else in this respect. Since all the groups in the Tauade area, and in the Sub-District as a whole, are roughly evenly matched, and equally inefficient in their mode of warfare and transport, there was not much that any one group could have done anyway, even if it had wanted to, to despoil another group of its resources in the long run. Where contiguous groups are all characterised by a low level of efficiency in their social organisation, and their environments are sufficiently undemanding to allow the satisfaction of what are generally accepted within the culture as normal requirements of life, there is no reason to expect competition, as opposed to mere violence.

It seems therefore that in situations like New Guinea, it is possible to have a multiplicity of small groups, incredibly inefficient by our standards of social organisation, staggering along for century after century, not really being able to do each other much harm, in a state of minimal social change. The only significant social changes would have been brought about by the peaceful introduction of new commodities, such as pigs, sweet potatoes, yams, tobacco, and perhaps the pandanus tree. It is significant that the sweet potato, which confers a genuine adaptive advantage on mountain dwellers who adopt it, because it will grow at higher altitudes than yams or taro thereby allowing them to use more of their land, was not jealously retained solely by the groups which introduced it. On the contrary, it was diffused, and the competitive advantage which it might have conferred upon groups which adopted it but refused to let their neighbours have it, was lost.

Only when faced with genuine competition, in the form of the Australian Administration, organised for true military and social efficiency, do we have a situation resembling that posited as normal by evolutionary theorists, and in which native society was hopelessly inadequate to meet the challenge. I am not therefore saying that competition between different societies does not take place - the conquests of the great empires of history, and more recently of the European colonial powers, are obvious examples of competing societies - merely that in large areas of the world in the past social inefficiency was so great that the possibilities of effective competition were very limited.

The further back one looks in time, moreover, the smaller the human population becomes, and the greater become natural resources in relation to it. The total human population has also increased more rapidly with the passage of time, and the rate of this increase has itself increased, especially after the introduction of agriculture and the domestication of animals. It is reasonable to believe, therefore, that the pressure on resources such as is described by ethnographers is a relatively recent phenomenon, where it exists at all, that is, and should not be assumed to have operated long before the present. It is clear that migration, rather than sitting tight and fighting it out, has generally been the preferred response to situations of overcrowding.

It is of course true that where some natural resources are beyond the technological capacities of a people to exploit them, they are to that extent non-existent, and that in consequence a culture of hunters and gatherers will require a greater land area to support itself than a community of advanced agriculturalists. Again, in some cases people have religious, legal and sentimental attachments to particular pieces of ground, and may be reluctant to move from them even to land which is more productive. Nevertheless, even when these important qualifications have been made, it is clear that the general pressure on resources will have tended to decrease the further back in time we go.

But even if, for the sake of argument, we grant that competition between societies exists at the primitive level, functionalists have assumed that existing institutions are in a state of adaptation to their natural and social environment. It is somewhat remarkable that they have ignored the possibility that natural selection might be taking place before their eyes, in the displacement of one society by another. Species did not become extinct with the rapidity of candles being snuffed out, nor do societies in most cases. Therefore just because a society has survived to be studied does not mean that it has done a good job of adaptation, or that it will not disappear in the future. Tortuous arguments to prove that the most unlikely cultural traits are really adaptive therefore seem to rest not upon any theory of natural selection, but upon its opposite, the belief that everything is for the best in the best of all possible worlds!

Moreover, by attempting to apply what they believe to be the principles of biological evolution, many functionalists in their determination to show that even such social institutions as warfare are adaptive, have adopted a view of natural selection which is more extreme in its rigidity than many biologists would claim for it in the study of animal populations. For example, G.C. Williams, a biologist, writes:

> 'A frequent practice is to recognize adaptation in any recognizable benefit arising from the activities of an organism. I believe that this is an insufficient basis for postulating adaptation and that it has led to some serious errors. A benefit can be the effect of chance instead of design' (Williams, 1966: 2).

> 'Ecological or physiological necessity is not an evolutionary factor, and the development of an adaptation is no evidence that it was necessary for the survival of the species' (28).

Moreover,

> 'The fact that a certain adaptation is necessary to the survival of a species has no bearing on its likelihood of evolving. We can say of every group of organisms that is now extinct that whatever adaptations were necessary for its survival were not, in fact, evolved' (Williams, 1966: 29-30).

Indeed, it is a truism that of all the characterstics of primitive societies which allowed them to be conquered so easily by centralised societies, their internal feuding and warfare was probably the most significant.

We may apply the lessons of the biological principles of natural selection to theories of social evolution as follows:

1. Because an institution exists, this does not mean that no other would have been sufficient in its place.
2. Because an institution exists, it does not follow that it had to.
3. Because an institution exists, it does not mean that it is the best one possible.
4. Because an institution needs to exist, in order for the society to survive, it does not follow that it will.

I referred earlier to societies as 'winners' and 'losers', but such distinctions in the long run are likely to have only transient significance, as Kipling reminds us,

> Far-called, our navies melt away;
> On dune and headland sinks the fire:
> Lo, all our pomp of yesterday
> Is one with Nineveh and Tyre.

Complexity is vulnerable, for all its triumphs, as the green algae have shown us; unchanged for 400 million years, they will outlast humanity. Perhaps, too, the last of all human societies will be tribal.

References

Carneiro, R.L. (1970). Foreword to *The Evolution of War*, edited by K. Otterbein. Cambridge, Mass.: HRAF Press.
Chagnon, N.A. (1967). Yanomamö social organisation and warfare. In *War*, edited by N.H. Fried, M. Harris and R. Murphy. New York: Natural History Press.
Chagnon, N.A. (1968). *Yanomamö : The Fierce People*. New York: Holt, Rinehart & Winston.
Collins, P.W. (1965). Functional analyses in the symposium 'Man, culture and animals'. In *Man, Culture and Animals: The Role of Animals in Human Ecological Adjustments*, edited by A. Leeds and A.P. Vayda. Washington: American Association for the Advancement of Science, Publ. 78.
Dampièrre, E. de (1967). *Un Ancien Royaume du Haut Obangi*. Paris: Plon.
Freeman, J.D. (1955). *Iban Agriculture: A Report on the Shifting Cultivation of Hill Rice by the Iban of Sarawak*. Colonial Research Study 18. London: HMSO.
Gluckman, M. (1963). *Custom and Conflict in Africa*, p. 4. Oxford: Blackwell.
Hallpike, C.R. (1972). *The Konso of Ethiopia: A Study of the Values of a Cushitic People*. Oxford: Clarendon Press.
Krapf-Askari, E. (1972). Women, spears and the scarce good: a comparison of the sociological function of warfare in two central African societies. In *Zande Themes*, edited by A. Singer and B.V. Street. Oxford: Blackwell.
Leach, E.R. (1950). *Social Science Research in Sarawak: A Report on the Possibilities of a Social Economic Survey of Sarawak*. Colonial Research Study 1. London : HMSO.
Leeds, A. and Vayda, A.P. (1965). Preface to *Man, Culture and Animals: The Role of Animals in Human Ecological Adjustments*. Washington: American Association for the Advancement of Science, Publ. 78.
Newcomb, W.W. (1950). A re-examination of the causes of Plains warfare. *American Anthropologist*, 52, 317-330.
Rappaport, R.A. (1968). *Pigs for the Ancestors: Ritual in the Ecology of a New Guinea People*. New Haven: Yale University Press.
Vayda, A. P. (1961). Expansion and warfare among swidden agriculturalists. *American Anthropologist*, 63, 346-358.
Vayda, A.P. (1967a). Maori warfare. In *Law and Warfare*, edited by P. Bohannan. New York: Natural History Press.
Vayda, A.P. (1967b). Research on the functions of primitive war. *Peace Research Society (Int.) Paper*, 7, 133-138.
Vayda, A. P. (1968a). Hypotheses about functions of war. In *War*, edited by N.H. Fried, M. Harris and R. Murphy. New York: Natural History Press.
Vayda, A.P. (1968b). Foreword to *Pigs for the Ancestors: Ritual in the Ecology of a New Guinea People*, edited by R.A. Rappaport. New Haven: Yale University Press.
Vayda, A.P. (1971). Phases of war and peace among the Marings of New Guinea. *Oceania*, 42, 1-24.
Wedgwood, C.H. (1930). Some aspects of warfare in Melanesia. *Oceania*, 1, 5-33.
White, L.A. (1947). Culturological versus psychological interpretations of human behaviour. *American Sociological Review*, 12, 686-698.
Williams, C.C. (1966). *Adaptations and Natural Selection*. Princeton: University Press.

16

ON GENETICS AND POLITICS

Theodosius Dobzhansky

There is a habit of thought perhaps as old as language itself that keeps getting in the way of our understanding of the history and nature of the processes of life. This is our tendency to think in terms of static types. Of course we must sort into categories the overwhelming diversity of phenomena we perceive and experience, and we do so in words like 'man', 'cat', or 'dog'. Such words do not refer to particular persons or animals but to abstract representatives of mankind, cat-kind, and dog-kind. Also, such words emphasize differences between 'kinds' as if there were rigid boundaries; they give no hint of what the 'kinds' may have in common. Nor do they take into account, or even suggest, the diversity within 'kinds' - the diversity of persons, of cats, and of dogs. Moreover, individual persons and animals change and grow old.

Typological Thinking

Nevertheless, man has long sought for ways to unify as well as classify this diversity - since long before Bronowski said, beautifully, that 'science is nothing else than the search to discover unity in the wild variety of nature - or more exactly, in the variety of our experience. Poetry, painting, the arts are in the same search, in Coleridge's phrase, for unity in variety. Each in its own way looks for likeness under the variety of human experience.

One tempting way to unify is to declare that the diversity and change are false appearances. Plato did so by his famous theory of ideas. He believed that God created eternal, unchangeable, and inconceivably beautiful prototypes, or ideas, of Man, Horse, and even such mundane and inanimate objects as Bed and Table; that individual persons, horses, beds, and tables are only pale shadows of their respective ideas; that acquiring wisdom means 'seeing' the ideas where formerly one saw only their shadows. Aristotle assumed only one cosmic idea, which manifests itself in the visible world. He believed that nature's 'purpose' was to realize the ideal form, and that all animals were variants of a single architectonic plan.

For more than 2,000 years - up to the time of Darwin - the organic world was viewed either as Plato or as Aristotle saw it, within the Western World. Either way was compatible with believing that living, and even nonliving, bodies constituted a 'Great Chain of Being' that ranged from lesser to greater perfection. Leibniz in the seventeenth and Bonnet in the eighteenth century felt satisfied that the Chain is single and uninterrupted. Bonnet saw it starting with fire and 'finer matters', and extending through air, water, minerals, corals, truffles, plants, sea anemones, birds, ostriches, bats, quadrupeds, monkeys, and so to man.

To Lamarck and to Geoffrey St. Hilaire in the nineteenth century, but not to their predecessors and contemporaries, the Great Chain implied evolution. Cuvier, dissenting, was of course absolutely right that there is no single plan of body structure common to all animals. Still, the hypothesis that living organisms are manifestations of a limited number of basic types or ideas of structure was useful because it inspired studies on comparative anatomy and classification. There is no doubt that such data, though collected for another purpose, did help to furnish a base for the theory of evolution.

Such are some of the pre-Darwinian roots of *typological thinking*. Their common quality is that they postulate, implicitly or explicitly, archetypes or ideal types.

Populational Thinking

The Darwin-Wallace theory of evolution shattered the basis of typological thinking over a century ago, but many biologists are still unaware of this profound implication. I agree with Ernst Mayr that 'the replacement of typological thinking by populational thinking is perhaps the greatest conceptual revolution that has taken place in biology'. My only cavil is that Mayr's 'has taken place' is over-optimistic, though I do believe that this conceptual revolution is well under way. It has proceeded so slowly because the difference between typological and populational thinking is as subtle as it is profound, but also because habits of thought are at least as hard to change as any other habits. I will try to show this difference, and then to indicate how it is represented in and confuses so much of our sociological and political thinking.

Darwin characterized his great work *On the Origin of Species* as 'one long argument'. The heart of this argument was 'that species are only strongly marked ... varieties, and that each species first existed as a variety'. This amounts to erasing any sharp lines between 'varieties' or 'species' by in effect saying that there exist within a 'species' the raw materials from which natural selection compounds new 'species', which are in turn subject to further transformation into other new 'species'. The transformations are not a false front or an illusion; they are real novelties because they take a variety of directions. Thus neither the 'varieties' nor the 'species' can be diverse manifestations of Platonic archetypes or ideas or of an Aristotelian tendency, for they are changeable in different ways. To the typologist, who is eager to classify and pigeonhole, the presence of intermediate forms between 'varieties', 'species', 'races' is a nuisance which one is tempted to shrug off whenever possible. But to the evolutionist borderline cases are a godsend. Darwin's argument was limited to affirming that evolution *had* taken place. For roughly the next four decades, until about 1900, studies in comparative anatomy, embryology, and paleontology concentrated on discovering and examining further evidence to confirm the argument. Such evidence is now so well known that it is a part of elementary, college, and high school courses of biology.

Then for about 30 years after the turn of the century there was a rapid growth of knowledge of basic genetics, stemming largely from Gregor Mendel's rediscovered work of 1865 on transmission of characteristics from one generation to another. Around 1930 a mathematical theory was deduced which explains *what causes* evolution to take place. It took account of Darwin's argument that natural selection was the mechanism; it introduced the idea of adaptation to environment as the 'pressure' that directed natural selection within a breeding population; and it incorporated the new hypothesis of gene mutations as explanation of the random appearance of entirely new characteristics within a population. Since then many scientists have demonstrated that the theory makes co-ordinated sense of experimental genetics, paleontology, zoological and botanical systematics, cytology, comparative morphology, embryology, anthropology, ecology, physiology, and biochemistry; and it has been strengthened by recent spectacular developments in molecular genetics.

This 'synthetic' theory (so called because it synthesizes) demonstrates that in a non-uniform environment there is no such thing as a typical, average, or ideal type within sexually reproducing, outbreeding populations of a species such as man. It demonstrates that such a biological species is a population of unique individuals (except for identical twins), carriers of *diverse* genotypes. ('Genotype' stands for the inherited, and hence heritable, components of an individual; 'phenotype' stands for the outwardly expressed characteristics.)

Now how great is the genetic diversity within a given species is only sketchily known at present. The genetic diversity within the human species in particular is still quite inadequately explored. Part of the problem relates to our discovering ever greater complexity in how 'genes' work. We have tried to explain the effects by hypothesizing dominant, semi-dominant, incompletely recessive, and completely recessive genes; polygenes - combinations that operate together to determine a characteristic; supergenes - linked groups of genes which determine complexes of traits inherited as units; pleiotropism - an individual gene having an effect on several characteristics which do not have any obvious developmental interdependence. The simple Mendelian duality of dominant and recessive genes has long since proved to offer a very inadequate explanation of reality. No doubt all of these postulates must eventually be reduced to molecular terms. But for our purposes at the moment, the main thing we must guard against is thinking in terms of one 'gene' for every 'trait' and one 'trait' for every 'gene'.

There is no doubt that the range of potential diversity, of potentially possible genotypes, within a species such as man is vastly greater than could ever be realized as actual genotypes. The number of genes in a human sex cell is not known, but it could hardly be less than the 10,000 estimated for *Drosophila*. If we assume only two variants, alleles, per gene (and many, or most, genes may have more than two alleles), this makes $2^{10,000}$ potentially possible genetically different gametes. (Each of the sex cells, the gametes, bears only one of the two sets of chromosomes of the organism.) Therefore the potentially possible zygotes (union of two sex cells, hence genotypes) would be $3^{10,000}$. Of course the actual genotypes realized are not just a random assortment of gene combinations, which such computations might imply, because of the complexity of how genes 'work', which I alluded to just above. Still, it should be apparent that 'potential' must exceed 'actually expressed' by astronomical proportions.

The main point to grasp about populational thinking in terms of the synthetic theory of evolution is that a *range* of diversity within a species is necessary for a range of adaptability to varying environments. Typological thinking is plainly un-evolutionary or anti-evolutionary because in varying ways it reverts to postulating an ideal or optimal type; and an optimal type could only be relevant to such a completely static and uniform environment as could pertain to few species - certainly not to man, though perhaps to such as oysters.

If the bulk of the genetic diversity in a species is balanced, the optimal genotype becomes a will-o'-the-wisp. There could be no one 'normal' genotype, but only arrays of genotypes which make their carriers able to live and reproduce successfully in the various environments the species inhabits. There would inevitably be ill-adapted, pathological variants at one extreme and exceptionally vigorous, outstandingly successful variants at the other extreme, the genetic elite. Then it is the diversity of genotypes and phenotypes in a population, including the diversity of behaviors, and the factors which maintain the diversity that should be studied, not any 'typical' or even statistically average behavior.

It is undeniable that some mutant genes are deleterious in all existing environments whether inheritance is homozygous or heterozygous. It is likewise undeniable that some kinds of heterozygous variants are maintained in a population by balancing selection even though inheritance of the homozygous condition may be lethal. The sickle-cell trait is perhaps one of the best-known examples of such a heterozygous condition being maintained. It appears that heterozygous inheritance of this 'gene' confers somewhat superior resistance to malaria while homozygous inheritance often leads to an anemic condition that frequently kills.

The Confusion of Political and Sociological Genetics

How does this subtle difference between typological thinking and populational thinking find its way into politics and sociology? First I must point out that though the roots of populational thinking are less easily traceable than the roots of typological thinking, they can be found in the Christian view that each individual soul is as valuable as any other; that it is the individual person who commits sins; that we possess free wills and are accountable for our actions. But the formal philosophical codification of human individuality came only in 1785, in Kant's doctrine that every human being is an end in himself. However, this doctrine is implicit in the belief that every man has certain inalienable rights, which belief became popular during the Age of Enlightenment, and which serves as the foundation of democracy.

In general, typological thinking about man goes mostly with conservative political persuasions, and the view that every man is an end in himself goes with liberal. But consistency is not one of man's hallmarks. Strangely enough, conservatives tend to emphasize that different people are genetically different, while liberals tend to assert that every man is at birth virtually a *tabula rasa*, a blank slate, and that all behavioral differences between men are the result of upbringing and education.

It is no exaggeration to say that some version of this *tabula rasa* theory is entertained, explicitly or implicitly, by most social scientists and by some influential schools of psychology, especially those with psychoanalytical leanings. It is attractive because it seems to uphold an optimistic view of human nature: though a lot of people behave stupidly, wretchedly, and viciously, this is because they were badly brought up and were spoiled by corrupting influences of badly organized society; a better organized society, better care, guidance, and education would make everybody behave with goodness and reasonableness, because that capacity is the normal and universal endowment of every representative of the human species.

Does it not become apparent that the *tabula rasa* theory is but another form of typological thinking? In this case only a single type for the whole species *Homo sapiens* is proposed.

John Locke made the classical statement of the *tabula rasa* theory, but he did not claim anything so rash as that all infants are born alike. What he did claim, rather, is that there are no inborn 'ideas'. He wrote: 'Let us then suppose the mind to be, as we say, white paper, void of all characters, without any ideas; how comes it to be furnished? . . . All that are born into the world being surrounded with bodies that perpetually and diversely affect them, variety of ideas, whether care be taken about it or not, are imprinted on the minds of children.' His expression of the *tabula rasa* theory had a great and abiding influence on the climate of ideas in which the civilized part of mankind lives. It was adopted by the thinkers of the Age of Enlightenment, from Voltaire and Helvetius, Rousseau and Condorcet, to Bentham and Jefferson. It has been, and continues to be, an important ingredient in the philosophy of democracy. But exaggeration and over-extension of the theory - to the erroneous conclusion that people are innately uniform lumps of clay molded only be environmental conditions - that interpretation of Locke, I think it can be demonstrated, makes nonsense of democracy.

Here is another example of typological thinking as it has become, in this case, woven into conservative political and sociological thought. The current civil rights movement in the United States has prompted the racists to devise a curious quasi-scientific justification of their social and political biases. Their argument is that Negroes, compared to whites, have a smaller average brain size and lower average scores on various intelligence and achievement tests. Whether these alleged differences are real, and if real whether of environmental origin, need not concern us here. The point is that not even racists deny that all these measurements vary among whites as well as among Negroes. The variation ranges overlap so broadly that the large brains and the high scores in Negroes are decidedly above the white averages, and the small brains and the low scores in whites are decidedly below the Negro averages. Now, the typological reasoning goes about as follows. All Negroes are said to be but manifestations of the same Negro archetype, and all whites of the same white archetype; no matter what his brain size or his intelligence score may be, an individual is either a Negro or a white and should be treated accordingly. There seems to be some subtle implication here that whatever genes determine 'Negroness' and 'whiteness' - 'polygenes', 'supergenes', or 'pleiotropic' - also determine the brain size.

The populational, and in this case liberal, approach is simply that an individual is a unique genotype (except, again, for identical twins) - a unique combination of a huge number of different characteristics which makes him different from any other person, be that a member of his family, clan, race, or mankind. Beyond the universal rights of all human beings, a person ought to be evaluated on his own individual merits.

The populational approach does not invoke misguided extension of the *tabula rasa* theory; it does not assume that human nature is uniform, thereby reducing individuality to the status of a veneer applied by infant-rearing practices and circumstances of a person's biography. That is starting with a valid premise of Locke's *tabula rasa* theory but going on to an erroneous conclusion. The valid premise that population thinking accepts is that the behavioral development of *Homo sapiens* is remarkably malleable by external circumstances. The geneticist is constantly forced to remind his colleagues, especially those in the social sciences, that what is inherited is not this or that particular phenotypic 'trait' or 'character' but a genotypic potentiality for an organism's developmental response to its environment. Given a certain genotype and a certain sequence of environmental situations, the development follows a certain path. The carriers of other genetic endowments in the same environmental sequence might well develop differently. But also, a given genotype might well develop phenotypically along different paths in different environments. In most abbreviated terms, the observed phenotypic variance has both a genetic and an environmental component.

How 'stabilized' or how 'plastic' any phenotypic expression might be varies from species to species, but in general what is necessary for survival and reproduction is rather 'fixed'. For instance, with very few exceptions, human babies are born with two eyes, a four-chambered heart, a suckling instinct, physiological mechanisms for maintaining constant body temperature, etc. However, sometimes stabilization is disadvantageous. If a *Drosophila* larva is given ample food, it develops into a fly of a certain size. If food is scarce, although above a certain minimum, the starving larva does not die, but pupates and gives an adult insect of a diminutive size. Also, the number of eggs deposited by a *Drosophila* female on abundant food and at favorable temperatures may easily be ten times greater than with scarce food and an unfavorable temperature. Evidently fixed body size and number of eggs produced would be disadvantageous. Natural selection has operated on the genotype to destabilize these characteristics and make them contingent on the environment in which an individual finds itself. It may be that the increased body size among many populations of human beings over the last few centuries (and particularly the last few generations) represents a similar mechanism. (Note the small size of medieval armor, and also the evidence from clothing and shoe manufacturers that nowadays people tend to be bigger than their grandparents, and even parents.)

Now the paramount adaptive characteristic of man is his educability - his capacity to adjust his behavior to circumstances in the light of experience - and that educability is a universal property of all nonpathological individuals. All individuals which belong to the adaptive norm of our species have this capacity of educability through symbolic thinking and communication by symbols, language. It is perhaps justified to say that human evolution has stabilized this capacity, although consequent overt, observable behavior is not stabilized. Locke went no further than that in his original *tabula rasa* theory, although it is easy to see how it could be exaggerated into the illusion that man at birth is a complete *tabula rasa* as far as his prospective behavioral development is concerned.

In reality, this educability goes hand in hand with the populational thinking which argues that genetic diversity enhances the adaptability of our species in particular. Any human society has diverse functions, and as civilization has developed and continues to develop, the diversity of vocations has increased and continues to increase enormously. The division of labor in a primitive society is distributed chiefly between sexes and among different age groups. In a civilized society it is distributed among castes and, ultimately, individuals. The trend of cultural evolution is obviously not toward making everybody have identical occupations, but toward a more and more differentiated occupational structure. What would be the most adaptive response to this trend? Certainly nothing that would encourage genetic uniformity. Although the genetically guaranteed educability of our species makes most individuals trainable for most occupations, it is highly probable that individuals have more genetic adaptability to some occupations than to others. Although almost everybody could become, if brought up and properly trained, a fairly competent farmer, or a craftsman of some sort, or a soldier, sailor, tradesman, teacher, or priest, certain ones would be more easily trainable to be soldiers and others to be teachers, for instance. And it is even more probable that only a relatively few individuals would have the genetic wherewithal for certain highly specialized professions, such as musician or singer or poet, or for high achievement in sports or wisdom or leadership. To argue that only environmental circumstances and training determine a person's behavior makes a travesty of democratic notions of individual choice, responsibility, and freedom.

Human educability is traditionally emphasized by those who espouse liberal political views, while genetic differences are harped upon by conservatives. As pointed out above, this is sheer confusion. The main tenet of liberalism is, it seems to me, that every human being, every individual of the species *Homo sapiens*, is entitled to equal opportunity to achieve the realization of his own particular potentialities, at least so far as compatible with realization of the potentialities of other people. Because human beings are individuals and not 'types', because they are all different, equality of opportunity is necessary. A class or caste society leads unavoidably to misplacement of talents. The biological justification of equality of opportunity is that a society should minimize the loss of valuable human resources, as well as the personal misery resulting from misplaced abilities, and thus enhance its total adaptiveness to variable environments.

17
THE NEW BIOLOGY: WHAT PRICE RELIEVING MAN'S ESTATE?

Leon R. Kass

Recent advances in biology and medicine suggest that we may be rapidly acquiring the power to modify and control the capacities and activities of men by direct intervention and manipulation of their bodies and minds. Certain means are already in use or at hand, others await the solution of relatively minor technical problems, while yet others, those offering perhaps the most precise kind of control, depend upon further basic research. Biologists who have considered these matters disagree on the question of how much how soon, but all agree that the power for 'human engineering', to borrow from the jargon, is coming and that it will probably have profound social consequences.

These developments have been viewed both with enthusiasm and with alarm; they are only just beginning to receive serious attention. Several biologists have undertaken to inform the public about the technical possibilities, present and future. Practitioners of social science 'futurology' are attempting to predict and describe the likely social consequences of and public responses to the new technologies. Lawyers and legislators are exploring institutional innovations for assessing new technologies. All of these activities are based upon the hope that we can harness the new technology of man for the betterment of mankind.

Yet this commendable aspiration points to another set of questions, which are, in my view, sorely neglected - questions that inquire into the meaning of phrases such as the 'betterment of mankind'. A *full* understanding of the new technology of man requires an exploration of ends, values, standards, What ends will or should the new techniques serve? What values should guide society's adjustments? By what standards should the assessment agencies assess? Behind these questions lie others: what is a good man, what is a good life for man, what is a good community? This article is an attempt to provoke discussion of these neglected and important questions.

While these questions about ends and ultimate ends are never unimportant or irrelevant, they have rarely been more important or more relevant. That this is so can be seen once we recognize that we are dealing with a group of technologies that are in a decisive respect unique: the object upon which they operate is man himself. The technologies of energy or food production, of communication, of manufacture, and of motion greatly alter the implements available to man and the conditions in which he uses them. In contrast, the biomedical technology works to change the user himself. To be sure, the printing press, the automobile, the television, and the jet airplane have greatly altered the conditions under which and the way in which men live; but men as biological beings have remained largely unchanged. They have been, and remain, able to accept or reject, to use and abuse these technologies; they choose, whether wisely or foolishly, the ends to which these technologies are means. Biomedical technology may make it possible to change the inherent capacity for choice itself. Indeed, both those who welcome and those who fear the advent of 'human engineering' ground their hopes and fears in the same prospect: *that man can for the first time recreate himself.*

Engineering the engineer seems to differ in kind from engineering his engine. Some have argued, however, that biomedical engineering does not differ qualitatively from toilet training, education, and moral teachings - all of which are forms of so-called 'social engineering', which has man as its object, and is used by one generation to mold the next. In reply, it must at least be said that the techniques which have hitherto been employed are feeble and inefficient when compared to those on the horizon. This quantitative difference rests in part on a qualitative difference in the means of intervention. The traditional influences operate by speech or by symbolic deeds. They pay tribute to man as the animal who lives by speech and who understands the meanings of actions. Also, their effects are, in general, reversible, or at least subject to attempts at reversal. Each person has greater or lesser power to accept or reject or abandon them. In contrast, biomedical engineering circumvents the human context of speech and meaning, bypasses choice, and goes directly to work to modify the human material itself. Moreover, the changes wrought may be irreversible.

In addition, there is an important practical reason for considering the biomedical technology apart from other technologies. The advances we shall examine are fruits of a large, humane project dedicated to the conquest of disease and the relief of human suffering. The biologist and physician, regardless of their private motives, are seen, with justification, to be the well-wishers and benefactors of mankind. Thus, in a time in which technological advance is more carefully scrutinized and increasingly criticized, biomedical developments are still viewed by most people as benefits largely without qualification. The price we pay for these developments is thus more likely to go unrecognized. For this reason, I shall consider only the dangers and costs of biomedical advance. As the benefits are well known, there is no need to dwell upon them here. My discussion is deliberately partial.

I begin with a survey of the pertinent technologies. Next, I will consider some of the basic ethical and social problems in the use of these technologies. Then, I will briefly raise some fundamental questions to which these problems point. Finally, I shall offer some very general reflections on what is to be done.

The Biomedical Technologies

The biomedical technologies can be usefully organized into three groups, according to their major purpose: (i) control of death and life, (ii) control of human potentialities, and (iii) control of human achievement. The corresponding technologies are (i) medicine, especially the arts of prolonging life and of controlling reproduction, (ii) genetic engineering, and (iii) neurological and psychological manipulation. I shall briefly summarize each group of techniques.

1. Control of death and life

Previous medical triumphs have greatly increased average life expectancy. Yet other developments, such as organ transplantation or replacement and research into aging, hold forth the promise of increasing not just the average, but also the maximum life expectancy. Indeed, medicine seems to be sharpening its tools to do battle with death itself, as if death were just one more disease.

More immediately and concretely, available techniques of prolonging life - respirators, cardiac pacemakers, artificial kidneys - are already in the lists against death. Ironically, the success of these devices in forestalling death has introduced confusion in determining that death has, in fact, occurred. The traditional signs of life - heartbeat and respiration - can now be maintained entirely by machines. Some physicians are now busily trying to devise so-called 'new definitions of death', while others maintain that the technical advances show that death is not a concrete event at all, but rather a gradual process, like twilight, incapable of precise temporal localization.

The real challenge to death will come from research into aging and senescence, a field just entering puberty. Recent studies suggest that aging is a genetically controlled process, distinct from disease, but one that can be manipulated and altered by diet or drugs. Extrapolating from animal studies, some scientists have suggested that a decrease in the rate of aging might also be achieved simply by effecting a very small decrease in human body temperature. According to some estimates, by the year 2000 it may be technically possible to add from 20 to 40 useful years to the period of middle life.

Medicine's success in extending life is already a major cause of excessive population growth: death control points to birth control. Although we are already technically competent, new techniques for lowering fertility and chemical agents for inducing abortion will greatly enhance our powers over conception and gestation. Problems of definition have been raised here as well. The need to determine when individuals acquire enforceable legal rights gives society an interest in the definition of human life and of the time when it begins. These matters are too familiar to need elaboration.

Technologies to conquer infertility proceed alongside those to promote it. The first successful laboratory fertilization of human egg by human sperm was reported in 1969 (Edwards *et al.,* 1969). In 1970, British scientists learned how to grow human embryos in the laboratory up to at least the blastocyst stage [that is, to the age of 1 week (Edwards *et al.,* 1970)]. We may soon hear about the next stage, the successful reimplantation of such an embryo into a woman previously infertile because of oviduct disease. The development of an artificial placenta, now under investigation, will make possible full laboratory control of fertilization and gestation. In addition, sophisticated biochemical and cytological techniques of monitoring the 'quality' of the fetus have been and are being developed and used. These developments not only give us more power over the generation of human life, but make it possible to manipulate and to modify the quality of the human material.

2. *Control of human potentialities*

Genetic engineering, when fully developed, will wield two powers not shared by ordinary medical practice. Medicine treats existing individuals and seeks to correct deviations from a norm of health. Genetic engineering, in contrast, will be able to make changes that can be transmitted to succeeding generations and will be able to create new capacities, and hence to establish new norms of health and fitness.

Nevertheless, one of the major interests in genetic manipulation is strictly medical: to develop treatments for individuals with inherited diseases. Genetic disease is prevalent and increasing, thanks partly to medical advances that enable those affected to survive and perpetuate their mutant genes. The hope is that normal copies of the appropriate gene, obtained biologically or synthesized chemically, can be introduced into defective individuals to correct their deficiencies. This *therapeutic* use of genetic technology appears to be far in the future. Moreover, there is some doubt that it will ever be practical, since the same end could be more easily achieved by transplanting cells or organs that could compensate for the missing or defective gene product.

Far less remote are technologies that could serve *eugenic* ends. Their development has been endorsed by those concerned about a general deterioration of the human gene pool and by others who believe that even an undeteriorated human gene pool needs upgrading. Artificial insemination with selected donors, the eugenic proposal of Herman Muller (1961), has been possible for several years because of the perfection of methods for long-term storage of human spermatozoa. The successful maturation of human oocytes in the laboratory and their subsequent fertilization now make it possible to select donors of ova as well. But a far more suitable technique for eugenic purposes will soon be upon us - namely, nuclear transplantation, or cloning. Bypassing the lottery of sexual recombination, nuclear transplantation permits the asexual reproduction or copying of an already developed individual. The nucleus of a mature but unfertilized egg is replaced by a nucleus obtained from a specialized cell of an adult organism or embryo (for example, a cell from the intestines or the skin). The egg with its transplanted nucleus develops as if it had been fertilized and, barring complications, will give rise to a normal adult organism. Since almost all the hereditary material (DNA) of a cell is contained within its nucleus, the renucleated egg and the individual into which it develops are genetically identical to the adult organism that was the source of the donor nucleus. Cloning could be used to produce sets of unlimited numbers of genetically identical individuals, each set derived from a single parent. Cloning has been successful in amphibians and is now being tried in mice; its extension to man merely requires the solution of certain technical problems.

Production of man-animal chimeras by the introduction of selected nonhuman material into developing human embryos is also expected. Fusion of human and nonhuman cells in tissue culture has already been achieved.

Other, less direct means of influencing the gene pool are already available, thanks to our increasing ability to identify and diagnose genetic diseases. Genetic counselors can now detect biochemically and cytologically a variety of severe genetic defects (for example, Mongolism, Tay-Sachs disease) while the fetus is still in utero. Since treatments are at present largely unavailable, diagnosis is often followed by abortion of the affected fetus. In the future, more sensitive tests will also permit the detection of heterozygote carriers, the unaffected individuals who carry but a a single dose of a given deleterious gene. The eradication of a given genetic disease might then be attempted by aborting all such carriers. In fact, it was recently suggested that the fairly common disease cystic fibrosis could be completely eliminated over the next 40 years by screening all pregnancies and aborting the 17,000,000 unaffected fetuses that will carry a single gene for this disease. Such zealots need to be reminded of the consequences should each geneticist be allowed an equal assault on his favorite genetic disorder, given that each human being is a carrier for some four to eight such recessive, lethal genetic diseases.

3. *Control of human achievement*

Although human achievement depends at least in part upon genetic endowment, heredity determines only the material upon which experience and education impose the form. The limits of many capacities and powers of an individual are indeed genetically determined, but the nurturing and perfection of these capacities depend upon other influences. Neurological and psychological manipulation hold forth the promise of controlling the development of human capacities, particularly those long considered most distinctively human: speech, thought, choice, emotion, memory, and imagination.

These techniques are now in a rather primitive state because we understand so little about the brain and mind. Nevertheless, we have already seen the use of electrical stimulation of the human brain to produce sensations of intense pleasure and to control rage, the use of brain surgery (for example, frontal lobotomy) for the relief of severe anxiety, and the use of aversive conditioning with electric shock to treat sexual perversion. Operant-conditioning techniques are widely used, apparently with success, in schools and mental hospitals. The use of so-called consciousness-expanding and hallucinogenic drugs is widespread, to say nothing of tranquilizers and stimulants. We are promised drugs to modify memory, intelligence, libido, and aggressiveness.

The following passages from a recent book by Yale neurophysiologist José Delgado - a book instructively entitled *Physical Control of the Mind: Toward a Psychocivilized Society* - should serve to make this discussion more concrete. In the early 1950's, it was discovered that, with electrodes placed in certain discrete regions of their brains, animals would repeatedly and indefatigably press levers to stimulate their own brains, with obvious resultant enjoyment. Even starving animals preferred stimulating these so-called pleasure centers to eating. Delgado (1969) comments on the electrical stimulation of a similar center in a human subject (p. 185).

'[T] he patient reported a pleasant tingling sensation in the left side of her body "from my face down to the bottom of my legs". She started giggling and making funny comments, stating that she enjoyed the sensation "very much". Repetition of these stimulations made the patient more communicative and flirtatious, and she ended by openly expressing her desire to marry the therapist.'

And one further quotation from Delgado (p. 88).

'Leaving wires inside of a thinking brain may appear unpleasant or dangerous, but actually the many patients who have undergone this experience have not been concerned about the fact of being wired, nor have they felt any discomfort due to the presence of conductors in their heads. Some women have shown their feminine adaptability to circumstances by wearing attractive hats or wigs to conceal their electrical headgear, and many people have been able to enjoy a normal life as outpatients, returning to the clinic periodically for examination and stimulation. In a few cases in which contacts were located in pleasurable areas, patients have had the opportunity to stimulate their own brains by pressing the button of a portable instrument, and this procedure is reported to have therapeutic benefits.'

It bears repeating that the sciences of neurophysiology and psychopharmacology are in their infancy. The techniques that are now available are crude, imprecise, weak, and unpredictable, compared to those that may flow from a more mature neurobiology.

Basic Ethical and Social Problems and the Use of Biomedical Technology

After this cursory review of the powers now and soon to be at our disposal, I turn to the questions concerning the use of these powers. First, we must recognize that questions of use of science and technology are always moral and political questions, never simply technical ones. All private or public decisions to develop or to use biomedical technology - and decisions *not* to do so - inevitably contain judgments about value. This is true even if the values guiding those decisions are not articulated or made clear, as indeed they often are not. Secondly, the value judgments cannot be derived from biomedical science. This is true even if scientists themselves make the decisions.

These important points are often overlooked for at least three reasons.
1. They are obscured by those who like to speak of 'the control of nature by science'. It is men who control, not that abstraction 'science'. Science may provide the means, but men choose the ends; the choice of ends comes from beyond science.
2. Introduction of new technologies often appears to be the result of no decision whatsoever, or of the culmination of decisions too small or unconscious to be recognized as such. What can be done is done. However, someone is deciding on the basis of some notions of desirability, no matter how self-serving or altruistic.
3. Desires to gain or keep money and power no doubt influence much of what happens, but these desires can also be formulated as reasons and then discussed and debated.

Insofar as our society has tried to deliberate about questions of use, how has it done so? Pragmatists that we are, we prefer a utilitarian calculus: we weigh 'benefits' against 'risks', and we weigh them for both the individual and 'society'. We often ignore the fact that the very definitions of 'a benefit' and 'a risk' are themselves based upon judgments about value. In the biomedical areas just reviewed, the benefits are considered to be self-evident: prolongation of life, control of fertility and of population size, treatment and prevention of genetic disease, the reduction of anxiety and aggressiveness, and the enhancement of memory, intelligence, and pleasure. The assessment of risk is, in general, simply pragmatic - will the technique work effectively and reliably, how much will it cost, will it do detectable bodily harm, and who will complain if we proceed with development? As these questions are familiar and congenial, there is no need to belabor them.

The very pragmatism that makes us sensitive to considerations of economic cost often blinds us to the larger social costs exacted by biomedical advances. For one thing, we seem to be unaware that we may not be able to maximize all the benefits, that several of the goals we are promoting conflict with each other. On the one hand, we seek to control population growth by lowering fertility; on the other hand, we develop techniques to enable every infertile woman to bear a child. On the one hand, we try to extend the lives of individuals with genetic disease; on the other, we wish to eliminate deleterious genes from the human population. I am not urging that we resolve these conflicts in favor of one side or the other, but simply that we recognize that such conflicts exist. Once we do, we are more likely to appreciate that most 'progress' is heavily paid for in terms not generally included in the simple utilitarian calculus.

To become sensitive to the larger costs of biomedical progress, we must attend to several serious ethical and social questions. I will briefly discuss three of them: (i) questions of distributive justice, (ii) questions of the use and abuse of power, and (iii) questions of self-degradation and dehumanization.

Distributive Justice

The introduction of any biomedical technology presents a new instance of an old problem - how to distribute scarce resources justly. We should assume that demand will usually exceed supply. Which people should receive a kidney transplant or an artificial heart? Who should get the benefits of genetic therapy or of brain stimulation? Is 'first-come, first-served' the fairest principle? Or are certain people 'more worthy', and if so, on what grounds?

It is unlikely that we will arrive at answers to these questions in the form of deliberate decisions. More likely, the problem of distribution will continue to be decided ad hoc and locally. If so, the consequence will probably be a sharp increase in the already far too great inequality of medical care. The extreme case will be longevity, which will probably be, at first, obtainable only at great expense. Who is likely to be able to buy it? Do conscience and prudence permit us to enlarge the gap between rich and poor, especially with respect to something as fundamental as life itself?

Questions of distributive justice also arise in the earlier decisions to acquire new knowledge and to develop new techniques. Personnel and facilities for medical research and treatment are scarce resources. Is the development of a new technology the best use of the limited resources, given current circumstances? How should we balance efforts aimed at prevention against those aimed at cure, or either of these against efforts to redesign the species? How should we balance the delivery of available levels of care against further basic research? More fundamentally, how should we balance efforts in biology and medicine against efforts to eliminate poverty, pollution, urban decay, discrimination, and poor education? This last question about distribution is perhaps the most profound. We should reflect upon the social consequences of seducing many of our brightest young people to spend their lives locating the biomedical defects in rare genetic diseases, while our more serious problems go begging. The current squeeze on money for research provides us with an opportunity to rethink and reorder our priorities.

Problems of distributive justice are frequently mentioned and discussed, but they are hard to resolve in a rational manner. We find them especially difficult because of the enormous range of conflicting values and interests that characterizes our pluralistic society. We cannot agree - unfortunately, we often do not even try to agree - on standards for just distribution. Rather, decisions tend to be made largely out of a clash of competing interests. Thus, regrettably, the question of how to distribute justly often gets reduced to who shall decide how to distribute. The question about justice has led us to the question about power.

Use and Abuse of Power

We have difficulty recognizing the problems of the exercise of power in the biomedical enterprise because of our delight with the wondrous fruits it has yielded. This is ironic because the notion of power is absolutely central to the modern conception of science. The ancients conceived of science as the *understanding* of nature, pursued for its own sake. We moderns view science as power, as *control* over nature; the conquest of nature 'for the relief of man's estate' was the charge issued by Francis Bacon, one of the leading architects of the modern scientific project (Bacon, 1955).

Another source of difficulty is our fondness for speaking of the abstraction 'Man'. I suspect that we prefer to speak figuratively about 'Man's power over Nature' because it obscures an unpleasant reality about human affairs. It is in fact particular men who wield power, not Man. What we really mean by 'Man's power over Nature' is a power exercised by some men over other men, with a knowledge of nature as their instrument.

While applicable to technology in general, these reflections are especially pertinent to the technologies of human engineering, with which men deliberately exercise power over future generations. An excellent discussion of this question is found in *The Abolition of Man*, by C.S. Lewis (1965).

'It is, of course, a commonplace to complain that men have hitherto used badly, and against their fellows, the powers that science has given them. But that is not the point I am trying to make. I am not speaking of particular corruptions and abuses which an increase of moral virtue would cure: I am considering what the thing called 'Man's power over Nature' must always and essentially be . . .
   In reality, of course, if any one age really attains, by eugenics and scientific education, the power to make its descendants what it pleases, all men who live after it are the patients of that power. They are weaker, not stronger: for though we may have put wonderful machines in their hands, we have pre-ordained how they are to use them. . . The real picture is that of one dominant age . . . which resists all previous ages most successfully and dominates all subsequent ages most irresistibly, and thus is the real master of the human species. But even within this master generation (itself an infinitesimal minority of the species) the power will be exercised by a minority smaller still. Man's conquest of Nature, if the dreams of some scientific planners are realized, means the rule of a few hundreds of men over billions upon billions of men. There neither is nor can be any simple increase of power on Man's side. Each new power won *by* man is a power *over* man as well. Each advance leaves him weaker as well as stronger. In every victory, besides being the general who triumphs, he is also the prisoner who follows the triumphal car.'

Please note that I am not yet speaking about the problem of the misuse or abuse of power. The point is rather that the power which grows is unavoidably the power of only some men, and that the number of powerful men decreases as power increases.

Specific problems of abuse and misuse of specific powers must not, however, be overlooked. Some have voiced the fear that the technologies of genetic engineering and behavior control, though developed for good purposes, will be put to evil uses. These fears are perhaps somewhat exaggerated, if only because biomedical technologies would add very little to our highly developed arsenal for mischief, destruction, and stultification. Nevertheless, any proposal for large-scale human engineering should make us wary. Consider a program of positive eugenics based upon the widespread practice of asexual reproduction. Who shall decide what constitutes a superior individual worthy of replication? Who shall decide which individuals may or must reproduce, and by which method? These are questions easily answered only for a tyrannical regime.

Concern about the use of power is equally necessary in the selection of means for desirable or agreed-upon ends. Consider the desired end of limiting population growth. An effective program of fertility control is likely to be coercive. Who should decide the choice of means? Will the program penalize 'conscientious objectors'?

Serious problems arise simply from obtaining and disseminating information, as in the mass screening programs now being proposed for detection of genetic disease. For what kinds of disorders is compulsory screening justified? Who shall have access to the data obtained, and for what purposes? To whom does information about a person's genotype belong? In ordinary medical practice, the patient's privacy is protected by the doctor's adherence to the principle of confidentiality. What will protect his privacy under conditions of mass screening? More than privacy is at stake if screening is undertaken to detect psychological or behavioral abnormalities. A recent proposal, tendered and supported high in government, called for the psychological testing of all 6-year-olds to detect future criminals and misfits. The proposal was rejected; current tests lack the requisite predictive powers. But will such a proposal be rejected if reliable tests become available? What if certain genetic disorders, diagnosable in childhood, can be shown to correlate with subsequent antisocial behavior? For what degree of correlation and for what kinds of behavior can mandatory screening be justified? What use should be made of the data? Might not the dissemination of the information itself undermine the individual's chance for a worthy life and contribute to his so-called antisocial tendencies?

Consider the seemingly harmless effort to redefine clinical death. If the need for organs for transplantation is the stimulus for redefining death, might not this concern influence the definition at the expense of the dying? One physician, in fact, refers in writing to the revised criteria for declaring a patient dead as a 'new definition of heart donor eligibility' (Rutstein, 1969, p. 526).

Problems of abuse of power arise even in the acquisition of basic knowledge. The securing of a voluntary and informed consent is an abiding problem in the use of human subjects in experimentation. Gross coercion and deception are now rarely a problem; the pressures are generally subtle, often related to an intrinsic power imbalance in favor of the experimentalist.

A special problem arises in experiments on or manipulations of the unborn. Here it is impossible to obtain the consent of the human subject. If the purpose of the intervention is therapeutic - to correct a known genetic abnormality, for example - consent can reasonably be implied. But can anyone ethically consent to nontherapeutic interventions in which parents or scientists work their wills or their eugenic visions on the child-to-be? Would not such manipulation represent in itself an abuse of power, independent of consequences?

There are many clinical situations which already permit, if not invite, the manipulative or arbitrary use of powers provided by biomedical technology: obtaining organs for transplantation, refusing to let a person die with dignity, giving genetic counselling of a frightened couple, recommending eugenic sterilization for a mental retardate, ordering electric shock for a homosexual. In each situation, there is an opportunity to violate the will of the patient or subject. Such opportunities have generally existed in medical practice, but the dangers are becoming increasingly serious. With the growing complexity of the technologies, the technician gains in authority, since he alone can understand what he is doing. The patient's lack of knowledge makes him deferential and often inhibits him from speaking up when he feels threatened. Physicians *are* sometimes troubled by their increasing power, yet they feel they cannot avoid its exercise. 'Reluctantly', one commented to me, 'we shall have to play God'. With what guidance and to what ends I shall consider later. For the moment, I merely ask: 'By whose authority?'

While these questions about power are pertinent and important, they are in one sense misleading. They imply an inherent conflict of purpose between physician and patient, between scientist and citizen. The discussion conjures up images of master and slave, of oppressor and oppressed. Yet it must be remembered that conflict of purpose is largely absent, especially with regard to general goals. To be sure, the purposes of medical scientists are not always the same as those of the subjects experimented on. Nevertheless, basic sponsors and partisans of biomedical technology are precisely those upon whom the technology will operate. The will of the scientist and physician is happily married to (rather, is the offspring of) the desire of all of us for better health, longer life, and peace of mind.

Most future biomedical technologies will probably be welcomed, as have those of the past. Their use will require little or no coercion. Some developments, such as pills to improve memory, control mood, or induce pleasure, are likely to need no promotion. Thus, even if we should escape from the dangers of coercive manipulation, we shall still face large problems posed by the voluntary use of biomedical technology, problems to which I now turn.

Voluntary Self-Degradation and Dehumanization

Modern opinion is sensitive to problems of restriction of freedom and abuse of power. Indeed, many hold that a man can be injured only by violating his will. But this view is much too narrow. It fails to recognize the great dangers we shall face in the use of biomedical technology, dangers that stem from an excess of freedom, from the uninhibited exercises of will. In my view, our greatest problem will increasingly be one of voluntary self-degradation, or willing dehumanization.

Certain desired and perfected medical technologies have already had some dehumanizing consequences. Improved methods of resuscitation have made possible heroic efforts to 'save' the severely ill and injured. Yet these efforts are sometimes only partly successful; they may succeed in salvaging individuals with severe brain damage, capable of only a less-than-human, vegetating existence. Such patients, increasingly found in the intensive care units of university hospitals, have been denied a death with dignity. Families are forced to suffer seeing their loved ones so reduced, and are made to bear the burdens of a protracted death watch. Even the ordinary methods of treating disease and prolonging life have impoverished the context in which men die. Fewer and fewer people die in the familiar surroundings of home or in the company of family and friends. At that time of life when there is perhaps the greatest need for human warmth and comfort, the dying patient is kept company by cardiac pacemakers and defibrillators, respirators, aspirators, oxygenators, catheters, and his intravenous drip.

But the loneliness is not confined to the dying patient in the hospital bed. Consider the increasing number of old people who are still alive, thanks to medical progress. As a group, the elderly are the most alienated members of our society. Not yet ready for the world of the dead, not deemed fit for the world of the living, they are shunted aside. More and more of them spend the extra years medicine has given them in 'homes for senior citizens', in chronic hospitals, in nursing homes - waiting for the end. We have learned how to increase their years, but we have not learned how to help them enjoy their days. And yet, we bravely and relentlessly push back the frontiers against death.

Paradoxically, even the young and vigorous may be suffering because of medicine's success in removing death from their personal experience. Those born since penicillin represent the first generation ever to grow up without the experience or fear of probable unexpected death at an early age. They look around and see that virtually all of their friends are alive. A thoughtful physician, Eric Cassell (1969) has remarked on this in 'Death and the physician':

> 'While the gift of time must surely be marked as a great blessing, the *perception* of time, as stretching out endlessly before us, is somewhat threatening. Many of us function best under deadlines, and tend to procrastinate when time limits are not set.
> ... Thus, this unquestioned boon, the extension of life, and the removal of the threat of premature death, carries with it an unexpected anxiety: the anxiety of an unlimited future.
>   In the young, the sense of limitless time has apparently imparted not a feeling of limitless opportunity, but increased stress and anxiety, in addition to the anxiety which results from other modern freedoms: personal mobility, a wide range of occupational choice, and independence from the limitations of class and familial patterns of work ... A certain aimlessness (often ringed around with great social consciousness) characterizes discussions about their own aspirations. The future is endless, and their inner demands seem minimal. Although it may appear uncharitable to say so, they seem to be acting in a way best described as "childish" - particularly in their lack of a time sense. They behave as though there were no tomorrow, or as though the time limits imposed by the biological facts of life had become so vague for them as to be nonexistent.'

Consider next the coming power over reproduction and genotype. We endorse the project that will enable us to control numbers and to treat individuals with genetic disease. But out desires outrun these defensible goals. Many would welcome the chance to become parents without the inconvenience of pregnancy; others would wish to know in advance the characteristics of their offspring (sex, height, eye color, intelligence); still others would wish to design these characteristics to suit their tastes. Some scientists have called for the use of the new technologies to assure the 'quality' of all new babies (Glass, 1971). As one obstetrician put it: 'The business of obstetrics is to produce *optimum* babies.' But the price to be paid for the 'optimum baby' is the transfer of procreation from the home to the laboratory and its coincident transformation into manufacture. Increasing control over the product is purchased by the increasing depersonalization of the process. The complete depersonalization of procreation (possible with the development of an artificial placenta) shall be, in itself, seriously dehumanizing, no matter how optimum the product. It should not be forgotten that human procreation not only issues new human beings, but is itself a human acitivity.

Procreation is not simply an activity of the rational will. It is a more complete human activity precisely because it engages us bodily and spiritually, as well as rationally. Is there perhaps some wisdom in that mystery of nature which joins the pleasure of sex, the communication of love, and the desire for children in the very activity by which we continue the chain of human existence? Is not biological parenthood a built-in 'mechanism', selected because it fosters and supports in parents an adequate concern for and commitment to their children? Would not the laboratory production of human beings no longer be *human* procreation? Could it keep human parenthood human?

The dehumanizing consequences of programmed reproduction extend beyond the mere acts and processes of life-giving. Transfer of procreation to the laboratory will no doubt weaken what is presently for many people the best remaining justification and support for the existence of marriage and the family. Sex is now comfortably at home outside of marriage; child-rearing is progressively being given over to the state, the schools, the mass media, and the child-care centers. Some have argued that the family, long the nursery of humanity, has outlived its usefulness. To be sure, laboratory and governmental alternatives might be designed for procreation and child-rearing, but at what cost?

This is not the place to conduct a full evaluation of the biological family. Nevertheless, some of its important virtues are, nowadays, too often overlooked. The family is rapidly becoming the only institution in an increasingly impersonal world where each person is loved not for what he does or makes, but simply because he is. The family is also the institution where most of us, both as children and as parents, acquire a sense of continuity with the past and a sense of commitment to the future. Without the family, we would have little incentive to take an interest in anything after our own deaths. These observations suggest that the elimination of the family would weaken ties to past and future, and would throw us, even more than we are now, to the mercy of an impersonal, lonely present.

Neurobiology and psychobiology probe most directly into the distinctively human. The technological fruit of these sciences is likely to be both more tempting than Eve's apple and more 'catastrophic' in its result. One need only consider contemporary drug use to see what people are willing to risk or sacrifice for novel experiences, heightened perceptions, or just 'kicks'. The possibility of drug-induced, instant, and effortless gratification will be welcomed. Recall the possibilities of voluntary self-stimulation of the brain to reduce anxiety, to heighten pleasure, or to create visual and auditory sensations unavailable through the peripheral sense organs. Once these techniques are perfected and safe, is there much doubt that they will be desired, demanded, and used?

What ends will these techniques serve? Most likely, only the most elemental, those most tied to the bodily pleasures. What will happen to thought, to love, to friendship, to art, to judgment, to public-spiritedness in a society with a perfected technology of pleasure? What kinds of creatures will we become if we obtain our pleasure by drug or electrical stimulation without the usual kind of human efforts and frustrations? What kind of society will we have?

We need only consult Aldous Huxley's prophetic novel *Brave New World* for a likely answer to these questions. There we encounter a society dedicated to homogeneity and stability, administered by means of instant gratifications and peopled by creatures of human shape but of stunted humanity. They consume, fornicate, take 'soma', and operate the machinery that makes it all possible. They do not read, write, think, love, or govern themselves. Creativity and curiosity, reason and passion, exist only in a rudimentary and mutilated form. In short, they are not men at all.

True, our techniques, like theirs, may in fact enable us to treat schizophrenia, to alleviate anxiety, to curb aggressiveness. We, like they, may indeed be able to save mankind from itself, but probably only at the cost of its humanness. In the end, the price of relieving man's estate might well be the abolition of man.

There are, of course, many other routes leading to the abolition of man. There are many other and better known causes of dehumanization. Disease, starvation, mental retardation, slavery and brutality - to name just a few - have long prevented many, if not most, people from living a fully human life. We should work to reduce and eventually to eliminate these evils. But the existence of these evils should not prevent us from appreciating that the use of the technology of man, uninformed by wisdom concerning proper human ends, and untempered by an appropriate humility and awe, can unwittingly render us all irreversibly less than human. For, unlike the man reduced by disease or slavery, the people dehumanized à la *Brave New World* are not miserable, do not know that they are dehumanized, and, what is worse, would not care if they knew. They are, indeed, happy slaves, with a slavish happiness.

Some Fundamental Questions

The practical problems of distributing scarce resources, of curbing the abuses of power, and of preventing voluntary dehumanization point beyond themselves to some large, enduring, and most difficult questions: the nature of justice and the good community, the nature of man and the good for man. My appreciation of the profundity of these questions and my own ignorance before them makes me hesitant to say any more about them. Nevertheless, previous failures to find a shortcut around them have led me to believe that these questions must be faced if we are to have any hope of understanding where biology is taking us. Therefore, I shall try to show in outline how I think some of the larger questions arise from my discussion of dehumanization and self-degradation.

My remarks on dehumanization can hardly fail to arouse argument. It might be said, correctly, that to speak about dehumanization presupposes a concept of 'the distinctively human'. It might also be said, correctly, that to speak about wisdom concerning proper human ends presupposes that such ends do in fact exist and that they may be more or less accessible to human understanding, or at least to rational inquiry. It is true that neither presupposition is at home in modern thought.

The notion of the 'distinctively human' has been seriously challenged by modern scientists. Darwinists hold that man is, at least in origin, tied to the subhuman; his seeming distinctiveness is an illusion or, at most, not very important. Biochemists and molecular biologists extend the challenge by blurring the distinction between the living and the nonliving. The laws of physics and chemistry are found to be valid and are held to be sufficient for explaining biological systems. Man is a collection of molecules, an accident on the stage of evolution, endowed by chance with the power to change himself, but only along determined lines.

Psychoanalysts have also debunked the 'distinctly human'. The essence of man is seen to be located in those drives he shares with other animals - pursuit of pleasure and avoidance of pain. The so-called 'higher functions' are understood to be servants of the more elementary, the more base. Any distinctiveness or 'dignity' that man has consists of his superior capacity for gratifying his animal needs.

The idea of 'human good' fares no better. In the social sciences, historicists and existentialists have helped drive this question underground.

The former hold all notions of human good to be culturally and historically bound, and hence mutable. The latter hold that values are subjective: each man makes his own, and ethics becomes simply the cataloging of personal tastes.

Such appear to be the prevailing opinions. Yet there is nothing novel about reductionism, hedonism, and relativism; these are doctrines with which Socrates contended. What is new is that these doctrines seem to be vindicated by scientific advance. Not only do the scientific notions of nature and of man flower into verifiable predictions, but they yield marvellous fruit. The technological triumphs are held to validate their scientific foundations. Here, perhaps, is the most pernicious result of technological progress - more dehumanizing than any actual manipulation or technique, present or future. We are witnessing the erosion, perhaps that final erosion, of the idea of man as something splendid or divine, and its replacement with a view that sees man, no less than nature, as simply more raw material for manipulation and homogenization. Hence, our peculiar moral crisis. We are in turbulent seas without a landmark precisely because we adhere more and more to a view of nature and of man which both gives us enormous power and, at the same time, denies all possibility of standards to guide its use. Though well-equipped, we know not who we are nor where we are going. We are left to the accidents of our hasty, biased, and ephemeral judgments.

Let us not fail to note a painful irony: our conquest of nature has made us the slaves of blind chance. We triumph over nature's unpredictabilities only to subject ourselves to the still greater unpredictability of our capricious wills and our fickle opinions. That we have a method is no proof against our madness. Thus, engineering the engineer as well as the engine, we race our train we know not where.

While the disastrous consequences of ethical nihilism are insufficient to to refute it, they invite and make urgent a reinvestigation of the ancient and enduring questions of what is a proper life for a human being, what is a good community, and how are they achieved. We must not be deterred from these questions simply because the best minds in human history have failed to settle them. Should we not rather be encouraged by the fact that they considered them to be the most important questions?

As I have hinted before, our ethical dilemma is caused by the victory of modern natural science with its nonteleological view of man. We ought therefore to reexamine with great care the modern notions of nature and of man, which undermine those earlier notions that provide a basis for ethics. If we consult our common experience, we are likely to discover some grounds for believing that the questions about man and human good are far from closed. Our common experience suggests many difficulties for the modern 'scientific view of man'. For example, this view fails to account for the concern for justice and freedom that appears to be characteristic of all human societies. It also fails to account for or to explain the fact that men have speech and not merely voice, that men can choose and act and not merely move or react. It fails to explain why men engage in moral discourse, or, for that matter, why they speak at all. Finally, the 'scientific view of man' cannot account for scientific inquiry itself, for why men seek to know. Might there not be something the matter with a knowledge of man that does not explain or take account of his most distinctive activities, aspirations, and concerns?

Having gone this far, let me offer one suggestion as to where the difficulty might lie: in the modern understanding of knowledge. Since Bacon, as I have mentioned earlier, technology has increasingly come to be the basic justification for scientific inquiry. The end is power, not knowledge for its own sake. But power is not only the end. It is also an important *validation* of knowledge. One definitely knows that one knows only if one can make. Synthesis is held to be the ultimate proof of understanding. A more radical formulation holds that one knows only what one makes: knowing *equals* making.

Yet therein lies a difficulty. If truth be the power to change or to make the object studied, then of what do we have knowledge? If there are no fixed realities, but only material upon which we may work our wills, will not 'science' be merely the 'knowledge' of the transient and the manipulatable? We might indeed have knowledge of the laws by which things change and the rules for their manipulation, but no knowledge of the things themselves. Can such a view of 'science' yield any knowledge about the nature of man, or indeed, about the nature of anything? Our questions appear to lead back to the most basic of questions: What does it mean to know? What is it that is knowable?

We have seen that the practical problems point toward and make urgent certain enduring, fundamental questions. Yet while pursuing these questions, we cannot afford to neglect the practical problems as such. Let us now forget Delgado and the 'psychocivilized society'. The philosophical inquiry could be rendered moot by our blind, confident efforts to dissect and redesign ourselves. While awaiting a reconstruction of theory, we must act as best we can.

What Is To Be Done?
First, we sorely need to recover some humility in the face of our awesome powers. The arguments I have presented should make apparent the folly of arrogance, of the presumption that we are wise enough to remake ourselves. Because we lack wisdom, caution is our urgent need. Or to put it another way, in the absence of that 'ultimate wisdom', we can be wise enough to know that we are not wise enough. When we lack sufficient wisdom to do, wisdom consists in not doing. Caution, restraint, delay, abstention are what this second-best (and,

perhaps, only) wisdom dictates with respect to the technology for human engineering.

If we can recognize that biomedical advances carry significant social costs, we may be willing to adopt a less permissive, more critical stance toward new developments. We need to reexamine our prejudice not only that all biomedical innovation is progress, but also that it is inevitable. Precedent certainly favors the view that what can be done will be done, but is this necessarily so? Ought we not to be suspicious when technologists speak of coming developments as automatic, not subject to human control? Is there not something contradictory in the notion that we have the power to control all the untoward consequences of a technology, but lack the power to determine whether it should be developed in the first place?

What will be the likely consequences of the perpetuation of our permissive and fatalistic attitude toward human engineering? How will the large decisions be made? Technocratically and self-servingly, if our experience with previous technologies is any guide. Under conditions of laissez-faire, most technologists will pursue techniques, and most private industries will pursue profits. We are fortunate that, apart from the drug manufacturers, there are at present in the biomedical area few large industries that influence public policy. Once these appear, the voice of 'the public interest' will have to shout very loudly to be heard above their whisperings in the halls of Congress. These reflections point to the need for institutional controls.

Scientists understandably balk at the notion of the regulation of science and technology. Censorship is ugly and often based upon ignorant fear; bureaucratic regulation is often stupid and inefficient. Yet there is something disingenuous about a scientist who professes concern about the social consequences of science, but who responds to every suggestion of regulation with one or both of the following: 'No restrictions on scientific research', and 'Technological progress should not be curtailed.' Surely, to suggest that *certain* technologies ought to be regulated or forestalled is not to call for that halt of *all* technological progress (and says nothing at all about basic research). Each development should be considered on its own merits. Although the dangers of regulation cannot be dismissed, who, for example, would still object to efforts to obtain an effective, complete, global prohibition on the development, testing, and use of biological and nuclear weapons?

The proponents of laissez-faire ignore two fundamental points. They ignore the fact that not to regulate is as much a policy decision as the opposite, and that it merely postpones the time of regulation. Controls will eventually be called for - as they are now being demanded to end environmental pollution. If attempts are not made early to detect and diminish the social costs of biomedical advances by intelligent institutional regulation, the society is likely to react later with more sweeping, immoderate, and throttling controls.

The proponents of laissez-faire also ignore the fact that much of technology is already regulated. The federal government is already deep in research and development (for example, space, electronics, and weapons) and is the principal sponsor of biomedical research. One may well question the wisdom of the direction given, but one would be wrong in arguing that technology cannot survive social control. Clearly, the question is not control versus no control, but rather what kind of control, when, by whom, and for what purpose.

Means for achieving international regulation and control need to be devised. Biomedical technology can be no nation's monopoly. The need for international agreements and supervision can readily be understood if we consider the likely American response to the successful asexual reproduction of 10,000 Mao Tse-tungs.

To repeat, the basic short-term need is caution. Practically, this means that we should shift the burden of proof to the *proponents* of a new biomedical technology. Concepts of 'risk' and 'cost' need to be broadened to include some of the social and ethical consequences discussed earlier. The probable or possible harmful effects of the widespread use of a new technique should be anticipated and introduced as 'costs' to be weighed in deciding about the *first* use. The regulatory institutions should be encouraged to exercise restraint and to formulate the grounds for saying 'no'. We must all get used to the idea that biomedical technology makes possible many things we should never do.

But caution is not enough. Nor are clever institutional arrangements. Institutions can be little better than the people who make them work. However worthy our intentions, we are deficient in understanding. In the *long* run, our hope can only lie in education: in a public educated about the meanings and limits of science and enlightened in its use of technology; in scientists better educated to understand the relationships between science and technology on the one hand, and ethics and politics on the other; in human beings who are as wise in the latter as they are clever in the former.

References

Bacon, F. (1955). *The Advancement of Learning,* Book 1, edited by H.G. Dick, p. 193. New York: Random House.
Cassell, E.J. (1969). Death and the physician. *Commentary,* 73, 76.
Delgado, J.M.R. (1969). *Physical Control of the Mind: Toward a Psychocivilized Society.* New York: Harper & Row.

Edwards, R.G., Bavister, B.D. and Steptoe, P.C. (1969). Early stages in fertilisation *in vitro* of human oocytes matured *in vitro*. *Nature*, 221, 632-635.
Edwards, R.G., Steptoe, P.C. and Purdy, J.M. (1970). Fertilisation and cleavage *in vitro* of preovulator human oocyte. *Nature*, 227, 1307-1309.
Glass, B. (1971). Science: endless horizons or golden age? *Science*, 171, 23-29.
Lewis, C.S. (1965). *The abolition of Man*, pp. 69-71. New York: Macmillan.
Muller, H.J. (1961). Human evolution by voluntary choice of germ plasm. *Science*, 134, 643-649.
Rutstein, D.D. (1969). The ethical design of human experiments. *Daedalus*, Spring, 523-541.

SUBJECT INDEX

Abortion, 44, 45, 46, 59, 60, 61, 63, 64, 65, 66, 70, 78, 80-82, 133, 135, 136, 275, 277
Anencephaly, 177-89

Behaviour
  biology of, 23-5
  and the brain, 193, 195, 196, 203-4
  control, 227-9, 277-9, 282, 284, 287
  criminal, 31, 214, 221-39, 283
  and environment, 269-70
  evolution of, 1-23
  and genetics, 90, 108-9, 117, 123, 127, 130-2, 136, 138, 139, 214, 221-4, 232-6, 268, 283
  sexual, 2-3, 5-20, 28, 34-8, 44-7, 60-1, 110, 251
  social, 228-32, 234-9
  and warfare, 242, 245, 248-9, 250-4
Biomedical engineering, 273-93
  see also Genetic engineering
Bonding, 7, 13, 16, 18-19, 23, 25-6, 28, 29, 30, 34-8
Brain
  evolution of, 4, 15, 17, 18-19, 20
  structure and function of, 191-207, 270, 278-9, 280, 287

Cloning, 277
Conditioning, 227-9, 278
Consanguinity, 184, 187
Contraception, 45-6, 60-61, 63, 64-6, 70, 71, 74-9, 80-83, 86, 138, 275
Criminal behaviour, 31, 214, 221-39
  and environment, 221-3, 232, 233
  and genetics, 221-4, 232-5, 236, 283
  and physical characteristics, 221, 235

DNA, 127, 129, 277
Dehumanization, technological, 284-92
Demography *see* Population
Depopulation, 50
Disease and disorder
  and biomedical engineering, 275
  and body constitution, 171-3, 186
  of the brain, 201-2
  and environment, 151-4, 163, 170-1, 174, 178-9
  and ethnicity, 163-74
  genetic, 108, 119, 122, 126-9, 131, 133, 135-9, 151-4, 161, 163, 169-71, 181-8, 268-9, 276, 277, 279, 280, 282-3, 286
  and population control, 43-5, 48, 58-9, 275-6, 279, 280, 286
  and race, 161-76, 181-2, 185
Dominance, 8-10, 13-20, 23, 28-31, 35, 36-7, 243

Dyslexia, 201, 202

Educability
  and environment, 209-19, 271-2
  and genetics, 86, 110, 209-19, 271-2
Education
  and ethnicity, 213-16
  and genetics, 86, 88, 99, 101, 214
  and intelligence, 201-2
  and population size, 74, 80
  and race, 214-16
Emotionality, 233-4
Environment
  and behaviour, 269-70
  and crime, 221-3, 232, 233
  and disease, 151-4, 163, 170-1, 174, 177-89
  and educability, 209-19, 271-2
  and genetics, 87, 89-101, 108, 110-14, 116, 118, 138-9, 163, 210-19, 221-3, 232, 233, 267-8, 270-2, 275
  and survival, 242-52, 256-63, 267-8
  see also Population, and environment
Epidemiology, 161-2
  see also Disease and disorder
Equilibration, 15, 19, 20
Ethnicity
  and disease, 163-74
  and education, 214-16
  and genetics, 163-74, 215
Eugenics, 176-7, 282, 283
Extraversion, 224-6, 232-8

Family
  and crime, 221
  genetics, 105-7, 133-4, 135, 136, 182-4, 277, 283, 286
  and kinship, 1-20, 33, 37-8, 44-51, 86, 93, 95, 97, 98-9, 109, 221, 231, 252, 255, 286-7
  size, 44-7, 60-1, 64-6, 75, 81, 86, 94, 101, 106, 142-3
Family planning *see* Contraception
Fertility, 42, 44-9, 53, 57-66, 76, 86, 101, 106, 108, 150, 158, 173, 211, 275-6, 279, 280

Genetics
  and aging, 275
  anthropological, 3, 7, 13-14, 141-60
  and behaviour, 90, 108-9, 117, 123, 127, 130-2, 136, 138, 139, 214, 221-4, 232-6, 268, 283
  and computers, 132
  and consanguinity, 184, 187
  counselling, 133-6, 277, 283
  drift, 147-51, 156, 158

SUBJECT INDEX

Genetics *(contd)*
  and educability, 86, 110, 209-19,
    271-2
  and education, 86, 88, 99, 101, 214
  engineering, 127, 129, 134-5, 276-7,
    279, 280, 282
  and ethnicity, 163-74, 215
  and intelligence, 85-6, 90-1, 100, 109,
    137-8, 186, 211-19
  isolates, 116, 147-51, 163, 174
  medical, 121-39
  and politics, 265-72
  publications, 124-5, 133
  and race, 100-101, 104-19, 136-7,
    161-74, 213-16
  reproductive, 61, 63, 65, 66, 86,
    130-7, 275-6, 283, 286, 292
  and selection, 85-101
  and sexual discrimination, 24-5,
    27, 29-31, 35
  teaching, 127, 134-7
  training, 125-7, 129
  see also Disease and disorder, genetic;
    Environment, and genetics; *and*
    Population, genetics
Great Chain of Being, 265-6

Handedness, 195, 202
Homosexuality, 45, 223, 224, 283
Hunting, 4, 6, 12, 13, 15, 17-19, 25-6,
  29, 35, 37, 42-4, 49-50, 52,
  246-8, 262

IQ, 210-18
Inbreeding, 91-2, 93, 110, 116, 118, 119,
  161
Intelligence
  and the brain, 198, 201-2, 270
  and education, 201-2
  and genetics, 85-6, 90-1, 100, 109,
    137-8, 186, 211-19
  and race, 270
  and selection, 86
Introversion, 224-6, 232-8

Language
  and the brain, 194, 195, 197, 198-9,
    202
  and race, 110
Learning and conditioning, 227-8, 236

Mating
  assortative, 85-101
  and genetics, 104-19, 141-5, 158
  see also Eugenics
Migration, 42-3, 48, 116, 147-8, 151,
  153, 161, 171, 174, 181-2, 262
Mutation, 93, 105, 119, 128, 131, 138,
  139, 141-3, 174, 185, 267, 268

Neuroticism, 224-6, 232-3

Overpopulation, 42, 57, 61-3, 71

Personality, 224-9
Physical characteristics
  and crime, 221, 235
  and disease, 171-3, 186
Politics
  and genetics, 265-72
  and population size, 51-2
Population
  boundaries, 51, 103, 109-11, 116,
    118-19, 157, 243-51, 256-63
  characteristics, 106-9, 113, 117
  classification, 107, 114-17
  clines, 113-14, 115, 152-3
  comparisons, 112-14
  control, 43-8, 58-9, 63-6, 69-83,
    275-6, 279, 280, 286
  defined, 106-7
  distribution, 143-58, 161
  and environment, 108-18, 143-7,
    151-8, 242-52, 256-63
  genetics, 103-19, 126-32, 137-8,
    141-58
  growth, 41-2, 45, 46, 48-51, 57-9,
    61-3, 69-76, 80-3, 109, 138,
    139, 143, 241, 275
  intergradation, 111-12, 118,
    154-6, 244
  and migration, 42-3, 262
  size and organisation, 47-52, 58-9,
    69-75, 80, 109, 145-7
  see also Depopulation *and*
    Overpopulation
Primates, 2-20, 27-9, 34, 35, 36, 37,
  103, 118
Psychopaths, 226-7, 231-2

Race
  defined, 162-3
  and disease, 161-76, 181-2, 185
  and education, 214-16
  and genetics, 100-101, 104-19,
    136-7, 161-74, 213-16
  and intelligence, 270
  intermixture, 103, 111-12, 118, 119,
    154-6, 163, 174, 184, 187, 244
  and mate selection, 89, 92, 95,
    98-101
  see also Eugenics
Reproduction
  genetic aspects, 61, 63, 65, 66, 86,
    139-7, 275-6, 283, 286, 292
  social impact, 57-66

Selection, 15-16, 24, 25, 27, 28, 37,
  85-102, 104, 106, 108, 114, 115,

SUBJECT INDEX

Selection *(contd)*
   118, 139, 147, 151-4, 211, 242, 260, 262-3, 267, 271
Sex
   behaviour, 2-3, 5-20, 28, 34-8, 44-7, 60-1, 110, 251
   chromosomes, 128, 129, 214
   discrimination, 23-38
   ratios, 63-4, 80
Spina bifida, 177-89
Sterilization, 78, 81, 283

Taboos, 2, 3, 16, 20, 32, 36, 231
Technology *see* Biomedical engineering
Thought and the brain, 198-201
Tools, 4, 6, 15, 17, 19, 41
Totemism, 2, 3, 16, 20

Warfare
   and boundaries, 51, 243-51, 256-63
   and economic advantage, 246-7, 256
   and environment, 242-52, 256-63
   and group solidarity, 252-5
   and population levels, 43-4, 248-51, 256
   primitive, 241-64
Weapons, 2, 4, 13, 14, 17, 19-20, 248